Reading Interests of Children and Young Adults

Compiled by
Jean Spealman Kujoth

The Scarecrow Press, Inc.
Metuchen, N.J.   1970

Copyright 1970, by Jean Spealman Kujoth
ISBN 0-8108-0307-0

"Some books are to be tasted,
others to be swallowed,
and some few to be chewed and digested."

      ----Francis Bacon

Introduction and Acknowledgments

This anthology is intended primarily for teachers, librarians, students of education and of library science, and others who work, or plan to work, with children or young adults and with books. The challenge "to get the right book to the right person at the right time" can be well met only if one knows what reading experiences are likely to be most valuable to what persons.

This book is a collection of recent research findings and observations by a number of experienced professionals including college faculty members, elementary and secondary school teachers, librarians, and authors of books for children and for young adults, most of them from the United States and some from other countries. The book aims to speed the search for helpful enlightenment on the subject of reading interests of children and young people from one to twenty years of age.

The fifty-five articles in the book are reprinted from thirty-five serial publications, mostly journals in the fields of education and library science. They discuss questions such as: What motivates children to read? What books do children and young adults like best, and why? What personal characteristics and social factors influence reading? What implications are there for those who want to make available to children and young adults the reading experiences that will be most valuable to them?

The book is divided into sections according to age groups, except for the last section, which concerns exceptional children. The apparent duplication of some of the sections is due to the fact that the articles are grouped as much as possible according to their scope rather than according to some neat-looking but ill-fitting artificial pattern.

The compiler expresses sincere thanks to the contributing authors, to the editors who granted permission to use copyrighted material, and to the libraries that made the material accessible.

                                        Jean S. (Mrs. Richard) Kujoth
                                        Milwaukee, Wisconsin

TABLE OF CONTENTS

(Note: The authors' positions listed below are not necessarily their current ones. They are the posts held at the time the articles were published and are included as clues to the authority and viewpoint of each article.)

Section One: Ages One to Eight   Page

Books Before Two: Some Observations on the
    Reading of the Very Young. Sylva Simsova
    (Finchley Public Library, England). Assistant
    Librarian 55:168-70, September 1962.   15

The Books the Boys Like, Reported by Their
    Mother. Mrs. Robert Mead (Friend of the
    Scribner Book Store, Norfolk, Connecticut).
    Publishers' Weekly 189:107-10, February 21,
    1966.   19

Dictionaries Before Six. Sylva Simsova (Lecturer,
    School of Librarianship, North-Western Poly-
    technic, London). Bookseller no. 3135:182-5,
    January 22, 1966.   27

Children's Reading Choices and Basic Reader
    Content. Ruth C. Smith (Candidate for Master's
    Degree in Education, University of Wisconsin-
    Milwaukee). Elementary English 39:202-9,
    March 1962.   33

A Study of Children's Book Choices. Bette J.
    Peltola (Graduate student and Instructor in
    Children's Literature, College of Education,
    University of Minnesota). Elementary English
    40:690-5+, November 1963.   44

Reading Interests of First Graders. Helen E. Rogers
    (Reading Teacher, Gary, Indiana, Public Schools)
    and H. Alan Robinson (Director of the Reading

	Page
Conference and Workshop in the Department of Education, University of Chicago). Elementary English 40:707-11, November 1963.	55
What Do First Graders Like to Read? Sister Mary Consuelo, O. S. U. (Director of Student Library, Ursuline College, Louisville, Kentucky). Catholic School Journal 67:42-3, February 1967.	65
Race, Illustrations, and Interest in Materials for Reading and Creative Writing. Monroe Rowland (Associate Professor, San Diego State College) and Patricia Hill (Teacher, Campus Laboratory School, San Diego State College). Journal of Negro Education 34:84-7, Winter 1965.	68
Expressed Reading Preferences of Second-Grade Children in Selected Schools in Colorado. Reviewed by Elizabeth N. Wade (Elementary Supervisor, Colorado Springs, Colorado). Childhood Education 40:494-5, May 1964.	75
Children's Hour, Children's Choice. Newsweek 67: 118+, June 13, 1966.	79

Section Two: Ages Six to Twelve

Children and Humorous Literature. Robin B. Bateman (Tutor Librarian, City of Leeds College of Education). School Librarian and School Library Review 15:153-6+, July 1967.	82
Influences on Primary School Children's Reading. R. S. Buzzing (Margaret Wix Junior School, St. Albans, England). School Librarian and School Library Review 11:584-6+, December 1963.	90
Reading Patterns of Children; What and Why They Read. Richard J. Hurley (Supervisor of Libraries, Fairfax County, Virginia). National Catholic Educational Association Bulletin 62:468, August 1965.	96

Children's Newspaper Reading. Lois V. Johnson (Associate Professor of Education, Los Angeles

	Page
State College). <u>Elementary English</u> 40:428-32+, April 1963.	98
Textbooks Versus Tradebooks--A Child's View. Patrick J. Groff (Professor of Education, San Diego State College). <u>School Libraries</u> 16:29-33, Summer 1967.	108

Section Three: Ages Six to Fifteen

Why and What Children Read. Helen S. Canfield (Supervisor of Work with Children, Hartford Public Library). <u>Library Journal</u> 85:4198-9, November 15; <u>Junior Libraries</u> 7:22-3, November 1960.	116
Why Children Like Horse Stories. Bernard Poll (Head, Children's Department, King County Public Library, Seattle). <u>Elementary English</u> 38:473-4, November 1961.	119
Nineteen All-Time Favorites. Roma Gans (Professor Emeritus, Teachers College, Columbia University). <u>Grade Teacher</u> 82:75-8, March 1965.	122
What the City Boy Reads. Iris Vinton (Director of Publications Department, Boys' Clubs of America, and author of many children's books). <u>Elementary English</u> 40:559-62, May 1963.	126
What Do Children Value? Richard Crosscup (Head of the High School English Department, Walden School, New York City). <u>Wilson Library Bulletin</u> 39:146-50, October 1964.	132
Critical Appraisal of Research on Children's Reading Interests, Preferences, and Habits. Ethel M. King (Professor of Education, University of Calgary). <u>Canadian Education and Research Digest</u> 7:312-26, December 1967.	142

Section Four: Ages Twelve to Fifteen

Reading and Reference Interests of Junior-High Students. Charles E. Johnson and J. Harlan

	Page
Shores (both of College of Education, University of Illinois). <u>Illinois Education</u> 51:374-6, May 1963.	157
Junior High Book Discussions. Nancy Elsmo (Racine Public Library). <u>Wisconsin Library Bulletin</u> 62:279-80, September-October 1966.	164
Publishers Hear YA Panel Talk About Reading Tastes. <u>Library Journal</u> 92:284+, January 15; <u>School Library Journal</u> 14:16+, January 1967.	167
Salient Elements of Recreational Reading of Junior High School Students. Anthony T. Soares (Assistant Professor of Educational Psychology, Boston College). <u>Elementary English</u> 40:843-5, December 1963.	169
Reading Content That Interests Seventh, Eighth, and Ninth Grade Students. Ann Jungeblut (Educational Records Bureau, New York) and John H. Coleman (Executive Analysis Corporation, New York; formerly Professor of Education and in charge of the Training School at Miami University, Oxford, Ohio). <u>Journal of Educational Research</u> 58:393-401, May 1965.	174
Reading Interests of Eighth-Grade Students. Beryl I. Vaughan (Teacher of Developmental Reading, Arlington High School, Indianapolis). <u>Journal of Developmental Reading</u> 6:149-55, Spring 1963.	192
The Reading Interests of Eighth-Grade Boys. Jo M. Stanchfield (Professor of Education, Occidental College, Los Angeles). <u>Journal of Developmental Reading</u> 5:256-65, Summer 1962.	200
A Study of Leisure-Time Reading Preferences of Ninth Grade Students. John Q. Adams (Assistant Professor of Secondary Education, University of North Dakota). <u>High School Journal</u> 46:67-72, November 1962.	209
Why Do Children Read? Ernest Roe (Senior Lecturer in Education, University of Adelaide). <u>Australian Library Journal</u> 13:3-14, March 1964.	217

Section Five: Ages Twelve to Nineteen

What Do They Read? David Jesson-Dibley (Senior English Master, Christ's Hospital), Robin Atthill (Senior English Master, Downside School) and Roland Earl (Headmaster, Hackbridge C. P. Junior Boys' School, Surrey). English 13:55-8, Summer 1960. ... 239

Deiches Studies of Pratt Library Examine Student Reading. Lowell A. Martin (Director of the Deiches Fund Studies). Maryland Libraries 29:9-11, Fall 1962. ... 247

A Study of Pupils' Interests: Grades Nine, Ten, Eleven, Twelve. Paul Witty (Professor of Education, Northwestern University, Evanston, Illinois). Education 82:100-10, October 1961. ... 251

"We Don't Even Call Those Books!" Esther Millett (Librarian, Westover School, Middlebury, Connecticut). Top of the News 20:45-7, October 1963. ... 260

Patterns of Young Adults' Reading; Meeting During the ALA Convention. Publishers' Weekly 190:29-32, August 8, 1966. ... 264

The National Library Week Conference: Teen-Age Reading. Publishers' Weekly 176:12-5, November 30, 1959. ... 269

Teen Reading Assessed in Scholastic's Survey. Publishers' Weekly 175:22-3, April 13, 1959. ... 277

What Do They Really Want to Read? Mary L. Smith (Sumner, Iowa, Community School) and Isabel V. Eno (Waverly, Iowa, Community School). English Journal 50:343-5, May 1961. ... 279

Analyzing Reading Interests. Dean C. Andrew (Academic Dean, Southern State College, Magnolia, Arkansas) and Curtis Easley (Superintendent of Schools, Taylor, Arkansas). Clearing House 33:496 501, April 1959. ... 284

A Study in Adolescent Reading. Joan W. Butler (Organizer, Work with Young People, Herts County Library). Library Association Record 58:387-9, October 1956. 295

What Young People Want to Know About Themselves. Evelyn Millis Duvall (Author of books about courtship and marriage; formerly Founding Director of the Association for Family Living, Chicago). Top of the News 13:39, December 1956. 301

Some Results of a Twelve-Year Study of Children's Reading Interests. George W. Norvell (Supervisor of English, New York State Department of Education). English Journal 35:531-6, December 1946. 303

What Does Johnny Read? Lois B. Hall (Librarian, North Caroline High School) and William N. Rairigh (Administrator, Kent-Caroline Public Libraries Association). Maryland Libraries 31:6-8, Fall 1964. 313

Anybody Got a Good Book? Thomas L. Kilpatrick (Librarian, Herrin Township High School). Illinois Libraries 44:282-4, April 1962. 318

Contemporary Literature Through the Eyes of Upper-Grade Pupils [in Russia]. L. S. Aizerman (credentials unknown. Literatura V Shkole, 1964, No. 5; Soviet Review 6:32-45, Spring 1965. 322

Tell It As It Is. Nat Hentoff (Author of novels including Jazz Country, Call the Keeper, and Our Children are Dying). New York Times Book Review, p. 3+, May 7, 1967. 349

"Well, What Did You Think of It?" Bruce C. Appleby and John W. Conner (both of Department of English, University High School, University of Iowa). English Journal 54:606-12, October 1965. 354

Section Six: Ages Fifteen to Nineteen

What High School Students Say About Good Books. Nick Aaron Ford (Head of English Department, Morgan State College, Baltimore). English

	Page
Journal 50:539-40+, November 1961.	365

Private Reading in the Fifth. W. Stephen Jones (now Head of English Department, Rydal School, Colwyn Bay, Wales--this is not the school the article refers to). Times Educational Supplement 2626:506, September 17, 1965. ... 370

Why Do They Hate the Classics? Lewis S. Gannett (formerly daily book critic for the New York Herald Tribune). Child Study 34:16-7, Spring 1957. ... 377

Free Reading and Book Reports--An Informal Survey of Grade Eleven. Donald R. Gallo (Doctoral Candidate, Syracuse University, Reading and Language Arts Center; formerly teacher of English, Westport, Connecticut). Journal of Reading 11:532-8, April 1968. ... 381

What Does Research Reveal About Reading and the High School Student? John J. DeBoer (Professor of Education, University of Illinois; Editor of Elementary English; Past President of the National Council of Teachers of English). English Journal 47:271-81, May 1958. ... 390

Reading Interests and Informational Needs of High School Students. J. Harlan Shores (Professor of Elementary Education, University of Illinois). Reading Teacher 17:536-44, April 1964. ... 407

Section Seven: Exceptional Children

The Library Looks at the Gifted. Howard W. Winger (Associate Professor, Graduate Library School, University of Chicago). Illinois Libraries 42:287-96, May 1960. ... 420

Reading Interests of Retarded, Reluctant, and Disturbed Readers. Louise Moses (Librarian, Juvenile Hall, Institutions Region, Los Angeles County Public Library). Claremont Reading Conference: 26th Yearbook, 1962, pp. 77-84. ... 433

Author Index ... 443

Subject Index ... 445

I: Ages One to Eight

Books Before Two: Some Observations On the Reading of the Very Young

Sylva Simsova

From The Assistant Librarian 55:168-70, September 1962. Article copyrighted by the author. Reprinted by permission.

A long time ago, before I had any experience of small children, a reader asked me to allow her two year old son to join the library. She claimed that he had been reading books with her for several months. I accepted her explanation with incredulity, thinking that she was showing off with her precocious child.

Since then I have discovered, with the help of my son, that toddlers do have an interest in reading. I shall try to describe the development of his reading between approximately 18 months and two years. I was sorry to find that D. M. White in her valuable study Books Before Five did not start to keep a record of her child's reading until she was two. She mentions, however, that her daughter was given books and showed an interest in them before the age of two. I would have liked to compare her record with my own observations.

The interest and the attitude shown by the parents towards the child's reading are among the decisive influences on its own development. A child liberally supplied with reading matter and living in a household in which books form part of the daily life of its inhabitants will be a more advanced reader than one whose parents never take their eyes off the television.

A child of 18 months has a small vocabulary and is unable to follow a story told by his parents. He recognizes some three-dimensional objects, but finds it hard to recognize two-dimensional pictures of them. He has to be taught the meaning of pictures just as later he will have to be taught the meaning of letters.

It takes some time before he distinguishes the shapes and colors of pictures and relates them to the objects of his experience in real life within the limits not only of his experience, but also of his vocabulary. As the first two words are the names of the two most important beings in his life, so also he starts his reading by calling every picture of a human being "Mummy" and "Daddy."

What the child reads does not matter in these early stages. There is no need to use books; reading matter is provided by newspapers and periodicals. The present style of advertisements with large real-life photographs is much appreciated by him.

Sooner or later he distinguishes between men and women and begins to add other objects of his experience to his reading. His recognition of them in picture form is not very accurate at first: every round object (including the letter O if sufficiently large) is "ball," every four-legged creature "bow-wow." This stage lasts for a long time and is closely linked with the growth of the child's vocabulary. Gradually the child develops greater accuracy and better perception of detail. But the main feature of this stage remains: the pictures are static, they do not represent action.

I would have expected a picture dictionary to be the ideal book for this kind of reading, but I found the illustrations in most picture dictionaries too small. The child likes large realistic pictures, preferably in color, the kind often to be found in books for grown-ups. My son's favorite book was Fishes of the World. Large color photographs, such as those in the Collins' New ABC in Colour-Photography, are best, especially if they show one object only. Photographs including too much action and detail such as Tales of the Riverbank, are too confusing. Pictures of animals dressed in clothes, in the style of B. Potter, are lacking in realism no matter how realistically drawn and the excellent illustrations of Ardizzone in the Tim series are lost on the child until he can begin to follow a story.

It is during the second stage that the child perceives or imagines action in pictures. He begins to buzz when he sees the picture of a car, to bark in front of the picture of a dog. At first the action is not necessarily related to the action in the picture (the car may be stationary), it is based on the association between the object and its activity. Then, one day, he sees the action, perhaps with the startling announcement over a picture of a car crash in a paper: "Car broken." Pictures begin to tell a story to him.

For a time each picture tells a story of its own; he is unable to follow a long story spread over several pages. Books with individual pictures depicting an action, e.g. well illustrated nursery rhymes, are ideal for this stage, but any book will do provided each picture is taken separately. To quote again a book not intended for small children which was however thoroughly enjoyed by my son in his own way: it was one of the Rathbone books dealing with scientific experiments and showing a chemist at work. He called it "the man who cooks" and read it over and over again.

Next comes the perception of an elementary dramatic situation spread preferably over not more than two pictures. I find, though, that the type of book answering this specification is comparatively rare and cannot think of a better example than a Czech picture book by E. Cepcekova and B. Hajducikova. It is a series of stories about two helpful characters, Teddy and Piggy. Each story is in two pictures: the first presents a problem, the second its solution. On one page Teddy and Piggy find a kitten lost in the snow and crying bitterly. On the next page they take it home in their sledge and everyone is happy. I shall never forget the intensity with which my boy followed this drama when he was ready to understand it: He would "miaw" sadly over the first picture and rejoice saying, "Home!" and "Daddy!" over the next one.

As the child's imagination begins to develop he acquires a sense of humor. He no longer wants the pictures to be fully realistic. He thoroughly enjoys Tom Kitten dressed up in his small trousers being naughty and smacked by his mother.

I expect that the next stage will lead to the enjoyment of a full story of the Ardizzone type, but that is something I still have to learn.

Earlier I have said that material other than books can be used for the first stages of a child's reading. Newspapers, periodicals, well illustrated adult books enlarge his vocabulary and teach him to understand pictures. Children's literature comes into its own when the child has the first inkling of a dramatic situation. Provided his parents help him to acquire the elementary techniques necessary for following a story in pictures, the need for children's books begins approximately at the age of two. My reader who brought her son to our library chose the right time for it.

The Books the Boys Like, Reported By Their Mother

Mrs. Robert Mead

From Publishers' Weekly 189:107-10, February 21, 1966. Copyright by R. R. Bowker Company. Reprinted by permission.

A wise friend once told me that children like to be read to so much that they would listen contentedly to the laundry list. There is no question that the mere possession of Mommy or Daddy for a few minutes, for his very own, holds great meaning for a child in this age of scurrying parents. (And the TV, unfortunately, is such an easy substitute for the busy mother.) However, a parent is in for a glorious revelation when he discovers that reading aloud to his children can be as relaxing and as pleasurable for him as for the children--if the laundry list is chosen for the amusement and entertainment of both the reader and his listeners.

We are a very reading family. Our two boys, Robin, who is seven, and Slade, who is four, have seen books around the house since they were babies, so have come by their reading enthusiasm by osmosis. We have had great success in reading to them together; our enthusiasm, coupled with Robin's, is transmitted to Slade, and he will listen happily--even if he doesn't always understand. At first I translated the more difficult words into his jargon, but he would have none of that. He was right, it was a mistake; for even if Beatrix Potter did write a different language from that which a child of today speaks, she has appealed to many generations without any editing on my part. And Slade likes to hear a new word--and discover the meaning of it.

Occasionally we indulge the boys with separate reading sessions because there are certain books which Slade loves and which Robin has heard so often that they can no

Reading Interests--Children and YA

longer hold his full interest. The most obvious title that comes to mind is Winnie the Pooh. Both boys chose Christopher Robin for their literary hero when each was four. The little books in Maurice Sendak's "Nutshell Library" are dog-eared both from being read aloud to Slade and from his own readings. Pierre: A Cautionary Tale is the most dog-eared of the four. On his shelf of favorites are also: A Hole Is to Dig, Who Took the Farmer's Hat? The Littlest Rabbit, Swimmy and the peep-show book of Little Red Riding Hood. He also pores over The Fox Went Out on a Chilly Night, the ballad illustrated with glorious pictures of autumn in New England, and The Cow Who Fell in the Canal, with drawings of Holland which are so realistic that Slade will feel very much at home one day when he goes there himself. M. Sasek's books have much of the same fascination for both boys, and they have eyed New York most critically and appreciatively, as they looked for all the spots Mr. Sasek pointed out in his This Is New York. Now they can hardly wait to go to Rome, Paris and London to find Mr. Sasek's other landmarks. His enthusiasm has rubbed off on both boys. Astrid Lindgren's Tomten and her Tomten and the Fox are lovely to look at and to read, and have brought a new world of folklore to them.

A wonderful learning-to-count book is One Snail and Me. The story and charming illustrations give the numbers an imaginative twist. Diligence is pleasingly taught in The Little Engine That Could.

Required reading for a small boy is The Giant Nursery Book of Things That Go. George Zaffo has left no vehicle unturned and the drawings are technical enough to be educational as well as fun.

Richard Scarry's Best Word Book Ever is the best word book ever. I find Slade poring over each picture with new interest and amusement each time. I always feel that Mr. Scarry created the book with a small child on his knee begging for this or that. Slade is delighted when Robin reads to him "Ant and Bee," "Mr. Willowby's Christmas Tree" and "May I Bring a Friend?"

Favorite Books for a
Very Young Reader

Robin has many favorites which he's read many times

Ages One to Eight

over, and the enthusiasm of doing it himself never seems dulled by the repetition. His favorite beginning reader was Red Fox and His Canoe, and what age doesn't enjoy Nathaniel Benchley? Else Minarik's Little Bear is another fine starter and has a fine follow-up with three more Little Bear tales. I'm afraid I cannot overlook Dr. Seuss who once made a smash hit with Horton Hatches the Egg, but Robin's interest in him has diminished ever since. However, as long as I was not required to read them aloud, I was pleased when Robin was in first grade and derived so much pleasure from reading The Cat in the Hat and Green Eggs and Ham to himself. There is a newly published book called Big Max which is a delight! It is a mystery story for the beginner to read and what could make a child feel more grown up? Robin also likes to read The Meanest Squirrel I Ever Met, Cats and Bats and Things With Wings (and he loves the illustrations), and Kathleen Lines' collection of nursery stories and Thornton Burgess' animal stories.

I must certainly not omit one of our elder child's favorite pastimes, which is leafing through the Encyclopaedia Britannica. I don't mean to imply that he is particularly precocious, but there are words and illustrations that fascinate him, and often a volume is brought to me with a request to read aloud. Although it seems awfully ponderous to me, he seems to derive great pleasure from the information provided in its rather stark style. The Golden Encyclopedia and Mary Elting's Answers and More Answers have always made good reading in small doses, and they do help answer some of the questions which I feel inadequate to answer myself.

Books that Should Never Go Out of Print

The books that I am particularly pleased he reads with as much pleasure as I did as a child, will, I hope, never go out of print. One is The Story About Ping. It is most interesting to hear the modern child's reaction to the story that takes place in China. China is a mysterious enemy land in his mind and he is fascinated to learn more about it. In my youth China was simply the country one came to when digging a very deep hole on the beach. The other book is The Little House, which is also perhaps particularly interesting to the child of today who is used to seeing the ever-expanding city everywhere. The house itself is as great a hero as any human or animal in any other book. My children are strongly attracted by the idea that objects, whether they be houses, tugboats, or steamshovels, have personalities and souls.

There is a great difference at this age between what we read to him and what he reads to himself. There is a pitfall here, however, to be avoided. Quite often an adult's nostalgia gets the best of him, and he produces a book that was the high point of his childhood, forgetting that his high point occurred at age 10, when his child is only seven. The Wind in the Willows and Alice in Wonderland were my mistakes, and I hope that my insistence has not ruined them for later on. Everyone's child is different and only the parent can judge from his child's particular tastes when is the right moment to introduce a particular book. However, there are unlimited other treasures to be discovered in the meantime. For example, there is a great camaraderie between our child and his father over Frank Baum's Wizard of Oz books. These were a highlight in Daddy's childhood, and he and Robin are busily reading their way through the 39 books. (It's hard to discern who is the more enthusiastic.) My favorite to read to him is Robin Hood. He also loves to hear Favorite Poems Old and New.

Some Modern Classics
That Are Re-Read

Among the books that we have found most successful for reading to both boys, Ferdinand and Wee Gillis are all-time favorites. Robert Lawson's illustrations are in a category by themselves, as his direct black and white drawings are so basically appealing. In general, I feel that it takes color to stir my children's interest, but Mr. Lawson's bold detailed pictures can enrapture any child. The Atwaters' Mr. Popper's Penguins is another most successful story. Much in the same category are the creations of Bill Peet. He has written and illustrated an amusing series of stories in verse form. The rhymes greatly appeal to both children, and I find them very clever and witty. Mr. Peet's greatest success has been Chester, the Worldly Pig and there are several others.

The de Brunhoffs' Babar books are perfect reading for different age levels. The adventure is most exciting for the elder and the general humor and wonderful illustrations are thrilling for young children. The new Babar Comes to America is, to me, the best. Perhaps it is my amusement at finding my old world childhood friend confronted with such modern, busy, materialistic Americanisms. Babar has come a long way from his poisonous mushrooms when he goes to find entertainment at Disneyland. However, our children love the fact that Babar has been to some of the places they have.

Both boys have sat spellbound by the frequent readings of Peter Pan. Mary Poppins is a sentimental favorite of mine, but I feared that the concept of a nanny would mean nothing to my children. How far from the occasional teen-age baby-sitter of today can you get? However, it is Miss Travers' timeless, magic-filled imagination that brings the story to life for everyone, and no one has asked why Mary was living with the Banks family. It is refreshing to find that children need not always "identify" and learn that some people live and think very differently from them.

E. B. White has brought many laughs and tears to a four- a seven-, a twenty-eight-, and a thirty-year-old. What skill a man has when he can entertain all ages with one story! There was an evening in our household when all of us sat weeping together over Charlotte's brave and tragic death in Charlotte's Web. Stuart Little also delights us, but it will be some time before we feel "emotionally up" to tackling "Charlotte" again. I wish E. B. White were here to describe the closed and lovely circle that is formed when parents and children cry and laugh together over a fine book.

The Books They Like

The following is a list of the books that Mrs. Mead reads to her children, with authors, illustrators, and publishers:

Alice in Wonderland by Lewis Carroll. Illus. by John Tenniel. Macmillan.

Answers and More Answers by Mary Elting. Illus. by Tran Mawicke. Grosset.

Ant and Bee by Angela Banner. Illus. by Bryan Ward. Watts.

Reading Interests--Children and YA

Babar Comes to America written and illus. by Jean de Brunhoff. Random.

Big Max by Kin Platt. Illus. by Robert Lopshire. Harper (I Can Read Book).

The Cat in the Hat written and illus. by Dr. Seuss. Random.

Cats and Bats and Things with Wings by Conrad Aiken. Illus. by Milton Glaser. Atheneum.

Charlotte's Web by E. B. White. Illus. by Garth Williams. Harper.

Chester, The Worldly Pig written and illus. by Bill Peet. Houghton Mifflin.

The Cow Who Fell Into the Canal by Phyllis Krasilovsky. Illus. by Peter Spier. Doubleday.

Favorite Poems Old and New edited by Helen Ferris. Illus. by Leonard Weisgard. Doubleday.

Ferdinand by Munro Leaf. Illus. by Robert Lawson. Viking.

The Fox Went Out on a Chilly Night illus. by Peter Spier. Doubleday.

The Giant Book of Things that Go written and illus. by George Zaffo. Doubleday.

The Golden Encyclopedia by Dorothy Bennett. Illus. by Cornelius De Witt. Golden Press.

Green Eggs and Ham written and illus. by Dr. Seuss. Random.

A Hole Is to Dig by Ruth Krauss. Illus. by Maurice Sendak. Harper.

Horton Hatches the Egg written and illus. by Dr. Seuss. Random.

Ages One to Eight

Lavender's Blue by Katherine Lines. Illus. by Harold Jones. Watts.

Little Bear by Else Holmelund Minarik. Illus. by Maurice Sendak. Harper (I Can Read Book).

The Little Engine That Could by Watty Piper. Illus. by George and Doris Hauman. Platt & Munk.

The Little House written and illus. by Virginia Burton. Houghton Mifflin.

Little Red Riding Hood illus. by Patricia Turner. Merrie Thoughts.

The Littlest Rabbit written and illus. by Robert Kraus. Harper.

Mary Poppins by P. L. Travers. Illus. by Mary Shepard. Harcourt, Brace & World.

May I Bring a Friend? by Beatrice Schenk de Regniers. Illus. by Beni Montresor. Atheneum.

The Meanest Squirrel I Ever Met written and illus. by Gene Zion. Scribners.

Mr. Popper's Penguins by Richard and Florence Atwater. Illus. by Robert Lawson. Little, Brown.

Mr. Willowby's Christmas Tree written and illus. by R. Barry. McGraw-Hill.

Nutshell Library written and illus. by Maurice Sendak. Harper.

One Snail and Me by Emilie Warren McLeod. Illus. by Walter Lorraine. Little, Brown.

Peter Pan by James M. Barrie. Illus. by Mora Unwin. Scribners.

Red Fox and His Canoe by Nathaniel Benchley. Illus. by Arnold Lobel. Harper (I Can Read Book).

Richard Scarry's Best Word Book Ever written and illus. by Richard Scarry. Golden Press.

Some Merry Adventures of Robin Hood written and illus. by Howard Pyle. Scribners.

The Story About Ping by Marjorie Flack. Illus. by Kurt Wiese. Viking.

Stuart Little by E. B. White. Illus. by Garth Williams. Harper.

Swimmy written and illus. by Leo Lionni. Pantheon.

This Is New York written and illus. by M. Sasek. Macmillan.

Thornton Burgess' animal books. Grosset & Dunlap.

The Tomten and the Fox by Astrid Lindgren. Illus. by Harald Wiberg. Coward.

Wee Gillis by Munro Leaf. Illus. by Robert Lawson. Viking.

Who Took the Farmer's Hat? by Joan L. Nodset. Illus. by Fritz Siebel. Harper.

The Wind in the Willows by Kenneth Grahame. Illus. by Ernest Shepard. Scribners.

Winnie-the-Pooh by A. A. Milne. Illus. by Ernest Shepard. Dutton.

The Wizard of Oz by L. Frank Baum. Illus. by W. W. Denslow. Reilly & Lee.

The World of Christopher Robin by A. A. Milne. Illus. by Ernest Shepard. Dutton.

Dictionaries Before Six

Sylva Simsova

From The Bookseller, no. 3135, pp. 182-5, January 22, 1966. Reprinted by permission.

My book.

Room 10 is a very nus Room and
I like sumthing Els in my CLASS.
I can mayk things and I luv howm
and it is going to bee the suma
holideys soon onli two mar days
and I em going to play with my
Sisar and tok with my Mumi and
We are going to have a hepy tum
at hom the End.

When I read this "book" written by my child at the end of his first school year it occurred to me that he needed a dictionary. I decided to treat my boy's need with appropriate seriousness and this article is the story of my search for a picture dictionary.

What words is a boy of five and a half likely to use in his writing? Looking through some of his other scraps of paper I found that his expressions range from common words like Reyl Wey (railway), to specific words like Tomcat (spelled correctly), technical expressions like 100-68 Muyals Lodon (168 miles from London), and proper names like Noth Wesan Politeknik (North-Western Polytechnic). For my purpose I selected nine words to make a checklist by which I could judge the usefulness of junior dictionaries.

The list included everyday nouns (sister, railway), abstract nouns (time), a technical term (miles), verbs (make, talk), adjectives (happy, nice) and the useful word: more. One of the words was in the plural to check how dictionaries can help the child to overcome the barrier of having no grammar.

With this checklist plus a list of criteria for judging picture dictionaries from Library Journal (April 15, 1963, p. 1725), I examined 26 junior dictionaries listed in the British National Bibliography for the period 1950-64. The dictionaries seem to fall into five groups:

A.   Word books with a limited vocabulary, each word being illustrated:

    Boyce, E. R.: Gay Way Picture Dictionary, (Macmillan, 2s. 6d.).
    Moore, L.: A Child's First Picture Dictionary. 1948 (Wonder Books, 3s. 6d.).
    Noel, J.: The "Easy Word" Picture Dictionary, 1954 (Philip & Tacey, 3s. 6d.).
    Waddington, M.: Cassell's Picture Dictionary (6s. 6d.).
    Walpole, E. W.: The Golden Dictionary (Publicity Products, 10s. 6d.).

B.   Selective dictionaries with a number of illustrations:

    Derwent, L.: The Picture Word Book (Collins, 3s. 9d.).
    Derwent, L.: Children's Picture Dictionary (Collins, 10s. 6d.).
    Moore, L.: The Golden Picture Dictionary (Adprint, 5s.).
    Waddington, M.: Cassell's Second Picture Dictionary (6s. 6d.).

C.   Dictionaries aiming at comprehensiveness, with some illustrations of meaning:

    Arkley, A. J.: A Children's Working Dictionary (Hamish Hamilton, 8s 6d.).
    Courtis, S. A. and Watters, G.: The Giant All-colour Dictionary (Hamlyn, 21s.).
    Courtis, S. A. and Watters, G.: Learn at Home Illustrated Dictionary (Golden Pleasure, 36s.).
    Mclean, I. M.: Words: A Simple Dictionary for Boys and Girls (Warne, 4s.).
    Robertson, J.: Odham's Junior Dictionary Illustrated (13s. 9d.).

Stoloff, A. J.: Kingsway Dictionary, 1956 (Evans, 12s. 6d.).

D.   Dictionaries aiming at comprehensiveness, with illustrations of the encyclopaedic type:

Chambers's Children's Illustrated Dictionary (10s. 6d.).
Finch, P. and Nicholas, C.: Newnes Pictorial Dictionary (90s.).
Wise, L.: The Wonder Book Dictionary (Ward Lock, 30s.).
Coulson, J.: Oxford Illustrated Dictionary (Clarendon Press, 50s.).

E.   A junior version of an adult dictionary with no illustrations:

Anderson, A. B. and Arkieson, J. E.: Chambers's School Dictionary (4s.).
Chellew, H.: The Children's Dictionary (Crosby Lockwood, 2s. 6d.).
Mackenzie, D. C.: Oxford School Dictionary, 1960 (O.U.P., 6s.).
Hulme, T. J.: Junior Writing Dictionary, 1962 (Black, 8s. 6d.).
Parr, D. K.: Collins New Cleartype Dictionary (4s.).
Thorndike, E. L.: Thorndike School Dictionary (U.L.P., 5s.).
Wright, W. D.: A First Dictionary (Nisbet, 4s.).

Contradictory Claims

A child under six knows, it seems, the letters of the alphabet and likes to experiment with putting them together in various combinations to express words. He does not, however, know the order of the alphabet. Although able to read many of the words defined in a dictionary he is unable to read or understand definitions. He prefers large print and numerous illustrations combined with a small format.

All these contradictory claims combined with the need for a large vocabulary make it extremely difficult to produce a dictionary for the very young child. Ideally, every word should be illustrated as in Group A. Unfortunately the limited vocabulary of dictionaries in this group makes them practically useless for a child who has a great deal to say. Two dictionaries (Boyce and Noel) did not have any of the words on my checklist, Waddington had one and Moore had four. The limitation in Boyce is easy to understand as it is a word list of the Gay Way series of reading books. The choice of words in Noel is rather arbitrary and unsatisfactory in spite of the good idea of a separate section for verbs. Waddington is very good, especially if used in combination with its second volume. Its total vocabulary is, however, too small. The selection of words in Moore is based on key words which appear with great frequency in readers.

The only dictionary in Group A which had all but one of the words in my checklist was Walpole. Every word was illustrated; the meaning of each was clarified by a simple definition or an example of use. It is altogether an excellent dictionary except for its format. I find it hard to imagine a child consulting it while trying to write, because of the large spread of its open pages.

Dictionaries in Group B do not have such a limited vocabulary. With the exception of Waddington, which has only three of the words in my checklist, they each have over half of the words. Moore includes only five of them, but has on the other hand some advantages: simple definitions, grammatical forms and large print, which all make up in part for the bad impression created by the poor paper and mediocre illustrations.

The choice in this group is between the two dictionaries by Derwent: <u>The Picture Word Book</u>, which is cheap both in price and in the impression it gives, and <u>The Children's Picture Dictionary</u>, which is well produced and costs more. The selection of words is equally good in both (Picture Word Book scores 8, <u>Children's Picture Dictionary</u> 6) and both have an alphabetization guide.

In the third category (C) one would expect a complete coverage of all the words in the checklist. Surprisingly this is not so: only Courtis and Robertson have all the words. Of these two, Courtis is far superior in its production.

The remaining three dictionaries exclude many everyday words which form the child's basic vocabulary and concentrate instead on difficult and unusual words. It is typical, for instance, that the word "nice" is not in any of them and the word "sister" only in one. Arkley's dictionary is a systematic course in dictionary technique with the stress on "keywords of today." As such it is useful and very well produced. McLean is a dull little book with long lines of type that tire the eyes and with small illustrations, the subjects of which seem to have been chosen quite arbitrarily. Stoloff has the advantage of large print, but its general approach is too grown up.

Dictionaries in the last two groups (D and E) are too advanced for my purpose and therefore I have examined them only superficially.

Having spent some time at the British Museum studying these dictionaries I bought in the end Derwent's <u>Children's Picture Dictionary</u> (after some hesitation in favor of Walpole) making a mental note that Courtis would be a suitable present for the sixth birthday if my experiments with the use of a dictionary were successful. This should be followed at a much later birthday by the <u>Oxford Illustrated Dictionary.</u>

<u>Perfectly Understood</u>

My next problem was: Can a child under six use a dictionary? Does he want to use it?

Children are adept at imitation and rather than criticize my son for his rather original spelling I have instead let him see how the dictionary helps me with my own. He seems to have understood the idea perfectly.

Alphabetization was also a problem. Even with a good alphabetization guide, i.e., one which shows the complete alphabet on every page, it looks a difficult task for a child to find words in alphabetical sequence. Yet, just as children often find their way through the most complex grown-up talk, they occasionally manage to grasp principles which to us seem far beyond their comprehension.

After his first excited early morning with the new dictionary my son came to me with a complaint that the dictionary was no good because it did not have the word "hippopotamus." He was right, the word was not there. Many other words were there, however, but that did not seem to make much difference as can be seen from Chapter 2 of his book which I received shortly afterwards and which reads:

> Chapter 2.
>
> Lona Caym a man cald Mr. Crrm
> Wht Whs a WISAD AND He truyd
> to do sum Magik But He Cunot
> Sepl The thing So He poot a nowt
> up and wen Mr. WICH Red IT He
> Said ESI pis Sow He DUN THE Sep.
>
> (Along came a man called Mr. Crrm
> what was a wizard and he tried to do
> some magic but he could not spell the
> thing so he put a nought up and when
> Mr. Witch read it he said Easy-peasy,
> so he done the spell.)

Children's Reading Choices and Basic Reader Content

Ruth C. Smith

From Elementary English 39:202-9, March 1962. Reprinted with the permission of the National Council of Teachers of English and Ruth C. Smith.

The reading interests of children can be ascertained to some extent through their free choice of reading material at the library. The purpose of this investigation, therefore, was to determine how nearly the interest categories found in basic preprimers and primers designed as an introduction to reading for first grade children matched the reading interests of these children as evidenced by their "free-choice" selection of reading material from the library.

Procedure

Two libraries were selected at which to record and tabulate children's reading choices while thirty-seven preprimers and twelve primers, representing twelve publishing companies, were used to analyze and tabulate the interest categories found in the basic readers.

The library selections of twenty-six first grade children from the Campus School, University of Wisconsin--Milwaukee, thirty-three from Manitoba School, a city public school, and fifty-one from Blessed Sacrament, a parochial school, were recorded. The children from the Campus School used the Campus School Library. The children from Manitoba and Blessed Sacrament Schools made their selection at the Jackson Park Branch Library of the Milwaukee Public Library. These libraries were chosen because first grade children came to the library as class groups. This insured that all children in these rooms would be included, thus providing a fairly representative selection of first grade children.

The preprimers and primers used for the analysis

were selected at the Curriculum Library of the University of Wisconsin--Milwaukee, and represented those most generally used in the schools. After a brief review of several of these preprimers and primers and consulting with a children's librarian, a list of twenty-three categories of reading interest was prepared. The books which the children selected were then assigned on the basis of their content to one of the interest categories. Likewise every story in the preprimers and primers was read and on the basis of its content assigned to interest categories from the same list as was used for the tabulation of children's library selections. A story was classified in as many interest categories as were found in the story.

The interest categories found in the preprimers and primers were then compared with the categories of interest found in the books which the children selected at the libraries.

Results

Results from the library study. Of the 566 books withdrawn in the fourteen library visits by the 113 first grade children participating in the investigation, the five interest categories which ranked the highest in the children's free-choice reading were: Humor-Fantasy; Real Animals; and Fairy Tales. The two categories which ranked the lowest in these children's choices were: Adventure-Mystery and Store-Money, while two of the twenty-three categories, Clothes and Food, were not selected by any of the children.

A comparison of the choices at the two libraries showed that stories about animals, humor and fantasy, and nature were included in the five highest categories at both libraries. Stories about travel, airplanes, and astronomy were chosen most often at the Campus School Library, while children at the Jackson Park Library chose most frequently stories about holidays, birthdays, and fairy tales.

Results from the preprimers and primers. Stories about Children-Parents predominated in the content of the preprimers and primers. (See Table III.) Of the 859 stories examined, 807 were assigned to this area. "Real Animals" was the center of interest in 497 of these stories, while 245 stories were chiefly about Toys. These three categories ranked first, second, and third with Play-Games and Humor-Fantasy ranking fourth and fifth.

Ages One to Eight

Table I

Children's Interests and Preprimer and Primer Content Ranked By Frequency

Children's Interest Area	Frequency	Preprimer & Primer Interests*	Frequency
1. Humor-Fantasy	123	1. Children-Parents	807
2. Real Animals	108	2. Real Animals	497
3. Nature-Science	62	3. Toys	245
4. Holidays-Birthdays	40	4. Games-Play	153
5. Fairy Tales	38	5. Humor-Fantasy	64
6. Wild West-Cowboys	22	6. Travel-Airplanes	63
7. Birds	21	7. Helpers-Workers	61
8. Travel-Airplanes	21	8. Holidays-Birthdays	58
9. Children-Parents	19	9. Food	51
10. Astronomy	15	10. Make-Do Things	50
11. Helpers-Workers	15	11. School-Books-Poetry	45
12. Games-Play	15	12. Store-Money	41
13. Space	11	13. Nature-Science	19
14. Toys	9	14. Birds	16
15. Indians	9	15. Clothes	13
16. Make-Do Things	9	16. Adventure-Mystery	0
17. Other Countries	8	17. Fairy Tales	0
18. School-Books-Poetry	7	18. Indians	0
19. Long Ago-History	7	19. Astronomy	0
20. Adventure-Mystery	6	20. Other Countries	0
21. Store-Money	1	21. Wild West-Cowboys	0
22. Clothes	0	22. Long Ago-History	0
23. Food	0	23. Space	0

*Preprimer and primer stories classified in more than one area if necessary.

In contrast to the prevalence of these five categories of interest in the stories, eight areas of interest were not found at all in the content of either the preprimers or the primers. (See Tables III, IV, and V.) Publishers and writers of first grade reading materials used in this study have not introduced stories about Adventure-Mystery, Fairy Tales, Indians, Space, Astronomy, Other Countries, Wild West-Cowboys, and Long Ago-History. A few stories were found to contain the low ranking interest areas of Clothes, Birds, and Nature-Science. The categories of reading interest which ranked the highest and lowest were the same in the preprimers and primers, resulting in very little change in interest content at the two reading levels.

Table II

Reading Interests According to Free Choice of Library Books

Interest Area	Times Selected	Per Cent of Total	Rank
1. Children-Parents	19	3.35	9
2. Toys	9	1.59	15
3. Real Animals	108	19.09	2
4. Games-Play	15	2.65	11
5. Adventure-Mystery	6	1.06	20
6. Holidays-Birthdays	40	7.06	4
7. Fairy Tales	38	6.71	5
8. Indians	9	1.59	15
9. Humor-Fantasy	123	21.73	1
10. Travel-Airplanes	21	3.71	7.5
11. Nature-Science	62	10.95	3
12. Space	11	1.94	13
13. Astronomy	15	2.65	11
14. Birds	21	3.71	7.5
15. School-Books-Poetry	7	1.23	18.5
16. Other Countries	8	1.41	17
17. Store-Money	1	.17	21
18. Wild West-Cowboys	22	3.88	6
19. Long Ago-History	7	1.23	18.5
20. Helpers-Workers	15	2.65	11
21. Make-Do Things	9	1.59	15
22. Clothes	0	0	22.5
23. Food	0	0	22.5

Total Selections 566
Choice of books by 113 children on 14 library visits.

Ages One to Eight

Table III

Interest Categories in Forty-Nine Preprimers & Primers

Interest Area	Number of Stories	Per Cent of Total	Rank
1. Children-Parents	807	93.94	1
2. Toys	245	28.52	3
3. Real Animals	497	57.85	2
4. Games-Play	153	17.81	4
5. Adventure-Mystery	0	0	19.5
6. Holidays-Birthdays	58	6.75	8
7. Fairy Tales	0	0	19.5
8. Indians	0	0	19.5
9. Humor-Fantasy	64	7.45	5
10. Travel-Airplanes	63	7.33	6
11. Nature-Science	19	2.21	13
12. Space	0	0	19.5
13. Astronomy	0	0	19.5
14. Birds	16	1.86	14
15. School-Books-Poetry	45	5.23	11
16. Other Countries	0	0	19.5
17. Store-Money	41	4.77	12
18. Wild West-Cowboys	0	0	19.5
19. Long Ago-History	0	0	19.5
20. Helpers-Workers	61	7.10	7
21. Make-Do Things	50	5.82	10
22. Clothes	13	1.51	15
23. Food	51	5.93	9
Total Stories	859		

Comparison of children's library reading choices and interest areas found in primers and preprimers. From the data presented in Table I and VI pertaining to children's selections at the library, it appears that children in these first grades are most interested in stories about humor and fantasy, a category selected 123 times and representing 21.73 per cent of the total number of books selected by the children. Yet of the 859 stories analyzed from the forty-nine preprimers and primers only sixty-four or 7.45 per cent of the total number of stories could be classified in this interest area. The preprimers contained eighteen stories or 3.86 per cent with a small element of humor present. The primers showed an increase of twenty-eight, or a total of forty-six stories classifiable as humorous, not significantly different from what was found in the preprimers.

Real Animal stories ranked second both in reading interest in the children's library choices and in the preprimer and primer content. This category was selected 108 times or 19.09 per cent of the total selections made by the children at the two libraries. The preprimers contained 285 stories about real animals and the primers 212, with a total of 497 animal stories, 57.85 per cent of the 859 stories considered. It is interesting to note, however, that the animal stories found in the preprimers and primers were chiefly about dogs and kittens while the trade books were about a variety of animals, both tame and wild.

Nature and Science stories were preferred by children sixty-two times which represented 10.95 percent of the total choices made. They ranked third in frequency of selection. However, in the preprimers and primers this interest area ranked thirteenth and represented only 2.21 per cent of the total number of stories. The preprimers contained only eleven stories out of 466 which were about nature, science or weather. The primers treated these subjects in only eight out of 393 stories.

Holiday and Birthday stories comprised 7.06 per cent of the children's library selections and 6.75 per cent of the preprimers and primer stories. They ranked fourth and eighth respectively. Fairy Tales which were not found at all in the preprimers and primers but which comprised 6.71 per cent of the children's selections, ranked fifth among their "free choices."

Eight categories of reading interest were not found in the content of the preprimers and primers. The following table shows the number of times each one was selected by the children when they chose their library books, the per cent of the total, number of choices, and the rank of their library selections.

Ages One to Eight

Interest Area	Times Selected	Percentage	Rank
1. Fairy Tales	38	6.71	5
18. Wild West-Cowboys	22	3.88	6
13. Astronomy	15	2.65	11
12. Space	11	1.94	13
8. Indians	9	1.59	15
16. Other Countries	8	1.41	17
5. Adventure-Mystery	6	1.06	20

The two categories of reading interest which were found in the readers used in this study but not selected by the children at the libraries were Clothes, which was found in thirteen stories and ranked fifteenth, and Food, found in fifty-one stories and ranked ninth.

Table IV

Interest Categories in Thirty-Seven Preprimers

Interest Area	Number of Stories	Per Cent of Total	Rank
1. Children-Parents	459	98.49	1
2. Toys	157	33.69	3
3. Real Animals	285	61.15	2
4. Games-Play	92	19.74	4
5. Adventure-Mystery	0	0	19.5
6. Holidays-Birthdays	21	4.50	7
7. Fairy Tales	0	0	19.5
8. Indians	0	0	19.5
9. Humor-Fantasy	18	3.86	10
10. Travel-Airplanes	36	7.72	5
11. Nature-Science	11	2.31	13
12. Space	0	0	19.5

Table IV (continued)

Interest Categories in Thirty-Seven Preprimers

	Interest Area	Number of Stories	Per Cent of Total	Rank
13.	Astronomy	0	0	19.5
14.	Birds	4	.85	15
15.	School-Books-Poetry	15	3.21	11.5
16.	Other Countries	0	0	19.5
17.	Store-Money	22	4.72	7
18.	Wild West-Cowboys	0	0	19.5
19.	Long Ago-History	0	0	19.5
20.	Helpers-Workers	15	3.21	11.5
21.	Make-Do Things	27	5.79	6
22.	Clothes	6	1.28	14
23.	Food	21	4.50	8

Total Stories 466
Total preprimers examined 37

Ages One to Eight

Table V

Interest Categories in Twelve Primers

Interest Area	Number of Stories	Per Cent of Total	Rank
1. Children-Parents	348	88.54	1
2. Toys	88	22.39	3
3. Real Animals	212	53.94	2
4. Games-Play	61	15.52	4
5. Adventure-Mystery	0	0	19.5
6. Holidays-Birthdays	37	9.41	6
7. Fairy Tales	0	0	19.5
8. Indians	0	0	19.5
9. Humor-Fantasy	46	11.70	5.5
10. Travel Airplanes	27	6.87	8
11. Nature-Science	8	2.03	14
12. Space	0	0	19.5
13. Astronomy	0	0	19.5
14. Birds	12	3.05	13
15. School-Books-Poetry	30	7.63	8.5
16. Other Countries	0	0	19.5
17. Store-Money	19	4.83	12
18. Wild West-Cowboys	0	0	19.5
19. Long Ago-History	0	0	19.5
20. Helpers-Workers	46	11.70	5.5
21. Make-Do Things	23	5.85	11
22. Clothes	7	1.68	15
23. Food	30	7.63	8.5

Total Stories 393
Total primers examined 12

Table VI

Comparison of Children's Library Reading Interests and the Interest Areas Found in Preprimers and Primers

Interest Area	Per Cent of Total Selections	Rank	Per Cent of Total Stories	Rank
1. Children-Parents	3.35	9	93.94	1
2. Toys	1.59	15	28.52	3
3. Real Animals	19.09	2	57.85	2
4. Games-Play	2.65	11	17.81	4
5. Adventure-Mystery	1.06	20	0	19.5
6. Holidays-Birthdays	7.06	4	6.75	8
7. Fairy Tales	6.71	5	0	19.5
8. Indians	1.59	15	0	19.5
9. Humor-Fantasy	21.73	1	7.45	5
10. Travel-Airplanes	3.71	7.5	7.33	6
11. Nature-Science	10.95	3	2.21	13
12. Space	1.94	13	0	19.5
13. Astronomy	2.65	11	0	19.5
14. Birds	3.71	7.5	1.86	14
15. School-Books-Poetry	1.23	18.5	5.23	11
16. Other Countries	1.41	17	0	19.5
17. Store-Money	.17	21	4.77	12
18. Wild West-Cowboys	3.88	6	0	19.5
19. Long Ago-History	1.23	18.5	0	19.5
20. Helpers-Workers	2.65	11	7.10	7
21. Make-Do Things	1.59	15	5.82	10
22. Clothes	0	22.5	1.51	15
23. Food	0	22.5	5.93	9

Total Library Selections 566   Total Stories 859

Summary and Conclusions

In this investigation to determine how nearly the children's free-choice reading interests matched the interests in the content of the preprimers and primers, it was found that when these children selected their reading material they showed preference for stories about humor, fantasy, animals, nature, science, holidays, birthdays and fairy tales. (See Table VI.).

The examination of the preprimers and primers showed a narrower span of reading interests than in the children's choices since eight of the twenty-three interest categories were not found in the content of the selected readers. The category Children-Parents was found in an unusually high percentage of the total stories examined and a great majority of the stories were found to be about children playing with their dog or kitten. Animal stories were also highly favored by the children in their selection of trade books; however, the kinds of animals were more varied and the stories more informational.

In summary, therefore, the data seems to indicate that generally the preprimers and primers which the children are required to read, and which are supposed to stimulate an interest and desire to read, do not really satisfy their reading interests as shown by their "free choice" of books at the library. Although this library investigation was made with a limited number of children and at only two libraries, the writer believes the data are significant in pointing out that the book content which is concentrated almost specifically upon children, parents, toys, play, kittens, and dogs is not adequately meeting the reading interests and needs of a great many children of today. The children's selection of books showed a knowledge, understanding of, and a desire to read stories about the Wild West, space, astronomy, nature, animal adventure, humor, fantasy, fairy tales, and travel.

It appears, then, that the broad span of children's reading choices serves as an indication of the need for book publishers and writers of children's first grade reading materials to expand the interest content beyond the child, his parents, and his toys, and include more of the child's everyday world and its activities. It seems reasonable to expect beginning readers to include more variety and better balance to meet the modern interests of young children.

A Study of Children's Book Choices

Bette J. Peltola

From Elementary English 40:690-5+, November 1963. Reprinted with the permission of the National Council of Teachers of English and Bette J. Peltola.

Every two or three years the American Institute of Graphic Arts sponsors a show of the children's books which are the finest from a graphic arts point of view. From the four or five thousand books published for children in the years 1958, 1959, and 1960, ninety-eight books were chosen to be included in the 1958-60 Children's Book Show. Not all of the ninety-eight were excellent in all three areas: illustration, design, and production; but the books in this show can be considered the outstanding books of the three-year period, as judged by persons concerned with the graphic arts and with books for children.

When reviewing the award list from the point of view of persons concerned about children's choices of books, it seemed reasonable to attempt to investigate the extent of agreement between the jury's choices and children's choices. It was decided to limit this particular study to the book choices of first-grade boys and girls. One hundred ninety-two first-grade children in schools at and near a large university in a mid-western city were selected as the group for study. Each child was shown eight pairs of books and asked to decide which book in each pair he would like to have the chance to read. The books chosen for use in the study included sixteen books from the catalog of the AIGA 1958-60 Children's Book Show. These sixteen books were ones which had animals as the center of interest or as the leading characters in the book and were books which might reasonably appeal to a first-grade age group. The other sixteen books were books published in those same three years, using animals as the center of interest or the main characters, and listed in the annual catalog, 3300 Best Books for Children. These books were also judged to be reasonably within

the interest range of boys and girls in first grade. The
books used in the study are listed in Table I.

Each pair of books which a child saw was made up
of one AIGA book and one non-AIGA book. An individual
interview was held with each child so that he would be
considering the books independently without being influenced
by what other children were choosing. This minimized peer
influence and tended to make findings about the appeal of
the book itself more valid. The child was free to handle
and examine the books before he chose, and never were
more than the two books from which he was choosing available to him. The books had been paired so that each of
the sixteen AIGA books was paired with all sixteen of the
non-AIGA books. In doing this, the design of the study
would allow one to examine the groups of books as a whole,
or to compare one individual book with the entire set of
the other group of books, but not to compare one book with
one other book from the other group. No child saw any
book more than once. Each book was seen by ninety-six
children. Each book was paired with every book on the
other list six times.

The following hypotheses were tested statistically:

1. First grade children choose AIGA books and
   non-AIGA books an equal number of times.
2. Books on the AIGA list which also appear in
   3300 Best Books for Children are chosen an
   equal number of times with books appearing
   only on the AIGA list.
3. Boys and girls choose AIGA books an equal
   number of times.
4. Children who are very interested in books and
   children who show little or no interest in books
   choose AIGA books an equal number of times.
5. Children who are good readers and children
   who are poor readers choose AIGA books an
   equal number of times.
6. Books at the top and at the bottom of a ranked
   preference list show no significant difference
   in the times each was chosen.
7. There is no effect on the design of the study
   due to the different set of books shown to each
   child.

The hypotheses were tested using an analysis of variance
technique and the "t" test.

Table I

Books Used in Study

AIGA selected books

*Brown, Marcia	Felice
*Brown, Marcia	Tamarindo
Brown, Margaret Wise	The Dead Bird
Cunningham, Julia	The Vision of Francois the Fox
*Duvoisin, Roger	Petunia Beware!
*Janice	Angelique
Joslin, Sesyle	Brave Baby Elephant
Kepes, Juliet	Two Little Birds and Three
*Lionni, Leo	Inch by Inch
*Littlefield, William	The Whiskers of HoHo
*Minarik, Else H.	Little Bear's Friend
Osborne, M.M., Jr.	Rudi and the Mayor of Naples
Snyder, Dick	One Day at the Zoo
Tresselt, Alvin	The Smallest Elephant in the World
Ungerer, Tomi	Crictor
*Will (Lipkind)	The Little Tiny Rooster

*These books are also listed in the 1962 edition of 3300 Best Books for Children

Best Books books

Conklin, Gladys	I Like Butterflies
DuBois, William P.	Otto at Sea
Eastman, Philip	Sam and the Firefly
Ets, Marie Hall	Cow's Party
Fatio, Louise	The Three Happy Lions
Fritz, Jean	How to Read a Rabbit
Hoff, Syd	Julius
Ipcar, Dahlov	I Like Animals
Jones, Lee	Simpson
Lubell, Winifred	The Tall Grass Zoo
Minarik, Else H.	Father Bear Comes Home
Selsam, Millicent	Plenty of Fish
Slobodkin, Louis	Wide-awake Owl
Stolz, Mary	Emmett's Pig
Titus, Eve	Anatole and the Robot
Webb, Clifford	More Animals from Everywhere

Findings

There was a significant difference at the .01 level between the number of times children chose AIGA books and the number of times they chose non-AIGA books. The non-AIGA books were chosen a significantly greater number of times. There was no significant difference in the number of times AIGA books on the Best Books list and AIGA books not on the Best Books list were chosen.

Girls chose AIGA books a significantly greater number of times than did boys. This difference was significant at the .05 level. There was no significant difference between the number of times children whose teachers say they are very interested in books, and children whose teachers say they have little or no interest in books, chose AIGA books. Nor was there a significant difference between the number of times good readers and the number of times poor readers chose AIGA books. Children in the first grade who were receiving reading instruction in third level or higher basal readers or whose teachers said they could read materials at the third reader level were those considered good readers. Poor readers were those children receiving basal instruction in a primer or below in May of the first grade.

The four books chosen most often and the four books chosen least often were found to be chosen a significantly different number of times. Simple inspection will show that those chosen most often were chosen about four times as often as the four chosen least often. An analysis of variance was used to investigate the possibility of some effects accruing from the design of the study. None of the effects investigated was found to contribute significantly; therefore, it was assumed that the design did not bias the findings.

Conclusions

Based on the findings of this study, there would seem to be an indication of several factors which may influence children's choices of books. At the first-grade level, the illustrations do seem to be important in children's selection or rejection of a book. In many cases, first-grade children must rely on the illustrations for knowledge of the subject matter of a book. For this reason the subject of the illustrations, and how well the illustrations portray the subject in continuity, is important. The jacket or cover may also influence children's selection, as is suggested by the number of children who were ready to choose Syd Hoff's Julius before they even opened the book.

Action and humor seem to be two inseparable ingredients which children look for in the illustrations in their books. A study of the choices the children made will show that those books which were most popular contain unusual characters and out-of-the-ordinary episodes. At the age of six or seven, humor is still found mainly in events or actions rather than in words. As one moves farther down the ranked list of books, there is less action and less of the unusual in the books.

It is not possible to make any conclusive statements about the effect of color on children's book choice from the information available from this study. However, it seems reasonable to be able to state that factors other than color seemed to be having more effect. Color seemed to be important as an integral part of the illustration, but it did not seem to be the selling factor of a book. Appropriateness of color for the mood of the illustration may influence what children choose or do not choose.

Although girls chose AIGA books a significantly greater number of times than did boys, it seems necessary to look more closely at boys' and girls' choices and not merely conclude that girls' tastes are more like those of the AIGA jury, and therefore more developed and sophisticated than are boys' tastes. Study of the ranked lists for boys and for girls shown in Table II will suggest some factors which may have been operating to influence this significant difference. The entire list of books, ranked for the whole group of children and for boys and girls separately, shows that the same four books are in the first four places, although the second, third, and fourth choices are different from list to list. Two of these four books were chosen by the boys a greater percentage of times than they were chosen by the girls. These two books are DuBois' Otto at Sea and Eastman's Sam and the Firefly. Both of these books contain stories and illustrations with excitement and adventure. That girls also like this type of story is indicated by the fact that these two books also appear in the girls' first four

Ages One to Eight

Table II
Ranked List of Choices by Entire Group, by Boys, and by Girls

Boys and Girls	%	Boys	%	Girls	%
Hoff	89	Hoff	88	Hoff	90
DuBois	80	Eastman	87	DuBois	73
Eastman	79	DuBois	85	Titus	68
Titus	73	Titus	76	Eastman	66
Ungerer	59	Webb	66	Minarik-B	65
Snyder	58	Snyder	62	Ungerer	62
Ets	57	Ets	60	Joslin	61
Fatio	57	Fritz	57	Minarik-AIGA	61
Minarik-B	57	Fatio	56	Lionni	59
Webb	57	Jones	55	Fatio	58
Fritz	53	Slobodkin	54	Stolz	56
Joslin	53	Underer	53	Ets	55
Stolz	52	Minarik-B	50	Snyder	54
Tresselt	52	Tresselt	50	Tresselt	54
Slobodkin	50	Littlefield	50	Selsam	51
Littlefield	49	Stolz	48	Janice	50
Minarik-AIGA	49	M.W.Brown	47	Fritz	49
Lionni	48	Joslin	46	Littlefield	48
Selsam	48	Lubell	46	Webb	47
M.W. Brown	47	Selsam	45	M.W.Brown	47
Jones	47	Ipcar	43	Ipcar	47
Ipcar	45	Conklin	42	Slobodkin	46
Conklin	43	Kepes	40	Will	45
Janice	41	Lionni	39	Conklin	43
Kepes	41	Cunningham	38	Kepes	41
Will	41	Minarik-AIGA	38	Duvoisin	40
Lubell	38	Felice	37	Jones	38
Duvoisin	36	Will	36	Tamarindo	30
Felice	31	Janice	34	Lubell	25
Cunningham	28	Duvoisin	34	Felice	25
Tamarindo	27	Tamarindo	26	Cunningham	25
Osborne	14	Osborne	10	Osborne	17

choices. However, a greater percentage of boys chose these books over AIGA books than did girls, and there may be even greater appeal for boys in this type of story than there is for girls. Or there may be greater appeal for girls than for boys in some other types of stories.

Both Webb's More Animals from Everywhere and Lubell's Tall Grass Zoo seemed to be more popular with the boys than with the girls. The other nonfiction books on the list, Snyder's One Day at the Zoo, Conklin's I Like Butterflies, and Ipcar's I Like Animals, did not show this difference in sex preference, but this trend cannot be ignored.

The books, Vision of Francois the Fox and Felice, seemed to be chosen more often by boys than by girls. Although the difference in percentage of choice for Felice was significant at the .05 level, perhaps neither book was chosen often enough by either boys or girls to make the findings valid. The same can be said of other books showing some difference in choice by boys and girls, but near the bottom of the ranked lists. The differences in number of choices for these less popular books are important, however, when considered together with the other books showing differences, because they tend to reinforce some ideas about suspected trends.

Four of the five books which the girls seemed to choose a greater percentage of times than did the boys are from the AIGA list. The one that was not on the AIGA list has a close relationship to the AIGA list, and all five will be dealt with together. The five books are Leo Lionni's Inch by Inch, Joslin's Brave Baby Elephant, Janice's Angelique, and Else Holmelund Minarik's Little Bear's Friend and Father Bear Comes Home (the non-AIGA book). There are several striking factors about these five books considered as a group. First, these stories are milder than those which were favored by the boys more than by the girls. Another factor which these five books seem to have in common compared with the seven books which the boys chose more often is the reading level. Among the books chosen more often by the boys there is one book in which there was an attempt made to control the reading difficulty, Eastman's Sam and the Firefly. None of the other six books chosen more often by the boys seems to have the same ease of reading or the appeal to select by reading as do the five books selected more often by the girls. Although it seems necessary to point out the difference in the readability of the books the boys or the girls chose more often, a study of the entire list of the choices of boys and of girls does not suggest that the girls were more influenced by readability than were the boys. However, this possibility cannot be ruled out.

That the books at the top and near the bottom of the boys' list and of the girls' list are much the same would seem to bear out findings of earlier studies that boys' and girls' interests are similar. The variability of the books in the middle two-thirds of the lists suggests that there may be some sex differences, however. There may be some basic interests that boys and girls share at this age such as the adventure, humor and peril of the four most popular books. Other factors seem to have exerted enough influence to cause quite an amount of variability in the entire ranked lists for boys and for girls. Whether the differences between girls and boys in choice of AIGA books over non-AIGA books are really differences in taste discrimination in physical appearance, or are in subject matter or other considerations cannot be definitely stated. This is an area for further study.

Although no significant difference in choice of AIGA books by first-grade children exhibiting high interest in books and by children exhibiting little interest in books was found, the possibility that such a difference exists cannot be ruled out; it may certainly exist for older children. Possibly at the first-grade level, the experience with books and the levels of appreciation of both groups of children are not different enough to actually create any difference in their choices. Perhaps, also, their similar general interests will tend to make them choose the same books more than their dissimilar amount of interest in books themselves will tend to make them choose different books. One cannot ignore the fact that the standards of appreciation of seven-year-olds are newer and full of wonder and less developed than are those of the AIGA jury. These seven-year-olds probably would tend to be more like each other than would some of them tend to be like the AIGA jury in their standards of appreciation.

Implications

The jury's comment in the catalog of the AIGA Children's Books 1958-1960 Show includes this statement:

> . . . the child . . . is after all the one most affected by all the factors considered here. A young child may not always realize why one book is beautiful and another is not, but early impressions most certainly do exert their influence throughout a lifetime.

If this statement can be accepted, and serious reflection will probably not allow it to be rejected, it has some serious implications for teaching. First, it must be realized that the jury for the Book Show was composed of leaders in the fields of graphic arts and of children's books. Children cannot be expected to have the same tastes as the jury. The jury's tastes and criteria for selection have been developed by years of experience. Children's interests are naturally different from the jury's and cannot be overlooked. Theirs is a fresh view of life and their interests and tastes are commensurate with the experiences they have had.

One of the most important, and probably often neglected, objectives of the reading program is to develop an interest in using books both for pleasure and for information. Inseparable from this objective is the necessity for developing a taste for the better books, magazines, and other reading materials. Taste develops slowly through exposure to fine things which are also understandable on the level of development of the individual. Just as children are taught appreciation of music, of art, and of literature, so can they be helped to develop an appreciation of good graphic production. If the most popular books in this study exemplify the point of graphic and literary enjoyment and sophistication at which the teacher finds the child, it is at that level that he must begin. He need not cater to that level, but should use it to develop better taste in literature and in book design.

Findings which show the popularity of books such as those indicated by this study should not imply a necessity to create more books of this type or to cater to this interest and taste. Such findings are an indication of the existing status and the implications point toward the efforts which might be made toward improving children's literary and graphic tastes. Some of the selections of the AIGA jury for the Book Show are perhaps more sophisticated than childlike, and the books in the Show were chosen for outstanding appearance and not for content. Persons working with children and with books must keep them both in mind. However, they still strive to make the finest products which children are capable of appreciating available to them so that they may grow in graphic and literary appreciation and taste.

Bibliography

1. Children's Books 1958-60. New York: The American Institute of Graphic Arts, 1961.
2. 3300 Best Books for Children, 1962 Edition. New York: R. R. Bowker Company, 1962.

AIGA Books

*3. Brown, Marcia, Felice. New York: Charles Scribner's Sons, 1958.
*4. Brown, Marcia, Tamarindo. New York: Charles Scribner's Sons, 1960.
5. Brown, Margaret Wise, The Dead Bird. New York: William R. Scott, Inc., 1958.
6. Cunningham, Julia, The Vision of Francois the Fox. Boston: Houghton Mifflin Company, 1960.
*7. Duvoisin, Roger, Petunia Beware! New York: Alfred A. Knopf, Inc., 1958.
*8. Janice, Angelique, New York: McGraw-Hill Book Company, 1960.
9. Joslin, Sesyle, Brave Baby Elephant. New York: Harcourt, Brace & World, Inc., 1960.
10. Kepes, Juliet, Two Little Birds and Three. Boston: Houghton Mifflin Company, 1960.
*11. Lionni, Leo, Inch by Inch. New York: Ivan Obolensky, Inc., 1960.
*12. Littlefield, William, The Whiskers of Ho Ho. New York: Lothrop, Lee and Shepard Company, 1958.
*13. Minarik, Else Holmelund, Little Bear's Friend. New York: Harper & Brothers, 1960.
14. Osborne, M. M. Jr., Rudi and the Mayor of Naples. Boston: Houghton Mifflin Company, 1958.
15. Snyder, Dick, One Day at the Zoo. New York: Charles Scribner's Sons, 1960.
16. Tresselt, Alvin, The Smallest Elephant in the World. New York: Alfred A. Knopf, Inc., 1959.
17. Ungerer, Tomi, Crictor. New York: Harper & Brothers, 1958.

*18. Will (Lipkind), The Little Tiny Rooster. New York: Harcourt, Brace and World, Inc., 1960.

*Those AIGA books which are starred are also included in the catalog, 3300 Best Books for Children, 1962 Edition.

19. Conklin, Gladys, I Like Butterflies. New York: Holiday House, Inc., 1960.
20. DuBois, William Péne, Otto at Sea. New York: Viking Press, 1958.
21. Eastman, Philip, Sam and the Firefly. New York: Random House, Inc., 1958.
22. Ets, Marie Hall, Cow's Party. New York: Viking Press, Inc., 1958.
23. Fatio, Louise, The Three Happy Lions. New York: McGraw-Hill Book Company, 1959.
24. Fritz, Jean, How to Read a Rabbit. New York: Coward-McCann, 1959.
25. Hoff, Syd, Julius. New York: Harper and Brothers, 1959.
26. Ipcar, Dahlov, I Like Animals. New York: Alfred A. Knopf, Inc., 1960.
27. Jones, Lee, Simpson. New York: Holt, Rinehart, and Winston, Inc., 1960.
28. Lubell, Winifred, The Tall Grass Zoo. Chicago: Rand-McNally, 1960.
29. Minarik, Else Holmelund. Father Bear Comes Home. New York: Harper and Brothers, 1959.
30. Selsam, Millicent, Plenty of Fish. New York: Harper & Brothers, 1960.
31. Slobodkin, Louis, Wide-awake Owl. New York: Macmillan Company, 1958.
32. Stolz, Mary, Emmett's Pig. New York: Harper & Brothers, 1959.
33. Titus, Eve, Anatole and the Robot. New York: McGraw-Hill Book Company, 1960.
34. Webb, Clifford, More Animals from Everywhere. New York: Frederick Warne & Company, Inc., 1959.

Reading Interests of First Graders

Helen E. Rogers and H. Alan Robinson

From Elementary English 40:707-11, November 1963. This article is based on a study conducted by Mrs. Rogers in partial fulfillment of the requirements for a Master's Degree, and is reprinted with the permission of the National Council of Teachers of English, Helen E. Rogers, and H. Alan Robinson.

What do first graders want to read? A comparison of beginning basal readers and easy-to-read trade books often reveals major differences in content emphasis. Beginning basal readers appear to be slanted especially toward the child and his activities in and around his immediate environment. Beginning trade books appear to encompass fantasy, fairy tales, mystery, space travel, etc., in addition to home, school, and community activities.

Rapid technological advances of recent years must certainly have increased the experiential background of the first graders. The major impact of television on the life of a preschool child may very well have changed the reading interests of first graders. Are first graders uninterested in reading stories limited to their daily activities? Do first graders really crave the additional kinds of experiences included in trade books? Do boys and girls have different reading interests? Do good and poor readers have different reading interests? Are first graders, exposed today to so many broad experiences, eager to read about current events?

With the foregoing questions in mind, a study was conducted with first graders in Gary, Indiana, during May, 1962, to test the following hypotheses:

Hypothesis One: First-grade children want books which will enrich and expand their knowledge of, and experience with the world in general, rather than have the books limited to the relating of stories about familiar daily activities of children like themselves.

Hypothesis Two: First-grade boys have already developed markedly different reading interests from those held by first-grade girls.

Hypothesis Three: First-grade children who are poor readers will have reading interests which are similar to those held by good first-grade readers.

Related Literature

In 1955, Harris[3] conducted a study with 248 first graders to discover their expressed reading interests and the adequacy of current basic readers in meeting these interests. In an interview situation he learned that first-grade children are interested in the same elements, whether the medium be reading, radio, television, or movies. Boys and girls were interested in cowboys and Indians, fairy tales, comics and funny stories, and pets and other animals. Girls seemed to like stories about children and stories about romance and marriage more than the boys; boys were more inclined to like stories about adult adventure and exciting events.

Girls chose basic reader content significantly more often than boys. Poor readers, in general, showed a significantly greater preference for basic reader content than good readers. No significant differences relating to level of intelligence were discovered.

Gunderson[2] worked with 21 second graders of the University Elementary School, University of Wyoming. She attempted to determine their reading interests by reading fourteen books to them and then asking which stories they liked and why. The results of this 1949 study showed that these children liked, most of all, stories which contained humor. Their other choices included stories with excitement, suspense, adventure, an element of magic or fancy, and a satisfactory ending in which justice triumphs.

In a 1946 study conducted by Witty and others,[5] the children in kindergarten and the first three grades were asked to name the stories they liked best. Their homeroom teachers wrote down the pupils' responses and reported them

Ages One to Eight

as homeroom choices. The list compiled from these responses showed stories of animals (wild or tame, real or fanciful) predominating. Fairy tales and humor followed in that order.

Norvell[4] conducted a study of the reading interests of children in grades three through six. Twenty-four hundred students were asked to classify selections as very interesting, fairly interesting or uninteresting. A total of 1,576 stories were involved in the survey. Norvell found that as early as the third grade girls' and boys' choices in reading differed. Girls enjoyed many boys' books, but boys rejected almost all girls' books.

Procedure

Design of the Study

In this study the reading interests of 275 first graders were ascertained through the use of a thirty-two-item questionnaire. The questionnaire was evaluated independently by three professional children's librarians and two experienced first-grade teachers. To test and then refine the questionnaire, a pilot study was conducted using six children not involved in the study itself. This group included two good readers, two average, and two poor readers. As a result of the pilot study, the questionnaire was modified to avoid encountering any reading difficulties, even for the poor readers.

Eight possible areas of reading interest were explored with four items on the questionnaire representing each area. Hence, the thirty-two questionnaire items in Figure I broke down into eight major categories: today's world, items 1, 5, 9, 13; family activities, 2, 6, 10, 14; historical events, 3, 7, 11, 15; make-believe themes, 4, 8, 12, 16; humorous situations, 17, 21, 25, 29; adventurous stories, 18, 22, 26, 30; anxiety situations, 19, 23, 27, 31; and happy activities, 20, 24, 28, 32.

Figure I

The Thirty-two Items on the Questionnaire

1. What an astronaut does

2. The things a family does
3. The way people lived long ago
4. An animal who could talk
5. A person on TV
6. A child who has a pet
7. Indians
8. A prince and princess in fairyland
9. Boys and girls who live in a faraway country
10. A birthday party
11. George Washington
12. A magic ring
13. Building a bridge
14. Grandmother's visit
15. Old-fashioned things
16. A friendly giant
17. Funny things that happen to a seven-year-old child
18. A haunted house
19. A child who is lost
20. A happy day at the beach
21. A funny "dress-up" party
22. A child exploring a cave
23. A day in the hospital
24. Fun at school
25. Funny things a pet does
26. A boy and girl who hear a mysterious noise
27. A pupil who didn't learn his numbers
28. A child who won a prize
29. A funny clown
30. An exciting airplane ride
31. A child who was afraid
32. A happy Christmas day

The questionnaire was administered to the 275 first graders by their classroom teachers in May of 1962. The presentation of the questionnaire to the children was prefaced by an explanation that there were no "right" answers to these questions, that different people like different things. Following this explanation, very careful directions on how to mark the answers were given using examples on the blackboard. Each item began "Would you like to read a book about ----." followed by "LIKE" and "NOT LIKE." The children were asked to circle the word or words that described how they felt about reading each kind of book. When the pupils understood the task, the teacher read each question aloud so that no child would encounter any word recognition difficulties.

Findings and Discussion

The entire group of 275 first graders appeared to have a wide variety of "likes," for the average number of items liked by the group of children was 25.5 out of a possible 32. Five story ideas were liked by at least ninety percent of the children. They were a magic ring, George Washington, a happy Christmas day, a friendly giant, and a funny clown.

For these first graders, their favorite type of story appeared to be make-believe. Only ten boys and one girl said they would not like to read about a magic ring, the most popular item on the questionnaire. These findings substantiate Frank's contention that "despite the controversy that has raged in the past few decades about fairy tales, the place of fantasy in the child's reading is nevertheless firmly established now, as it has always been."[1]

Figure II

Areas of Reading Interest Demonstrated by
275 First-Grade Pupils

Order of Preference	Category
1	Make-believe
2	Happiness
3	Humor
4	Adventure
5	History
6	Family
7	Anxiety
8	Today's World

Figure II shows the story ideas grouped in the eight categories and the categories ranked in order of popularity.

Hypothesis One appears to be refuted partially, for the children ranked last their desire to read about events and people in the world-at-large; but they also ranked family activities low (sixth). These first-grade children turn to reading for entertainment but seem to have not yet developed the desire to use reading as a tool for gaining information about today's world nor do they appear to look to reading as a mirror for reflecting their own lives.

The least liked category was today's world. The questionnaire was administered shortly after the historic orbit of John Glenn and so "astronaut" was a familiar concept to these children. Yet reading about an astronaut ranked 26.5, thus falling in the last quartile of popularity. Other questions in this category were not popular. Ranking 21st, yet the favorite item in this category, was reading about boys and girls who live in a faraway country.

Reading about a person on TV rated 30th on the 32-point scale. For this population, it appeared that seeing people on TV did not create an interest in reading about them. At least the interest wasn't strong enough to take precedence over many other topics. It must be noted, however, that there was no mention made in this study of wanting to read a book which had been dramatized on TV. It may be that historical events or fiction appearing on TV would create a desire to read about them while TV personalities had less appeal for this group. The item about "building a bridge" was least liked of all items on the questionnaire, ranking thirty-second.

The place of the family activities category deserves special attention. Most basal reader materials at first-grade level seem to feature stories that fall into this category. Yet there are many other ideas for stories that are rated more interesting by first graders. In fact, only stories with anxiety-causing plots or dealing with today's world were less popular. The results of this study seem to indicate that stories of fantasy, adventure, happiness, humor, and history might generate more interest in reading than do family activities.

Sex Differences

Hypothesis Two has been substantiated--reading interests of the boys seem markedly different from those of girls in the first grade. These differences are depicted in Figure III.

Figure III

Order of Interest by Categories
As Shown by Boys and Girls

Order of Preference	Boys	Girls
1	Adventure	Make-believe
2	History	Humor
3	Make-believe	Happiness
4	Happiness	Family
5	Humor	Adventure
6	Today's World	History
7	Anxiety	Anxiety
8	Family	Today's World

  The greatest contrast appeared in the family activities, adventurous, and historical categories. Boys seemed to prefer stories with adventurous and historical themes, while girls ranked family life stories higher than boys. The greatest difference on any single story idea involved the desire, or lack of desire, to read about Indians. Boys ranked reading about Indians below only George Washington, a friendly giant, and a magic ring, while girls liked it better than only one item, building a bridge. In contrast, Harris[6] found cowboys and Indians liked by both boys and girls.

  Boys were much more interested than girls in the specific story ideas of an exciting airplane ride, what an astronaut does, and a child exploring a cave. These results are in harmony with Harris' study which found boys liking adventurous and exciting stories better than girls.

  Turning to the themes of stories that girls ranked noticeably higher than boys, we find a funny dress-up party, grandmother's visit, things a family does, and a prince and princess in fairyland high up on the list. It would appear that girls have more interest in fantasy, home life, and romance than do boys even as early as first grade. These differences may possibly reflect a traditional picture our culture appears to have for the sex roles--girls generally favor home and family, rejecting violence and danger; boys frequently seek out adventure and excitement.

Reading Ability

Hypothesis Three appears to be valid within the scope of this study. The reading interests of these good and poor readers are similar, but because of the small number of poor readers (youngsters who were receiving instruction in May, 1962 in a primer or preprimer), extreme caution must be taken in making any generalizations. Twelve percent (33) of the group (275) fell in the poor reader classification, thirty-nine percent (107) in the average classification, and forty-nine percent (135) in the good reader (2^1 or higher book) classification. Figure IV shows the categories as ranked by these good and poor readers.

Figure IV

Order of Interest by Categories
As Shown by Good and Poor Readers

Order of Preference	Good Readers	Poor Readers
1	Make-believe	Make-believe
2	Humor	Happiness
3	Happiness	Adventure
4	History	Humor
5	Adventure	History
6	Family	Anxiety
7	Anxiety	Family
8	Today's World	Today's World

Need for Further Study

1. We need to know on what basis acceptances or rejections were made. For example, was "Indians" rejected by the girls because it brought to mind ideas of violence rather than ideas of adventure, excitement, and our cultural heritage? Or on what basis was a "funny dress-up party" evaluated? Was it regarded as humorous because the word funny was used? Or did the word dress-up predominate the pupils' evaluations and did fantasy become the determining factor for liking or not liking?

2. The questionnaire used in this study was extremely limited in ascertaining the interests of children in reading about people and events on the contemporary scene. Perhaps future questionnaires of this type ought to delve more deeply into interests related to prominent living people and current events.

3. Much more exploration probably needs to be made of interests related directly to the space age. A variety of questions in this area might throw more light on those aspects of space and space travel which appear to interest first-grade children.

4. An expression of interest may not be sufficiently strong to lead to the actual reading of a book. We need further study to determine how closely the expressions of interests are allied to the actual reading habits of these children, keeping in mind the limiting factor of the books available.

5. It might be particularly valuable to study the expressed interests of children prior to kindergarten, in kindergarten, and at the beginning of first-grade instruction. Since eighty-eight percent of the children in this study were completing the second half of the first-grade reading material or were already in second-grade readers, their reading interests may have been molded by these reading experiences. Studies prior to any reading instruction might point to areas of interest which undergo changes as a result of instruction or materials of instruction.

Bibliography

1. Frank, Josette, Your Child's Reading Today. Children's Book Committee, The Child Study Association, 1960.
2. Gunderson, Agnes G., "What Seven Year Olds Like in Books," Elementary English, 30 (March, 1953), 163-166.
3. Harris, James M., The Expressed Reading Interest of First Grade Boys and Girls and the Adequacy of Current Basic Readers in Meeting These Interests, Doctoral Dissertation, Cornell University, 1955.

4. Norvell, George W., What Boys and Girls Like to Read, Silver Burdett Co., 1958.
5. Witty, Paul, Ann Coomer, Dilla McBean, "Children's Choices of Favorite Books: A Study Conducted in Ten Elementary Schools," Journal of Educational Psychology, 37 (May, 1946), 266-278.

What Do First Graders Like To Read?

Sister Mary Consuelo, O.S.U.

From the Catholic School Journal 67:42-3, February 1967. Copyright by Bruce Publishing Company. Reprinted by permission.

What do first graders like to read? A survey was made of the reading tastes of 29 first graders during their second semester of grade one at Sacred Heart Model School, a campus laboratory school at Ursuline College, Louisville, Ky.

The children's reading scores from standardized tests were studied to ascertain reading levels. Titles correlating with the unit themes in the basic reading program for each group were selected. From these books each child chose what he wanted to read. If these books did not appeal to the young patrons, an effort was made to satisfy their interests from among other titles. Less guidance was needed as the semester progressed and the children became more competent in choosing suitable books.

Learn Library Tasks

During the scheduled weekly library period, these first graders were trained to charge out their own books and to file the book cards on the card sorter for the librarian. This procedure freed the teacher and the librarian to assist the children with their selections. A record was kept of the titles read by each child on individual borrower's cards, which were inserted in book pockets bearing each child's name. These pockets were posted on the class bulletin board in an attractive setting that varied from month to month.

An oral book report was required by the first grade teacher to check reading comprehension. The book report was chiefly in the form of a dialogue about the book and gave

Animals 41%
Religious 4%
Science 5%
Miscellaneous 7%
Fairy 10%
Realistic 33%

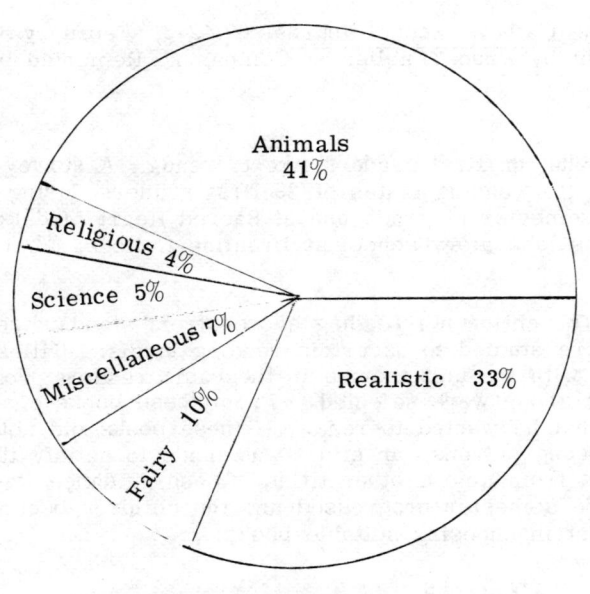

Class As a Whole

Ages One to Eight   67

the child permission to select another book. Many children made frequent and even daily, unscheduled visits to the library, usually before morning classes.

In the survey it was found that 41 percent of the books read by this first grade were animal stories; 33 percent were realistic stories; 10 percent fairy tales and fantasy; 7 percent, miscellaneous; 5 percent, science; and 4 percent, religious.

In the animal story group, Wanda Gag's Millions of Cats was the most popular, and in the realistic group, Phyllis Krasilovsky's The Old Man Who Didn't Like to Wash His Dishes.

The study also revealed that reading maturity was probably a significant factor in the percentage of fairy tales and fantasy read in each reading group. Group one, composed of the most mature readers, showed a preference for animal and realistic stories (38 and 32 percent respectively). They chose 15 percent of their titles from fantasy and fairy tales as compared with 6 percent for group two and 7 percent for group three. Possibly this is a normal reaction since fantasy frequently requires creative insight of the reader. Maturity also seemed to be a deciding factor in the area of science books. Group one read one and one-half times as many science books as group two, and almost three times as many as group three.

Race, Illustrations, and Interest in Materials
for Reading and Creative Writing

Monroe Rowland and Patricia Hill

From the Journal of Negro Education 34:84-7, Winter 1965. Reprinted by permission.

Approximately ten percent of the children of the United States are Negro--yet they are reading materials peopled almost solely, if the illustrations are taken as a criterion, by Caucasians. Materials for other subjects reflect this same bias. One might well consider: "What is the interest of the nation's Negro children in materials so illustrated?" "What would be the interest of the nation's Caucasian children in materials illustrated with Negroes?" Prejudice is learned early. Allport reports that:

> . . . it takes him (the child) the first six to eight years of his life to learn total rejection and another six years or so to modify it to fit the complex adult creed which attempts to combine ethnocentrism with democracy.[1]

This study was undertaken in an attempt to answer the question: Is the racial content of school materials related to the interest of children in them? In less precise terms: How interested are children in reading or using materials illustrated with individuals who are either totally rejected by the reader or who totally reject him?

The answer to this question may be significant since attitudes and interests have so frequently been found to be related to achievement. Groff[5] notes that ". . .reading comprehension of the individual child as he reads is influenced. . .by his attitudes toward the content type of materials being read." Crossen[3] observes that unfavorable attitudes interfere with critical reading skill. Hinze[6] established the relationship between the emotional tone of words and their interpretation. A number of similar studies (2, 4, 7, 8, 9, 10) have indicated a significant relationship between attitudes and achievement in other school subjects. The existence of this relationship underlies the need to know to what extent the racial content of school materials influences the interest of children in them.

The hypothesis of the study was that the interest of children in materials for reading and creative writing would be influenced by the racial content of those materials and the race of the child.

Design of the Study

Subjects

The children studied were in a first grade in a racially mixed school attendance area--an area apparently well-integrated and static in population composition. There were fourteen Caucasian children, seven boys and seven girls, and seventeen Negro children, seven boys and ten girls. The teacher was Caucasian. Little intelligence data were available on the children although their Pintner-Cunningham Primary Reading Test scores ranged from the second to the seventh stanine.

Procedures

Materials--The classroom teacher prepared two sets of materials for reading: one set illustrated with Negroes, the other with Caucasians. The materials consisted of twelve pairs of pictures and their accompanying stories mounted on red construction paper. The stories in each pair were identical. The pictures, clipped from magazines, were as nearly identical as possible in content, quality, and attractiveness with only the race of the characters depicted varying. Only black and white illustrations were used. Fourteen similar pairs of materials were prepared for creative writing. Although essentially the same as the reading materials, they lacked stories; it was the task of the children to create their own.

Administration--The reading materials were placed on the reading shelf with pairs in adjacent positions. Each pair was separated by the space of a foot from other pairs. At appropriate times, the children were instructed to go to the reading shelf and to choose a story to read. Whenever one member of a pair was selected, its mate was removed to eliminate the possibility of a forced selection. Each child was given six opportunities to select reading materials.

Creative writing materials were handled similarly. The children were told to examine all of the materials before they selected the one about which they wished to create a story. Each child had six opportunities to select writing materials. All choices of children were recorded.

The selection of any one of a pair was interpreted as indicating a greater interest in that item than in its counterpart.

Analysis--In addition to simply describing the selections of the children, the writers characterized certain children as "committed" to selecting either Caucasian or Negro materials. Since selection patterns of 6-0 or 5-1 could occur by chance only eleven per cent of the time, such patterns were identified as "committed" for either reading or creative writing choices. Patterns ranging from 9-3 to 12-0 could occur by chance only seven per cent of the time and were likewise classified as "committed" with respect to the twelve selection opportunities the pupils had in combination. Analysis was then undertaken of the patterns of selection commitment with the test for difference in proportions.

Findings

Patterns of Selection

Reading- Reading selections of both Caucasian and Negro children ranged from six Caucasian choices (6C) and no Negro choices (0N) to only one Caucasian choice (1C) and five Negro choices (5N). The median pattern for Caucasian children was 4C-2N. The median selection pattern for the Negro children was 3C-3N.

Creative Writing--In creative writing, the Caucasian selection patterns ranged from 6C-0N to 2C-4N. The Negro children ranged in their selection patterns from 5C-1N to

Ages One to Eight   71

1C-5N. The median pattern of the Caucasian children was the same as in reading, 4C-2N. Similarly the median pattern of the Negro children was identical with that in reading, 3C-3N.

<u>In combination</u>--When choice patterns were combined for reading and writing it was found that the range of patterns for Caucasian children was from 11C-1N to 4C-8N. The range of selection patterns of Negro children was somewhat narrower--from 9C-3N to 3C-9N. The median pattern of the Caucasian children was 8C-4N. The median pattern for the Negro Children was 7C-5N.

When these selection patterns of Negro and Caucasian children were statistically compared with the Kolmogorov-Smirnov test, no significant differences were found.

Patterns of Commitment

Six Caucasian children were "committed" to selecting Caucasian materials in reading; one was committed to selecting Negro materials. Only two Negro children were committed to selecting Caucasian materials in reading, while one was committed to the selection of Negro materials. In creative writing, three Caucasian children committed themselves to selecting Caucasian materials, while none committed to the use of Negro materials. On the other hand, three Negro children committed themselves to the use of Caucasian materials for creative writing and two committed to the use of Negro materials. In the combined situation, it was found that five Caucasian children were committed to Caucasian choices while none were committed to Negro choices. In contrast, two Negro children committed to the use of Caucasian materials and three committed to the use of Negro materials.

Table I, on the following page, reports these data.

Table I

Frequency With Which Children Committed to the Use of Racially Illustrated Materials in Reading, Creative Writing, and in Combination

	Reading Materials		Creative Writing Materials		Combined Materials	
	C*	N*	C	N	C	N
Caucasian Children (N=14)	6	1	3	0	5	0
Negro Children (N=17)	2	1	3	2	2	3

*C= Committed to choice of Caucasian materials.
N= Committed to choice of Negro materials.

The data on commitment to a given selection pattern were recast in four different ways: (1) commitment to selection of materials illustrated with the user's own race; (2) commitment to the selection of materials illustrated with the race other than the user's own; (3) commitment to the selection of materials illustrated with Caucasians; and (4) commitment to the selection of materials illustrated with Negroes. When this was done, some new facts emerged. They are listed below:

1. A significantly (.01) greater proportion of Caucasian children than Negro children committed to the use of reading materials illustrated with their own race.

2. A significantly (.05) greater proportion of Negro

children than Caucasian committed to the use of creative writing materials illustrated with the opposite race.

    3. A significantly (.05) greater proportion of Caucasian children than Negro committed to the use of reading materials illustrated with Caucasians.

    4. In the combined situation, a significantly (.05) greater proportion of Negro children committed to the use of Negro materials.

Conclusions and Implications

    The hypothesis was accepted: the interest of children as measured by their voluntary selections, in materials for reading and creative writing was influenced by the racial content of the materials and the race of the child. The ambivalence of the selections and commitments of the Negro children, as contrasted with the definite position assumed by many of the Caucasian children, is a point of significance.

    With the relationship between interest and achievement firmly established, and the tendency noted for interest to be related to the racial content of the materials, it would seem desirable to increase the production of materials illustrated with a variety of racial types. Although no relationship has been established between racial content and achievement, the logical step is not difficult to take.

    Perhaps several kinds of research are indicated. Certainly the sample on which this study was based was a small one, the community was integrated, and the materials were limited in number, content, and purpose. Other studies might well be undertaken in communities of a different nature--in which the Negro occupies a different position. Larger groups should be used and materials should cover a broader range. In addition, it may not be undesirable to attempt to study the validity of the writers' logical step from racial content to interest to achievement.

Bibliography

1. Allport, Gordon W. The Nature of Prejudice. New York: Doubleday and Company, 1958, p. 22.

2. Carey, Gloria L. "Sex Differences in Problem-Solving Performance as a Function of Attitude Differences," The Journal of Abnormal and Social Psychology, 56:256-60, March, 1958.
3. Crossen, Helen J. Effect of the Attitudes of the Reader Upon Critical Reading Ability. University of Chicago, 1947.
4. Feierabend, Rosalind L. "Review of Completed Research," Research Problems in Mathematics Education. p. 3-48. U.S. Dept. of Health, Education, and Welfare. Monograph No. 3, Washington: Government Printing Office, 1960.
5. Groff, Patrick J. "Children's Attitudes Toward Reading and Their Critical Reading Abilities in Four Content-Type Materials," The Journal of Educational Research, 55:313-17, April, 1962.
6. Hinze, Helen K. "The Individual's Word Association and His Interpretation of Prose Paragraphs." Journal of General Psychology, 44:193-203, January, 1961.
7. Kurtz, John J. and Esther J. Swanson. "Student, Parent, and Teacher Attitude Toward Student Achievement in School," The School Review, 59:273-9, May, 1951.
8. McCandless, Boyd R. and Alfred Castaneda. "Anxiety in Children, School Achievement, and Intelligence." Child Development, 27:379-82, September, 1956.
9. Plank, Emma N. "Observations on Attitudes of Young Children Toward Mathematics," Mathematics Teacher, 43:252-63, 1950.
10. Shearin, Deloris. A Comparison of Attitude Toward Arithmetic and Arithmetic Achievement in Grade Six. Unpublished paper, San Diego State College, 1962.

Expressed Reading Preferences of
Second-Grade Children in Selected Schools in Colorado

Reviewed by Elizabeth N. Wade

From Childhood Education 40:494-5, May 1964. Review of James O. Butler's "Expressed Reading Preferences of Second-Grade Children in Selected Schools of Colorado," an unpublished doctoral dissertation, University of Oklahoma. Reprinted by permission of Elizabeth N. Wade and the Association for Childhood Education International, 3615 Wisconsin Avenue, N.W., Washington, D.C. Copyright 1964 by the Association.

A study by James O. Butler, currently under way in the Colorado Springs Public Schools, will attempt to determine the reading preferences of 185 second-grade children in three elementary schools in varying socio-economic areas.

The various facets of children's reading have long been of concern to educators and investigators. The vast array of research in the area of reading interests of children implies the advancement of knowledge concerning the relation of interests to reading. Many questions yet remain unanswered, and authorities in the field of education question the suitability of reading material as related to the interests of primary children.

Tabulations of the first portion of the Butler study indicate some deviations from the conclusions of previous studies which established the widespread belief that animal personification in stories is the favorite theme of primary children and that sex differences generally do not appear in reading preferences before age nine. Recently authorities acknowledged that children's interests may be influenced by societal changes in the culture and by new media of communication.

In his study Mr. Butler is determining the reading preferences of second-grade children through isolation and control of the following factors: (a) readability, (b) accessibility and (c) range of content area.

Answers to the following questions will be sought:

    1. What are the expressed reading preferences of second-grade children as revealed by expressed choices in eight categories of reading content areas?
    2. Do these preferences reflect a shift in emphasis from those revealed in earlier studies?
    3. What effect do the following intrinsic and extrinsic factors reflect in expressed preferences?

Sex	Social Class
Intelligence	Reading Competence

<u>Expressed Reading Preferences</u>

The basic instrument used in attempting to answer these questions consists of twenty-four books read orally by the teacher, over a period of approximately six months, to the children involved in the study. These twenty-four books were selected from an original number of forty-eight books by a panel knowledgeable in reading interests of this age group. The twenty-four books represent eight reading interest categories, each containing three titles. Interest categories are as follows: fairy tales, animal stories, biography, science and nature, stories of home and school life, poetry, fantasy, and children of other lands.

Books selected for each of the categories above contained known high interest producing factors to establish a uniform range of book titles of comparable interest level. In an effort to diminish a biased effect caused by previous familiarity with the books, selections were made from books published after January 1, 1960.

The books were subdivided into sets, each set including one title from each interest category. The sets were read in random order, both between sets and between categories, to second-grade pupils in three schools. The three schools represent poor and excellent socio-economic environments.

Preliminary tabulation of a portion of the responses to be secured in the study indicates that children representing different socio-economic environments may have marked differences in the type of books preferred. It further indicates that there are differences in reading preferences between boys and girls.

Data secured by ranking the preferences expressed by 185 children upon completion of the first set of books is shown in the table on page 78.

The table shows that animal stories were rated not higher than third choice by children in all three environments, boys rating them fourth and below.

Girls and boys from the culturally deprived area rated stories of children of other lands first and third respectively, while both the boys and girls from good and excellent environments rated the same category quite low.

Boys and girls from good and excellent environments rated stories of fantasy and fairy tales their first and second choices. Children of poor environment rated both of these categories low with the exception of fantasy, ranked second by girls. Most authorities in the field of children's literature place fairy tales in a higher grade than second.

Children in the poor environment rated stories of home and school life high, while the others rated them quite low.

Other interesting ratings may be noted, such as the low rating by all groups given to stories of science and nature.

At this point in the study of reading preferences of second-grade children, there is indication that recent changes in our society and new media of communication, such as radio and television, are influencing the reading interest of young children. The seven- and eight-year-old has broader interests than in former years. This is reflected in differences in types of books selected by boys as compared to girls . . .

Interest Category	Poor Environmental Conditions Boys	Poor Environmental Conditions Girls	Good Environmental Conditions Boys	Good Environmental Conditions Girls	Excellent Environmental Conditions Boys	Excellent Environmental Conditions Girls
Fairy Tales	Fifth	Fifth	Second	Second	First	Second
Animal Stories	Fourth	Eighth	Seventh	Third	Fourth	Fourth
Biography	Second	Seventh	Third	Sixth	Fifth	Seventh
Science-Nature	Eighth	Sixth	Fifth	Eighth	Seventh	Eighth
Home--School Life	First	Third	Fourth	Fifth	Sixth	Fifth
Poetry	Seventh	Fourth	Sixth	Fourth	Third	Third
Fantasy	Sixth	Second	First	First	Second	First
Children of Other Lands	Third	First	Eighth	Seventh	Eighth	Sixth

Children's Hour; Children's Choice

From Newsweek 67:118+, June 13, 1966. Copyright Newsweek, Inc., June, 1966. Reprinted by permission.

Every year, a couple of dozen different prizes are passed out among the current crop of children's books. Everybody, from publishers to the PTA, takes a shot at picking the two or three, out of the 2,000 to 3,000 written annually, that will become battered and beloved bookshelf regulars; but hardly anybody asks the kids themselves. In winnowing out this year's half ton of books published for 4- to 8-year-olds, Newsweek enlisted the aid of several youngsters. Each was given four books and asked to pick a favorite. They offer the following opinions:

The Deer At Our House. By Erskine Caldwell. Illustrated by Ben Wohlberg. Collier Books. $2.95. "I like it because it is more better than any book I read already," states Karl Jay Anglin, 6 1/2, "better even than the library. You didn't know that deer like to eat peaches? Well they do. And they ate up all the peaches and left the seeds outside. I like a book because it is good to read, but when I read sometimes my breath gets a funny taste in it, because it is in my throat."

A Tale of Stolen Time. By Evgeny Schwartz. Translated by Lila Pargment and Estelle Titiev. Illustrated by Nonny Hogrogian. Prentice-Hall, $3.75. "It's about this little boy named Peter," says Kathleen Lake, 6 1/2, "who wastes time and things and doesn't do his work. There are some kids in my school like that, but not me. I like all the pictures because they have such funny hair."

What You Can Do With a Word. By J. Williams Illustrated by Leslie Goldstein. Collier Books $2.95. George Melrod, 7, says, "I read this one because it looked the shortest. It's about this boy who works for a witch but he didn't like working all the time and she made a machine

that made words but after awhile she told him to throw it
out and he did but later he came back and got it. I like
funny stories best."

Seven-year-olds explain, but younger children just
react. "I just better have this one," states Christopher
Roman, 4, of ABC of Cars and Trucks (by Anne Alexander.
Pictures by Ninon MacKnight. Doubleday. $3.25). "I
know what that is; that's a fire engine. It has a flat tire
and another flat tire and another flat tire. Is this the front
end? You know what? I'm hungry." Cathy Truman, 3 1/2,
picked Did a Bear Just Walk There? (by Ann Rand and A.
Birnbaum. Harcourt, Brace & World. $3.75) "because
it's new. It's good because I want it. Look, he hasn't got
all his body! Wow, that's a crocodile. I touched him."

Kids are just as definite about what they don't want.
"Let me tell you what's wrong with this" (Just One Apple.
by Janosch. Walck. $3.75), says Wilcox Snellings, 7.
"Well, it's by this man from Poland and maybe he had
different ideas about things, but the king's too little; he's
just a man with a crown on. Kings shouldn't look like
that." Billy Betsch, 5, liked the nursery rhymes in
Maurice Sendak's Hector Protector and as I Went Over the
Water (Harper & Row, $4.25), but turned it down because
"the pictures are silly."

The only thing a child asks of a book really is that
it be "good." What should a good story be? "A little bit
hard for me to read. Magic is nice," says Kathleen. "A
story doesn't have to have magic in it, but it should tell
you things," says Wilcox. "Words and animals in them,"
says Karl. Billy wants bad men or Batman. "Monsters,
but not scary monsters," says George. "I don't like scary
stories."

In general, the current crop is probably no better or
no worse than usual. Some of the books are charming,
some are dull, too many are condescending, a few are silly,
some are meant to entertain, some to instruct and some to
carry obscure moral points--but it could be, in trying to
enchant their little readers with adult ideas of what a children's book should be, that publishers are overlooking their
richest source of new material. They might be a bit surprised to find how many mite-sized storytellers are authors
as well.

Billy and Anthony Fusco, 7, both paint books--"all kinds," says Anthony, "mostly pictures and no words; that's best." Karl has written two, one about a horse named Sammy and the other about a boy and his pet goldfish. Wilcox has finished his third, 38 laboriously lettered pages of an epic of outer space that begins, "A 100 days after Jesus Christ was born. There was no Pluto but in space there was an egg colored olive. And when astronauts went into space they got out and chased the egg. But however fast they ran the egg ran faster. On the 122 day after Christ was born the egg burst open and then the astronauts called the planet Pluto. Then the astronauts found out that inside the egg that burst into the planet called Pluto had a little baby inside of it but the baby was a little bit different than us of course. But the astronauts where old fashion and could only stay 79 weeks."

And Kathleen specialized in punny stories: "If I tell you this one you'd probably laugh all day. It's about this princess named Spy-ring and she married a prince named Spy-ring and they had a little baby named Sweat-drop!"

II: Ages Six to Twelve

Children and Humorous Literature

Robin B. Bateman

From The School Librarian and School Library Review 15: 153-6+, July 1967. Published by the School Library Association. Reprinted by permission.

Comparatively little has been written on laughter and the kinds of humor which provoke it. On children's laughter and sense of humor, which form such a large part of a child's psyche, the standard works on child psychology are surprisingly reticent. The analysis of that elusive element which makes something comical to a child could be a fascinating study and possibly one of considerable importance. I am here concerned with what in literature children find funny. A little consideration of the question shows that there is a distinction between the humorously written story or poem which children read with pleasure and happy anticipation, and those phrases and passages of a work which occasion outright merriment. J.L. Brisley's Milly-Molly-Mandy Stories (Harrap) is an amusing book which provokes appreciative smiles, whereas "you balance an eel on the end of your nose" produces, when it produces anything at all, audible laughter. It is this literary provocation to laughter which I propose to consider here.

The children used for this study were mainly 6-11 years old, that is, children who have become familiar with the written word as a means to enjoyment, but have not yet acquired either adolescent inhibitions or adult tastes. The school classes which provide the bulk of the evidence were 10-11-year-olds, 8-year-olds and 7-year-olds, all with a socially mixed intake. A brief summary of the research method, if one can glorify curiosity by such a term, may be helpful to put the findings and tentative conclusions in the current light:

1. Discussion with young children and young adults about what they could remember as funny in children's books

Ages Six to Twelve

which they had read produced a mass of facts and opinions.

2. Consideration of the whole field of humor and children's books in the light of the insight gained produced some initial hypotheses.

3. These hypotheses were tested by reading passages to children in class, and noting their reactions. Readings were interspersed with discussions of what other books were thought funny by the children. At the end of each class session, there was a secret ballot to discover which passages among those read the children had thought most funny.

4. The whole mass of evidence was collated and tabulated, and the earlier hypotheses amended or substantiated.

There seem to be six different sets of circumstances in literature which provoke mirth in the young, and the response to them varies with age and with intelligence.

1. The Funny Incident

Slapstick and banana-skin humor appeals to some extent to all ages. As one matures, the attraction is diminished proportionately as other forms of wit are recognized, and even dies altogether when overlaid by a more sophisticated appreciation of what can be funny. In the young and the immature the reaction to banana-skins is universal and immediate. Hence, of course, the popularity of comics like Beano. Dr. Bernstein ("Language and Social Class," British Journal of Sociology, XI) has shown that the working-class language code tends to make the concrete more relevant than those situations which point to reflective, abstract relationships. I believe this may also apply to the unsophisticated. This would explain to a large extent why incidents are for the young so much more generally an occasion for laughter than sarcasm, puns or other more abstract comic conceptions.

> The next (film) was a comedy. It began by a solitary workman engaged upon the repainting of a door, and ended with a miscellaneous crowd of people, all covered with paint, falling downstairs on top of one another. It was amusing. William was riotously and loudly amused.

The William stories, from which the quotation is taken, are classic cases of incident humor for children. In these, the reader remains an outsider, and does not associate himself with the unfortunates who bear the brunt of William's activities.

Gene Zion's Harry the Dirty Dog (Bodley Head), which could be described as an amusing series of incidents, was second in popularity with 7-year-olds (first was Dr. Seuss's story "Pale Green Pants," which is referred to later).

"In which Pooh Invents a New Game" (A. A. Milne's The House at Pooh Corner, Methuen), from the arrival of Eeyore floating upside-down under the bridge, kept 8-year-olds amused and laughing. They enjoyed Eeyore's sarcastic comment and indeed the whole of the conversation between the animals. But it was "Looking very calm, very dignified, with his legs in the air, came Eeyore from beneath the bridge"; the splash of the stone Pooh dropped; Eeyore reappearing, wet, at the side of the river; the description of how Tigger "hooshed" him into it in the first place--in fact the action--which produced the more immediate and pronounced response. (The 11-year-olds also enjoyed the tale but, I think, with rather a tolerant amusement for something which they felt was too young for them.)

The children's reaction to Billy Bunter is particularly interesting. Poor Bunter suffers as a result of most of the pranks which are played on him. The pranks are funny, but only if the reader identifies himself with the chums, and not with the unfortunate Bunter. For the sympathetic child who feels for Billy Bunter, the pranks are not funny. Gross states that sympathy, which is a mature emotion, "prevents the enlivening effect of the comic" (quoted in The Nature of Laughter, J. C. Gregory, Kegan Paul, 1924).

Two parallel sequences from Nurse Matilda by Christianna Brand (Brockhampton) demonstrate this preventive effect very well. In one, Nurse Matilda's action results in puppies being force-fed by the naughty children. "And Francesca was stuffing baby-food down the dogs' throats, stuff, stuff, stodge, stodge and the dogs were full up with baby-food right to the top." In the other, the naughty children are themselves forced to continue stuffing porridge into

Ages Six to Twelve

their own mouths. To the 8-year-olds, the latter was screamingly funny, the former definitely not: the children's feeling for animals was too strong for them to think that any such maltreatment was amusing. Force-feeding of the children was very funny, however, because the situation could be seen to be patently ridiculous, and thereby laughable; "Up and down flashed their egg spoons choking down egg on top of porridge; and on top of the egg came more and more of that dreadful bread and butter and jam . . . and then the porridge started all over again . . . The children puffed and blew, their cheeks bulged, their eyes goggled. . ." The description of the dolls being decapitated was accorded a nearly tearful reception.

Incident entanglement, too, is a source of laughter, but only in children of 10 upwards. Younger children find a number of coincident sequences in a story too bewildering to contend with. The older child evidently revels in such complexities. "Billy Bunter is funny because of the way things all get mixed up" (10-year-old boy). The sequence of events leading up to the midnight feast in Enid Blyton's Fifth Form at St. Claire's (Methuen) produced an uproar of laughter from 10-11-year-olds even when considerably abridged in my retelling.

2. The Comic Pictorial Image

I am here concerned with the image evoked in the mind by words, not by illustrations. Three points emerged from the inquiry. First, the image abruptly evoked with an economy of words produces spontaneous laughter, and is considerably more effective than the image which has been built up sentence by sentence. This is not a novel conclusion, for we all know how effective is the sudden twist in a joke, and the surprise ending of a funny story. "You balance an eel on the end of your nose" was immediately effective with the 6-7-year-olds, who did not laugh at any except one of the other verses of "You are old Father William", none of these being evocative pictorially. The exception was "Be off or I'll kick you downstairs" which produces a banana-skin image--and, consequently, guffaws.

Second, the comic image makes more impact on the young than on the older reader. Whereas the 10-11-year-olds were evidently amused and even delighted by Eric Link-

later's portrait of Gunner Boles (The Pirates in the Deep
Green Sea, Macmillan) with his "bald head, a red nose, red
patches of hair above his ears, and red side-whiskers, and
in his mouth. . .a short clay pipe from which came little
puffs of smoke as if he were a steamer," their reaction
was nothing compared with the uproar with which 7-year-
olds greeted the description of Nurse Matilda's "Fierce
round face with its boot-button eyes and its nose like two
potatoes." The youngest class's reaction to "You balance
an eel. . ." is noted above; the 8-year-old class included
a few children who laughed loudly; the 10- and 11-year-olds
did not respond at all.

     Third, the ludicrous element is a powerful additional
stimulant. Nurse Matilda's nose provides evidence of this,
but even more so does the passage in the same chapter
relating how the tea ran back into the teapot. This was
very funny to the 8-year-olds.

3. The Sense of Superiority

     Gregory states that a sense of superiority is a
laughter maker; so much so, evidently, that some psychologists have in the past considered that laughter indicated
the assumption of superiority, and that "gratified animus"
was the prime cause of laughter. Superiority may have
occasioned adult laughter in the past (see Pope's self-defen-
sive diatribe against those who laughed at his deformity)
but civilization has brought adults to look with sympathy
on the difficulties and ignorance of others. In children
and the unsophisticated, merriment is still often the reaction to the predicaments of others. The older the child,
the less the predicaments of others are thought funny.

     But there are many literary occasions when a gentle
pleasure in one's superiority can bubble over in the young.
Mary Plain's assumption (Gwynedd Rae's All Mary, Rout-
ledge) that the plural of "visit," when one added an 's',
was "svisit" was very funny to 8-year-olds. That the
plural of "pit" was "spit" was even more uproarious--en-
hanced, no doubt by the "forbidden" word. Pooh and Piglet
looking for a Woozle is similarly funny. A 5-year-old
commented on "Pooh Builds a House" that it was funny
"because they were so daft."

When Milo (Norton Juster's The Phantom Tollbooth, Collins) buys the word "quagmire" at the stall in the word market, because he liked the sound of it "although he had no idea what it meant," the reaction from the bright children in the 10-11 class was immediate.

Enid Blyton is evidently aware of this aspect of children's humor. In the St. Claire's series, the French girls give the opportunity for laughter. They say "chattertin" for "chatterbox," and "wasp in her hat," for "bee in her bonnet," but I was interested to note that the 10-11 class evidently thought this a poor attempt at humor.

4. Ludicrous Nonsense

Nonsense in itself is insufficient to produce more than quiet amusement. If nonsense produces a funny mental picture (see above) or if a nonsense word sounds funny, it is sufficient. Otherwise it needs the additive of the ludicrous or the ridiculous. As Santayana states in a study of the attitude of youth to humor, "to be ridiculous is part of the fun" (Soliloquies in England and Later Soliloquies, Constable, 1922). Gregory remarks on the "laughing relish of absurdities." It seems to me that, to be ludicrous, nonsense needs to be anchored to known realities, so that it can be seen in relation to reality.

"Jabberwocky" produced no guffaws in any age group. Nurse Matilda, which is ridiculous and far-fetched, but deals with comprehensible realities, was voted the funniest of the books I dealt with by 7 out of the 36 8-year-olds. Dr. Seuss's "Pale Green Pants" (The Sneetches and Other Stories, Collins) was voted the funniest by far by all the classes of children, and indeed the conception of "pale green pants with nobody inside them" was hilarious, especially with 5-7-year-olds, to whom the "naughty" word gave evident thrills at its daring. The same author's "Sneetches," which at the child's level is similar nonsense, but not being linked with reality, not so ludicrous, was voted best by 10 out of 69, as against 41 out of 69 for "Pale Green Pants." (I write "at the child's level," because the children would be unaware of the social comment in the plot.)

Two riddles substantiate this point. "Why does a

stork stand on one leg?--because it would fall down if it lifted it up," was received with hilarity by 10-11-year olds, though less so by the 8-year-olds. "What is big, red, and eats rocks?--a big, red, rock-eater" produced no reaction. Incidentally, I was puzzled by the absence of laughter in 6-7-year-olds to the stork joke, until questions revealed the fact that none of these children knew what a stork was.

5. Subtlety

It has often been remarked that the best children's books appeal to adults as well as to children. So far as humor is concerned, it seems evident that what appeals to the adult passes by the child, and what the child enjoys may be thought of poor quality by the adult.

The finer points of Eeyore's sarcasm in the Poohsticks episode pass unnoticed. "I'll give you three guesses, Rabbit. Digging holes in the ground? Wrong. Leaping from branch to branch of a young oak-tree? Wrong. Waiting for somebody to help me out of the river? Right. Give Rabbit time, and he'll always get the answer" was thoroughly enjoyed, from the bright 8-year-olds up. The bitter humor of "If it goes on snowing for another six weeks or so, one of them will begin to say to himself, 'Eeyore can't be so very much too Hot about three o'clock in the morning'" was not noticed unless the reader specifically pointed the remarks by his intonation. Once spotted, it was very much appreciated.

Puns need to be outrageous to be noticed at all, and even then they are food only for the really bright child. The Phantom Tollbooth, which was reported by a 10-year-old with a high I.Q. to be the funniest book ever "because it has jokes all the way through," passed over the heads of most children, except for its most obvious jokes. Children laughed at the Watchdog and at Short Shrift when shown the drawing, but the additional point that the latter is the name of an officer of the law went unnoticed. Short Shrift, in his capacity as judge, asks Milo, whom he is sentencing to prison, "Now, would you like a long or short sentence?" "A short one, if you please," said Milo. "Good, I always have trouble remembering the long ones. How about 'I am'? That's the shortest sentence I know." After the two top children in the class of 11-year-olds had noticed the joke, there was a crescendo of laughter, as its impact moved

Ages Six to Twelve

round the classroom. Presumably most of the class would have missed even such a simple joke as that, if they had been reading to themselves. However, the proportion of jokes at all levels was enough, in spite of the wit that was not noticed, for the whole of the letter market chapter to be acclaimed by the 10-11-year-olds as one of the two funniest stories which I had read to them, equal with "Pale Green Pants."

6. Summary

My main conclusions may be summarized as follows:

(a) The funny incident inevitably provokes laughter.
(b) The comic pictorial image is extremely potent, particularly in the very young.
(c) The child's pleasure in words as words extends for the very young to the conception of words as sounds, but this is not so with older children.
(d) The misuse of words by a character, or other signs of a character's ignorance, produces an active sense of superiority in the child, and is thereby a frequent source of laughter.
(e) Nonsense by itself is not sufficient to produce laughter; nonsense needs to be ludicrous to be effective.
(f) Subtlety, and particularly in puns, is noticed only by the very intelligent.

Influences on Primary School Children's Reading

R. S. Buzzing

From The School Librarian and School Library Review 11: 584-6+, December 1963. Reprinted by permission.

What is the child's reaction when first he is confronted with a book? He seems to pause, think and then reach out for it. If its impression upon him is now good, he wants to read it. What, however, is he in fact doing in that initial "thinking" period? He seems to be deciding whether the book will offer him a source of enjoyment or be of some use to him. Such a confronting can be accidental--the casual picking up of a book lying about or on the bookshelf--or it can be deliberate, i.e. introduced by an adult, teacher, parent, librarian. There is sometimes a third motive for reading, namely, to master the skill. Very young children, on learning a new sound or movement, will repeat it endlessly until they have mastery over it. Similarly some children will exercise the reading skill just to gain mastery over this form of expression. These might be called the fundamental motives for reading, but we must not overlook the vital need to encourage children to develop from these earlier motives.

One such development is seen as books begin to be chosen because they offer an outlet. Sometimes the outlet is purely hedonistic, the story is amusing or exciting. This may be because it embodies something the child would simply love to do but cannot in fact do. The reading of books concerned with childish escapades may predominate for such reasons. This early interest will probably lead to a much closer identification with the heroes of books, especially those who meet with and overcome real difficulties. Children seeking such identification will prefer deeper books, e.g. those by Rosemary Sutcliff, Rhoda Power or Hans Baumann, where they identify themselves with "historical" heroes. By the ages of ten and eleven such identification with heroes may well be taking place with members of the Kon-Tiki or Everest teams.

Sometimes too there is another outlet, a form of escapism. Younger children who are surrounded by a limiting, frustrating or unprepossessing environment often seek to escape into the world of fantasy by reading fairy tales and similar stories. Many good books are to be found in this range, especially in the O.U.P. and Dent collections. However, there are many children who live in much happier surroundings who welcome the world of fantasy and gentle make-believe. Developing children attracted to this type of material will begin to demand and appreciate stories by Alison Uttley and Patricia Lynch. Then many will progress to books like the "Borrowers" series of Mary Norton, the "Land of Narnia" adventures by C.S. Lewis, and The Hobbit and the "Ring" cycle by J.R.R. Tolkien.

A second major development is that of reading to obtain information. Children of junior age are frequently collectors of many things, and books which encourage this collecting instinct are in considerable demand. This is true not only of books on stamps, coins and butterflies, but also of those on less common subjects such as brass rubbings and heraldry. The motivating force for the child here is his innate curiosity which demands to know the whys and wherefores of life. This kind of reading can be for enjoyment as much as for strictly utilitarian purposes. There are children who want to learn for learning's sake (the budding intellectuals?), and there are those who seek learning because it enables them more clearly to understand where they are going or how a thing works.

A third major impulse to read is that of filling up time. When a child is bored, perhaps because he cannot be active in bad weather, he may well turn to a book as an antidote to boredom. Sometimes, of course, the filling up of time by reading is an antidote to other forms of work. A child may wish to escape his share of the chores about the house or classroom, and so he picks up a book to read. At such times the apparent grip of a book upon the child's imagination and concentration is truly phenomenal!

In all that has been written so far it is suggested that the child is activated by internal motives or impulses.

He has chosen to read for one or more of several reasons, but mainly because in himself he wants to read. It is now fitting to turn and see if there are any external factors which influence children to read. In seeking to establish these factors it is apparent that some of them have been mentioned already. In the first paragraph it was stated that children might be deliberately confronted with books. Here is an important external factor: teachers to a marked degree and parents to a lesser degree expect children to read. Children may very well then be expected to "go through the motions" of reading because it is expected, the done thing. Perhaps it is time for the daily period of reading; perhaps the child is encouraged to read because somehow, quite mysteriously, it is hoped that this will improve his chances in the selection process. In this sense reading is not merely inflicted, it can correctly be called compulsory or even punitive. Such influences for reading might well be considered second-rate, and with justification, but they must not be ignored just because the motive is suspect.

Another external stimulus lies in the child's leisure pursuits. One who is enthusiastic about fishing will want to raid the library shelves to find a book on the subject. A second child may have an interest awakened in modeling and through this interest, which originated elsewhere, come to seek books on the subject. Both of these are examples of actual happenings--and there was a most reproachful look from the child whose search for a fishing book went unrewarded (this lack of provision has long since been remedied!). Here is the factor of utility re-emerging, for know-how will bring a greater efficiency--surely a very commendable and welcome impulse to improve. Even the much maligned mass media of newspapers, comics, radio and television do from time to time have the very beneficial side-effects of sending children scurrying for books. In my own experience, for example, television programs on sport have helped juniors to realize their need to develop skills. Similarly, programs on natural history have stimulated research into animal behavior and geographical studies of other lands. The result of viewing has been a searching of the shelves next morning for the "do-it-this-way" or other kind of information book. These influences have also resulted in children seeking further information simply as an intellectual exercise or again merely for the pleasure that searching affords. Often enough the casual reference to, say,

Ages Six to Twelve

the <u>Oxford Junior Encyclopaedia</u> for information on one topic has led to seemingly chance interest in another topic dealt with in the same volume. The provision of time for browsing is a matter demanding serious consideration and I shall return to it later.

Other external influences are far too frequently neglected and close attention might profitably be given to them. Children will often be influenced to read by hearing a good excerpt from a book. If the reading is lively, interesting and well delivered, many children will want to read the excerpt for themselves. This then leads to reading on in the book and even back in the book until the whole is read. In the past year I have been able in this way to stimulate first-year juniors by reading to them excerpts from <u>The Good Master</u> by Kate Seredy, <u>Jascha</u> by Franz Hutterer, and even <u>Prince Caspian</u> by C.S. Lewis. Similarly my own third-year class has been arrested by the ballads about Kon-Tiki and Everest by Ian Serraillier, and by excerpts from <u>Old Possum's Book of Practical Cats</u> by T. S. Eliot. Then propaganda pinned up in the library has also proved very useful; I refer in particular to the excellent O.U.P. series of posters on children's authors and children's artists.

Again, a child may want to read a book after hearing one of his peers saying how much <u>he</u> enjoyed the book. This stimulus through recommendation is one which has borne much fruit in my experience. It must be remembered that children will frequently listen without prejudice to one of their own number and follow his advice where they would have reservations about an adult's opinions. We have a system in class whereby children fill in a form after reading a book. One question asks the child to state whether he would recommend the book to other children and for what reasons. (If he rejects the book he also says why he does not wish to recommend it.) As a result of the information thus acquired, children are from time to time asked to choose and read excerpts to the class. A girl dissolving into laughter as she read one of Pippi Longstocking's adventures drew demands for those books. A boy reading an excerpt from <u>Tom-Toms in Oworo</u> by René Guillot brought an as yet unsatiated demand for his books. By this means during the past year children have had their attention drawn to books by Cynthia Harnett, Rosemary Sutcliff, Geoffrey

Trease, C. Day Lewis, Tove Jansson, Arthur Ransome, William Mayne, Monica Edwards, Ronald Welch--the list is not exhausted. Significantly, too, there has been a developing awareness that if one book by an author is enjoyed then other books by the same author may offer similar enjoyment.

Finally, there is an outstandingly important influence upon the child and his attitude towards reading--and it is the one which seems to be forgotten far too readily--namely that of example. In the family circle and indeed in the school circle where all those present sit down to read, or naturally spend a significant portion of their spare time in reading, the child in turn is likely to follow the same pursuit. It is almost a reflex action on his part. Here it is the matter of atmosphere which is important, the reading being done without any sense of artificiality. Even as one would expect in the home that parents and children should be reading together, so with older juniors one might experiment in having the teacher and children reading their own books at the same time. There can still be reference to the teacher when necessary, or the teacher can still find opportunities to hear the children read. The primary child is so obviously sensitive to atmosphere and naturalness that it is essential to develop the conveyed impression that reading is a natural habit. It thus becomes worthwhile in its own right and so impressed upon the child's mind that it may well be the most important single factor of all in influencing him to read. Reading then becomes enjoyed for its own sake, as an outlet, pleasurable in itself, and practical--in fact as a major key to the following of a fuller life.

All the foregoing, however, begs the question of where the child is to find the books. Of the utmost importance is the school's own collection of books. If each classroom library is well endowed with books of the best quality, and if attention is regularly drawn to the fact that these books are there--by using some of the methods suggested above, or by using others--then progress will be made. This progress will be further enhanced if alongside the regular reading times there are frequent opportunities for browsing during school and play times. It is imperative that there should also be a first-class central collection of books, both fiction and non-fiction, for borrowing purposes. The central collection should contain further examples of the work of authors represented in class libraries and also a wider range of authors and books than a class library can contain for reasons of space, expense and so on. A good central collection must also be regularly and imaginatively advertized.

In my experience close cooperation between school and city or county library branches brings enormous dividends. Our city children's librarian visits the school upon request or receives classes from the school at the library. There she talks to them, arousing curiosity, setting simple library projects. She has also helped me considerably by recommending authors and books which I had not met. Parents are advised that this cooperation exists, and they then are able to encourage children to visit the city library for reading during leisure and holiday times.

Parents, too, often fail to realize the interest which children have in establishing their own personal libraries at home. From the earliest reading days children can begin to set up their own collections. Many suitable books are obtainable at reasonable prices in these days of paperbacks, and the Puffin books are especially useful. Active and financial encouragement from parents is a potent aid in influencing children to read, but parents themselves often need to be stimulated and made aware of opportunities by teachers.

The purpose of this article is to call for a renewed and reinvigorated approach to the question of children and their reading, especially stressing the vitally interrelated influences of example and accessibility. Given these, we are some way on the road to success in encouraging children to read simply because they are interested in books and authors.

Reading Patterns of Children; What and Why They Read

Richard J. Hurley

From the National Catholic Educational Association Bulletin 62:468-9, August 1965. Published by the Association. Reprinted by permission.

Three recent movements in reading have focused attention upon the importance of knowing the reading patterns of elementary school children: the Initial Teaching Alphabet, the early home-parent teaching of reading, and more especially the increasing emphasis upon individualized reading where skills are part of motivated reading. Librarians and others ask, "Knowing how to read, what is the next step?" In spite of some research, what we don't know exceeds what we do know.

Although children are individuals and differ as to sex, age, intelligence, environment, reading ability, and instinctive elements, there is an amazing consistency in patterns of reading interest, beginning in preschool. The early influence of parents reading to the child, of helping a child build a library, and of the child's own bookcase, have important results in school. Likewise, reading experiences in the elementary grades lead to a pattern of liking or disliking books which becomes fixed in the fifth grade. By this grade, we recognize boys' and girls' patterns as distinct and almost mutually exclusive--the reluctant reader who may be a potential dropout, the slow, and the gifted reader. The latter has been neglected whereas he is of high priority because of future leadership. He reads earlier, reads more, reads a greater variety of books, and almost matches girls who, in general, read rings around boys.

There are such basic interests as humor, animals, and mystery. A feature of the pattern in the elementary school is the rapid change of interest from grade to grade as represented by animals--humanized animals, talking animals, real animals, or pets, farm animals, zoo animals, wild animals. Girls prefer horse stories and boys dog stories. Sixth grade for some children is dominated by the series such as the "Hardy Boys" and "Nancy Drews." Ultimately they grow bored with the formula and turn to more literary reading: if not, they should be nudged. Science fiction deserves greater attention as a motivator for reluctant reading boys. Adventure is the best loved type of story. Idealism reflects itself in the consistent reading of biography. We know little about the religious book reading as reflected in research.

Children's Newspaper Reading

Lois V. Johnson.

From Elementary English 40:428-32+, April 1963. Reprinted with the permission of the National Council of Teachers of English and Lois V. Johnson.

Children's reading and use of the newspaper should be viewed in the context of the varied mass media which are inseparable parts of children's daily lives. Newspapers are, of course, only one of the mass communication media which continuously impinge upon the developing child.

Children have gained the basic beginnings of reading in the primary grades and by grades four, five and six are typically in a period of expanding power in their reading development. The curriculum in these grades makes increased reference to broadening horizons in the child's world. Increased reading skills, broadened interests, and greater scope in the curriculum make relevant and investigation of children's interests in and use of the newspaper.

Problem and Procedure

The purposes of this study were to explore some aspects of the newspaper reading habits and interests of children in grades four, five and six, including such specific points as the extent to which children read newspapers, the parts or sections of the newspapers which they read or do not read, their use of the newspaper in the subjects of the school curriculum, and their understandings and explanations of the different treatment of the same news material by different papers.

A questionnaire was constructed after consultation with classroom teachers on the content and suitability of the questions. The reading difficulty was maintained below the reading grade level. A pilot study to test the questionnaire was made in two schools with 110 children, 63 boys and 47

Ages Six to Twelve

girls, in the three grade levels. The questions proved to be understandable, suitable to the purposes of the study, and unambiguous. The results from the pilot groups were similar in content, form and completeness to those obtained from the groups used in the study.

There were 564 children in the study, 295 boys and 269 girls, in three public schools in an urban area. Scores on standardized tests showed normal ranges of reading achievement in all groups. The socio-economic areas of the three schools were such that all children could be expected to have the usual experiences with mass media, including newspapers, in their home environments. Metropolitan daily papers and local weekly and semi-weekly papers were common.

The regular classroom teachers administered the instrument, which was given without previous class preparation or discussion. The teachers followed written instructions in introducing the questionnaire to the children. They reminded the class that many children were interested in news, that the questions asked what interested each individual, and that it was not a test. Because of the procedural precautions, it was felt that the children's responses were candid and as complete as possible.

Interpretation of the Data

The majority of the children in grades four, five and six indicated in their responses that they "sometimes" read newspapers. While 70 per cent were irregular or "sometimes" readers, 24 per cent reported that they were regular readers, and 6 per cent said they did not read newspapers. (The children who responded "yes," i.e., that they were regular readers, substantiated their answers by describing a current item that they had read.) Children increasingly read the newspaper from grade to grade. The numbers of children who do not read showed a corresponding decline from year to year, with 20 at grade four, 10 at grade five and 3 at grade six. There were no significant differences between boys and girls.

The part of the newspaper which the children "usually read" and "liked best" was the funnies or comics. This was the most frequent answer for the three grades. A related question, asking what other parts of the paper were read, drew multiple replies from many children. In answer to this latter question, the comics were often mentioned by children who had not previously named them as the part they "liked best." (The total responses to the two questions are given in Table I.)

Table I

Parts of the Newspaper Which Children Read and Liked

Parts of the Newspaper	Grade 4 (N=167) No. %	Grade 5 (N=205) No. %	Grade 6 (N=192) No. %
Funnies, comics	110 45	171 48	153 40
News, first page news	67 26	102 29	115 30
Sports	59 23	73 21	97 26
Television	16 6	7 2	18 4

The "news" or "front page news" was second in frequency for all grades with each succeeding grade showing more interest. Sports news was third for all grades, with an increase in sixth grade. Other parts of the newspaper which children read and liked were: the television page, ads or advertisements, weather, movies, and the family section. A few items were named by only one child and probably represented special individual interests. Included in these single items were: automobiles, churches, and a special column that would be indicated by the author's name.

Children were, of course, acquainted with the parts of the paper which they regularly read. To investigate children's awareness of the total newspaper with its wide variety of material and topics, they were asked, "What parts of the paper do you never read?" The completeness and precision of their responses indicated that children were aware of the contents of the total paper. They listed "ads" most frequently--sometimes specifying "sales" and "classified ads"--as a part of the paper which they did not read. Girls

Ages Six to Twelve

in considerable numbers said they did not read the sport section. Of the 34 fourth graders who were nonreaders of sports, all were girls, in fifth grade 93 per cent were girls and 75 per cent in sixth grade. The relation of this expressed disinterest in sports by the girls to the typical separation of girls' and boys' game and physical activities and interests at these age levels can only be noted, as this study has no evidence on the point.

Children's awareness of the total newspaper and its contents was partially shown by the range of parts which they said they do not read. They named: the front page, politics, crime, funnies and comics, fashion, real estate, editorial, finance and business, magazine section, columns, home and family sections, television, theater, movies, weather, and society.

The children had had only incidental experiences with contrasting reports of the same news. They were told that, "Sometimes the same news story is reported differently by two different newspapers," and were then asked, "Why?" There was a progressive increase in the number of answers at each grade level. At fourth grade approximately 40 per cent gave answers, at fifth grade 55 per cent, and at sixth grade 80 per cent.

The reasons given by the children for the differences in reporting of the same material were as follows:

1. Some children answered, "Because it is important." These answers, found in grade four, showed only partial understanding. A similar level of incomplete understanding was evident in the answers, "Because some people get one newspaper," and "Because some people don't get the same paper." This reply was frequent in grade four and a few similar ones occurred in grade five.

2. The fact that the reporters were individuals was given as a reason. "Two different reporters," and "Because of different reporters," were common answers.

3. The perceptions of the reporter was given as a reason at all grade levels. Fourth graders said, "Each sees differently," "They hear it differently," and "They do it as they see it." Similar answers were given in grades

five and six. Examples from sixth graders are: "The newsmen see it differently or they put more detail in it." "Two reporters are on the job and they think differently. So out come two different stories." "One person thinks it's different from the other. Or maybe they are both wrong." Other children mentioned individual differences in "minds," "opinions," and "imaginations." Examples are: "The different newsmen have different opinions." "Because they have their own imagination just as you and I have."

    4. Sources of information and the effects of time and place were recognized by the children as producing varied interpretations. Answers included the following: "They get their news from different places and the people tell them different stories." "They hear it differently and get there at different times." "Some people are gone when one of them arrived." "They get their information from different places and people and at different times." "If one newspaper misses a little of the story, the other newspaper gets it." "Different reporters go to different people to get the story. People tell the story in their own way and it is printed in that way."

    5. The necessity of avoiding copying or "cheating" was offered as a reason by a few pupils. Typical statements were: "They tell it different so as not to cheat." "They are not to copy." "So they will not think they copied one another."

    6. The writing itself was seen as a cause of differences by a few pupils at each grade level. Fourth graders wrote: "The men put what has happened into their own words." "Two reporters copy the subject down differently." "Some make it longer and use harder words that mean the same thing." Fifth graders said: "Some reporters put together differently." "They get the same things so they write different." A sixth grader said: "They might get the same story but they have different ideas how to put it."

    7. Deliberate attempts to be different, interesting and exciting were given as reasons. A fourth grade girl said, "They don't want to have the same story." The factor of interest was given as shown in the following examples: "They want to make it interesting." "They might want to make it more interesting." "The newspapers print it differ-

ent to get more people interested in it. Sometimes they don't tell the truth." Other explanations for differences that were deliberately achieved were: "Sometimes newspapers alter the story to make it more exciting." "Sometimes a reporter will dramatize a story." "They have different opinions on the subject. Some of them exaggerate."

8. Economic reasons, including "company" ownership and competition in sales, were reasons that some pupils cited. "They are made by two different paper companies," was the explanation of a sixth grade boy. Examples of some fourth grade responses are: "They are reported differently because they are different companies." "Why, because their company has different ways of doing it." "If all papers did all of the stories the same, all the papers but one would go out of business." "One newspaper wants more people to buy his paper than other papers and exaggerates the story."

9. Editorial positions and policies were perceived by a few children. Examples of a hazy understanding on the part of fifth graders are: "There are different kinds of newspapers." "I think they like different sides of the story." Sixth graders were more specific: "Different editors have different beliefs." "Because of differences of opinion of editors of the papers toward the news." "One's a Democrat and one's the other." "Because like in the elections some newspapers were Democratic and some were Republican. So they wrote good things about the ones they were for."

In another question the children were asked in what school subjects they thought they had been helped by their reading of newspapers. Analysis of the responses shows the number of subjects in which the pupils believed they were helped. (Table II.)

The majority of the children (approximately 75 per cent) said that their reading of the newspaper had helped them with school subjects and work. Of these, about one half (53 per cent) reported they had been aided in one subject, while smaller numbers named two, three and four subjects in which they had been helped.

Table II

Number of School Subjects Helped by Newspaper Reading

Number of subjects	Grade 4 (N=167) No.	%	Grade 5 (N=205) No.	%	Grade 6 (N=192) No.	%	Total (N=564) No.	%
0	60	36	47	23	42	21	149	27
1	79	48	117	58	94	49	290	53
2	18	11	27	13	41	23	86	15
3	5	3	9	4	11	6	25	4
4	3	2	4	2	2	1	9	1

While most children found the newspaper helpful in school work, approximately 25 per cent stated that it had been of no help. There was a decline in the percentage of pupils who found the paper of "no help" from 36 per cent in fourth grade to 23 per cent in fifth and 21 per cent in sixth grade. Conversely, this indicates increasing use of the newspaper at successively higher grade levels. The finding of the numbers of children who did not use the paper in school work was consistent with the previous finding of the numbers of children who did not read or who were irregular newspaper readers.

One analysis of the question, "In what school subjects has reading of the newspaper helped you?" has been given. (Table II.) Another analysis of the responses to the same question yields the subjects that the children named. The school subjects of social studies and reading were most frequently mentioned as benefiting from newspaper reading. Current events, while of low frequency in replies from fourth grade, was increasingly mentioned by fifth and sixth graders. Spelling, language and science were less often named by the children. (Figure I.)

Figure I

School Subjects Helped by
Newspaper Reading

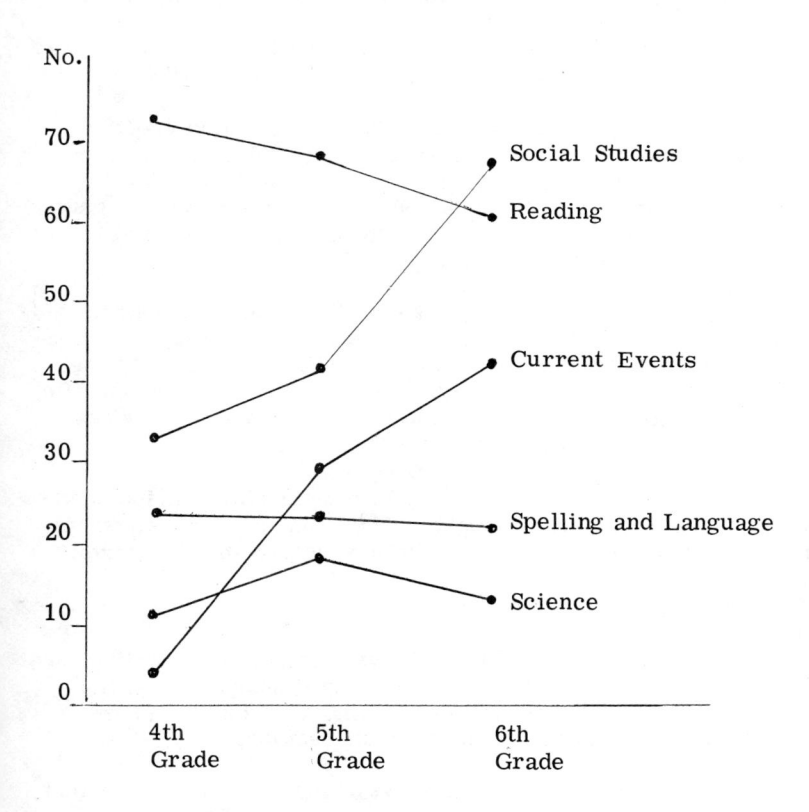

```
No.
70 —
                                    Social Studies
60 —                              • Reading
50 —
40 —                            • Current Events
30 —
20 —                            • Spelling and Language
10 —                            • Science
 0
      4th        5th        6th
     Grade     Grade      Grade
```

The high rating of reading as a subject helped by newspapers is understandable from the child's viewpoint in the following illustrative comments: "It helps you read better." "When I read the newspaper, it helps me read better in school." "I think just reading the paper helps to be better readers." "It helped me to learn to read and write." "It helped me learn hard words in reading." "Reading because it helps me pronounce many words." "It helps me in reading and understanding my teacher."

The pupils often named the separate fields of history and geography as well as the more inclusive term, "social studies." Examples of replies are: "It has helped me to know more about world problems." "It tells about the countries we study." "It helps in understanding the news of our country in a way to be History." Specific uses of newspapers by individuals are illustrated by the following: "In my study of missions." "In my fire project."

In explaining their use of the paper for current events, some examples of answers are: "What is going on in the world." "Learning what has happened this day." "When we have current events and the teacher brings it up, I will know the news." "In current events we get higher grades and it tells you a lot."

Some children answered that they had been helped in spelling, writing, language and grammar. They commonly indicated their use of the paper in science class by the name of the subject, "science." Examples of more specific references are: "Things that have been invented." "When we were studying about the universe in science."

Miscellaneous answers from single children included those from a girl who thought, "The funnies have helped me in art," and a boy who said, "It has helped me in sports."

Summary

Children in grades four, five and six in reporting on their reading of newspapers showed increases from grade to grade, with most children reporting that they read the newspapers "sometimes" rather than regularly.

The comics, major news stories, and sports, in that order, were the most frequently read parts of the paper. In identifying the parts of the newspaper which they did not read, the children indicated awareness of the content of newspapers.

The explanations which children gave for different reports of the same materials in several newspapers included: perceptions of the reporters, sources of information, language used in writing, deliberate attempts to be different, economic reasons, and editorial policies. The ability to give reasons showed a development progression.

The majority of the children named one or more school subjects in which they had been helped by newspaper reading. The subjects most frequently named were reading, social studies, and current events.

Textbooks vs. Tradebooks--A Child's View

Patrick J. Groff

From School Libraries 16:29-33, Summer 1967. Published by the American Association of School Librarians. Reprinted by permission.

The questionnaire used in this study was designed to test some of the long-prevailing sentiments and traditions that surround the use of the basal reading textbook--the reader. While there seems little doubt that at least two out of three elementary teachers view the reader as "absolutely necessary" in their classrooms, some adults see it as tawdry, humdrum, crassly commercial stuff, with little sensibility in its content toward the real problems of the modern world. Knowing this, the questionnaire attempted to get a feedback on these matters from those most intimately affected by the reader's pages--the children. It asked children, in concepts and language they could understand, to validate the feelings of one or the other of the two groups of adults concerned with the reader--the teachers and the critics. The results speak for themselves.

Do children in the intermediate grades, who have had experience with both readers and tradebooks, prefer one of the two types of reading material over the other? If so, for what reasons?

Middle-grade children's answers to these queries were investigated through the use of a 35-item questionnaire that required their forced-choice answers of either "Reader" or "Library Book" (used to mean tradebook). The questionnaire ended by asking these children to:

Check which one you like to do more:

........Read a library book by myself.
........Read my reader and talk about it with other boys and girls in my reading group.

The children were then asked to freely respond with the reasons for their choice between these two reading activities and materials.

The Children

There were 634 children who completed the questionnaire. Of these, 353 were in the sixth-grade; 257 were in the fifth-grade; and 24 were in the fourth-grade. There were 317 boys and 317 girls in the total group studied. The children were from twenty-one classrooms in eight different schools in four different school districts, and from a college elementary school. While they were all from middle-class schools, only five classes of children in the study attended schools that had libraries.

Table I

Percentages of Responses to Items in the Questionnaire By 634 Children

1.	Which one can you read faster?	L	73
		R	27
2.	Which one tells more about things that could happen?	L	61
		R	39
3.	Which one tells more about things you like to read about?	L	83
		R	17
4.	Which one do your friends like better?	L	87
		R	13
5.	Which one has more words you do not know?	L	62
		R	38
6.	Which one has better pictures?	L	44
		R	56
7.	Which one is more exciting and interesting?	L	85
		R	15
8.	Which one do you learn more from?	L	38
		R	62
9.	Which one would you rather take home to read?	L	86
		R	14
10.	Which one would your teacher rather have you read?	L	34
		R	66

11. Which one tells more about real things?   L   54**
      R   46
12. Which one tells how to make other people like you?   L   52*
      R   48
13. Which one has more funny parts in it?   L   73
      R   27
14. Which one tells you how to get things you want?   L   64
      R   36
15. Which one keeps you wondering what will happen next?   L   85
      R   15
16. Which one tells you how to be a good boy or girl?   L   41
      R   59
17. Which one sounds better when it is read aloud?   L   60
      R   40
18. Which one has the characters do more things and talk more?   L   64
      R   36
19. Which one is more about a boy and girl like yourself?   L   54**
      R   46
20. Which one do you remember more things from?   L   64
      R   36
21. Which one tells you how to do more things?   L   60
      R   40
22. Which one is harder to read?   L   61
      R   39
23. Which one do you want to read more in school?   L   73
      R   27
24. Which one do girls like better?   L   78
      R   22
25. Which one would you rather read aloud to someone?   L   60
      R   40
26. Which one has print that is easier to read?   L   33
      R   67

Ages Six to Twelve

27.	Which one makes you want to read for a longer time?	L	86
		R	14
28.	Which one is easier to understand?	L	44
		R	56
29.	Which one makes you more curious about things?	L	80
		R	20
30.	Which one has a better looking cover?	L	53*
		R	47
31.	Which one do boys like better?	L	87
		R	13
32.	Which one makes you want to figure out answers to things by yourself?	L	59
		R	41
33.	Which one tells you to work hard at school and at home?	L	22
		R	78
34.	Which one tells you what to do when you cannot get what you want?	L	50*
		R	50
35.	Which one would your Mother or Dad rather have you read?	L	56
		R	44

Legend: All numbers represent %'s.
  L: Response to "Library Book."
  R: Response to "Reader."

* Difference between L and R %'s not significant.
** Difference significant at .05 level.
  All other differences significant at .01 level.

Findings of the Study

    1. For each of the 35 items in the questionnaire (see Table I) there was calculated the percentage of the children who responded with one or the other of the two forced-choice responses: "Reader" or "Library Book." For instance, 73 per cent of the children answered the question, "Which can you read faster?" with "Library Book." Of the

same group, 27 per cent answered the same question with "reader." Table I indicates these percentages. The statistically significant differences* between the percentages of responses is also indicated there.

    2. The coefficients of correlation* between the frequency of the children's responses to "Library Book" in the total questionnaire and (a) the children's reading ability and (b) their intelligence were obtained. These correlations are presented in Table II.

Table II

Coefficients of Correlation Between Frequency of Response To "Library Book" and Reading Ability and Intelligence Quotients
F-L

	N	r		N	r
Reading--Boys	244	.343	I.Q.-Boys	238	.308
Reading--Girls	236	.278	I.Q.-Girls	232	.215
Reading--Boys and Girls	*480	.299	I.Q.-Boys & Girls	*470	.252

Legend: F-L: Frequency of response to "Library Book."
    *: Only this number of reading scores and I.Q.'s were available

These low correlations suggest there is very little relationship between reading ability or IQ and preferences for tradebooks by children.

    3. The frequencies of the voluntary answers by the children to the free-response question at the end of the questionnaire are presented in Table III.

Conclusions

    1. The major question of the study, "Do intermediate-grade children prefer tradebooks over reading textbooks," was answered in the affirmative. A large majority of the children indicated they enjoyed tradebooks more than readers. When asked the concluding question, "Which do you like to

do more, read a library book or a reader?", 84 percent of the children chose "library book." One might assume this per cent favoring tradebooks would be even higher than found here if all the schools in the study had libraries.

2. As seen from Table III, the main reason for this preference for tradebooks was that these books were seen to be more interesting, exciting, entertaining and suspenseful, or were thought to be easier to identify with than were readers. Being allowed to read at one's own speed and having the freedom to choose the material to be read, procedures ordinarily associated with the reading of tradebooks, were also indicated to be important reasons for the preference for this kind of book. These comments affirm some recent judgments of readers made by adult critics of these textbooks.

As seen from Table I, this preference for tradebooks was also indicated in responses to items in the questionnaire, such as question 7: "Which one is more exciting and interesting?" to which 85 per cent of the children responded, "Library Book." The preference for reading at one's own speed was also indicated by the response to question 27: "Which one makes you want to read for a longer time?" to which 85 per cent responded, "Library Book," or question 1: "Which one can you read faster?" to which 73 per cent responded, "Library Book." The wish to have the freedom to choose the material they read was suggested in the response to question 9: "Which one would you rather take home to read?" to which 86 per cent responded in favor of tradebooks, or question 3: "Which one tells more about things you like to read about?" to which 83 per cent responded in favor of tradebooks. Disapproval by the children of an increased use of readers was indicated by the responses to question 23: "Which one do you want to read more in school?" to which 73 per cent responded in favor of tradebooks.

3. There seemed a rather strong image in the children's minds, however, that teachers preferred readers to tradebooks, as indicated in the responses to question 10: "Which one would your teacher rather have you read?" to which 66 per cent responded, "Reader." On the other hand, the children tended to agree that members of both sexes and their friends favored tradebooks over readers. (See

the percentage of responses to questions 4, 24, and 31 in Table I.) The children were more or less equally divided in their opinions as to which type of book their parents rather have them read. (See question 35 in Table I.)

4. There were some significant differences between the boys' and the girls' opinions about tradebooks and readers; on 49 per cent of the questions there were significant differences between the opinions of the sex groups. Girls tended to be less critical of readers than boys.

Table III

Categories and Frequency of
Free Response Comments to
"Which Do You Like
To Read More?"

	Total L	R
More interesting, exciting	244	25
Can read at one's own speed	92	0
Dislike of reading group	91	0
Like reading group	0	60
Freedom to choose material	58	0
Better variety of books, stories	47	9
One learns more	45	37
Easier to read	27	9
More complete, detailed	20	0
More challenging	11	0
Better format	7	1
Totals	642	141
%'s	82	18

Legend:
  L: Comments favorable to "Library Book."
  R: Comments favorable to "Reader."
    Total number of comments will not correspond to number of subjects as some subjects gave no free-response, while others made as many as four distinct comments.

Implications of the Study

One must assume that children's interests in and attitudes toward the learning environment are central to the processes of teaching them not only to read, but to want to read. This study suggests that greater use of tradebooks as versus readers be made in school since children respond to them more favorably.

It also suggests that the role of the librarian in this matter should be enlarged since he is in a strategic position to help children develop taste and sensitivity toward good tradebooks.

The study indicates, as well, that librarians need to be especially prepared to guide children to books in keeping with their reading abilities (see items 5, 22, and 28). The study hints at an apparent disapproval by children of some aspects of the format of tradebooks (see items 6 and 26). These matters can be brought to publishers' attention.

Perhaps most importantly this study implies that an educational environment that depends largely on reading material that most children find second-rate cannot be condoned. The school librarian can be helpful in making this point clear when discussions of book budgets for readers versus tradebooks arise.

---

* For the reader unfamiliar with statistics, very simply, significant differences are true differences and not those that could happen due to chance factors. A correlation is the relationship between two sets of scores. If one child scored the highest on two measures, another child the next highest, etc., the r would be 1.00. They usually seem to be less than 1.00.

III: Ages Six to Fifteen

Why and What Children Read

Helen S. Canfield

Reprinted from Junior Libraries, November 1960, copyright (C) 1960 by the R.R. Bowker Company.

Why do children read? As a children's librarian, I had my own theories and so did my colleagues on the Hartford Public Library Staff. Our opportunity to find out from the boys and girls themselves their reasons for reading came during National Library Week, when the library and the Police Athletic League were co-sponsors of a "Why I Like To Read" contest among the city's school children in grades 4-9. During the three week period, about 1,000 essays were submitted and judged. These are the reasons that the boys and girls mentioned.

> By opening a book I can travel without moving a step from home.
>
> I pretend I am the hero and have the adventures he does.
>
> I enjoy myself and learn at the same time.
>
> I like to read because when I am lonely it satisfies my loneliness.
>
> It gives me confidence in myself when I am downhearted.
>
> I love the excitement, the adventure, the people found in books.
>
> Educational books help me with my school work.
>
> I enjoy reading for the thrill of gaining more knowledge.

Ages Six to Fifteen

> Daily repetitions makes one's life seem dull, but you can escape via a library card and a book. Then you will share the hardships, interests, trials, romances and achievements of others. Their lives become a part of yours.
>
> It gives me something to do when it rains and I can't play baseball.

To generalize, the children were reading for vicarious experience, for knowledge, for relaxation, for solution to personal problems.

These were the reasons the children gave for why they read, but what books, what specific titles, were their favorites? Again we had an opportunity to ask them. During Children's Book Week, we asked the boys and girls who visited the main library and branches to vote for their favorite book. The voting was completely free and anonymous. There were no adult suggestions, no signing of ballots. At the end of the week the ballot boxes were opened and the ballots, some 4,500 in number, were tallied. We saw immediately that their reading interests were very broad and distributed about equally between fiction and non-fiction. Then certain titles began to reappear and the final count showed that the following books were the most popular (not necessarily in the order of popularity):

<u>Lassie Come Home</u>, <u>Thirty Seconds Over Tokyo</u>, <u>Pinocchio</u>, <u>Adventures of Tom Sawyer</u>, <u>Little Women</u>, <u>Black Beauty</u>, <u>Cat in the Hat</u>, <u>Stuart Little</u>, <u>Peter Pan</u>, <u>Winnie the Pooh</u>, <u>Exploring Mars</u>, <u>Fifteen</u>, <u>Freddy the Detective</u>, <u>Rabbit Hill</u>, <u>Sue Barton</u> series.

What do these books have in common? First of all, there is one central character with whom the reader can easily identify. Each book has a strong theme and the majority have good plots. Some are fantasy; others, humor, but all have a positive and optimistic approach to life.

We hesitate to draw any conclusions from the contest and the balloting. Certainly these were not scientific investigations and they weren't meant to be. However, we think the following observations might be permitted. For many Hartford children, reading is an important free time activity and their public library is their major source for books. Their reading interests range far and wide, strongly influenced by current events, television programs, and school assignments. Although frequently the last book read, reflecting momentary interest and of ephemeral quality, was listed as "My Favorite Book," those which received the most votes had been read and remembered. These, too, were better quality books.

Why Children Like Horse Stories

Bernard Poll

From Elementary English 38:473-4, November 1961. Reprinted with the permission of the National Council of Teachers of English and Bernard Poll.

Even a useless explanation of the apparently insatiable desire of children for horse stories would be better than none at all. If not practical, it might at least offer us perspective and patience.

It is of course not true that horse stories have more of those qualities which appeal to children than do other kinds of stories. Stories about horses share with others those elements which are attractive to children: excitement, suspense, action, plot, a strong character with which to identify, and so on. A satisfactory explanation of why children demand horse stories, as heavily as we know they do, must show why it is the stories with the horse as the main character and not other types, which are in greatest demand.

Consider the tremendous security in having as the object of one's affection and interest a mammal who seems to return one's love no matter what whim, irritation or little perversion distort one's feelings toward it! Imagine never to be rejected when one falls short, but always to be loved with utter consistency. If is a delicious thought, for a child quite irresistible, momentous and, probably, rarely fulfilled even in much better times and cultures than our own. The horse is a larger mammal with whom the child can identify, one with whom he can rest with utter security.

My solution, then, is that the horse, and therefore the horse story, attracts children because of the role it plays in fulfilling these needs. The qualities of writing and features of plot and development, therefore, are irrelevant to an explanation of why children like horse stories. They want horse stories because they need what the horse symbolizes.

This feeling of children toward the horse is also evidenced in children's desire for pets. A boy and his dog is the traditional symbol of uncompromising, unqualified interchange of affection. Horses are better because they are larger, stronger, and more powerful. They overwhelm with their strength and love, or are felt to do so by children.

No proof is offered for this hypothesis. Evidence could be brought to bear, perhaps by comparing the reading interests of children in other cultures or children in areas which have not had associations with the horse. My appeal, for the truth of this view, is to your intuitive inspection based on your own experience with children.

These needs on the part of children, which horse stories may tend to fulfill, are certainly not conscious. Nothing could be more ridiculous than to assume that children are conscious of any of this reasoning. If the truth of the view rests in any degree upon conscious decision or awareness, even remotely like this explanation, on the part of children, then it is certainly wrong. But unconscious motivation is now a truism of psychology. It needs only to be proved in a particular instance.

Other animals as central characters beside the horse, could probably fill this role. Whales and bears, for example, might do this, but they usually suffer by being unknown in their psychological traits, like the really affectionate whale, or they may be thought to be dangerous, like the unjustly maligned bear (see Seton's great Biography of a Grizzly).

The wise and serious doctor in Butler's great book The Way of All Flesh prescribes for Ernest . . . "a course in the larger mammals. Don't let him think he is taking them medicinally, but let him go to their house twice a week for a fortnight, and stay with the hippopotamus, the rhinoceros, and the elephants, till they begin to bore him. I find these beasts do my patients more good than any other." The doctor's patients were both too sophisticated for horse stories, and their problems perhaps more urgent and of a somewhat different nature. The idea, however, is the same: acquaintance with those animals fulfills a basic need and therefore helps cure a condition.

This hypothesis implies no necessary aspersion on parents. They have their conditions and problems which may be reflected in their reading demands.

It does have the advantage of focusing one's attention on the social basis for demands for types of books. Societies have neurotic patterns as do individuals and what people read is symptomatic of their problems. It is an exciting advantage, which I am claiming for this view, that it stimulates thinking about the social milieu of book demands.

In the meantime, as a practicing children's librarian, my policy is to provide as many copies as my budget and other quality demands allow, of the best horse stories, Smoky and King of the Wind, to name two among long-time favorites.

Nineteen All-Time Favorites

Roma Gans

From Grade Teacher 82:75-8, March 1965. Copyright by Teachers Publishing Corporation. Reprinted by permission of the author.

"What do you suppose Jerry put down as the most important thing he did in school this first semester?" asked Miss Tanner, Jerry's second grade teacher. "Reading Ferdinand."

"What?" asked the principal, registering surprise, "is that old book still being read?"

"Yes, and loved," Miss Tanner answered.

Most of us can recall books that were high on our list. At five I loved my copy of Little Red Riding Hood, which had to be read to me, even if the pictures of the wolf were considered "too terrifying for a child" by an aunt. A brother wore his copy of Aesop's Fables thin in spots where his fingers gripped the pages.

Today's children can have access to thousands upon thousands of books, some good and some rubbish. Children can and do read hundreds of books in a year. That is, they do if they are in one of that too small percent of elementary schools with a library and if they have a psychologically sound reading program rather than one which is narrow and skill-centered. When children have time, books, and encouragement to read as a regular part of classroom life from kindergarten through the elementary school, they will pursue book reading avidly.

Their interest in books varies, as does ours. Some they read with a fair degree of interest. Some they skim through lightly. Some they read, re-read, and ponder over --and never forget.

Ages Six to Fifteen

Obvious Preferences

Anyone close to a group of children in school need not probe to discover what books run high on the interest scale. Children make their preferences obvious. I can still hear the kindergarten children in a school in New York squeal with delight over Marjorie Flack's The Story About Ping. They asked the teacher to read the book again and again. Some children asked their parents for a copy as a Christmas gift. During browsing time when children took a book to look at while resting, Ping was so popular that the school had to buy extra copies. Wanda Gag's Millions of Cats met almost the same popularity. And The Night Before Christmas by Clement Clarke Moore was a poem children wished to have included in their May Pole program.

Doubtlessly, kindergarten teachers from across our land will nod at these observations and say, "Just like my kindergarteners."

When we notice such genuine delight with a story or poem we naturally wish all children might have a similar chance to enjoy it. Although some stories and poems have wide, almost universal appeal, teachers are wise to remember that there are always some mavericks in groups who latch on to their own pet books, not joining the majority. And woe to the teacher who may say, "You should like this book. Everybody does."

First grade favorites

First graders express strong likes and often develop marked fondness for certain books, as do youngsters in the kindergarten. In a first grade, just before Christmas, two books--one Ruth Krauss's A Hole Is to Dig which had been a favorite with older brothers and sisters, the other a very recent one, Where's Wallace? by Hilary Knight--evoked great interest. Both books will stand the critical test of worthiness by specialists in children's literature.

So with the other grade groups, certain books, old or recent, win the abiding pleasure from a majority in the class. In many a second grade Mr. Popper's Penguins by Richard and Florence Atwater has earned the children's whole-souled approval. Some stories must be read aloud by the teacher again and again, and later on, are eagerly read by youngsters themselves. Mike Mulligan and His Steam Shovel and Jareb by Virginia Lee Barton continue to be popular in this respect.

Although reading interests grow wider as children move into third grade and some differences between boys' and girls' preferences appear, certain books still gain general popularity and an affection for them that seems to last. Mary Poppins, The Poppy Seeds, and Little Pear have given many children of this age enjoyment.

You may say, "Yes, this is true of younger children. To them good books are still an innovation. But how about that age between ten and the teens when sophistication begins to set in?"

Sophisticated choices

The best suggestion is to visit a classroom in which many good books are available and ask what books the children recommend to readers of their own age. You will hear such comments as, "Charlotte's Web. Nobody should miss that!" and "Madeline is the best book in the library!" and "Exploring by Astronaut is a perfect science book!" Not only will this age group reveal deep personal interests in certain books, but they also will demonstrate hard salesmanship to entice others to read and endorse their own prized selections. When such lively response is not forthcoming, one might appropriately assume either that a good selection of books is not available to the children, or the curriculum, or the teacher--or both--put a damper on joyful reading.

An important fact about books that children like is that they cannot be tidily assigned to a grade level. Once a child has acquired a fair degree of independence in his reading skills, he covers a wide range in his random reading. A fourth grader may top his list with a book rated high by fifth and sixth graders. Older youngsters may show equal enthusiasm for a selection prized by younger children. In one school, Madeline by Ludwig Bemelman was voted "the most popular book" by fourth, fifth and sixth grades. In each of these grades, different books were strong seconds, again revealing error in assuming that one book is the book for all of an age.

In fifth and sixth grades, deep interests in the field of science, history, or crafts arise. Some children of this age spend most of their reading time with books and other publications related to those interests. Factual rather than story books are often mentioned as their favorites. Such preferences reveal the zest for learning children acquire under a good school-and-home influence.

At times, a teacher or parent may question whether an all-inclusive absorption with the factual is desirable, with no evident interest in other reading. Often, with children as with adults, a whole-hearted attention to a new interest is not only natural, but also essential to develop enough satisfaction to continue the interest. Contacts with other boys and girls in the group, who are pursuing books that pique their interests, stimulate wider reading later on.

In the intermediate grades, many youngsters are able to read books primarily for adults. Marjorie Kinnan Rawlings' The Yearling was read and re-read in one sixth grade. In that same group were three boys who considered John F. Kennedy's Profiles in Courage the best book they had ever read.

Important observations

An examination of children's interest in books from kindergarten through their elementary years will very likely point up some important observations. First, children who are exposed to good books develop strong attachments to certain books. These attachments may be highly personal, but strong, and doubtlessly lasting in their effect. Second, books that in general evoke strong appeals have fine literary quality, and children tend to agree with evaluation specialists. Some highly prized books may be old-timers, others quite new, proving that good books continue to please children, generation after generation. Finally, if children continue to have access to a wide array of good books and have time to read them, their interests and strong preferences continue to develop, no matter how exciting and absorbing their lives become. Each, with his own tastes influencing his preferences, is building into his background a rich never-to-be forgotten store of memories about choice books.

What the City Boy Reads

Iris Vinton

From Elementary English 40:559-62, May 1963. Reprinted with the permission of the National Council of Teachers of English and Iris Vinton.

    Take a walk through a crowded part of the city where many families live close together, and you will in all likelihood come across a building with the words Boys' Club in the name over the entrance. If it's a weekday and not too late at night, the Club will be open. Here you'll find the boys from the surrounding neighborhoods. They'll be doing things boys like to do in their free time--from athletics to holding a meeting, from arts and crafts to sitting around in the Club library, reading or talking about books with their librarian or advisor.

    Just now it is the reading with which we are concerned. These many thousands of boys, dwellers in the not-so-desirable areas of our cities--what do they read, what are they interested in reading, what do they know, think, feel about books?

    We can let them speak for themselves, for the national reading program of Boys' Clubs of America (called Junior Book Awards), has provided the medium through which these city boys have been expressing their own opinions of current books for the past 18 years. Here, along with some comments by librarians and advisors, are some of the things they have been saying recently.

About science books

    Space science is a popular subject, as might be expected, for its popularity reflects the general interest of the nation. The comments of two 14-year-olds are typical of boys from about ten to the late teens: "I like to know about the latest in space science today." "I enjoyed reading

Ages Six to Fifteen 127

about and seeing the pictures of the rockets I have heard about in the news of the day." "I never knew so many things were in outer space until I read this book. A real adventure for man," said an 11-year-old.

"But," said a boy of 13, "I think I prefer science fiction books for enjoyment."

He was not alone in linking fact and fiction in his space reading. Riding the wave of popularity with the factual books on rockets, satellites, space probes, astronauts, missiles, and the like are fictional moon landings, stories of teams of boys playing sports tournaments in interstellar space, and of star-hopping pilots. One boy's comment expressed the general attitude: "This book (science fiction) gave me an idea of what space travel could really be like. I would recommend it to anyone who likes science or space travel (fiction) books." The boys are entirely aware of the difference between space science and space fiction, but find them equally "adventurous," "spine tingling," "fascinating," "full of lots of interesting, exciting things."

With the exception of natural science (excluding chemistry and physics), the sciences make little direct appeal through books. "It's okay, but I'm not too interested in chemistry, math, or whatever it is," say the boys. "Not interested, too technical"; "Over my head. A good book for anyone who wants to learn about - - - -"; "Very educational, but didn't interest me enough to finish the book."

A clue to this general disinterest in science books is given in a comment by Mrs. Ann Annemann of the Lawndale Boys' Club in Chicago: "When boys (9 to 13) saw the cover (book on rocks), they would reach for the book, look through it, then seem disappointed, making remarks, such as, 'I have a rock collection, but none like these,' or 'maybe they should have been in color.' Some boys didn't think they were rocks shown in the pictures. So, we had a session and I tried to tell them about the scope of rocks and rock hunting. A few were impressed, but, on the whole, they were not.

"Then boys from our two science groups were exposed to the book. They took a different attitude about it. They looked at it from the experience gained in their groups. They felt the book would be a great help. A 13-year-old showed me a rock collection he had bought at a museum and pointed out how easy it was to read and remember the names of the different rocks, etc. He would like to have the book."

Apparently boys want and need the immediate experience with science to enlist their interest in the printed word. However, books of easy experiments may hold disappointment for the lone experimenter. A boy of ten reported that he liked one of the you-can-do books. "It was easy to understand, but I tried some of the experiments without much success." Another, the same age, reported that he and his older brother followed the books and enjoyed doing all the experiments because they found the materials they needed around the house. Most boys found experiments most satisfying when they "tried them out" with friends and a group advisor at the Club, with father, mother (many times), older brother or sister.

About birds, bugs, and beasts
(fact or fiction)

Books about animals, insects, or birds usually get eager response from all ages. They rank along with space science in popularity. An immediate relationship seems to be set up between boy and the creatures in the book. "I would like to have a beaver for a pet or a raccoon," announced an 11-year-old after doing some reading about them. "Only I don't think these animals would be happy in the city." A book on beavers aroused this curiosity in an older boy: "They eat twigs like we eat celery. Do their teeth get so big because of this?"

A book on ants aroused enthusiasm from those from ten to fourteen. "Interesting for older boys, too, who like bugs," said one aged ten. An older boy commented, "Amazon ants are fiercer fighters than human Amazons. I know some pretty tough girls, though."

Inspired by Darwin and the voyage of H.M.S. Beagle, a youngster declared, "I wish I could go to South America and dig up lizards." Another, aged 14, was amazed that "the Indians of South America don't even have feathers. They don't wear as many clothes as our Indians did. Not so cold there, I suppose."

A book on insects stimulated a 14-year-old to start his own collection. "The author gives complete instructions on how to mount and preserve them," the boy reported. "I just have some common ones now, but I am going to hunt for a lot more in the park."

A book on water mammals brought forth much enthusiasm. It was declared "fascinating," "amazing," and "a beautiful book" by boys 10, 11, 12. They were excited about it even though some of them found it a little hard to read because of the big, scientific words.

Boys enjoyed reading about birds. "I liked it a lot, although we don't have too many birds here in the city," said a boy of 12. "I never knew there were so many different kinds before."

Shores and beaches interested the 9, 10 and 11-year-olds. An 11-year-old added this to his general comment. "I would like to live at a fishing place, but I would like to have plenty of friends there." Used to having many friends close to him in the city, he was greatly impressed by the loneliness of the beaches and of fishing.

The horse story and the dog story are always loved by the 8 to 14's. However, the books about which they expressed the warmest feelings were those in which the horse or dog overcame a serious handicap. For instance, stories of a blind colt and of a blind dog had top rating. "The colt learned to smell and hear to protect himself from enemies," said a boy of ten. "Then the boy trained him for riding when they found out the blind colt was very smart." A reader of nine, telling about another handicapped horse, said that "the author did a very good job of describing how horses felt. I was happy the horse lived to have such a wonderful life."

Horses and dogs lead into Westerns, which seem to give readers from the youngest to the oldest "something to dream about." Bandits robbing the stagecoach, cattle rustling, round-ups, rodeos, life on the ranch and range with all the Western trappings, are enjoyed. "Rodeo is a romantic Western sport," declared a ten-year-old. "I've never been to a rodeo, but I hope to go someday." Stories of the West (fact as well as fiction) are "real good books with lots of action (not necessarily gun action); fit in with

TV shows I've seen," boys say. They also like mystery in their Western as well as generally wanting more "just good mystery stories."

Some likes and dislikes

There are responses that these city boys make to various kinds of books and reading year after year. Most of these seem to have to do with "knights," "careers," "silly stories," "too childish for me stories," "sports," "other people, other lands."

Generally, they "don't like stories about knights." They are "strange" and "most of the adventure ridiculous."

The so-called career story or "how-to-get-to-be" book seems to afford little stimulation for the reader. He may want to be a postman, engineer, doctor, or have a fantasy about being an astronaut or great entertainer, but he never can quite see himself involved in the work or study necessary to get where he wants to be. He sees himself at the goal immediately. Therefore, he says: "It didn't sound true." "Dull! Dull! Dull!" "Somewhat interesting." "Pretty good, but I don't think I want to be that."

By "silly stories" boys from 7 to 10 or so mean those fantasies which they enjoyed very much because they were "full of imagination," "funny, made me laugh," and were "real crazy" or "kind of corny." Boats, machines, or inanimate things which "act like people" are thought to be corny but fun to read about. Stories or rhymes about creatures never seen on land or sea arouse enthusiasm, particularly if the pictures are "nutty," "crazy," "comical." Tricks and magical happenings, such as making food suddenly appear when needed, arouse favorable comment. But, most of all, they like the hero to get out of dangerous or ticklish situations by quick thinking or overcoming the villain by outwitting him.

Major criticism of stories of present day boys (or boys and girls) is that they are "too childish" and "didn't keep me interested." They often think the characters unreal or "dumb" to act or behave as they do. All this seems to have nothing to do with language, for the criticism comes from skilled as well as unskilled readers. In order to avoid a too negative opinion they often pick out parts of

Ages Six to Fifteen

books to which they can relate, such as "I liked the games they played," "I found out that a rich boy can be a regular boy," or that certain actions or characters reminded them of something they had seen in the movies or on TV.

On the other hand, books about children in foreign lands who overcome hardships, struggle to achieve a goal, have particular customs, manners and ways of doing things, capture attention and readers express the opinion that the people in the book were "no different from us." Boys respond to the characters by being sad, silly, happy, courageous, or afraid, with them.

Of all the sports, boys seem to like baseball best and to enjoy stories about the game as well as biographies of famous players. No boy will take a sports story that he feels is unrealistic, for most of them know far too much about sports to be interested in storyline or characters obviously manufactured. Boys 9 to 12 express much more eagerness for good sports stories, however, than older boys who are inclined to want adult books on the subject.

If boys' comments on their reading together with their special likes and dislikes suggest a trend, perhaps it is that general trend towards books to which they, as city boys, can relate, whose values they can understand and appreciate, or with which they can establish some real association. These boys take their books personally. "I want a book for me," says the city boy.

What Do Children Value?

Richard Crosscup

Reprinted by permission from the October 1964 issue of the Wilson Library Bulletin. Copyright 1964 by the H.W. Wilson Company.

The field of books written especially for children is a field about which I know very little. It is true that I have taught sixth, seventh, and eighth grades and have had considerable experience with children as young as eight and nine years old in camping situations. But, though the camping work involved considerable cultural activity, including dramatics, bedtime reading and storytelling, I have almost never drawn on children's books as sources. I have tended to confine myself to folk material, or to adult authors who write from a folk base. With sixth, seventh, and eighth graders, I have used adult books almost exclusively, or again, folk material. In one sixth-grade class, I had a number of girls who were poor readers. I established a few sessions per week to work with them on their reading skills. I borrowed some books written for girls their age from the elementary school library, but the girls couldn't stomach them, so we read Greek mythology instead. The mythology was very successful and led not only to emotionally satisfying reading sessions, but also to some creative results, including a beautiful dramatization of the story of Pygmalion and Galatea.

I mention these things, not by way of expressing hostility to books written for children, but by way of demonstrating my ignorance of the field. Let me list here a very few of the novels, documentary books, short stories, and poems, mainly adult material, to which my sixth, seventh, and eighth graders have responded with deep receptivity. I mention only works which have inspired creative results, that is art work, creative writing, creative dramatics, choral reading, etc., on the assumption that such activ-

132

ities give us some objective expression of the influence of
the works read and studied. Here, then, are some suggestions: Homer, The Odyssey; Pearl Buck, The Good Earth;
Sean O'Casey, Juno and the Paycock; Shakespeare, Romeo
and Juliet. Some short stories which have proved
most satisfactory include: Washington Irving, "The Devil
and Tom Walker," and Jack London, "The House of Mapuhi,"
a story of epic quality. Some adult works could not be
handled in their entirety, but were very valuable as sources
of specific chapters or selections. Among them are: Peter
Buck, Vikings of the Sunset, a documentary about the people
of Polynesia; Lady Frazer's abridgement of her husband's
great work, under the title, Leaves from the Golden Bough;
and a chapter or so of Roderick Random by Tobias Smollett.
There is at least one book written for children which I
cannot omit in this context, a small semidocumentary called
Stories of the Underground Railroad. Then there are three
works which are hard to classify: Mark Twain, The Adventures of Huckleberry Finn; Marjorie Rawlings, The Yearling;
and Sholom Aleichem, Adventures of Mottel, the Cantor's
Son. Perhaps these books were originally written for children; if so, I can't tell the difference.

    In the area of poetry, here are a few poems which
children have loved and which have inspired creative activity: Samuel Coleridge, The Rime of the Ancient Mariner;
William Blake, "Tiger," "London," "The Sick Rose," and
"The Chimney Sweeper" (the one from the Songs of Innocence; the one from Songs of Experience is too difficult);
A. E. Housman, "Is My Team Plowing?"; Langston Hughes,
"The Negro Speaks of Rivers" and "Merry-go-round"; James
Weldon Johnson, "The Creation"; Paul Lawrence Dunbar,
"The Caged Bird"; Robert Frost, "The Road Not Taken"
and "The Runaway"; Shelley, "Ozymandias"; Edna St. Vincent
Millay, "The Harp Weaver" and "The Buck in the Snow";
Wilfred Owen, "Dulce et Decorum Est"; and Eleanor Wylie,
"Velvet Shoes." Translations from Sappho, from The Greek
Anthology, even from some of Anacreon and Juvenal, and
from Chinese poetry, especially Ezra Pound's translation
of "The River Merchant's Wife" by Li Po, have also been
effective. Many readers may wonder whether these works
represent the books which children choose for their own
individual reading. To a degree, yes; perhaps to a larger
degree, no. Some of these works were introduced, not by
the teacher, but by students. However, for the most part,
I can vouch for their validity only in the context of the

classroom dialogue.

     The individual reading of students is a different kettle of fish. There are many things children do, things they spend a lot of time on, which may seem worthless to adults. When I was about fourteen or fifteen, I used to put my father in a state of frenzy during our Sunday afternoon automobile drives by counting Mercers, Wintons, and Stutzes. Yet this was at the very time that the existence of the poet Shelley broke on my consciousness like an unintermittent flash of soundless white lightning. Many parents are very puritanical in this connection. That is, they think that everything a child does has to produce values. Nature, however, dictates otherwise, and we must recognize that these apparently neutral activities are necessary, that they fill deep needs whose etiology we do not understand. Much of a child's individual reading will have this neutral, undefined character. His reading interests will be full of vagaries, contradictions, seemingly strange and unaccountable twists. One ten-year-old girl, now a student at Vassar, used to have only two categories on her reading list: the poetry of Edna St. Vincent Millay and every available book about the Brooklyn Dodgers. The classic story is the one about the book on penguins--before publication, it was circulated among a number of children for their reactions. One boy wrote: "This book tells me more about penguins than I care to know." But, I am sure that there were other youngsters who read the book and then looked for more material about penguins! There are obsessive factors in children's behavior, in their intellectual interests, and in their reading habits, about which we know very little. In short, almost any book produced for children by responsible, decent, and adequately skilled people has a certain validity.

     However, it is primarily those things which will help develop in the child a strong self, a strong subjectivity, with which I wish to concern myself. More than two months ago, I delivered a paper at a conference dealing with the child and his education in the scientific-nuclear age. Some of the remarks I made then seem appropriate here.

          For the transcendentalist Thoreau...the important thing is the individual--what he <u>is</u>, not what he <u>has</u> or <u>does</u>. That is, the <u>central</u>

values are to be found in inner experience.
This inward life, this human condition...
is perhaps only rarely beautiful and is often
stifled and mean or ugly and violent. Our
task, as I see it, is to examine why, in our
times, this is so and what can be done to
make man's experience more satisfying to
himself. What are the values, the trans-
cendent values, if you will, by which man's
consciousness can feel itself fulfilled?

When we speak of values, we speak of such
things as friendship or love or loyalty or
courage or truth, and these terms are of
great convenience for communication. But
when we speak of the inner life and its
relationship to the outer world, we speak of
an intense, ongoing process. The role of
education, if it is to deal with values...is
to help the individual shape that ongoing
process in a valuable way. We must also
recognize, I think, that this ongoing process,
this shaping of subjectivity, is also total and
irrefrangible. If we think that, in teaching,
we separate the biological, the intellectual,
and the emotional, we are mistaken. Our
very classroom manner works on the subjectivity of the student. When we are dull, we
free him, perhaps, for erotic fantasies; when
we are most dynamic, we may confirm his
anxieties. Even the reaches of the intellect
are extensions of feelings. "Mathematicians,"
said a mathematician, "are lonelier than poets."

Writers and editors understand the concept that life
and its meanings are primarily inward things. When one
writes a book, the flow of imagery objectifies itself almost
not at all, that is, only in a fine tracery of blotches on a
plane of some thin substance. But the human mind is so
constituted (to quote Aristotle) as to make it possible for
the reader to translate that tracery of blotches into another
flow of imagery: the reader's own imagery, affected by,
and even deeply synthesized with, the author's. When my
students and I read a book, we enter into an even more
primitive kind of communication, bypassing the technological
advances of printing and the phonetic alphabet. The exper-

ience of the book and the discussion of it may prove a very intense experience, deeply modifying all future imagery, influencing all future behavior, conditioning all future emotion, and future human relationships. In short, what is published may have a great influence, or it may have no influence at all. What parents have said, or have in other ways conveyed to children of two or three or four, may support what has been published for the child of eleven and what I may say to the child of fifteen. What parents have said or have failed to say, or what our general culture has conveyed or has failed to convey, may have stifled the inner life of the child, or have rendered it so turbulent, that we cannot reach him except at great pains, if at all. The point is, that if we love life, we have to try.

We cannot, in dealing with children, begin with a set of values and think that children will take to our values as a duck takes to water. We must rather ask ourselves: What do children value? What do we and children share in our common humanity? As I prepared this address, I asked myself: What, as I remember them, were the things in the books and stories and poems mentioned here, which caused them to affect young people deeply? From this examination I derived a list of the values which I think young people find most stirring in their reading. All of the works mentioned contain several of these values; a few contain all or almost all of them. Here, then, are the things which I think children between the ages of ten and fourteen want from their reading:

1. They like warmly described accounts of the unfolding of human personality, illustrating the uniqueness of individuality. They enjoy the humorous, the comical, the poignant or disquieting portrayals of human situations, or situations involving beasts, with whom children, perhaps more than we, feel a natural consanguinity. Most of the works I listed reflect this value. Little need be said about it, so obviously is it one of the central ones of our literary heritage. Realize for a moment the impact on young people of the first line of Langston Hughes' "Merry-go-round":

> Where's the Jim Crow section of this
>   merry-go-round, Mister?
> Cause I want to ride.

2. These children want themes dealing with the realities and choices by which a person relates to life, even, for example, the realities of separation, sorrow, or death. Although it is the idyllic quality of The Yearling that makes the young love this book, it is also the realism of the situation, the necessity of slaying the deer, that takes hold of a young person's soul on a deeper level, and confronts him with the anguish inherent in deep pleasure, in love, as he will confront it in actuality as he matures. It seems to me, too, that young people are stirred by a similar counterpoint in Wilfred Owen's antiwar poem, "Dulce et Decorum Est," in which the beauty of the imagery is juxtaposed to the horror of the gas attack. It is not a pleasant work, but then neither is "Oedipus Tyrannus."

3. Themes which challenge conscience, involving choices, in terms of human values, between right and wrong, justice and injustice, also attract the young. Certainly, in today's world, young people of eleven or twelve do not have long to go before life presents them with the most serious questions of conscience: choices which involve the question of their participation in the decency or the degeneracy of human society. Perhaps one of the greatest fictional accounts of the struggle of conscience, and certainly the greatest involving a child, is Huck Finn's inner conflict over the freeing of Jim. Huck's formal conscience tells him that if he frees a slave, he will go to hell. And he decides to go to hell, an assertion of the primacy of conscience over conscience! That is, of the primacy of humanity over the still, small voice of cant!*

4. Children want stories, which, though clear and lucid on the primary level of meaning, also have a second level, with symbolic meanings, or philosophical implications. Such books and poems challenge their minds to probe the writer's meaning and to see more than lies on the surface. Frost's "The Road Not Taken " excites this kind of probing, as does Eleanor Wylie's "Velvet Shoes," and William Blake's two-sentence poem, "The Sick Rose."

> O Rose, thou art sick!
> The invisible worm
> That flies in the night,
> In the howling storm,
> Has found out thy bed
> Of crimson joy,
> And his dark secret love
> Does thy life destroy.

    5. Children enjoy a literature which describes the ritual of passage: the wanderings of a human being (or possibly an animal) through a variety of experiences, during the course of which the person is fulfilled or profoundly changed. Such literature includes <u>The Odyssey,</u> <u>The Rime of the Ancient Mariner,</u> <u>The Good Earth,</u> <u>House of Mapuhi,</u> <u>Vikings of the Sunset,</u> and, of course, <u>The Adventures of Huckleberry Finn.</u> An important segment of <u>The Yearling,</u> also belongs in this class. In general, love stories and love poetry are not particularly wanted by children at this stage, except perhaps by some girls. Nevertheless, <u>Romeo and Juliet</u> is on our list, because it also represents something of a rite of passage. So, too, <u>The River Merchant's Wife</u> is ritualistic in this same sense. It takes the form of a letter written by a young woman of sixteen to her husband, who is away on a business trip. In her letter she reviews their life together, first as children living next door to each other, and then as man and wife in a marriage arranged by their parents.

> At fourteen I married My Lord you.
> I never laughed, being bashful.
> Lowering my head, I looked at the wall.
> Called to, a thousand times, I never looked back.
> At fifteen I stopped scowling,
> I desired my dust to be mingled with yours
> Forever and forever and forever . . .

    6. Another appeal comes from books evoking images of natural beauty: of forest and river, of rain and snow, of mountain and ocean, of tilled field and wild flowers, of day and night, of raccoon and horse and deer. I put this value last, that is, in a position of prime importance, not because it is more important than the other values, but because it is an area of great philosophical confusion. There is a general tendency to speak of spiritual values as good and material values as bad; since aesthetics involves the

pleasure we take from arrangements and organizations of matter, it tends to be placed in an ambiguous position. Renaissance artists and writers resolved this contradiction, to a degree, through neo-Platonism, but never completely resolved their guilt feelings, so that we find much of the medieval palinode even in Sidney, Shakespeare, and Donne. The truth, as I see it, is this: that matter is omnipresent and real, but meaningless, except as human consciousness gives it meaning. Our human inwardness, on the other hand, is a mire in which we wallow, except as it stems from and relates back to objective, material reality. Einstein's life work was as inward, as alone, as the inward processes of some wretched soul lost in fantasy. But his inward processes (together with those of Galileo and Newton before him, and many others before and since) have put projectiles and even human beings in space and brought them back to earth. In a superficial way, Lear is improbable and not very close to what we normally think of as actuality--that is, it is primarily a work of the imagination, yet the centuries since it was written have established its greatness as a burning vision of reality.

I do not claim that beauty is the highest human value, but only that it is among the highest and that not to think so is to debase life. I am just as adverse to using aesthetically tawdry material with young people as I am to using material which is tawdry in human relationships. Unfortunately, thanks to television, our children are inundated in their homes with a flood of material which is tawdry in both. The only technological advance which has established its right to respect is, it seems to me, printing. And yet, in a few hours spent visiting one bookshop and one newsstand, one could easily collect a mass of data which would call into question even this benign judgment. Teachers, authors, publishers of children's books, and librarians must struggle against the debasement of children, and in this struggle we must give each other support.

There remain three areas of special concern: the problem of children from culturally deprived homes, the problem of the cultural, anti-egghead lag of boys, and the problem of economically deprived children, that is, the children in slums and ghettos. About the first, the children from culturally deprived homes, let me say only that the problem exists, to a startling degree, in schools for the children of the prosperous, especially if one distinguishes between culture and the pretensions or trappings of culture. In regard to the second, the special problem of boys, it seems to me that we must find or create materials which will provide a strong counterthrust against the seductions of the quasi-scientific. In our school, I feel we have had a high degree of success in this area. Most of our boys who will become physicists, physicians, mathematicians, etc., also write poetry and tend to supplement their other studies in college with a lot of work in literature and the humanities. It is not that boys lack deeper feelings, but rather that they are abashed about their deeper feelings, and too much of what we give them caters to that abashment.

About the third problem, the problem of the children in slums and ghettos, I want to quote again from the paper I presented at the conference on the child and his education in the nuclear age:

> If I seem to talk too much about the high culture and not enough about shaping the subjectivity, for example, of the slum child, it is in part because I feel that it is the great humanistic tradition which is still our greatest source of values. But it is also because I believe that the same things are possible with children in the slums. Do any of you know how easy it is to get little boys and girls in Harlem, nine to twelve years old, to do creative things such as painting and dance and dramatics? Do you know how swiftly the slum child moves to the high culture when his time is ripe? The slums not only breed violence. They breed artists and writers and visions of reality. This is one of the great facts of the human spirit.

I feel that this statement has an important truth, but it fails to state another important truth: the situation is terribly, terribly bleak, and providing good books, and good teachers to supplement the books, is perhaps our most challenging problem. It is a problem whose solution, as I see it, calls for great honesty and daring. Writers, publishers, and teachers must be prepared to write, publish, assign, and discuss books in which such children can see some depth of applicability to the content of their own lives.

* To encourage in young people the development of a deep humanity, expressing itself in acts of conscience, is to put young people in serious danger. On Tuesday, June 23, as I was typing this paper, a radio news broadcast announced the disappearance--presumably the brutal murder--of three young men involved in the civil rights struggle in Mississippi. One of them, a boy of twenty, was one of the students in the sixth, seventh, and eighth grade program to which this paper makes so much reference. His parents, interviewed on television and in the press, have not wavered, even slightly, in reaffirming those values with which we are concerned here.--
                                                    The Author

Critical Appraisal of Research on Children's Reading Interests, Preferences, and Habits

Ethel M. King

From the Canadian Education and Research Digest 7:312-26, December 1967. Reprinted by permission.

Much effort is expended today in developing new and more efficient methods of teaching reading, and in evaluating the reading achievement of pupils. Evaluation of the total reading program, however, should be concerned with assessing more than the acquisition of reading skills. This evaluation should also include an assessment of the development of children's reading interests and habits. Curriculum guides in reading usually include some objectives related to the development of interests and the establishment of habits of reading, voluntarily, a wide variety of good literature. This kind of broad objective is perhaps one of the most important today because of the number of people who can read but don't. The process and the results of reading become equally important goals since they are interdependent.

What are the factors which influence what children are reading? A great many investigators have attempted to answer this question. Some begin by studying the attitudes of children, reasoning that a child's attitude towards reading is of prime importance in learning to read and in establishing habits of reading. Attitudes are general predispositions toward reading which are developed or modified with experience.

More specifically, the stimulus or generator of activity is the individual's interest in reading. Interest has been defined as "a characteristic disposition, organized through experience, which impels an individual to seek out particular objects, activities, understandings, skills or goals, for attention or acquisition."[9] Interest in reading develops with the skills and abilities of learning to read and is generally proportionate to the meaning a child receives from reading.

According to Kopel, "What makes an activity interesting is not that it is 'easy' but rather, that it is challenging--which means that it presents obstacles that can be overcome-- necessarily through effort."[16] The responsibility of the teacher, then, is to nurture an interest in reading by his own enthusiasm for reading and by skillfully guiding the pupils in a stimulating reading program.

While competency in reading affects interests in reading, particular interests, or special oompetencies in other areas of learning, are often important determinants of reading interests. For this reason, studies of reading interests frequently become much broader in order to include a general study of children's interests.

Reading interests are not necessarily the same as reading preferences.

> The difference between a preference and an interest is that the preference is relatively passive, while the interest is inevitably dynamic. A preference is a readiness to receive one object as against another; it does not induce us to seek out the object. In contrast, the basic nature of an interest is that it does induce us to seek out particular objects and activities.[9]

For example, a child might express a preference for Wind in the Willows over the Bobbsey Twins but not be interested in reading either one.

After pursuing reading interests, the reader will develop reading tastes. Harris points out that "Children do not develop discrimination by being allowed contact only with superior reading matter. . . . Taste develops through comparison and contrast, not from ignorance."[11]

As taste in reading improves, it is probable that interest in reading will increase. Such an increase may well lead to more reading and this repetition of an act which satisfies a motivating condition may determine reading habits.

If we accept as one of the objectives of elementary education the development of children who want to read, then knowledge of significant research findings can contribute to improved selection and use of books. The history of research in children's reading interests dates back to the beginning of this century. Over 300 studies in this area have since been completed. With the findings that have been accumulating, certain trends and characteristics can be identified.

Kinds of Studies

Many studies have been conducted on the general interests of children and their relationships to reading interest. Other studies have been concerned with changes in reading interests according to chronological age, sex differences, and intelligence. A third group of studies are those determining children's preferences in form, style, and format. Finally, there are studies which have tried to determine the reading habits of children.

Reading Interests

Reading Interests and General Interests

A number of the studies of reading interests are concerned with the general interests of children and the way these are reflected in reading interests. A commonly accepted assumption is that an individual's reading interests at any given time will be largely influenced by the kind of person he is, the kinds of activities he engages in, and the ideas about which he likes to think and talk. The topics favored by one reader may be rejected by another. Readers' preferences will change as new interests, reflecting increased maturation, are developed.

Reading interests do not necessarily reflect children's informational needs. Over 1,000 children were asked by Baker [1] to write questions they would like to ask. The responses indicated an emphasis on animal life, communication, and the earth. In analysing the science interests of intermediate grade children, Young[40] found that the universe, animals, earth, human growth, and weather ranked high. Shores[30] found that boys asked questions more in the field of science, particularly about geology, geography, and rockets. Girls, on the other hand, wanted information on foreign countries, history, authors, and artists. Intermediate grade pupils are more interested in reading to find the specific information needed rather than to read an entire book on the general topic. Shores concluded that children are not necessarily interested in reading the same things about which they ask questions. To find the answers to their questions, children often use sources of information other than reading.

Librarians report that the basic reading interests of children have changed very little over the years. However, topics of current interest, such as outer space, are reflected in the reading choices of children. Current movies may influence the popularity of certain books.

Until recently, studies of children's interests did not reflect the effect of watching television programs. Larrick[18] believes that urban and rural children may be developing interests which are more alike as a result of having the opportunity to watch the same television programs. After a study on general interests of children, Howes[12] concluded that television viewing ranks first among preferred activities. If such is the case, preferences in television programs could be expected to have a significant effect on the reading interests, preferences, and tastes of young children. Mauch and Swenson[25] reported that among recreational interests, reading ranked fourth.

Reading Interests and Chronological Age

The typical reading interests of children at different stages of development have been the concern of many investigators.

Studying interests of kindergarten children, Cappa[3] reported a preference for fanciful stories over realistic ones, providing they were not completely unrealistic. In spontaneous group discussions, children of seven revealed to Gunderson[10] that they enjoyed humor, excitement, suspense, adventure, magic, and a satisfying ending.

The content of stories selected by primary grade children will be largely realistic stories about everyday activities. They tend to favor fairy tales, animal stories, nature stories, humorous tales, comics, and how-to-do-it books. In the intermediate grades, pupils prefer adventure, animal stories, tall tales, family-life stories, famous people, sports, humor, science, and social studies.

Rudman's study,[29] using questionnaires to children, parents, teachers, and librarians, indicated that children generally enjoy stories of action, mystery, adventure, horses, and dogs. Interest in mysteries, recreation and sports continues to increase, and interest in cowboy stories and fairy tales decreases.

A very comprehensive study of children's interests was conducted by Norvell[26] with 24,000 children in New York State from grades three to eight. Some Mother Goose rhymes were enjoyed throughout the elementary grades, and others were rejected by grade three. Fables and fairy tales were popular in grades three to five and after that myths, legends, and folk tales were favored. Animal stories ranked first and biography second with children from grade three to six.

Recent studies reveal a trend among children of younger ages toward maturing faster in their reading interests. McAulay[20] identified more mature interests in social studies materials among younger children as being probably due to the influences of television, radio, movies, and travel.

Reading Interests of Boys and Girls

Studies of children's interest in reading reveal few differences between the sexes up to age nine. Young boys, however, generally show an unusual interest in stories about trains.

One of the classic studies in the field of reading interests was published in 1925 by Terman and Lima.[33] These two investigators described the typical interests of boys and girls at each age level, from pre-school through adolescent years. Girls preferred fairy tales, poetry, and sentimental fiction, while boys favored adventure and vigorous action.

In studying responses of 3,000 children, ages 10 to 15, Thorndike[34] reported that boys of all ages were more interested than girls in science, invention, sports, and violent adventure. In contrast, girls favored stories of home life, romance, school adventures, fairy tales, and animals.

Later Lazar,[19] investigating sex differences in reading interests, outlined the rank-order of preferences of boys as mystery stories, adventure, detective, history, invention, science, nature and animal, fairy stories, biography, novels, stories about home and school, and poetry. Girls listed, in descending order, mystery stories and stories of home and school activities.

Norvell[26] corroborated the findings of earlier studies which indicated that sex differences in children's reading interests appear at about age nine. Girls were found to enjoy many boys' books, but boys did not enjoy almost all girls' books. Boys were interested in the following: detective stories, humor, physical struggle, history, courage and heroism, invention, and science. Favorites among the girls were stories of: home and school life, domestic animals and pets, sentimental fiction, mystery, the supernatural, and fairy tales. During the middle grades, boys responded unfavorably to description, didacticism, fairy tales, romantic love, sentiments, physical weakness in males, and females as the leading characters in the stories. Girls disliked violent action, description, didacticism, slightly younger children, and fierce animals.

McKenzie studied the reading interests of pupils in Medicine Hat, Alberta. He found "Sex differences in reading interests appeared in Grade 4, and increased appreciably in Grades 5 and 6. In the latter grade the girls outnumbered the boys two to one in their choice of mystery books and children's stories, whereas the boys nearly reversed the score in preferences for non-fiction."[23]

Several other studies have been in general agreement with these findings on sex differences in reading interests.

Reading Interests and Intelligence

Intelligence is an important factor in determining what children read. Thorndike[34] studied the reading interests of thousands of children grouped according to superior (median I.Q. about 123), average, and weak pupils (median about 92). The superior group indicated interests more like pupils in the slow group who were two or three years older. Lazar,[19] too, found that the choice of books did not vary much with bright, average, and dull pupils. The patterns of reported reading interests were much the same for all groups. Within a class, however, the areas of interest of more intelligent children will be more mature than the less intelligent children.

The types of reading preferred by less able pupils, according to Stone,[32] varies only slightly from those preferred by average and bright pupils. The most notable exception is humor which is chosen less by dull pupils. While the slow-learning child has interests which are slightly immature for his chronological age, nevertheless, they are usually more mature than those of younger children of the same mental age. As a result, this group tends to select books which are at a reading level that is too difficult for them.

Summary of Factors Influencing Reading Interests

1. Reading interests tend to change as new interests are developed.

2. Reading interests do not necessarily reflect informational needs.

3. Audio-visual aids may play an important role in changing reading interests.

4. Primary grade children prefer fairy tales and realistic stories based on everyday activities and animal stories.

5. In the intermediate grades, pupils prefer mystery, adventure, animal stories, family life stories, biographies, sports, science, and social studies.

6. Children appear to be maturing faster in their reading interests.

7. There are few sex differences in reading interests up to age nine.

8. Definite differences in reading interests among girls and boys become apparent after age eight.
    a. Boys read more non-fiction than girls.
    b. Girls read more poetry than boys.
    c. Both boys and girls rank adventure, action, mystery,

animal stories, patriotism, and humor high in their preferences.
  d. Boys prefer stories of science, invention, and vigorous action.
  e. Girls prefer stories of home and school life, sentimentalized fiction, and fairy tales.
  f. Boys have a wider range of interests than girls.
  g. Girls will read a book considered to be of interest to boys but the reverse is seldom true.
9. The reading interests of children who are above average in intelligence mature faster than those of slow learners.

Reading Preferences

Factors influencing reading preferences have been studied in many different ways: pupil's reasons for choosing books, kinds of reading materials, literary form, style of writing, type of print, and illustrations.

Reasons for Selection

From studies which included 600 intermediate grade pupils, Humphreys[13] listed the reasons why children selected books. A recommendation from a personal friend was the reason stated most frequently.

A number of studies, such as those by Wightman,[36] Coast,[4] and Cappa,[2] indicated that the teacher's enthusiasm for literature is an important factor in the development of reading preferences.

Kinds of Reading Material

The reading interests, preferences, and habits of children are influenced by the amount and kind of materials they read. In addition to reading books, children often devote much time to reading comics and magazines.

Interest in reading comic books begins in the primary grades and continues beyond the elementary school. Witty and Sizemore[39] found 90 per cent of the pupils ages 8 to 13 read comics regularly.

In another study, Witty[37] concluded that boys tend to read more magazines than girls. A number of adult magazines enjoy popularity with children.[17]

Literary Form

Children throughout the elementary grades show a preference for narrative material. Fiction is preferred and read more frequently than non-fiction.

Girls show a greater interest in poetry than boys. Mackintosh[22] reported that the qualities children liked most in poetry were: rhyme, emotional tone, vocabulary, story, and descriptions. According to Norvell's study,[26] children preferred humorous poems and poems about animals.

Style of Writing

Factors which appeal to children in the style of writing have changed very little. In 1921, Dunn[8] described the preferred qualities as: surprise, action plot, repetition, and liveliness.

Primary grade children favor a story with a good plot and lots of action. Humor and nonsense rank high in their preferences.

Summarizing several studies, Jordan[14] concluded that the following characteristics were favored: action, adventure, mystery, excitement, and humor.

For factual and informational books to be popular with young readers, they must be simply written.

Type of Print

Young children prefer larger type and a page which is uncluttered. With growth in reading skills, their preferences change. Type size should decrease from 18 to 14 points in grade one to 12 points in grade six.[7] Sometimes books with smaller print may be judged to be more "grown-up." If a child is seeking approval, he may select a book more on the basis of what he thinks is expected of him rather than what he actually prefers.

Illustrations

Again, many studies have been conducted on the effect of various characteristics of illustrations on reading preferences. Whipple's study[35] indicated that preference for a book increases with the following factors: the proportion of the illustrations that depict action, along with the color, size of illustration, and number of illustrations. Other studies support the finding that the children prefer colored pictures to black and white ones. Whether a picture is colored or not is less important than the success of the picture in making the content appear real or life-like.[28, 24] Interpreting research findings in terms of the more recently published children's books is difficult because of the marked changes that have taken place in the last five years in the kinds of illustrations.

Summary of Factors Influencing Reading Preferences

1. Personal recommendations rank high in determining the selection of reading materials.

2. Pupils read a variety of reading materials including books, comics, and magazines.

3. Prose form, particularly narrative, is preferred to poetry.

4. Children prefer stories with a good plot, much action, and humor.

5. Colored pictures are preferred to black and white ones.

6. Realism tends to be a more important factor in illustrations than color.

Reading Habits

The Committee on Children's Recreational Reading in Ontario concluded that "reading problems are largely solved by making good books available in abundance and by directing children in their approach to them, and that where there is no great interest in books on the part of the central authorities, reading standards decline."[5] This point of view emphasizes the importance of making books available if we are to establish desirable reading habits.

In interviewing children about their reading habits, McCracken[21] found children could seldom give specific reasons when asked why they liked to read. All the avid readers, however, said they had liked reading and had had books around ever since they could remember. Once a good supply of books is available, children develop their own preferences, tastes, and methods of selection. The books preferred are not necessarily the same books as adults would choose or that adults think children would like, as studies such as Rankin's [27] on Newbery award-winning books have shown.

A number of studies have revealed an increase in the number of books read voluntarily by children each year to the end of the elementary grades. Cutright and Brueckner,[6] for example, found an increase in library books withdrawn from grades three to six. In addition, they found that the number of books borrowed from libraries was directly related to the distance the pupils lived from the library.

Terman and Lima[33] found that gifted children read three or four times as many books as children of average ability. In the study by McKenzie,[23] the upper third of the class, as determined by a reading test, read twice the number of books read by the lowest third. Witty and Lehman[38] also found that the amount of voluntary reading done by bright children far exceeded that done by other children.

Summary of Reading Habits

1. The amount of reading increases up to the end of the elementary grades.

2. Girls read more than boys (See Reading Interests).

3. Bright children read considerably more than children with a lower I.Q.

4. Home influences are important in establishing reading habits. The amount and quality of reading are related to the number and kinds of books, magazines, and newspapers in the home.

5. Easy access to good school libraries and public libraries is an important influence in establishing desirable reading habits. . . .

... The teacher needs an understanding of the interests of children generally, and his own class specifically. Since each child in a classroom will not have the same interests, we must pursue the matter further to discover the particular interests of each child. A knowledge of the general trends, as indicated by research findings, helps a teacher to anticipate the interests and preferences of pupils. Smith[31] sums it up by saying, "The reading interests with which children come to school are our opportunity, but the reading interests with which they leave school are our responsibility."

References

1. Baker, Emily L. Children's Questions and Their Implications for Planning the Curriculum. New York: Bureau of Publications, Teachers College, Columbia University, 1945.
2. Cappa, Dan. "Kindergarten Children's Spontaneous Responses to Story Books Read by Teachers," Journal of Educational Research, 52 (October, 1958), 75.
3. Cappa, Dan. "Types of Story Books Enjoyed by Kindergarten Children," Journal of Educational Research, XLIX (March, 1956), 555-557.
4. Coast, Alice B. "Children's Choices of Poetry as Affected by Teacher's Choices," Elementary English Review, 5 (May, 1928), 145-147.
5. Committee on Children's Recreational Reading in Ontario. The Recreational Reading Habits of Ontario School Children, Study Pamphlets in Canadian Education, No. Ten. Toronto: Copp Clark, 1952, 6.
6. Cutright, Prudence and Brueckner, Leo J. "A Measurement of the Effect of The Teaching of Recreational Reading," Elementary School Journal, XXIX (October, 1928), 132-137.
7. Dechant, Emerald V. Improving the Teaching of Reading. Englewood Cliffs: Prentice Hall, 1964.
8. Dunn, Fannie W. Interest Factors in Primary Reading Material. Contributions to Education, No. 113, New York: Bureau of Publications, Teachers College, Columbia University, 1921.
9. Getzels, Jacob W. "The Nature of Reading Interests," Developing Permanent Interest in Reading. Supple-

mentary Educational Monographs, No. 84. Chicago: University of Chicago Press, 1956, 7, 5.
10. Gunderson, Agnes G. "What Seven-Year-Olds Like in Books," Journal of Educational Research, L (March 1957), 509-520.
11. Harris, Albert J. How to Increase Reading Ability. New York: Longmans Green, 1956, 491.
12. Howes, Virgil E. "Children's Interest--A Keynote for Teaching Reading," Education, 83, (1962), 491-496.
13. Humphreys, Phila. "The Reading Interest and Habits of 600 Children in the Intermediate Grades," Language Arts in the Elementary School, 20th Yearbook of Department of Elementary School Principals, 20:6 (1941), 421-428.
14. Jordan, Arthur M. Children's Interests in Reading. Contributions to Education. No. 107. Teachers College, Columbia University, 1921.
15. Karlin, Robert. "Library-Book Borrowing vs. Library-Book Reading," The Reading Teacher. 16 (November, 1962), 77-81.
16. Kopel, David. "The Nature of Interests," Education, (April, 1963), 497-502.
17. Kramer, Sister M. Immaculata. "Children's Interests in Magazines and Newspapers," I, Catholic Educational Review, XXXIX (June, 1941), 343-358. II, Catholic Educational Review, XXXIX (June 1941), 348-358.
18. Larrick, Nancy. A Teacher's Guide to Children's Books. Columbus, Ohio: Charles E. Merrill Books, 1960.
19. Lazar, May. Reading Interests, Activities and Opportunities of Bright, Average, and Dull Children, Contributions to Education, No. 707. New York: Bureau of Publications, Teachers College, Columbia University, 1937.
20. McAulay, J. D. "Interests of Elementary School Children," Social Education, XXVI (April, 1962), 199-201.
21. McCracken, Ruth U. "What Makes a Difference?" Childhood Education (March, 1962), 319-321.
22. Mackintosh, Helen K. "A Critical Study of Children's Choice in Poetry," University of Iowa Studies, Studies in Education, VII, No. 4 (September, 1932).

23. McKenzie, Edwin. "Reading Interests of Pupils in the Intermediate Grades in the Public Schools in a Small Urban Center," Alberta Journal of Educational Research, 8 (March, 1962), 33-38.
24. Malter, Morton S. "Children's Preferences for Illustrative Materials," Journal of Educational Research, XLI (January, 1948).
25. Mauch, Inez L. and Swenson, Esther J. "A Study of Children's Recreational Reading," Elementary School Journal, L. (November, 1949), 144-150.
26. Norvell, George W. What Boys and Girls Like to Read. Morristown: Silver Burdett Co., 1958.
27. Rankin, Marie. Children's Interest in Library Books of Fiction, Contributions to Education, No. 906. New York: Bureau of Publications, Teachers College, Columbia University, 1944.
28. Rudisill, Mabel F. "Children's Preferences for Color versus Other Qualities in Illustrations," Elementary School Journal, LII (April, 1952), 444-451.
29. Rudman, Herbert C. "The Informational Needs and Reading Interests of Children in Grades Four Through Eight," Elementary School Journal, 55 (1955), 502-512.
30. Shores, J. Harlan. "Reading Interests and Informational Needs of Children in Grades Four to Eight," Elementary English, 31 (December, 1954), 493-500.
31. Smith, Dora V. "Current Issues Relating to Development of Reading Interests and Tastes," Recent Trends in Reading. Edited by W. S. Gray. Supplementary Educational Monographs No. 49. Chicago: University of Chicago Press, 1939.
32. Stone, C. R. "Grading Reading Selections on the Basis of Interests," Educational Method, 10 (1931), 225-230.
33. Terman, Lewis M. and Lima, Margaret. Children's Reading: A Guide for Parents and Teachers. New York: Appleton-Century-Crofts, 1931.
34. Thorndike, Robert L. Children's Reading Interests. New York: Teachers College, Columbia University, 1941.
35. Whipple, Gertrude. "Appraisal of the Interest Appeal of Illustrations," Elementary School Journal, 53 (1953), 262-269.
36. Wightman, H. J. "A Study of Reading Appreciation," American School Board Journal, L (June, 1915), 42.

37. Witty, Paul A. "Studies of Children's Interests--A Brief Summary," I, Elementary English, 27 (November, 1960), 469-475; II, Elementary English, 27 (December, 1960), 540-545, 572; III, Elementary English, 28 (January, 1961), 33-36.
38. Witty, Paul A. and Lehman, Harvey C. "A Study of Reading and Reading Interests of Gifted Children," Journal of Genetic Psychology, XL (June, 1932), 473-485.
39. Witty, Paul A. and Sizemore, Robert A. "Reading the Comics: A Summary of Studies and an Evaluation," I, Elementary English, XXXI (December, 1954), 501-506; II, Elementary English, XXXII (January, 1955) 43-49; III, Elementary English, XXXII (February, 1955), 109-114.
40. Young, Doris. "Identifying and Utilizing Children's Interests," Educational Leadership, 13 (December, 1955), 161-165.

IV: Ages Twelve to Fifteen

Reading and Reference Interests of Junior-High Students

Charles E. Johnson and J. Harlan Shores

From <u>Illinois Education</u> 51:374-6, May 1963. Copyright by the Illinois Education Association. Reprinted by permission.

Few would hold that children's interests and verbally expressed needs should serve as the sole or even primary foundation for the curriculum, but many wisely maintain that knowledge of what interests youth or what youth says it wants is needed by professional educators as an essential tool in the continual task of updating and improving methods of teaching. This knowledge is particularly helpful when used as a guide for grading content or selecting materials.

Realizing that the interests of any age group change gradually with societal changes, and that little attention has been given to the interests of junior-high-school youth as a group, the authors, with the endorsement of the Illinois Junior High School Principals Association, designed research to learn the reading interests and reference needs of junior-high-school students. (This study was supported financially by Grolier, Inc., New York, publishers of informational books and encyclopedias.)

What would junior-high-school students like a book about? What do they want to ask about? What do they look up in connection with their school work--and in connection with out-of-school interests? With what reference tasks are they unsuccessful? What kind of encyclopedia do they think is best? What do they want to look up in an encyclopedia? To provide at least partial answers to these questions was the purpose of this study.

To provide data for the study, responses to an inventory were obtained from 1521 junior-high-school students --approximately an equal number from each of six different junior high schools located in widely differing areas of Illinois.

There was nearly equal distribution of pupils among the seventh, eighth, and ninth grades. About one third completed the inventory in English classes, another third in science classes, and the remaining third in social science classes.

The inventory contained seven questions:

1. If someone were to give you a book as a present (not a dictionary or encyclopedia), what would you like it to be about?

2. Every student must from time to time look up information needed for use in school. What did you look up recently (not in a dictionary) in connection with school work? Tell exactly what you wanted to find out.

3. Most people sometime or another need information for their own use and not in connection with school work. What did you look up recently (not in a dictionary) that was not needed for school work? Tell exactly what you wanted to find out.

4. I'm sure you can remember trying to look up something recently (not in a dictionary) and not finding what you wanted. Tell exactly what you were looking for and couldn't find.

5. What kind of encyclopedia do you think is best?

6. If you had a good encyclopedia by your side and were told to look up anything that you wanted to find out about, just for your own use, what topic would you look up?

7. If you had a very good friend who could answer any question you asked, what would you ask about?

Six items were open-ended--that is, they required that the pupil write a statement in response. Item 5 was not; it provided five alternatives from which the pupil was to select one. The alternatives ranged from "A set which gives nearly all of the space in each topic to an overview of the topic and to telling what the topic is about. Almost no space is given to lists and tables of facts." to "A set which gives nearly all of its space in each topic to lists and tables of facts about the topic. Almost no space is given to an overview of the topic and to telling what the topic is about."

A classification form was developed for tabulating responses. Finally, the original form was revised and the result was a three-place classification containing 188 items arranged in 14 major categories. These categories, the first of three steps in the classification scheme, conform only roughly to any logical organization of content and are only generally suggestive of the data classified within each. The second step in the scheme--the minor categories--and the third step--the minor sub-categories--are more closely descriptive of the students' behavior, interests, and needs. For example, the major category of literature includes such minor categories as fiction, drama, and biography: fiction in turn includes such minor sub-categories as mysteries, adventure, and historical fiction. This three-place scheme frequently results in double or triple entries--i.e., a reading interest classified as mystery would be represented by a number and percentage in this minor sub-category, but it would also be a part of the entry for the minor category of fiction, and fiction in turn would form a part of the major category of literature.

The data were summarized in terms of the total number of responses to each question. Both the number of responses and the percentage that this number is of the total responses to the question were reported. Categories receiving less than one third of 1 percent were not reported.

Reading Interests

What do junior-high-school students want to read about? Half of the responses were in fiction (50%)--especially mystery, stories about young people, adventure, and romance. However, students also report strong reading interest in science (18%) and the social sciences (11%). Interests in biological science were stronger than those in the applied and physical sciences. In the biological sciences students wanted books about animals, especially horses or dogs; in the applied sciences, automobiles; in physical sciences, chemistry or astronomy. Prominent among social science interests were history, famous people, war, and cultures.

When reading interests in science were combined with those in science fiction, this made a strong interest area (21%). The same was true to a lesser extent with history and historical fiction (5%) and sports and sports stories (8%).

In the major categories, both boys and girls showed first preference for literature, second for science, and third for social science. Boys placed recreation and hobbies next, while girls ranked vocations fourth. When numbers of responses were compared, the girls showed greater preference for literature than did the boys, even though it was the boys' first choice; the boys showed greater preference for science, social science, and recreation and hobbies than did the girls.

Questions

What do junior-high-school students want to ask about? The majority of the responses were for science (26%) and social sciences (23%). Students had more questions about the physical sciences than the biological sciences. They were particularly concerned with space exploration and astronomy. In the social sciences they wanted to ask about the complex of concerns with U.S.-Soviet relations as these matters are related to keeping peace. They have many questions about personal and social adjustment (18%)--the opposite sex, teen-age problems, and their own personal future. They were also concerned about sports and hobbies (7%), vocational choice (6%), high school (4%), and religion (3%).

Boys wanted to ask more questions in the sciences and in recreation and hobbies; the girls, in personal and social adjustment. In major categories, the order of boys' responses was science, social science, personal and social adjustment, and recreation and hobbies. For the girls the order was social science, personal and social adjustment, and science.

Encyclopedias and Reference Work

Most of these students would like the encyclopedia to divide its space equally between general information and specific facts (56%). The next most frequent choice (27%) was for a set which gives most of its space to an overview of the topic and to telling what the topic is about, and only a small amount of space to lists and tables of facts about the topic. Ten percent of the group would like to see most of the space given to specific facts. Only a small percentage chose the extreme position of giving nearly all of the space in each topic to either general information (3%) or specific facts (4%). Boys and girls did not differ much in the distribution of their responses.

Most (82%) of students' school-assigned reference work is either in the social sciences (45%) or in science (37%). Considerably less attention is devoted to reference work in literature (7%). In the social sciences, reference assignments are concerned with cultures, geography, famous people, history, and government. Less attention is devoted to war and social problems.

Students are doing more reference work about biological science than applied or physical science. They are finding out about birds, the human body, insects, botany, and wild animals. They are also doing reference work about disease, health and hygiene, astronomy, and geology and physical geography. In literature, they are finding out about authors, poetry, and mythology. Girls and boys both reported the same type of school assignments.

What do junior-high-school students look up that is not in connection with school work? In the main they look up science (37%) and social science (26%) topics. Less attention is given to sports and hobbies (13%), and considerably less to literature (4%), arts (4%), vocations (3%), personal and social adjustment (3%), and religion (3%). There is only a scattering of reference interest in the other major areas.

"Out-of-school" reference in science is devoted much more to biological (16%) and applied science (14%) than to physical science (5%): Students want information about disease, health, and hygiene; animals, especially dogs, birds, and horses; automobiles; and astronomy and space travel. In the social sciences, they are doing reference work about famous people, geography, cultures, history, war, and political ideals--especially communism. In the area of sports and hobbies, they look for information about sports and sewing and cooking.

In only one category did boys and girls differ in their responses: in sports and hobbies boys had a considerably larger percentage of responses: although this was not one of the three leading areas of concern for either group.

As one would expect, the most unsuccessful reference attempts were in those areas where the most reference work is done--either in connection with school work or with out-of-school concerns. In school assignments, students reported more than three fourths (77%) of their unsuccessful references in social science, science, and literature. Sports and hobbies, a strong out-of-school area, was next (8%). Only a small percentage (2%) of the total unsuccessful attempts was in the area of personal and social adjustment. Apparently junior-high-school students do not use references for these concerns--but would rather talk about than read about them. Girls and boys differed very little in their responses.

What would these youth like to look up in a "good encyclopedia?" Their desires are closely akin to what they report looking up in the out-of-school situation: Science (37%), social sciences (33%), sports and hobbies (11%), vocations (7%), arts (4%), and literature (2%) make up nearly all of the total response (94%). Boys and girls differed somewhat in their responses. Boys responded most frequently in science and second in social sciences; girls responded most frequently in social sciences and second in science. There was a near balance of choices in the other major categories.

Teacher Prediction of Interests

As a supplement to this study, 105 of the teachers of the pupils involved were asked to respond to the inventory as they thought the pupils would answer. There was approximately equal representation of teachers from each of the six junior high schools and from the seventh, eighth, and ninth grades. By subjects, 30 teachers taught English, 47 social science, and 28 science.

Concerning read-about interests, the teachers' judgments in the first three major categories were the same and in the same order as responses of the pupils. However, there were differences with regard to distribution of responses. Both teachers and pupils named literature first-- but it accounted for 71 percent of the teachers' responses and only 55 percent of pupils' responses. In the second area, science, there was little difference in the distribution of responses--teachers, 17 percent; pupils, 18 percent. The third area, social sciences, accounted for only 5 percent of teachers' responses, but 11 percent of pupils' responses.

Concerning ask-about interests, teachers thought pupils would first ask questions in the area of personal and social adjustment (46%); next, science (20%); and third, social sciences (16%). Pupils' responses placed science first, social studies second, and personal and social adjustment third.

Teachers tended to think that pupils wanted an encyclopedia which gives most of its space to an overview of topics and a small amount of space to lists and tables of facts (59%). However, pupils preferred one which gives about half the space to an overview of topics and half to lists and tables of facts. Neither group gave more than 5 percent of the responses in the categories at the extremes.

Since responses to the other items on the inventory were dependent on school subjects and the sample of teachers was not representative, further comparisons of teachers' and pupils' responses were not made.

In general the reading interests and informational needs of junior-high-school boys and girls are similar. However, there is a tendency for boys to show greater interest in science and sports and hobbies than girls, and for girls to show more interest in social science topics than boys.

Junior High Book Discussions

Nancy Elsmo

From the Wisconsin Library Bulletin 62:279-80, September-October 1966. Reprinted by permission.

Perhaps most of us without direct contact and experiences in working with 12 and 13-year-olds mentally envision them discussing only the latest hit record and/or the fad in hip-huggers. It was something of a revelation to those of us at the Racine Public Library who led and observed the first Junior Great Books meeting in the winter of 1960, to see and hear the youngsters become vibrantly and enthusiastically interested and involved in discussing a book. When the Children's Department undertook this activity, it was decided to attempt reaching this somewhat neglected age group in book and library spheres, the junior high school "inbetweeners." We felt that a small discussion group for seventh and eighth grade students interested in reading might be the stimulus needed to keep some from veering entirely away from good independent reading before their encounter with the exacting rigors of a high school study schedule and social whirl. At the very least, this project acquaints the participants with literary selections they may not attempt to read on their own. We also feel that the sessions have given these young people the chance to develop their powers of self-expression. A natural, informal atmosphere was the goal to achieve a free flow of ideas and exchange of opinions, and though the meetings frequently have begun stiff and formal, the participants soon realize that no one is being graded or degraded for what he says, and the ice melts.

In 1963, the Great Books Foundation copyrighted its own Junior Great Books with suggested readings for fifth to ninth grades, and kits of paperbacks which can be purchased from the Foundation. Our own arrangement and choice of classics has proved so satisfactory that we have retained much the same program with which we began in 1960.

Participants are chosen in cooperation with public and parochial junior high schools in the Racine area. The number of names submitted by each librarian or English teacher is in direct ratio to the school's enrollment. Pupils are not selected on an IQ basis, but rather on the basis of reading capability and interest. There are two groups meeting alternate weeks, allowing everyone two weeks to read the selection for the next meeting. The seventh graders meet for a series of five discussions, and the eighth graders for a series of six. Of the 30 to 35 students invited by the library to join the group, some 20 to 25 stay with the program for the whole series. Paperbacks of all titles used are furnished by the library and charged out to the participants two weeks in advance of each meeting. The physical setup of the library meeting room for these sessions is the same as it is for Great Books meetings. Our sessions last from 50 to 80 minutes, depending on the enthusiasm of the leader and participants for the book they are discussing.

We have found it preferable to have a different leadder for each session. This tends to make the program less class-like and provides a different approach for each discussion. The opinions, impressions and criticisms of the students are first and foremost; each leader is advised to avoid lecturing and to have a few discussion topics ready to broach. Teachers, librarians and interested people in the community are enlisted to act as leaders; almost all of them have found the experience rewarding and return year after year to lead discussions.

A few of the titles we have found most successful are London's Call of the Wild, Twain's Huckleberry Finn, Poe's Great Tales, Crane's Red Badge of Courage, Shaw's Pygmalion, and Frank's Diary of a Young Girl. In discussing the books, the groups have usually been interested in general concepts and broader themes, e.g. the ideologies of Nazism and Communism, stimulated by Diary of a Young Girl, while Swiss Family Robinson prompted discussion of group survival as opposed to individual survival.

Books used in seventh grade discussion groups are: Jack London--Call of the Wild; Anne Frank--Diary of a

Young Girl; Mark Twain--Huckleberry Finn; Edgar Allan Poe--"Masque of the Red Death," "Fall of the House of Usher," "Murders in the Rue Morgue," "The Gold Bug," and "The Raven" from Great Tales and Poems of E.A. Poe; and Johann Wyss--Swiss Family Robinson.

Books used in eighth grade discussion groups are: Stephen Crane--Red Badge of Courage; George B. Shaw--Pygmalion; Charles Dickens--Oliver Twist; James Ullman--Banner in the Sky; Henry Thoreau--Walden; and Harriet B. Stowe--Uncle Tom's Cabin.

"There should be a general clash of opinion and rather sharp debate . . . we shouldn't linger on small details," stated one participant in a questionnaire. "I like being able to express my opinions on the book without fear of offending someone. It's like a debate." Another offered this comment, "I have made many friends with my fellow discussioners and the books . . . I'm sure being in the 'club' will help me get started somewhere as a writer, as I wish to be . . ." Though these youngsters reflect the adults with whom they come in contact, frequently their insights and criticism are so penetrating that the listener wonders if the world might not be better off with children running its affairs.

Publishers Hear YA Panel Talk About Reading Tastes

Reprinted from School Library Journal, January 1967, copyright (C) 1967 by the R. R. Bowker Company.

The elusive reading tastes of the so-called "young adult" group are a well-known phenomenon, but one that publishers can't often examine first hand. At a recent Children's Book Council luncheon in New York, they had that chance when a panel of half a dozen seventh and eighth graders talked about everything from book jackets to ethical values in literature.

The sample was hardly large enough, and rather too bright to be representative. (Almost all books panned by one child were defended by another.) But some of the candid comments were eye-openers:

Books they put down in the middle: To Kill a Mockingbird, because it was "all slow and boring"; Mary Poppins, because "nothing like that could ever happen"; Little Women, because "I didn't want to waste a lot of time feeling sorry for people."

None of the children said they paid attention to age and grade annotations from publishers when picking out books, though one looked at type size and format. Several went more often to adult books in bookstores and libraries than to young adult sections. And most said they preferred books with heroes their own age or older.

Exciting covers and intriguing titles were most often mentioned as inducements to reading a book. "I don't pay much attention to the beginning of the book" quipped one girl. "Some of the worst things in books are in the first paragraph."

Books they found particularly pertinent to their problems: Jazz Country by Nat Hentoff (Harper, 1965); Harriet the Spy by Louise Fitzhugh (Harper, 1964); and With Love from Karen by Mary Killilea (Prentice-Hall, 1963; pap. Dell).

Books that changed their attitudes: West Side Story by I. Shulman (pap. Dell, Pocket Books); North to Freedom by Anne Holm (Harcourt, 1965); and the stories of Mark Twain. The one Negro girl on the panel didn't like Mary Jane (Dorothy Sterling, Doubleday, 1959) because she "didn't want to read about that stuff," but praised Berries Goodman (Emily Neville, Harper, 1965), about a boy who befriends a Jewish child at school.

All of the students said they bought books for themselves, both hard cover and paperback.

Salient Elements of Recreational Reading of Junior High School Students

Anthony T. Soares

From *Elementary English* 40:843-5, December 1963. Reprinted with the permission of the National Council of Teachers of English and Anthony T. Soares.

"Literature is not an object of study, but a mode of pleasure; it is not a thing to be known, but to be lived."[1] Woodberry made this statement way back in 1922. Yet, forty years later, educators are still concerned largely with work-type reading material or with teaching reading skills in the classroom, ignoring the tremendous impact of reading for enjoyment only.

There are many benefits derivable from reading. First, reading offers pleasure and entertainment. Reading can help individuals to obtain psychological and emotional relief. It helps us to experience and to achieve many things vicariously. It offers information and example to help us to resolve our problems. It helps us to determine what roles we are to assume in life and how to carry out these roles. Reading touches on many aspects which relate to our daily lives. When these assumptions become realities in reading, the result may be satisfaction, pleasure, and tension-reduction. As a consequence, we are interested in what we are reading.

Too often, however, pupils' interests are not considered when reading material is assigned or suggested. Indeed, when it is considered at all, research has shown that there is a decided discrepancy between what experts consider to be interesting and what the students themselves profess to be interesting (Bishop, 1952; Norvell, 1958; Schubert, 1953; Shores and Rudman, 1954; Witty, 1948). Existing anthologies are not even based on differences in grade level, intelligence, or sex. Hence, an effort to stem this situation should be exerted soon--probably beginning with the junior high school, since it has been found that the amount of reading done starts to decline during the junior high school years.

If the amount of reading accomplished is related to the last grade attended, as Gray (1960) maintains, then the reading of students who leave school during, or on completion of, the junior high school years, is affected more than that of those who attend school beyond these years. Whether junior high school is the termination of a student's education or the transitional stage between the elementary grades and high school, there can be no question as to the important function of reading during these years.

To cast some light upon this problem of reading interests of junior high school students, a research study was recently undertaken for the purpose of determining whether short stories, rated high in interest by junior high school students, contained elements which did not appeal equally to all students when grouped on the basis of intellectual ability, grade level, or sex.[2] Sixty stories were rated by 1,653 subjects, and the top fifteen stories were analyzed on the basis of 33 elements. Further analysis was made to discover what elements were in the stories which had high appeal for each of the various intelligence, grade, and sex groups, and also how these different groups compared with one another.

In general, these were the results: all groups seemed to prefer the narrative type of story, told by an omniscient author who stressed the theme of bravery and cowardice rather than plot or character in his stories. The favorite story had to be realistic, set in contemporary times, and was most often about animals, sports, or teen-age problems. The most interesting story was high on physical action and contained one main character--a very attractive male teenager of unknown status. It was written in a clear style, with a single unifying effect--i.e., the subject was the basic interest, permeating the entire story--and concrete language (rather than abstract), and offered an implicit rather than an explicit moral. Furthermore, all groups appreciated an introduction which gave clues for interpreting the story, and illustrations one-half page in size, with one color besides black and white. They enjoyed some description and some conflict in the story, but tolerated only a few footnotes and a little humor. They definitely did not want to read stories about children as main characters and preferred stories without trick devices and satire.

The high intelligence group differed from the average and low intelligence groups in preferring suspense to a greater extent. In contrast to the other two groups on the content of the stories, the high intelligence students showed little liking for nonfiction, but they did enjoy adventure stories. The average group was the only one which indicated some liking for fantasy. It is interesting to note that only the low intelligence group (as well as the boys) manifested an interest for science stories. Both the high and average groups enjoyed stories in which plot was stressed, whereas the low group chose the theme of the story as the emphasis of the author. The low group, in contrast to the other two intelligence groups, preferred fewer footnotes and less conflict and reacted unfavorably toward stories with humor.

In the comparison of the grades, it was found that the ninth grade did not necessarily enjoy stories with the author as the main character. The eighth grade tended toward the ninth in its preferences and interests--more so than toward the seventh. In contrast to the other two grades, the seventh tolerated less description of persons and could still enjoy animal stories to a greater extent. The eighth grade enjoyed description of place much more than the other two grades.

In some respects, the sexes were more sharply defined. Though both enjoyed animal stories, the girls chose stories about teen-age problems; the boys were more interested in sports stories. The boys favored stories with suspense, physical action, and external conflict. If conflict was included in the stories found to be more interesting to the girls, then it was of the internal variety. Furthermore, the girls tolerated more dialogue and actually enjoyed sentiment in their stories. The sexes were also sharply differentiated on the type of moral included in the story--with the boys somewhat favoring the explicit type and the girls definitely preferring the implicit moral.

Some of the results might have been expected. For instance, the fact that the seventh graders could still enjoy animal stories a great deal indicates that their interests are somewhat closer to younger children than those of eighth and ninth graders. Older students, with the onset of puberty affecting more of their number, collectively have interests more in keeping with teenagers.

Another expected result could have been the tendency for all junior high school students to stay away from stories with "children" as the main characters. They prefer to identify with older characters so that they can "practice" being teenagers and develop their self concept as older students, both to themselves and to others.

Less expected, perhaps, could well have been the result showing the interest for science stories by the low intelligence group. It might have been a spurious result, or occurring because of the calibre of the science stories included in the testing. But it could also cause modern educators to ponder their desire--often so out of proportion --for bright students to demonstrate interest in science as a harbinger of a career in that area. Perhaps the need is not yet felt among students of junior high school age.

It is necessary for more research to be done with reading interests of students of different intelligence, grade, and sex. Perhaps then will teachers, librarians, parents, anthologists, and other adults concern themselves with reading material from the students' point of view and personality, as well as ability. And perhaps then, students will not have to read quite as many short stories which they find uninteresting, unrewarding, uninspiring, and unappreciated.

References

1. Woodberry, George E. The Appreciation of Literature. New York: Harcourt, Brace, 1922, p. 14.

2. Complete data can be found in the original paper of the author, Interest and Content in Some Recreational Reading of Junior High School Students, University of Illinois Library, Urbana, Illinois, 1962.

Bibliography

1. Bishop, M., "Pupils' Interest Areas in Reading." Wilson Library Bulletin, 27, 1952.
2. Gray, W. S., "Reading." Encyclopedia of Educational Research. (3rd ed.) N.Y.: Macmillan, 1960.
3. Gray, W. S., "Summary of Investigations Related to Reading," Journal of Educational Research, 53, 203-222, 1960.
4. Norvell, G. W., What Boys and Girls Like to Read. Morristown, N. J.: Silver, Burdett, 1958.
5. Schubert, D. G., "A Key to Reading Retardation," Elementary English, 30, 518-520, 1953.
6. Shores, J. H., and H. C. Rudman, What Are Children Interested In? Urbana, Illinois: Spencer Press, Inc., 1954.
7. Witty, P., "Reading in the High School and College." In NSSE 47 Yearbook, Part II, 1948.
8. Woodberry, G. E., The Appreciation of Literature. New York: Harcourt, Brace, 1922.

Reading Content That Interests
Seventh, Eighth, and Ninth Grade Students

Ann Jungeblut and John H. Coleman

From the Journal of Educational Research 58:393-401, May 1965. Copyright by Dembar Educational Research Services, Inc., Madison, Wisconsin. Reprinted by permission.

This study reports on the interest-aversion ratings by students in grades six through ten on 155 prose selections, of 275-400 words in length. The desirability of having quantitative interest-aversion information ratings on the actual reading content for these students may be outlined briefly.

Reading deficiencies among far too many students with an English-speaking background have been amply documented, among others, by Gray,[6] to Bond and Tinker,[1] De Boer,[2] and Smith and Dechant.[5] These young people can hardly become students in any meaningful sense of the word. They are severely handicapped for informing themselves by study of printed matter. Reading for pleasure is largely denied them for lack of facility in reading. They need help that would enable them to read comprehendingly.

When youngsters arrive at the seventh, eighth, or ninth grade with substantial deficiency in reading, the remedy needs to be applied there. The difficulty is that time for it is lacking when the need is imperative. Nevertheless, studies have shown that a substantial proportion of these students can achieve significantly improved facility in reading through efficiently planned systematic practice.[3]

Using interesting content in such a reading program is highly desirable. Research tends to confirm everyday experience in this respect. Smith and Dechant take into account the effects of such factors as differences in ability, and then summarize the findings of investigations in this area thus: "The more interesting the material to the reader, the better his comprehension tends to be."[5]

Ages Twelve to Fifteen   175

This principle is generally accepted. Uncertainty has arisen as to whether a given selection which purports to interest students does appeal to them.

At best, studies of students' general interests offer inadequate guides in this respect. Evidence bearing upon how well students like each specific selection is needed. In this study, the hope was to find 32 selections for each of grades 7, 8, and 9 from 51 or 52 of those judged to be potentially interesting to students at each of the three grade levels. The length of the selection suits the requirements of an efficient developmental reading plan.

The Rating Procedure

The selection was presented on the left of a double page. Just below it was the sentence, to be checked: Could you read the selection? Yes ----- No----. Of 29,119 returns, 830 (2.85%) checked "No" to this question. The rating scale was placed next. Students were asked to read and then rate selections on a six-point response scale: Like very, very much; Like quite a lot; Like a little; Dislike a little; Dislike quite a lot; Dislike very, very much. Students placed an X in a circle next to the statement that indicated their rating. Students were not asked to give their names in order to grant the freedom of anonymity to their choices. They were asked to circle numbers giving their age and grade, and to place an X after boy or girl.

The second page, facing the selection, contained six sets of one completion and five multiple choice exercises based on the selection. These involved vocabulary, best title, main idea, facts, outline, and conclusions. On the basis of poor answers to the exercises, it was assumed that approximately another 825 students did not comprehend a particular selection well enough to give it a significant rating. Thus, nearly 27,500 ratings were analyzed.

School officers and teachers in Michigan, New York, New Jersey, Ohio, Oregon, Pennsylvania, South Carolina and Wyoming graciously agreed to assist in these studies. The investigations were conducted in February-March, 1961 and 1962. The precise number of students participating cannot be stated because ratings were anonymous and there were absentees. It is estimated that 4088 students in 146 classrooms participated as follows:

Grade	Classrooms	Average of Selections Rated
6	14	6
7	35	7
8	46	7
9	35	9
10	26	8

    The selections were originally chosen for educational merit and potential interest. The Lorge Readability Index was calculated for each selection as an initial indication of best grade placement. Some selections were taken from school texts and supplementary sources. The large majority of the selections were written, however, by persons who make their living by writing.

    Each selection was rated by students in three consecutive grades, 6-7-8, 7-8-9, and 8-9 and 10, except for the selections prepared for Grade 10 which were rated only by students in Grades 9 and 10. This procedure generally provided substantial ratings over a span of five years in age for both sexes. The grouping of selections was rotated so that no two classes rated the same set of selections. Teachers were asked to present units twice a week. Some further comment is needed in this connection.

    Average rather than advanced or retarded classes were sought to do the rating. The assumption was that retarded readers would be likely to have interests similar to their age peers. Exigencies made it advisable to accept some known classes in remedial reading. Others were not announced, yet the answers to the exercises clearly indicated substantial reading deficiency for a considerable proportion of students. This provides added confidence that selections rated sufficiently liked would have appeal for those students in need of improving their skills in reading.

    A rating of "like very, very much" was given a value of 5; "like quite a lot," 4, and so on, to compute the medians.

Ratings of Two Biographical Selections

With these factors in mind, a dual purpose will be served by analyzing the ratings of two selections in detail. Interest studies have shown that students at this age range like biography. The question is whether any and every well written biographical sketch interests them.

Both biographical selections under discussion were written by professional journalists. Each passage was taken from a longer biographical sketch that appeared in newspapers. The first one described the manner in which a well-known symphony orchestra conductor, Leonard Bernstein, set about getting his first piano lessons from an outstanding teacher. Soon his teacher, a woman, was not able to schedule any other students after his lesson because he wanted to know so much that she never knew when he would go home. The selection goes on to tell that he kept his mother up until all hours of the night playing improvisations for her. He is described as having a pleasant manner of getting his own way. The narrative moves, but it is concerned with boyhood incidents of a musician now devoted largely to classical rather than, say, music that people whistle readily. How would twelve-, thirteen-, fourteen-, or fifteen-year-old youngsters react to it?

The selection was rated by 188 pupils in grades 6, 7, and 8. The Lorge Readability Index of the passage, 5.4, suggests that its structure is reasonably uncomplicated and easy for pupils of these age levels. Nevertheless, four pupils (2.1%) indicated that they could not read the selection. Scoring the exercises also made it clear that some additional pupils were retarded in reading skills.

For the selection on Leonard Bernstein, the median interest ratings for grades 6, 7 and 8 were 4.3, 4.3, and 3.9 respectively. The median ratings of 4.3 means that more than half of the sixth and seventh graders rated this selection either "like very, very much" or "like quite a lot." In this particular case 58% of the boys and girls in these grades rated the passage this high.

Here it is interesting to note that George W. Norvell[4] has found that a particular literary selection well liked in a given grade level will usually be well liked by pupils two or three grade levels above or below that grade. The me-

dians suggest that this biographical passage could be used
for remedial reading instruction with the expectation that it
would appeal to a large proportion of sixth, seventh, and
eighth graders.

The second selection discusses with some brilliance
the trials of a superb actor-comedian who is known, however, to a relatively limited group. The point, of course,
is not his fame, but how interesting a discussion of his
artistry is to fourteen-, fifteen-, and sixteen-year-olds. It
is brought out in the selection that for twenty years drama
critics have commended his performance over any play that
he has acted in. The tenor of the passage may be sensed
in the following paragraph.

> 'In a certain way,' he confided, 'I became a
> comedian out of necessity'--this Menasha
> Skulnik not quite five feet high, who looks
> like a tailor in a fairy story, but who commands a stage with magnificence. 'Sometimes when I played a serious part the audience
> used to laugh. I used to get red under my
> make-up. I would come out and say something like, 'No, you shall not do this,' and
> the audience would laugh. So I decided I
> was a comedian.' And the world agreed with
> him.

This selection, too, is relatively easy for juniorhigh-school age pupils as its Lorge Readability Index is also
5.4 A total of 194 pupils in grades 8, 9, and 10 rated it.
The median interest ratings for these grade groups were
3.3, 3.6, and 3.4. More than half of the pupils, then,
rated the passage with some degree of liking. However,
approximately 12% of the older pupils rated it in one of
the two strongest "dislike" categories.

In addition to the median ratings, the percentages of
pupils who indicated one of the three "liking" ratings were
computed. For the selection on Leonard Bernstein, the
percentages in grades 6 through 8 were 72, 90, and 76,
respectively. Chance factors may have raised the percent
liking in the seventh grade. Nevertheless, more than 75
percent of the seventh and eighth graders and at least 70
percent of the sixth-grade boys and girls rated this selec-

tion with some degree of liking when they could have given an anonymous rating of dislike.

For the second selection, the percentages of liking in grades 8, 9 and 10 were 62, 70, and 68. These ratings are not seriously negative. On the other hand, this selection does not seem to evoke the degree of lively interest that many selections did. Even though the general topic is biography, and even though the passage is written in relatively uncomplicated structure, the fact is that it was not especially well-liked by students thirteen to sixteen years old. This might be due to the author's style, the incidents reported, the nature of the concepts involved, pupils' lack of experience in seeing live actors on the stage, or a variety of other factors. Be that as it may, regardless of its literary superiority, the selection does not evoke the degree of interest associated with wide appeal for youngsters at these age levels.

Ratings by Grade and Topic

Tables 1-4 list selections in which the total of "like" ratings equalled or exceeded 75 percent. RI, in the tables, refers to the Lorge Readability Index. Median interest ratings are also given. Differences in medians serve to indicate whether preferences tend to be stronger for boys or girls, or about equal for both. Selections are classified under general topics. Not all of the selections were well liked, as Table 5 shows. Nevertheless, selections were found with high interest ratings. They should stimulate students in these grades to find more satisfaction in reading, when these selections are utilized in a systematic reading improvement program, than would be the case with content rated less appealing.

Thirty Selections Not Well Liked

Differences in the interest-aversion ratings, Table 5, on these selections are informative. Twenty-four of the 30 selections were rated with some degree of liking by a majority of the students. Nevertheless, the proportion of pupils expressing a liking are distinctly less than those found for the 126 other selections. Consequently these 24 selections are considered less likely to stimulate retarded readers favorably than others which have been, or could be, found.

Only five of the 155 selections were given more aversive than liking ratings. The case of selection 12 in this set is interesting. It was written by a talented professional writer. It appeared in a well-known national women's magazine. The discussion was oriented solely to girls, but it detailed ways that a sense of humor could help to cope with getting disagreeable things done with a minimum of wear and tear on one's emotions and relationships with others.

This selection held the possibility of giving some troubled early teenagers clues for handling some of their frustrations. Nevertheless, they disliked it, while four possibly equally "preachy" selections by another author and very popular singer, were rated well-liked. Neither the general topic nor the literary qualifications of an author seem to furnish an adequate guide to choosing reading selections when we wish for assurance that the selection will appeal to students.

Selections 12 and 13 of this "not well liked" group were written by the same author. Older students may like selection 13. The percentage of students rating selection 13 as liked increases from grade 8 to 10, as Table 5 shows. In Grade 10, 78 percent of the girls rated it liked, though 8.8 percent of the 194 raters checked that they could not read this selection with a Readability Index of 6.2.

Selections 7 (commercial geography) and 26 (termites) were rated liked by 75 percent or more raters in at least one grade. None of the ratings, however, occurred at the "like very, very much," level. These selections could be used. However, selections given more enthusiastic ratings seem more desirable. Selection 21 (sardine fishermen) meets this criterion. Ratings by 11th and 12th grade students are desirable. Selection 19 (famous writers when they were in college) also meets this criterion. It is best liked by girls, 87 percent of whom in the 9th grade and 80 percent in the 10th, rated it liked as compared to a little more than 50 percent of the boys.

Two of these 30 selections, 22 (birds, insects, and animals in winter) and 24 (worries of the wheat farmer), were rated well liked by sixth graders, but were not rated as well liked by older students.

Ages Twelve to Fifteen

Table 1.- Classification of Selections Interesting to Students
7th Grade
(Median number of ratings per selection, 219)

		Topic			
Total	RI	B	G	Both	% Like

1			Biography		
	5.4	3.9	4.5	4.3	90

2		Behavior in social situations			
	5.0	4.2	4.6	4.4	88
	6.3	3.8	4.4	4.1	91

3			Folklore		
	6.2	4.9	4.7	4.8	96
	6.3	4.1	4.6	4.4	91
	7.3	5.1	5.0	5.0	96

2			Geography		
	5.3	4.0	4.4	4.2	84
	7.3	3.7	4.0	3.8	85

6			History		
	5.0	4.0	3.9	4.0	78
	5.1	4.4	4.3	4.3	79
	5.4	4.3	4.3	4.3	91
	5.8	4.4	4.4	4.4	85
	5.9	4.6	4.3	4.4	89
	6.2	4.5	4.1	4.2	85

3			Narrative		
	4.8	4.2	4.3	4.2	79
	5.2	4.1	4.4	4.3	83
	5.9	4.1	4.7	4.3	90

4			Miscellaneous		
	5.1	3.5	3.7	3.6	76
	5.3	4.1	4.3	4.1	86
	5.7	4.3	4.1	4.3	87
	6.8	4.9	4.5	4.7	88

Table 1.-(cont'd)

Total	RI	B	G	Both	% Like

Science and Natural History

2 Anthropology

| | 5.8 | 4.1 | 3.9 | 4.0 | 85 |
| | 5.9 | 4.3 | 4.1 | 4.2 | 89 |

4 Biology, chemistry, physics

	5.7	4.2	4.0	4.2	89
	5.9	3.9	3.8	3.8	80
	5.9	4.5	4.0	4.3	88
	6.5	4.1	4.1	4.1	84

5 Plants and Animals in relation to agriculture & industry

	5.1	4.2	4.0	4.0	82
	5.7	4.1	4.1	4.1	84
	6.4	3.8	4.3	4.1	80
	6.6	3.9	3.8	3.9	76
	7.1	4.3	3.9	4.1	86

3 Relation of plants and animals to growth of civilization

	5.5	3.9	4.1	4.0	85
	5.8	3.6	3.9	3.8	78
	6.1	4.2	4.1	4.1	84

Table 2.- Classification of Selections Interesting to Students
8th Grade
(Median number of ratings per selection, 194)

Total	RI	B	G	Both	% Like
			Topic		
4			Folklore		
	6.2	4.3	4.4	4.4	97
	6.2	4.6	4.3	4.5	96
	6.7	3.9	4.7	4.4	97
	7.0	4.3	3.4	3.9	78
5		History--political, economic			
	5.8	4.0	4.0	4.0	92
	6.0	3.8	4.1	3.9	88
	6.2	4.2	3.9	4.0	85
	6.5	4.4	4.1	4.2	88
	6.6	3.8	3.8	3.8	80
4			Miscellaneous		
	5.3	3.7	4.1	3.9	85
	5.8	3.7	4.2	3.9	80
	5.8	3.8	3.7	3.8	77
	6.5	4.0	3.8	4.0	83
4			Narrative		
	6.2	3.9	4.0	3.9	79
	6.3	4.0	4.2	4.1	93
	6.5	4.4	4.6	4.5	94
	7.9	3.9	3.8	3.8	83
		Science and Natural History			
2			Biology		
	6.0	4.2	3.6	3.9	86
	6.5	4.0	3.4	3.8	78

Table 2.-(continued)

Total	RI	B	G	Both	%Like
5	Economic geography and industry					
	6.4	4.0	3.8	3.9	83
	7.0	4.0	4.4	4.3	94
	7.1	4.4	4.0	4.2	89
	7.3	3.6	3.8	3.7	83
	7.4	3.8	4.2	4.0	87
3	Narrative				
	6.3	3.8	4.1	4.0	85
	6.4	4.2	4.1	4.2	87
	7.4	3.8	3.6	3.7	80
4	Physical Science				
	5.6	4.8	4.0	4.4	91
	6.4	4.2	4.2	4.2	89
	6.6	4.3	3.8	4.1	84
	7.3	4.2	3.8	4.0	84
1	Vocational				
	5.9	3.2	4.3	3.9	76

Table 3. - Classification of Selections Interesting to Students
9th Grade
(Median number of ratings per selection, 177)

			Topic		
Total	RI	B	G	Both	% Like
4			Biography		
	5.8	3.5	4.1	3.8	81
	6.3	4.0	3.8	3.9	80
	6.6	4.1	3.9	4.0	84
	7.5	4.6	4.4	4.5	88
4		History and Social Problems			
	6.4	3.7	3.7	3.7	81
	6.8	3.8	3.8	3.8	94
	7.5	3.7	3.7	3.7	90
	8.3	4.0	3.8	3.9	81
6			Miscellaneous		
	4.6	4.0	4.1	4.1	82
	4.9	3.8	4.3	4.0	86
	5.8	3.2	4.1	3.7	84
	6.6	3.7	4.1	3.9	82
	6.6	4.0	3.4	3.7	77
	6.7	3.2	4.0	3.7	75
8			Narrative		
	6.3	3.6	3.8	3.7	83
	6.3	3.4	4.2	3.8	78
	6.7	3.9	3.9	3.9	88
	7.0	3.8	4.2	4.1	88
	7.2	3.9	4.0	3.9	87
	7.2	3.8	4.2	4.0	78
	7.4	4.5	3.9	4.2	89
	7.5	3.8	4.0	3.9	88

Table 3.-(cont'd)

			Topic		
Total	RI	B	G	Both	% Like

Science and Natural History

4 Biology

	6.3	3.6	3.8	3.7	83
	6.3	3.9	3.8	3.8	82
	6.8	4.2	4.0	4.1	92
	7.0	3.7	4.0	3.8	81

2 Economic geography (historical and contemporary)

| | 6.4 | 4.1 | 3.8 | 3.9 | 94 |
| | 7.1 | 3.8 | 3.5 | 3.6 | 81 |

1 Plants, Agriculture and History

| | 7.0 | 3.9 | 3.7 | 3.8 | 83 |

2 Physiology

| | 6.1 | 3.6 | 3.9 | 3.7 | 82 |
| | 6.7 | 3.9 | 4.0 | 4.0 | 86 |

2 Weather

| | 6.7 | 3.9 | 3.6 | 3.7 | 83 |
| | 7.2 | 4.3 | 3.9 | 4.1 | 94 |

1 Sports

| | 6.6 | 4.9 | 3.9 | 4.4 | 96 |

1 Vocational

| | 6.8 | 4.0 | 3.6 | 3.8 | 81 |

Table 4.-Classification of Selections Interesting to Students
10th Grade
(Median number of ratings per selection, 125)

Total	RI	B	G	Both	% Like
1			Architecture		
	7.2	4.2	4.4	4.3	89
5			Biography		
	6.2	3.6	4.0	3.9	81
	6.7	3.7	3.7	3.7	75
	7.0	3.6	3.7	3.6	80
	7.2	3.2	3.7	3.5	73
	7.8	3.8	3.5	3.6	79
1			Book Review		
	7.6	3.9	3.4	3.6	73
1			History		
	7.1	3.6	3.4	3.5	71
1			Miscellaneous		
	6.6	3.3	3.8	3.6	76
6			Narrative		
	5.9	3.9	4.5	4.2	95
	6.1	4.2	4.0	4.1	85
	6.9	3.3	3.6	3.4	71
	7.1	4.6	4.2	4.3	95
	7.2	4.5	4.1	4.3	97
	7.6	3.6	3.4	3.5	67

Table 4.-(cont'd)

Total	RI	B	G	Both	% Like
4		Science and Natural History			
	6.9	3.8	3.8	3.8	83
	7.0	3.5	3.8	3.6	79
	7.2	3.4	3.8	3.5	75
	7.2	3.6	3.8	3.6	78
4		Social Problems--national and international			
	6.7	3.8	3.5	3.7	75
	6.8	3.5	3.6	3.5	73
	7.0	4.2	3.4	3.8	80
	7.1	3.7	4.2	3.9	81

Ages Twelve to Fifteen

Table 5.—Selections Rated As Not Well Liked
(Median interest ratings of boys and girls combined by grades)
Numbers followed by % show the per cent of "like" ratings

Code	RI	6	7	8	9	10
Biography						
1	5.4			3.3 62%	3.6 70%	3.4 68%
2	5.5			3.4 65%	3.5 67%	3.5 67%
3	7.1				3.1 54%	3.2 56%
History						
4	5.0	3.6 64%	3.4 65%	3.4 68%		
5	5.5	4.4 83%	3.6 71%	3.5 71%		
6	6.0				3.3 61%	3.1 53%
7	6.1		3.1 55%	3.7 67%	3.5 79%	
8	6.5			3.4 68%	3.6 66%	
9	6.6			3.4 67%	3.3 61%	3.3 66%
10	6.8		3.4 78%	3.6 75%	3.4 74%	
11	7.6				3.0 50%	3.3 61%
Miscellaneous						
12	5.8		2.9 43%	2.6 41%	3.3 60%	
13	6.2			3.2 56%	3.5 60%	3.4 70%
14	6.4		2.9 48%	2.6 40%	3.4 61%	
15	6.8			3.2 57%	3.5 66%	3.4 72%
16	7.2				2.9 40%	2.6 39%
17	7.2				3.3 57%	3.3 64%
18	7.3			2.6 50%	3.1 52%	2.5 38%
Narrative						
19	6.5			3.2 62%	3.8 75%	3.6 71%
Occupational						
20	6.2		3.7 82%	3.3 63%	3.6 80%	
21	7.2			3.5 70%	3.6 75%	
Science						
22	5.5	4.1 89%	3.9 71%	3.5 70%		
23	5.5	3.7 73%	3.6 72%	3.7 71%		
24	5.9	3.6 75%	3.7 72%	3.3 66%		
25	6.7			3.6 67%	3.4 64%	3.4 71%
26	6.9				3.5 73%	3.5 75%
27	7.0				3.1 53%	2.2 26%
28	7.2			2.9 34%	3.2 69%	3.0 50%
29	7.2				3.4 68%	3.1 52%
30	7.3				3.2 56%	3.1 44%

Selection 8 was rated by two grades. Two school systems found it necessary at the last moment to change participating classrooms. Even so, 80 to 84 percent of the girls gave this discussion of women's rights a rating of liking. Only 3 of 228 raters said they couldn't read it. If a selection on the same topic with more appeal to boys could not be found, this one could be utilized as one that does appeal to girls.

Selection 20 (workers in a lumber camp) illustrates an interesting point. It was rated by students in grades 7, 8, and 9. Two school systems substituted two 8th grade remedial reading classes for regular classes. The respective percentages of "like" ratings are 82, 63, 80. Yet only one of 225 raters said he could not read the selection with an RI of 6.2. Students immediately below and above the grade with the retarded readers rated it well-liked. So did the "normal" class in their grade.

Summary

Student ratings indicate that the style and content of 102 selections of up to 400 words appeal differentially to 7th, 8th and 9th graders. Selections of this length meet the requirements for an efficient, systematic program for developing facility in reading at these age levels. The scope of topics is comprehensive though not all-inclusive. Nevertheless, the ratings suggest that these selections could contribute to motivating retarded readers to improve their reading skills. Then they would be better equipped, with further stimulation from school, libraries and other sources, to explore other printed materials of unique interest to them.

References

1. Bond, Guy L. and Tinker, Miles A. Reading Difficulties: Their Diagnosis and Correction (New York: Appleton-Century-Crofts, Inc. 1957), pp. 7-8.
2. DeBoer, John J. "What Does Research Reveal about Reading and the High School Student." English Journal, XLII (May, 1958), pp. 274-5.

3. Guiler, Walter S., and Coleman, John H. Reading for Meaning, Teacher's Manual (New York: J. B. Lippincott Co., 1955), pp. 2-3.
4. Norvell, George W. The Reading Interests of Young People (New York: D. C. Heath and Company, 1950) p. 262.
5. Smith, Henry P., and Dechant, Emerald V. Psychology in Teaching Reading, (New York: Prentice-Hall, Inc., 1961), pp. 1, 2, 6.
6. Thirty-Sixth Yearbook of the National Society for the Study of Education, Part I, 1937, p. 15.

Reading Interests of Eighth-Grade Students

Beryl I. Vaughan

From the Journal of Developmental Reading 6:149-55, Spring 1963. Reprinted with permission of Beryl I. Vaughan and the International Reading Association.

One of the major purposes of this study was to try to obtain a general picture of the reading interests of the majority of eighth-grade students attending Arsenal Technical Junior High School. . . .

A group of 134 students, representing seventy-five per cent of the eighth-grade enrollment at Tech Junior High School, was chosen to participate in this study. There were sixty-seven boys and sixty-seven girls with IQ scores ranging from 65 to 159, as determined by the Henmon-Nelson Intelligence Test. The boys and girls were then separated into intelligence groupings and classed as bright, average and dull, depending upon whether their IQ score fell in one of the following ranges: 111-159, 90-110, 65-89.

The questions relating to book choices were presented in the form of selections of actual book titles and tabulated according to such general interest categories as "Adventures of the Big Ten" and "Hunting for Buried Treasure," to represent adventure. In like manner, twelve categories were disguised with title choices and each student was asked to choose five (see Tables I, II, and III). Interest choices, such as humor, religion, home and family, etc., were also sought in three preferences (see Tables IV, V, and VI).

Newspaper section and magazine choices were included in this study in order that all reading media be recognized as a possible influence on the reading choices of junior high school students. The schedules were administered with a minimum of explanation in order to obtain a self-analysis of reading interests. All students were told that their responses would be of value in planning reading pro-

Ages Twelve to Fifteen

grams for future students of Arsenal Technical Junior High. The information in the various tables represents a general picture of the reading interests of this particular group.

Table I

Books Liked Best by Sixty-Seven Boys & Sixty-Seven Girls

Category	Boys Total*	Rank	Girls Total*	Rank
Mystery	60	1	40	3
Science	51	2	15	9
Invention	42	3	10	12
History	35	4	30	5
Biography	32	5	23	7
Detective	30	6	27	6
Adventure	24	7	11	11
Nature	17	8	13	10
Home and School	16	9	67	1
Fairy Tale	12	10	35	4
Novels	11	11	47	2
Poetry	10	12	20	8

* Weighted Totals-- 1st choice 5
2nd choice 4
3rd choice 3
4th choice 2
5th choice 1

Table II

First Choices of Books Preferred By Bright, Average, and Dull Boys

Bright, Percentage		Average, Percentage		Dull, Percentage	
Adventure	22.2	Detective	26.9	Detective	21.7
Invention	22.0	Adventure	11.5	Biography	17.3
Science	16.7	History	11.3	Fairy Tales	13.1
History	16.5	Invention	11.1	Mystery	13.0
Home & School	11.1	Mystery	8.9	Science	8.8

Table III

First Choices of Books Preferred By Bright, Average, and Dull Girls

Bright, Percentage		Average, Percentage		Dull, Percentage	
Home&School	22.2	Home&School	24.0	Home&School	27.0
Mystery	12.8	Novels	16.5	Fairy Tales	15.8
Detective	12.5	Poetry	16.0	Detective	15.5
History	12.3	Detective	12.8	Biography	15.3
Biography	12.1	Biography	12.0	History	11.5

Detective stories, ranked sixth on both the boys' and girls' lists, were chosen by forty-five percent of the boys and forty percent of the girls. Contrast this with Table II where students are grouped according to IQ, and we find that the bright boys did not select this category at all in their first choices. However, average and dull boys preferred this type of reading, and all girls seemed to enjoy it, although ranking it lower. This would suggest that while most of the students read detective stories, the bright boys preferred other types of literature.

Ages Twelve to Fifteen 195

As a group, boys prefer mystery and science, with invention, history, and biography next, while girls prefer stories relating to home and school, novels and mystery. This suggests that boys of this age are less interested in the love element or the fanciful tales than the girls. Although the novel was ranked second by girls, only 16.5 percent of the average girls (see Table III) included it in their preferred list.

Home and School category was interpreted to mean the stories of teen-agers. Of course, the love element may be, and often is, included in this type of story. All girls ranked this category first, but only 11.1 percent of the bright boys chose Home and School first.

Books of Adventure were not ranked high in the general choices on Table I, yet Adventure was chosen by bright and average boys in their first three choices.

Poetry was ranked last by the boys, while the girls ranked it in eighth place. It was interesting to note that only the dull boys chose poetry; the bright and average boys left this space blank.

Biography was listed as a preference by approximately forty percent of the total number of eighth-grade students taking part in this study. The preference for historical and biographical interest may indicate that this group enjoys true stories almost as well as make-believe tales.

Table IV

Reading Interest Choices of
Sixty-Seven Boys and Sixty-Seven Girls

Interest Choice	Boys Total	Percent	Girls Total	Percent
Adventure	49	73	33	49
Mystery	43	64	38	57
Humor	32	48	26	38
Animals	15	22	10	15
Historical Background	14	21	14	23
Love	12	18	45	67
Home and Family	7	11	16	24
Religion	3	4	8	12

Table V

Interest Choices of Bright, Average, and Dull Boys

Bright, Percentage		Average, Percentage		Dull, Percentage	
Mystery	93.7	Adventure	92.1	Mystery	64.2
Adventure	87.5	Mystery	52.0	Adventure	46.1
Humor	81.2	Humor	40.2	Love	39.2
Animals	25.0	Animals	24.5	Humor	37.1
Historical Background	18.8	Historical Background	20.8	Animals	18.3

Table VI

Interest Choices of Bright, Average, and Dull Girls

Bright, Percentage		Average, Percentage		Dull, Percentage	
Humor	61.1	Love	59.2	Love	95.6
Mystery	55.5	Adventure	50.0	Mystery	78.2
Adventure	50.0	Humor	43.0	Adventure	47.8
Love	27.9	Mystery	38.4	Home and Family Life	21.8
Home and Family Life	16.6	Home and Family Life	30.9	Historical Background	20.6

In the interest choices, both boys and girls enjoy books with humor. The bright girls ranked humor first, and both bright and average boys ranked it third. Animal stories are enjoyed by boys more than girls. Mystery ranks high for both girls and boys, and stories with historical background are popular. Historical background and Home and Family Life have a lower interest rating than they received in book choices. However, the Home and School book choice may have had a different connotation for the student from Home and Family. The individual background of the student may have influenced the choice.

Ages Twelve to Fifteen

The intelligence factor for the boys' interest choices was not too much different from the general sex grouping. However, the difference between girl and boy interest is the greatest where the love factor is shown. Many other interests are common to both.

Magazines. Fourteen magazines were presented as possible choices in this study. Sports Illustrated was chosen by fifty-two percent of the boys, but by only four percent of the girls. Approximately the same percentage of the boys chose comics as did the girls--both thirty-five percent: however, it was interesting to note that ninety-one percent of the dull boys chose comic magazines in contrast to the Science Fiction choice of the bright boys.

Although the love-interest magazines are preferred by the girls generally, the bright girls prefer Life, Look, The Saturday Evening Post, and Reader's Digest over Screen Play and comics. The Average and Dull Girls chose Modern Romance, True Story and comics, in that order, as preferred magazines.

Newspapers. The significance in this tabulation seems to lie in the fact that among the 134 families involved, nearly all subscribed to one or all of the Indianapolis newspapers. Five percent of the boys and seven percent of the girls indicated that their families also took such papers as The Louisville Journal, The New York Times, and The Chicago Tribune.

The comic section of the newspaper was preferred by both boys and girls. The sport section was ranked second by the boys, but the girls enjoyed news and stories.

Editorials in the newspaper seemed to be liked least by boys and girls. This would suggest a lack of serious reading at this age and grade level. Perhaps a greater interest in motivation and this type of reading in the classroom would stimulate critical reading in all areas. Many junior high students depend on television and radio to fill in the blank spaces on the "why" of current events.

Library. The largest group owning library cards was the average group. It should be a matter of concern to the classroom teacher, as well as the parents of these children, that the junior high student makes little effort to take advantage of library facilities that are within walking distance of his home.

The dull boys and girls show a greater reluctance to read or use the library cards. Perhaps a special section in the school library, devoted to their interests, would be rewarding. Many students in this lower intelligence group display a genuine effort to master basic concepts and enjoy reading at a lower level of difficulty.

The use of library cards and the availability of a library were considered significant because outside reading or the lack of it may help to determine where to begin a guided reading program.

Summary

There is a marked contrast in the general preferences of boys and girls. Boys prefer mystery and science, while girls prefer stories of home and school and love interest. Only fifteen percent of the girls liked books about invention, but sixty-seven percent of the boys chose this type of reading. Sixty-seven percent of the girls preferred stories with love, but only eighteen percent of the boys chose this category. The girls liked the make-believe type of story, as well as the love interest type, to a much greater extent than the boys, yet the dull boys preferred some of this type of reading.

Poetry, ranked twelfth by the boys and eighth by the girls, would suggest further guidance in this reading area.

Both boys and girls prefer history and biography to many other interest choices--the boys rating these categories slightly higher than the girls.

The comic magazine is high on the list of reading for both boys and girls, but the greatest preference is shown by the 91% of the dull boys who chose this type of magazine. Most boys ranked Sports Illustrated as first choice. Girls preferred Modern Romance and True Story, but the bright girls contrasted sharply with this preference. Hunting and Fishing ranked fourth for all boys, but last or fourteenth for the girls.

Since most of the families of these 134 students subscribed to newspapers, some type of reading material is available in their homes. This might suggest that a greater interest in reading could be stimulated by more classroom discussion of newspaper organization and content.

In the groupings studied, the choices seem to support the view that there is a wider divergence of interest factors present in the sex comparison than in intelligence comparisons. The intelligence factor is important, however, in future planning, as there are significant implications of interest deviations.

The Reading Interests of Eighth-Grade Boys

Jo M. Stanchfield

From the Journal of Developmental Reading 5:256-65, Summer 1962. Reprinted with permission of Jo M. Stanchfield and the International Reading Association.

Through his ability to read maturely, every youth should have the right to partake of the treasures of the past and present and to unlock those of the future. As John Gardner said in the education section of Goals for Americans, "Some subjects are more important than others, but reading is the most important of all."

Learned adults are not the only persons concerned with the importance of reading in our culture today. Junior high school boys interviewed by the author showed a sincere feeling about the necessity of being able to read well. They volunteered remarks such as these: "You can't do anything in school if you can't read." "Definitely I'd like school better if I could read O.K." "You're half blind when you can't read all the stuff, and you get behind the others." "I wish some one had got me started reading better when I was in the lower grades."

In order to develop effective reading skills, an individual must read; to read widely, he must be interested in reading. To discover reading interests, therefore, is a key problem. While it is true that numerous studies and articles on reading interests have been published during the last few decades, there has been little evidence available to show the relationship of reading interests to reading achievement. What are the reading interests of eighth-grade boys and do these interests differ according to varying reading competencies? A recent study by the author of this article provides tentative answers to these questions.

Fifty-one eighth-grade boys of differing reading abilities

were selected from Los Angeles City Schools for individual interviews. This number was composed of three sub-groupings of seventeen boys each: superior readers, average readers, and poor readers. The reading comprehension scores on the California Achievement Tests formed the basis for dividing the boys.

A method of stratified random sampling was used to select the names from the test score sheets. The sampling involved checking every third name on the lists of scores. The sampling was stratified to the extent that the boys so chosen had to meet other requirements necessary for the data, namely: (1) The IQ range should be between 90 and 120. (2) The physical health of the interviewees should be good. (3) The emotional adjustment of the boys selected should be normal. (4) The interviewee should come from an American-born family in order to assure an English-speaking background. (5) The home environment of the interviewees should provide a cross section of socio-economic levels, ranging from lower middle-class to upper middle-class. The sampling was further restricted by the fact that equal numbers of boys had to be chosen from the names on the score sheets of those reading above, at, and below grade level.

The group of interviewees was limited to boys because boys throughout the nation have far more frequent and severe reading problems than girls. For example, the statistics for the remedial reading classes for one of the largest city school systems in the nation revealed that over three-fourths of the students in these classes were boys. Further, by eliminating a comparison of the sex factors, it was possible to secure data with fifty-one boys that would produce reliable computations at the .05 level of confidence.

Interviewing in Depth

In order to study boys' reading interests with depth and intensiveness and to secure the most valid responses possible, the interview technique was chosen rather than the questionnaire procedure. The interview had advantages over the questionnaire in that the researcher was able to clarify meanings for the interviewee, stimulate his thinking processes, and encourage him in the articulation of these responses. . . .

In answering all the questions, the boys were first encouraged to talk without interference or restriction in a "free-response" situation. Then the interviewer suggested other possible responses; and the boys, after careful thought decided on their final answers. Some boys were vociferous in their answers and definite in their preferences. Others were quiet and reflective, with a quality of moderation in their choices. Still others were almost compulsive in their need to explain how and why they differed in their likes and dislikes from expectations of parents and teachers. During the discussion, the boys were urged to ask questions about any items which they did not understand. For instance, to clarify certain reading categories or literary characteristics, the interviewer gave examples of specific stories or situations. Somewhat past the midpoint of each interview, a relaxing interruption was afforded by the opportunity for the boy to stand up, walk to a nearby table on which were displayed three dozen books, pick up the books, and look through them. He did this before attempting to answer the question, "When you look at a book, what things help you to choose this particular book?" The books included a variety of interesting titles, attractive cover designs, appealing title pages, engaging tables of contents, exciting chapter headings, colorful pictures, black and white pictures, different book shapes and sizes, and degrees of vocabulary difficulty.

Throughout each interview, the writer followed a general program of topics to be covered and information to be secured, but at all times tried to speak in an extemporaneous, conversational manner with humor, enthusiasm, and zest (which proved to be no small challenge after weeks of day-in-day-out interviewing, especially with the low achievers who were considerably less than enthusiastic about anything pertaining to reading). It was hopeful that the boys would give honest, sincere responses, more readily elicited in a relaxed, emotionally satisfying atmosphere. That this was accomplished to some degree was evidenced by remarks of principals and counselors that the boys "got a big kick" out of the interviews and that other boys wanted to be chosen to talk with "the lady from the university."

Interpreting the Data: Categories of Reading Interests

The data in Table I showed that two categories were tied for first place in the boys' preferences: "exploration and

Ages Twelve to Fifteen

expeditions" and "outdoor life." A high degree of interest was also evident in tales of "fantasy," "everyday life adventure of boys," "historical fiction," "sea adventure," "sports and games," "war," "humor," "science fiction," "mystery," and "outer space."

The eight-grade boys showed less interest in "fables," "animal adventure," "occupations," "animal fiction," "cowboys and westerns," "mathematics," "riddles and puzzles," "birds and insects," "plants," and "teen-age romance." The least interest was apparent in the categories of "fairy tales," "music," "family and home life," "plays," "art," and "poetry."

Table I

Categories of Reading Interests
Eighth Grade Choices

	Rank	Category Name	Mean*
1.	1.5	Explorations and Expeditions	1.12
2.	1.5	Outdoor Life	1.12
3.	3	Tales of Fantasy	1.16
4.	4	Everyday Life Adventure of Boys	1.18
5.	6.5	Historical Fiction (their own age)	1.20
6.	6.5	Sea Adventure	1.20
7.	6.5	Sports and Games	1.20
8.	6.5	War	1.20
9.	9.5	Humor	1.24
10.	9.5	Science Fiction	1.24
11.	11	Mystery and Detective	1.26
12.	12	Outer Space	1.29
13.	13	Legends and Myths	1.37
14.	14	Prehistoric Life	1.39
15.	15	Hobbies--How to Do Things	1.41
16.	16	Heroes of Long Ago	1.43
17.	18.5	Folk Tales	1.45
18.	18.5	History	1.45
19.	18.5	Inventions--Machines	1.45
20.	18.5	Science Experiments	1.45
21.	21	Primitive Peoples	1.51
22.	22	Pioneers and the Frontier	1.55
23.	23	Aviation--Jets, Rockets, Missiles	1.57
24.	24	Automobiles and Hot-rods	1.59

Table I (cont'd)

Rank		Category Name	Mean*
25.	25	Travel	1.63
26.	26	Snakes and Reptiles	1.68
27.	27	Sea Life	1.72
28.	28	Biography	1.74
29.	29	Bible Stories	1.76
30.	30	Communication	1.78
31.	31	Foreign Lands and Peoples	1.84
32.	32	Transportation	1.88
33.	33.5	Geography	1.90
34.	33.5	Weather and Climate	1.90
35.	35	Fables	1.92
36.	36.5	Animals--Animal Adventure	1.96
37.	36.5	Occupations	1.96
38.	38	Animal Fiction	1.98
39.	39	Cowboys and Westerns	2.06
40.	40	Mathematics	2.20
41.	41	Riddles and Puzzles	2.27
42.	42	Birds and Insects	2.29
43.	43	Plants	2.31
44.	44	Teen-age Romance	2.41
45.	45.5	Fairy Tales	2.43
46.	45.5	Music	2.43
47.	47	Family and Home Life	2.47
48.	48	Plays	2.53
49.	49.5	Art	2.78
50.	49.5	Poetry	2.78

* Means indicate the degree of interest in response to the question, "How often would you like to read a story or book about--?" "Very often" has a weight of 1; "sometimes," 2; "not very often," 3; and "never" 4.

A broad range of interest was reflected in the choices of the boys. For example, they showed an equal amount of interest in four quite disparate reading topics: "folk tales," "history," "inventions and machines," and "science experiments." They were apparently becoming interested in foreign lands and peoples. The category of "travel" also showed a relatively high degree of interest. Although the topic of "automobiles and hot-rods" was high in appeal, an even higher degree of interest might have been anticipated because of the expressed interest of the boys in owning and driving such vehicles.

There were no significant differences in the preferences of the superior, average, and poor readers. This was one of the most interesting facets of this survey, for many people seem to take for granted that boys with differing reading abilities, even though at the same grade level, will have different reading interests. At least this opinion could be inferred by the kinds of reading materials foisted upon the below-average readers.

The significance of the means in Table I is that of showing the degree of interest in the various choices of the boys, a fact not clearly evident from the rankings. For instance, the category of "Primitive Peoples" ranked 21st, but the mean of 1.51 showed that approximately half the boys included the subject in the "would like to read very often" group. Likewise, "Art" and "Poetry," which ranked at the bottom of the list, were of interest to some of the boys; or the mean would have been 4 instead of 2.78. A similar conclusion may be made about the significance of the means for Table II, Characteristics of Reading Interests.

Table II

Characteristics of Reading Interests
Choices of Boys in the Eighth Grade

Rank		Characteristic	Characteristic No.	Mean*
1.	2	Excitement	19	1.00
2.	2	Suspense	18	1.00
3.	2	Unusual experiences	7	1.00
4.	4	Surprise or unexpectedness	10	1.02
5.	5.	Liveliness and action (fast moving events)	13	1.04
6.	6	Fantastic, fanciful, or weird elements	12	1.12
7.	7	Funny incidents	9	1.20
8.	8	Frightening or scary incidents	15	1.27
9.	9.5	Physical courage	14	1.33
10.	9.5	Ridiculous or exaggerated elements	20	1.33
11.	11	Information	3	1.37

Table II (cont'd)

Rank		Characteristic	Characteristic No.	Mean*
12.	12	Moral Courage	8	1.51
13.	13.5	Friendship and loyalty	6	1.53
14.	13.5	Hardships	11	1.53
15.	15	Happiness	15	1.59
16.	16	Heroism and service	16	1.61
17.	17	Qualities such as anger, hate, cruelty, fighting, bragging	17	1.88
18.	18	Sadness	4	2.00
19.	19	Family love and closeness	5	2.18
20.	20	Familiar experiences	2	2.41

* Means indicate the degree of interest in responses to the question, "How much do you enjoy stories or books which portray--?" "Very much" has a weight of 1; "some," 2; "not very much," 3; "not at all," 4.

Characteristics of Reading Interests

As shown in Table II, three characteristics tied for first place in the preference of the eighth graders, "excitement," "suspense," and "unusual experiences." "Surprise or unexpectedness" was also a favorite. Other items of high interest were "liveliness and action," "fantastic, fanciful, or weird elements," "funny incidents," and "frightening or scary events."

Less interest was shown in "physical courage," "ridiculous or exaggerated elements," "information," "moral courage," "friendship and loyalty," "hardships," "happiness," and "heroism and service." The least amount of interest was evident in qualities such as "anger, hatred, cruelty, fighting, and brutality," "sadness," "family love and closeness," and "familiar experiences."

War stories had a great appeal for the boys, but only in the idealized sense; they did not care for the brutality, fighting, and horror of war. It was evident that they were highly interested in unusual experiences and not very much interested in familiar, commonplace happenings. They also showed little interest in stories that expressed sadness or affectionate family relationships. The boys' enthusiasm and liking for excitement, suspense, surprise, and the action of fast-moving events were obvious.

Here again, there were no significant differences in the choices of the boys reading above grade level, at grade level, and below grade level. Regardless of differing reading abilities, they were all interested in the same kinds of literary qualities.

Increasing Teacher Effectiveness

Many teachers who work with adolescent boys are already aware of the intensity of the feelings of the underachievers in reading. During the course of the interview, many of these boys would not readily admit that they were poor readers; they simply said that they didn't like to read and weren't interested in reading. Some were openly hostile and aggressive in their dislike of school and all things connected with reading. According to the junior high school counselors, many of these boys were disciplinary problems. Other eighth-graders in the low achievement group in reading were quiet, bleak, unresponsive, rather sad characters who seemed to give the impression that school life was too much for them. From the writer's experience in interviewing boys at lower grade levels, as well as those in the eighth grade, it was apparent that the effect of frustration was cumulative and heightened at the junior high school. Therefore, to remedy this situation with eighth-grade boys presents a tremendous challenge and a great responsibility. What a tragedy that ways were not found to insure sufficient remediation at younger ages for these eighth-grade boys and others like them!

All of the boys interviewed seemed to have a sincere feeling about the importance of being able to read well. They volunteered remarks such as these: "It takes too long to do your homework when you can't read very well." "Other kids laugh if you stumble over words when you're reading out loud." "If I could read faster, I'd get better grades and my old man wouldn't ride me so." "Guess I'll never make it to college if I don't improve my reading." "My dad wants me to be a lawyer, but I could never read all those books."

These observations indicated that the boys felt that skill in reading was an important and essential quality for success in school, in college, and even in a chosen life profession. It would seem highly desirable that all junior high school teachers develop a good attitude toward reading by talking about interesting books, by reading fascinating books aloud, by displaying appealing books, by advertising challenging books on bulletin boards, and by providing every opportunity for students to become exposed to various types of literature that might motivate them to read. Such techniques practiced by junior high school teachers in every subject area would give the remedial reading teacher an invaluable springboard from which to teach the basic reading skills to the under-achievers.

Because of the striking similarity between the reading interests expressed by the low achievers and those by the average and high achievers, it would seem highly important to re-examine the materials of instruction used in the reading improvement classes. It may be there is an urgent need for easy-to-read books on a variety of topics interesting to eighth-grade boys. The boys who read poorly commented thus: "Sure, I like to read books about outer space, but I can't pronounce the words." "The books I can read and understand are too silly and babyish." "I hate the reading improvement classes--the books are all little kid stuff." "Why don't they write easy books about science fiction?" "I love baseball stories, but it's no fun when you have to stop to figure out too many words." "Wish I could read what it says under the pictures in my science book." This last remark by an eighth-grade boy indicates the need for books in the content fields to be written on easy levels of reading ability so that the retarded reader will have access to the same challenging subject matter as his more fortunate classmates. . . .

A Study of Leisure-Time Reading Preferences of Ninth Grade Students

John Q. Adams

From the High School Journal 46: 67-72, November 1962. Published by the University of North Carolina Press for the School of Education of the University of North Carolina. Reprinted by permission.

One of the basic facts revealed by historical research is that reading is an indispensable means of mass communication in a civilized society. Another significant fact is that from the earliest times reading has served two radically different ends. On the one hand, it has been a great unifying force, tending to unite social groups by providing common vicarious experiences and by cultivating common attitudes, ideals, interests, and aspirations. On the other hand, it has served as a disintegrating force, tending to intensify differences between social groups.

A third idea that merits emphasis is that the reading materials produced during any period of history are greatly influenced by the social setting in which they develop. The materials published over a period of time reflect vital cultural trends or changes. As such materials are read, they influence the thinking of both group leaders and the masses, and may promote or retard social change.

Studies involving analysis of the contents of magazines read by ninth grade students in a large metropolitan area show that materials vary all the way from modern classics to the cheapest type of sensational materials. Studies of the circulation of magazines show that the eight or ten which are usually recognized as superior in character have relatively small circulation and that the so-called popular middle-grade magazines are published in greatest numbers. There is general agreement among investigators that the current-events type of magazine contains material that is more cosmopolitan and valuable than is true of the typical newspaper. Inquiries made among children and parents reveal the fact that a surprisingly large number of magazines of the cheap sensational type are subscribed for regularly or purchased at the news stand. The prominence of these magazines on the home library table suggests the urgent need for campaigns among teachers to elevate reading tastes and to stimulate interest in magazines of a better class.

Because of varied likes and dislikes expressed by the pupils in the investigator's ninth grade World Geography-English Core program, a questionnaire was administered to discover the real leisure-time reading interests of these pupils.

The questionnaire was given to a group of sixty ninth grade pupils of Hawthorne High School, Hawthorne, California. Hawthorne is a typical, middle-class suburban community in the Los Angeles area. The pupils were not required to sign their names to this questionnaire, since they were to feel that their answers would not be checked against them in any way. The respondents were later identified by handwriting analysis. The pupils were asked to be as honest as possible. The questions were worded simply, so that each pupil could proceed by himself.

The results from this questionnaire indicated, in the main, that the respondents were serious and in earnest, and tried to the best of their ability to answer the questions honestly.

Each pupil was asked to list his favorite magazines. In all, forty magazines were listed.

The Findings

The findings of this investigation on "Leisure-time Reading" were organized in terms of (a) rank of preferred magazines, (b) quality rating assigned to magazines, (c) relationship of quality ratings of magazines read and the respondent's I.Q., (d) frequency of preference by respondents for individual magazines, and (e) general information data on respondents.

The magazines that were ranked highest by the pupils are presented in Table I. Examples are provided of the individual magazines that appear in each of the twelve categories.

Table I

Examples of magazines, identified by ninth grade pupils in response to a leisure-time reading questionnaire, ranked according to preference.

Rank	Magazine Category	Individual Magazine Titles
1	Teen-age	Dig, Seventeen
2	Comic	Mad, Horror
3	Stage and Screen	Photoplay
4	True Romance	True Story, True Confession
5	Mechanical	Popular Science, Road and Track
6	Weekly Pictorial	Life, Look
7	Weekly	Saturday Evening Post
8	Outdoor Sport	Skin Diver, Yachting
9	Digests	Readers' Digest, Coronet
10	Women's Fashion	Bazaar, Vogue, Charm
11	Women's Home	McCall's, Good Housekeeping
12	Suggestive Picture	Playboy, Escapade

According to recent studies made on leisure-time reading of high school students, comic books rank first or second in reading preference. The results of this study demonstrate this to be the case as far as the group under study is concerned. Reader's Digest and The Saturday Evening Post received very high preference ratings in other studies, but were rated low in this one.

Teen-age magazines, especially Dig and Seventeen, rated very high, and they were not even mentioned in other recent studies.[1] The fashion magazines for women--Bazaar, Vogue, etc.--were read by many of the girls, but were not mentioned in any other studies. Another surprising feature of this study was the preference of many of these boys for the "sexy" or suggestive pictorial magazines--Playboy, Escapade, etc. This was not the case in any of the other studies.

The discrepancies between this study at Hawthorne

High School and the other three mentioned might have something to do with the period when the studies were made. Punke's study was made in 1937, Witty's in 1943, and Andersen's in 1951. The leading magazines (Dig and Seventeen) were not even being published at the time of these studies, and the same thing is true of the "sexy" magazines which are of very recent origin.

The investigator divided the magazines read by the respondents into four categories. A number representing a quality rating was assigned to each magazine. The higher quality magazines were assigned number (4), and the lowest quality magazines were assigned number (1). The resulting ratings appear in Table 2.

Table 2

Quality ratings assigned to magazine categories

Magazine Categories	Quality Rating
Comic	1
Suggestive	1
Stage and Screen	2
Scandal (Confidential)	2
True Romance	2
Mechanical	2
Travel (Holiday)	3
Science-Fiction	3
Weekly Pictorial	3
Teen-Age	3
Outdoor Sports	3
National Geographic	4
Current Events	4
Church	4
Weekly (Post)	4
Men's Adventure	4
Digest	4
Women's Fashion	4
Women's Home	5

Next, the investigator ranked the magazine categories according to the number of respondents that included the category among their top five preferences. The results of this ranking procedure appear on Table 3.

Ages Twelve to Fifteen

Table 3

Magazine categories ranked according to the number of respondents that included the category among their preferences.

Category of Magazine	Number of Respondents Including This Category Among Their Preferences
Teen-Age	60
Comic	55
Stage and Screen	45
True Romance	40
Mechanical	35
Weekly Pictorial	33
Weekly	26
Outdoor Sports	25
Digest	24
Women's Fashion	21
Women's Home	14
Suggestive	9
Travel	7
Science-Fiction	6
Scandal	5
Current Events	5
Men's Adventure	4
Church	3

All of the respondents included Teen-Age magazines in their leisure-time reading preference list. Comic, Stage and Screen, and True Romance category magazines also seemed to occupy an important part of their reading time. Sex, sensationalism, and escape seem to be the preferences expressed by the respondents.

Each pupil handed in to the investigator a list of his five favorite magazines. A number was assigned to each magazine. The total number for the five magazines and the I.Q. of the respondents was used as the basis for a "scatter diagram." The only conclusion that could be drawn from the diagram was that there is no apparent correlation between the I.Q.'s of the twenty boys and forty girls and leisure-time reading interests.

Next, the investigator compiled personal data from each respondent's cumulative record. This data appears in Table 4.

Table 4

Personal data information compiled from the cumulative records of the sixty respondents.

Name	Sex	I.Q.	Reading Skills	Subject Grade	Quality Rating
P.B.	F	97	-	C	14
C.C.	F	102	+	B	12
M.M.	F	100	+	C	12
V.P.	M	109	+	B	9
F.R.	M	107	+	B	18
R.R.	M	104	-	C	12
S.S.	F	125	+	B	13
C.S.	F	130	+	B	12
P.T.	F	86	-	C	12
T.G.	F	113	+	C	11
J.T.	F	105	-	C	16
L.T.	F	111	+	B	13
J.U.	F	112	+	C	11
S.V.	F	130	+	A	10
B.S.	F	93	-	C	0
L.W.	F	99	-	C	16
S.W.	F	101	-	B	13
G.W.	F	100	-	C	17
D.W.	F	93	-	B	13
K.W.	F	103	+	B	14
C.A.	M	131	+	B	10
R.A.	M	101	-	A	12
C.B.	M	83	-	C	11
N.B.	F	111	+	B	13
W.C.	M	128	+	B	16
D.C.	F	96	-	B	15
L.C.	F	104	+	B	16
M.C.	F	80	+	C	14
J.D.	M	114	+	B	12
S.F.	M	87	+	B	17
P.G.	F	118	+	C	14
L.H.	F	131	+	A	15
P.H.	M	86	-	C	12

Ages Twelve to Fifteen

Table 4. - (cont'd)

Name	Sex	I.Q.	Reading Skills	Subject Grade	Quality Rating
J.K.	F	92	-	D	12
C.M.	F	103	+	B	16
B.M.	M	87	-	D	7
C.R.	M	128	+	A	14
D.W.	M	94	+	C	11
M.G.	M	118	+	D	11
J.A.	M	118	+	B	13
R.B.	M	81	-	C	11
D.B.	F	115	+	B	16
K.B.	F	102	+	B	9
C.B.	F	87	-	C	11
G.B.	M	103	+	B	8
R.C.	M	116	+	B	10
B.C.	F	112	+	C	16
D.C.	M	91	-	B	15
I.C.	F	117	+	B	10
K.D.	F	116	+	B	18
D.D.	F	121	+	B	16
L.D.	F	124	+	B	17
M.G.	F	102	+	B	11
L.H.	F	103	+	C	9
H.H.	F	110	+	B	13
S.H.	F	109	+	B	10
V.J.	F	91	-	C	10
S.L.	F	110	+	B	10
M.M.	M	132	+	A	19
J.W.	F	107	+	C	15
D.G.	F	103	+	C	13
L.R.	M	108	+	B	8

The respondents' names were coded. The + or - symbol appearing in the Reading Skills column is based on the California Mental Maturity Test Data. It represents above or below average accomplishment in reading skills. The Subject Grade is the individual's grade in the World Geography-English Core for the winter quarter. The Quality Ratings range from 5-20, depending upon the quality of each of the five preferred magazines that the student reads. The zero rating was given one girl, because she stated that she never reads outside of school.

Summary of Findings

The findings of this study of leisure-time reading preferences make apparent the tremendous interest in sex, sensationalism, and escape from reality found in our adolescents today. It seems that in our struggle to develop reading skills we neglected to build in them a value system that would allow them to discriminate.

The findings suggest also that interest of teen-agers rather than ability determines what they read during early adolescence at least in a middle-class setting. No longer can we identify comic books and movie magazines with low ability students. It is apparent from this study that average as well as high ability students, once out of the ever watchful eye of the teacher, receive great personal satisfaction from reading magazines of questionable value.

Why Do Children Read?

Ernest Roe

From the Australian Library Journal 13:3-14, March 1964. Reprinted by permission.

It is obvious enough, though in our own enthusiasm we do not like to admit it, that many children do not read; that indeed many prefer almost any activity to reading. Sometimes they lack the skill, so that reading is inevitably associated with frustration and failure in school and is, therefore, the last pastime they would undertake for pleasure; sometimes they find other activities or passivities--sport and watching television for instance--more rewarding; sometimes the status of reading is low in the groups in which they spend most of their time; sometimes they have been mishandled by parents or teachers or even by librarians; and sometimes all these and other reasons may be applicable simultaneously. Much has been said and written about the importance of reading and I shall not add to it here. However, it may be that, because its importance seems to us self-evident and because we regard it as axiomatic that all children ought to read, we fail to ask certain basic questions about children and reading.

One of these questions is "Why do children read?" It seems to me just as sensible to ask "He likes reading--what's wrong with him?" as to pursue the question "He doesn't like reading--what's wrong with him?" But though librarians and others concerned with books and education frequently ask the second question, it rarely occurs to them to ask the first. Yet some answers to it might much increase their understanding of their task. This is not to say that I think concern over why children do not read is useless --far from it. Librarians might worry about it much more than they do; in fact, when I suggest that they frequently ask what is wrong with children who do not read, I suspect that the question is apt to be rhetorical and that from a position

of superior enlightenment they look upon the non-reader as
a strange species. While wondering idly what made him
like that they do not seriously seek to understand the reasons.

But understanding of why children do not read may
come, partly at least, through understanding why they do
read and it is the latter question on which I propose to concentrate. I would like to re-emphasize, however, because
it is basic to my discussion, that just as some individual
children have excellent reasons for reading, so do other
individual children have excellent reasons for not reading.
And it is important not to confuse such a statement of fact
with our more usual statements of value and purpose; that
is, whether children ought to read or whether it is or may
be good for them to read is beside the point. This or that
individual child at this point in time because of his past
experiences, his present environment and state of development has excellent reasons for liking/not liking to read the
books we kindly provide for him.

To understand why certain children like to read, we
need to appreciate the extent and complexity of the differences among individual children. An important part of the
research into the role of libraries in education which I have
been conducting during recent years has been many discussions with children. These discussions have not only been
important in the sense of the information they have provided;
they have also been of absorbing interest and delight. The
situation of one who is an "outsider" interviewing children
is particularly happy. He is not their teacher or their
parent; he is able to enjoy everything about them and it
costs him nothing; there is no shadow from past or future
over his relationship with them. More than once I was
conscious that something about a child I found fascinating,
hilarious or quaint, might well have been a source of profound irritation to someone who had to cope with the same
child every day. But the conversations I had with them
provided vivid illustrations of the differences among individual children, underlined the difficulties and dangers of
making facile generalizations about that convenient abstraction called "The Child," and were a salutary experience for
me. Although people involved in education preach eloquent
sermons about individual differences, these can rather easily
become theoretical and the stark truth of what we are saying
slips away from our consciousness. In fact, teachers' a-

wareness of the "need to cater for individual differences" (one of the most pervasive of all educational platitudes) has a struggle for survival because many feel that in coping with large classes, examinamania and the rest, what they can actually do about individual differences is severely limited.

The librarian may escape some of these difficulties. Even the harassed school librarian with too many children chasing too few books, comes to know at least some children as individuals because she has contact with them away from the classroom group and because she can scarcely help learning something about their individual interests, if only through the books they read. The children's librarian in a public library should be much more favorably situated. She has no direct link, either psychologically or geographically, with school and formal lessons; she is able to meet each child as an individual, without labels or preconceptions; and she ought to be in an excellent position to appreciate and cater for individual differences. But again, I know there are practical difficulties; again too many children, too few books, not enough staff, and above all too many children at the same time--for example, Saturday morning--for individuals to have a fair chance.

Perhaps then, the librarian, though her prospects for appreciating individual differences are better than those of most teachers, is still at a considerable disadvantage compared with the fortunate interviewer; at a disadvantage, that is, in appreciating, in the sense of enjoying, and also in the sense of understanding children as individuals. In the latter sense, the librarian is handicapped not only by the practical difficulties already noted but often also because her training is deficient.

However, the interviewer, though he possesses a smattering of such knowledge and has time to think about the individual children he has talked to and what they have told him, also has his frustrations. He may understand something of their past and present; but since his contact with them begins and ends within a very short period of time he cannot put the knowledge he has acquired to practical use, except perhaps by passing it on to others--and this entails much risk in that their misinterpretations may be added to his and through failures of communication a child may be thoroughly misunderstood.

But perhaps by attempting to portray a few individual children to librarians-in-general he may illustrate the range of individual differences, and may also demonstrate some features or peculiarities which may be met and better understood in other children, and in doing so suggest some of the reasons why children read.

Without further preamble, here are some of the brief case studies I made of individual children in their first year at secondary school. I have, of course, used fictitious names but the children are real enough!

Gary is a cheerful, talkative boy, eldest of 4 children. His father is a mechanic and the family live in a still uncompleted house in a semi-rural suburb. The father has been building the house himself, in his spare time, for the last 10 years. The house, a car and a small boat appear to have absorbed any "surplus" from the father's income over the years. The boat has to be transported on a trailer pulled behind the car about 10 miles to the sea whenever members of the family go sailing, but they often do this, even though the house remains unfinished. Although Gary's parents own very few books, they are both keen readers and borrow from the Public Library. They enrolled Gary at the Children's Library when he was 6 years old and his two younger sisters also belong to it. (The fourth child is still a baby). The whole family has a regular week-end "library expedition" and visits the city on either Saturday or Sunday expressly for this purpose. Gary commented that "Dad and I just read and read and read" and explained that his mother could not read quite as much as they, because, with four children, she had limited spare time. However, she was particularly interested in reading because she had never had much chance to read when younger. This was because, although she had done very well at school, she had had to leave early and assume considerable family responsibilities. Gary said that she often reads the books he gets from the library, and he obviously has complete trust in her judgment when it is a matter of choosing books. As he put it: "Mum comes in handy. She knows my age." His parents read to him every night when he was a small child, and he was able to recall many of the books they had read to him.

Gary is in the top stream at high school, has an I.Q. about 124, and was placed 10th out of 36 in the class in a recent examination. His teachers assess him as essentially a normal boy and rate highly his enthusiasm both for school work and other interests, his sociability and his fertility of imagination. His own comments on school included the following points: he likes Woodwork and Science particularly, has no particular dislikes, though on the whole does not enjoy school as much as in the previous year (his last year at primary school); the library at the school is only beginning--it is a new school--and has been stocked with books brought by the children themselves; the library is looked after by Mr. --------, the Sports Master; his English teacher gives his class a period a week for reading, but has never recommended any books or shown much interest; Gary has "got into trouble reading in school" (when he should have been doing something else) and has been criticized because he "writes too lengthy in essays"; he believes that from reading "you get good words and this shows up in your compositions"; school and homework "take up a lot of time" and he wishes he had more time both for reading and for "some outdoor life with his dog."

Gary thinks he would like to be a writer or a woodwork teacher, or perhaps a naturalist or a botanist. He reads a lot because--and this is the order in which he gave reasons-- "you like to be able to express yourself," "you can find out things," "it's a good hobby," and "just for something to do." He likes adventure stories, books about ancient Greece and Rome; and he often gets from the library books of which there are extracts in his school text books. He once became very interested in electric trains after reading a book about them but reluctantly abandoned any ambitions to acquire one because "they're too costly." But after reading Swallows and Amazons he developed a keen interest in boats and now shares this with his father. Among other interests are tennis, baseball and a youth club which he attends once a week; the family has no television set and takes little interest in radio programmes but the whole family goes to the cinema about once a month "if there are any good films on."

Finally, Gary reads about 3 books a week, and says regretfully that he had "time to read a bit more than that last year"; he shows an extensive knowledge of and liking for good quality authors, and by the criteria used in this study was one of the best readers interviewed.

Comment:

The evidence suggests that the quality of his family life is particularly significant in Gary's reading development. Not only are there specific influences such as the keen interest of his parents in reading but also a generally favorable and stimulating atmosphere. The family spend much of their leisure together, as a unit--the weekly library expedition, the sailing, the visits to the cinema, the parents reading to the children. The mother values reading highly and wants it for her children because her own love of it was frustrated when she was a child. The impression given by the boy's own story and his account of his family is one of liveliness and mutual affection and creative energy--the father is building his own house, yet has not sacrificed everything to this task; there is "messing about in boats"; there is vicarious experience through reading; there is little interest in "manufactured" entertainment, such as radio and television; Gary's possible future occupations are all of a creative nature and he wants to express himself, to find out things.

By contrast the school's influence appears to be quite insignificant. There is little, if any, reading stimulus from the school library or from his English teacher, and Gary chafes a little under the restrictions of school and homework--has been in trouble for reading at the wrong time, has had his undisciplined self-expression in essays curbed, finds school and homework taking up too much time. Yet, since he has a healthy appetite for experience, he is open to influence from the school; his belief that reading helps with compositions (probably, on evidence from other children, a teacher's comment rather than his own conclusions), and his pursuit of books quoted in school textbooks, are evidence for this. Like many other good readers Gary belies the stereotype of "bookworm" in his energetic devotion to other interests, including outdoor life.

Peter, in appearance and manner and, as it turned out, in much else, was a striking contrast to Gary. He was round-shouldered, morose and initially uncommunicative. His parents were divorced some years ago and he lives with his mother, elder brother (15) and sister (20) in a lower socio-economic area close to the city. His mother works in a small factory and his sister is a nurse. There are very few books in the home, though he is sometimes given books for his birthday. He can remember being read to occasionally as a child but the only encouragement he now receives is his mother's admonitions not to read so much because he has to study for examinations.

His school report discloses that he was originally in the top stream but was demoted to a lower stream "because he did not work." His I.Q. is about 112 and in his present class he was placed 42nd out of 47 last term. Generally his teachers find him an unsatisfactory pupil, indifferent, unsociable, and Peter's comments about school indicate that his teachers' feelings are fully reciprocated. "I don't care for it much--and it's getting worse" was the way he summed up school. The only subject he likes is Science, though he tolerates English because of the reading involved. His English teacher gives "reading homework," allows time in school for boys to describe the books they enjoy, criticizes their choice and recommends many books himself. Peter became more animated when the school library was mentioned; he uses it almost daily, the librarian has shown him how to find what he wants, and he reads about 4 books a week. He joined the Children's Library on his own initiative three or four years ago, because he was afraid he couldn't get enough books, but has not used it extensively this year because the school library has met most of his requirements.

Peter would like to become a pilot, but is doubtful whether he will ever be able to obtain the necessary qualifications. He dislikes sport, does not go to the films or watch television and listens only to "hit parades" on the radio. His hobbies are making model airplanes and collecting stamps but most of his time, he says, is spent on homework and reading. His friends "think he's a bit mad because he reads so much"; they read only comics. He likes reading because "it's just something to do." He went on to explain that he enjoyed the books because they are often exciting, but then reiterated "I mainly read because I haven't much else to do." His favorite books are historical fiction, and he has developed a special interest in Roman Britain and in Norman times through reading novels with those settings. He also likes books which deal with war and with aircraft. He dislikes books with "a gang of kids" as the main characters because the things they do are "a bit unreal." Conversely, a book like He Went with Christopher Columbus appeals to him because it is "more real."

Some of the best authors writing for Peter's age group have written historical fiction and he has read many books of very good quality; his reading is particularly striking in terms of quantity, however, and he appears to have been reading for some years at a high and steadily increasing rate which is now around 200 books a year. His final comment was that he "often gets bored when he hasn't got a book to read."

Comment:

The evidence suggests that for Peter reading is primarily a means of escape from the unattractiveness of his daily life at home and school; possibly too a psychological refuge from his own anxieties and feelings of inadequacy. It was clearly impossible in the time available to discover how the loss of his father has affected him and his general family situation, but the impression was strong that the other three members of the household are too busy in their several ways to be much concerned with each other or with Peter--an impression not at all of hostility, but of indifference. In any case, there is certainly no active influence in the home, whether by urging or example, encouraging Peter to read in the way in which Gary, for example, is encouraged.

Peter's attitude to school is plain enough. How he felt about his demotion can only be surmised; if he sees himself as a failure he is possibly concealing deep feelings of inadequacy beneath a mask of indifference. It is relevant that, although his ambition to be a pilot seems quite strong, he is already prepared for failure. The school library appears to be an oasis in a desert of harsh academic demands upon him.

Another factor which may be significant is that Peter's interests and pastimes are all of a solitary nature. Reading, building model airplanes, stamp collecting, and even homework, are all done alone, whereas sport, which is social, he dislikes. It is significant, too, that one apparently so intent on escaping from reality should despise some books as "unreal"; it seems that as long as he can get away from this time and place he does not need fantasy and finds the impression of reality reassuring; historical fiction is eminently suitable for providing reality at a safe distance.

The above interpretations are tentatively advanced in the belief that Peter is one of a number of keen readers for whom reading is primarily a means of escape. The school he attends is one of the very few in South Australia with a trained librarian who spends almost all her time in the library, and a stock of books from which much material of poor quality has been excluded. There is not much doubt that this librarian--and her library--are in a position to exert considerable influence on Peter. If at present they are meeting a deep psychological need for escape, various important questions arise--for example, what can or should the librarian do, and what can books do, to help Peter to stop running away? At least perhaps it is reason for satisfaction that Peter's needs are being met with books of good quality, whereas in other schools and with other "librarians" he might have to subsist on a different diet.

Ruth, who lives in one of the poorer socio-economic areas of the city, is the second of 5 children. Her father is employed by a small firm of painters and decorators. There are few books in the home--Ruth thought about 30-- but her parents still buy books occasionally. Her father buys "murder things" and religious books, and her mother religious books also. Ruth "always has her nose in a book" and her parents complain when she reads in a poor light. They are Methodists and the Bible was read to her when she was small; there is much Bible-reading in the house and it is read regularly to her little brothers aged 5 and 3.

At High School she is in the top stream, her I.Q. about 120, and she was placed 30th out of 45 in a recent examination. She enjoys school, likes all subjects, and described the school library as "marvelous." She spoke at length about her English teacher who, she said, "reads a lot." This teacher lends books to the class, has recommended many, urges them to tell other children about what they have read, and often sets them to "find out things overnight." She also makes them every week write about books they have read and liked. "I read so many I get them confused," commented Ruth. "You think a book's good until you begin to write about it."[1] "The teacher sometimes puts up a list of books she thinks are good but," said Ruth, "I don't always agree."

When Ruth's own reading and interest in books were discussed, she reeled off the names of eight authors and several titles immediately and the conversation was punctuated with comments on a number of others. One of the authors mentioned was a classic and all the others, and all the titles, were of good quality contemporary fiction. She borrows frequently from the Children's Library, the school library, the local Institute library and "all over the place"-- from friends, from teachers. She has several friends who are keen readers and they recommend to each other. Ruth reads a book a day.

She plays hockey, basketball, softball and table tennis. She belongs to Girl Guides, a Church Youth group, the Red Cross, Crusaders (another church group) at school, and a gymnastics club. The family has no television but she often listens to the radio and her favorite programs are plays, quizzes and "My World." She sometimes goes to pictures, when there are religious films--Ten Commandments and the Story of Ruth, for example--but her parents judged Ben Hur not suitable. "I cry a lot at the pictures," she said. She cannot manage to do all she would like because she gets lots of colds and earaches and has a troublesome knee because she was "hit by a car a couple of years ago."

Conversations with Ruth were very lengthy and the main impressions were of exceptional vitality, lively intelligence and wide interests and a cheerful gusto for everything in life. She likes reading for many reasons--"you find out so much, learn a lot, it's relaxing, you learn about other people--how they used to live, it helps you to understand other people," and "when you're told off, you can go and read a book." Through reading Rosemary Sutcliff's Outcast she became interested in the Roman Empire and so, at the commencement of her secondary education, decided to study Latin. She thinks reading has helped "tremendously" with study at school, because "you have to pick up facts of your own, and not depend on one book." She criticised Enid Blyton's books because they "don't give you anything to think about." She said that "it's a lot of rot, life going marvelously and people being lucky all the time" and that in books "not everybody must be a model of innocence."

Ruth's teachers regard her as a "quite unusual" child with exceptional ability at oral self-expression and only a little less so at written self-expression. She was also rated very highly on sociability, imagination, and enthusiasm for activities and interests other than school work. On the latter, however, her teachers were unimpressed. The final summing-up on Ruth by her class teacher, who is her English teacher, was in four words--"A menace. Very lazy."

Comment:

On the evidence presented, any suggestions as to how Ruth has become the exceptional reader and interesting personality she undoubtedly is could only be extremely tentative.

Her home does not appear to have given her a "good start" in the sense that a child of professional parents in a home full of books is often given a good start. Yet a number of the children interviewed who apparently had the most favorable of home backgrounds had not developed into good readers. Ruth's parents do read, but to what extent reading mainly from the Bible and religious books provides an atmosphere in which a keen and wide interest in reading may develop, is unknown.

Evidence on her school background also has some thought-provoking features. For example, Ruth made her English teacher appear quite an enthusiastic promoter of reading, whereas other children taught by her gave a somewhat different impression. On the other hand, Ruth seems not to have been altogether appreciated at school if the teacher's view of her as a "menace" and "very lazy" is any criterion. A similar lack of appreciation has been noted in respect to other good readers interviewed. Since there is much emphasis on children being quiet and docile and on cramming for examinations, it is not surprising that Ruth may be seen as a "menace"--non-conformist and potentially disruptive. She talks too much, she is interested in too much and no doubt lacks application to some of the tastes of an examination-oriented class. If she is "very lazy" in any sense of the term, it can only be in respect to a very narrow range of school activities; otherwise the description is so inept as to be ludicrous.

It is, perhaps, significant that Ruth appears quite unaffected by the school's overt or potential hostility. Her gusto is such that she enjoys almost every experience. She was more receptive than anyone else in the class to the English teacher's attempts to encourage reading, even though she could be critical of them. She appreciates everything from the school library to the Girl Guides, from hockey to quizzes on the radio. Further study of her development over the next few years should be illuminating, but clearly the influences which have made her the exceptional reader she is are extremely complex, and these brief speculations have scarcely begun to unravel them.

John lives with his parents, three brothers and a sister, in a small house in an older suburb. He is the second child of a family who moved to the city from a remote country district two years ago, and his father, formerly an unsuccessful builder, is now a salesman in a hardware store. His parents have a bookcase full of old books, including "school stories" dating from their own and their parents' schooldays. They have no time to read themselves nowadays but they want John to read. They urge him to go to the library "because it will help with his education." His mother compels the older children in the family to read to the little ones.

His father is in poor health and was recently "ill with hepatitis brought on by worry." His mother, as the ensuing account will clearly show, makes all the decisions. John has no ideas about a future occupation but "Mum wants me to stay at school as long as I can." Information about the boy's home background was also contained in an unusually long report from his teachers; for example, "John comes from a respectable home but his parents are from the West Coast and have no education...He is never kept clean and this results in some degree of unpopularity among the rest of the children in the class."

John is in the second top stream in a large high school, was placed 33rd out of 45 in a recent examination, and has an I.Q. of 123. He was placed bottom of the class in English. His teachers comment that his parents' lack of education "is always reflected in the boy's vocabulary and ability to express himself. He is unable to cope with any work which requires initiative and his year's work has not borne out his I.Q."

John's most vehement complaint against school was that he "doesn't like essays because he can't think of anything to write." He borrows books from the school library, but takes no part in extra-curricular activities and cares little for sport. (His teachers also commented on his lack of interest in sport). Of his English teacher he said "She's got a degree in English and thinks we ought to read too" and "She tells us just about every day to read but doesn't tell us what to read." However, she does "read bits out of books to them," including some short stories and some translations from Caesar. Latin and Math were mentioned by John as his best subjects.

He reads library books "only after homework." He never goes to films because "Mum doesn't like me going." The family has no television because "Mum doesn't like it—it would spoil our school work," but he is allowed to go to his grandmother's house to watch during holidays only. Sundays are spent at Baptist Church and at Sunday School, and he goes to the Boys' Brigade on Friday nights. He listens to the radio "a lot," especially to serials.

He joined the Children's Library because "Mum wanted me to." He likes reading adventure books and showed acquaintance with some authors and titles of good quality. He said that he reads "to fill in time" but added, rather grudgingly, that he "likes books." He remarks in a tone of great surprise that "some children don't even like reading." He reads more now than in previous years "because Mum's brought me to the Children's Library, that's why!" --said resentfully rather than with satisfaction. However, his reading is still small in quantity and he reads about two books each month.

Comment:

On the classification basis used in this study, John is just on the "good reader" side of the arbitrary dividing line because of the proportion of good quality books and authors listed by him. He made acquaintance with them by way of borrowings from the Children's Library; the books he read from the school library were of poorer quality, and the books at home even more so. But he is a good reader with some reluctance and the situation is a particularly interesting and somewhat unusual one.

Mrs. -------, uneducated herself and married, it seems, to an ineffectual and/or unlucky husband, is fiercely ambitious for her children and sees education as the golden key which will unlock all doors for them. The way she has kept all the family's old books may be significant of a lifetime respect for "book-learning" and a belief that books are precious possessions--attitudes not uncommon in uneducated lower-class families of a generation or two ago. She drives John to read, to join libraries and declares her intention of keeping him at school as long as possible. Homework comes first and television is seen as a menace to school work.

John, though his measured I.Q. is quite high, is handicapped by his origins, particularly in English, and it is scarcely surprising that he "lacks initiative." His mother has left him little scope for any. Towards his mother's pressure and her ambitions for him he is ambivalent. Some comments are resentful, others acquiescent; but though he feels he has been pushed into libraries and forced into reading, he seems to enjoy what he reads. It may well be an echo of his mother's values that his first comment on his teacher was that she had a degree in English. Again, there was some resentment of his teacher joining forces as it were with his mother and continually urging him to read.

The methods by which John has become a good reader could scarcely be recommended for general use. In fact, whether he will remain any kind of a reader must be regarded as doubtful. He may react violently sooner or later against books. Or he may remain sufficiently passive to go on bowing to his mother's will and become, to her delight, a "white-collar" employee and contented bookworm. What in these circumstances the books he reads are doing for him is also problematical. Follow-up studies should be illuminating.

Julian's father has a high administrative post in the chemical industry, the family live in one of Adelaide's most "desirable" suburbs, and Julian, who is the eldest of three children, attends an independent school. There are few books in the home and Julian said his parents "don't read at all except newspapers and magazines" but they are continually insistent that he should read. His father borrows books from the Children's Library for him and his mother recently gave him a book which cost Ł4. It was "very hard reading" but "since Mum gave it to me I had to read it, but it took a whole term to read." Julian likes paperback books, but "Mum won't let me buy paperbacks." He was "pushed on to" reading. "If Mum and Dad didn't insist, I would never have read a book." His two sisters, aged 10 and 8, are great readers and borrow books "ten at a time."

Julian was in First Year last year but, because he was one of the youngest and his results were moderate, is repeating First Year in the top stream. In the most recent examination he was placed 20th out of 32. No I.Q. score is available. He describes the school library as a "junk heap," dislikes English because "it's the same old sort of book all through school," and likes Science and Math best, though "it depends what day it is." His English teacher urges them to read, and reads out a list of suggestions at the beginning of term. Those Julian could recall were all either classics or adult books. The teacher says they should try to read 10 books a term. Julian likes books about chemistry, plants, animals and birds, nonsense stories, science fiction and gory murders. His main source of nonsense stories and science fiction is his English teacher who recommends and lends him paperbacks--and the examples quoted were of very poor quality fiction. He thinks reading helps him with compositions and general knowledge and said that the National Geographic Magazine "puts me on to new ideas." He was, when interviewed, "just off to the Museum to look into how you grow carnivorous plants." Finally, he thought that "having a lot of homework makes you read more; it leaves no time for anything else but does leave you time to read."

Julian likes tennis but not football, and also goes sailing. He listens to the radio "a lot." He is permitted to go to only "good" films and the family has no television "because Mum says it's all American rubbish."

Both of Julian's parents had telephone conversations with the interviewer in which they voiced their concern that he read so slowly, lacked comprehension of what he read and that this handicapped him in his school work. They were very grateful that "someone was taking an interest" and hoped the interviewer could "turn him into a really good reader."

Comment:

Julian's parents have good intentions but lack the skill and knowledge necessary to make them effective. This is true of many of the teachers encountered in the course of this investigation, but the influence of determined parents may be much more powerful and also much more damaging. The home, though prosperous, is not "bookish," and the pressure the parents put on Julian to read is not supported by any example they themselves set. It is a factor in Julian's resistance to reading that his parents' attitude is "do as we say" rather than "do as we do." His parents also make much use of censorship. Paperbacks, films and television all come under their outspoken disapproval in varying degrees. Furthermore, his mother presented him with a long boring book which he had to read. The somewhat antagonistic note of Julian's references to his parents and the rather contemptuous tone in which he described his sisters as "great readers" might well have some significance. It seems to him his sisters are highly approved and he is not. They read "good" books; he is discouraged from reading some of the books he likes. It would not be surprising if he were inclined to regard a penchant for good books as feminine, as a "sissy" inclination; an attitude which the school he attends may help to reinforce.

The evidence from the school may have some other significant features. Julian's aggressive remarks may be related to some shame, certain defensive attitudes, connected with his having to repeat First Year. The English teacher encourages them to read but fosters adult tastes, and he lends Julian books which are very attractive to him, not least because they enable him to circumvent parental censorship. A friend's supply of paperbacks is even more obviously valuable for this purpose.

But as usual, the situation has its complexities. Julian is resisting pressure from his over-anxious parents who nag him ceaselessly, who want him to be "cultured"; but he likes reading, he has use for it in pursuit of his interests, and he is in no danger, as John probably is, of reacting violently against books. He wants to read on his own terms without any conscious aim at self-improvement. His parents' eagerness that he should read more good books because his slowness at reading handicaps him in school

Ages Twelve to Fifteen

work, is almost comical. The evidence leaves little doubt that his "slowness" is due to lack of interest; he is slow with dull school books (like the English one he described), and he was painfully slow with his mother's present! He reads loans from his teacher and his friend rapidly enough.

It is doubtful whether, if Julian's parents could be persuaded to leave him alone, this would provide a perfect solution. There is room for doubt whether his teacher's influence will greatly enrich his reading experience. Like many other children studied, Julian could gather a splendid harvest from books, if only there were adults, either parents or teachers or librarians or all three, with the necessary skill, knowledge--and tact--to help him.

Barbara is the eldest of three daughters of the head of a firm of accountants, lives in an exclusive suburb and attends an independent school. Though comparatively wealthy, the home appears quite uncultured. Barbara gave a cheerful description of her father's reading--the newspapers and "mostly the stock exchange news and the sporting pages" and her mother's--"all the women's magazines and the bridge notes." There are few books in the home, the parents lead a busy social life, with many parties, and when at home watch television. They neither encourage nor discourage Barbara from reading, though she quoted a remark by her mother that she "seemed to be quite a bookworm lately." Her two younger sisters "read a bit but not much" and are more interested in tennis and television.

Barbara was placed 3rd out of 27 in a recent examination in one of three unstreamed First Year classes and has an I.Q. of 108. Her teachers speak highly of her liveliness, enthusiasm and sociability and a final comment reads "Jolly, extrovert, very friendly, most helpful in class." Barbara herself says she "loves school" though she wishes there was less homework so that she had more time for reading. Her most obvious enthusiasm was for the school library which she described at length. She was "not much of a reader" until the beginning of this year when she "found out at last what she's been missing." Miss _____, the librarian, had given her a book to read and she liked it so much she went back and asked for another like it.

Since then Barbara has read "lots and lots of books" and she thinks Miss _____ is "marvelous because she always seems to know what you want. Miss _____ must have read every book in the library." Her English teacher is keen that they should read, but says little about it. She sometimes reads them "bits out of good books, so that we'll want to read them." Also, "she knows a lot about Shakespeare."

Barbara quoted the authors and titles of some of the best quality contemporary children's fiction and made a mixture of childish and sophisticated comments about them, from "I don't like _____ (a character in a book); he was horrible" to "it was fantastic, like a different world altogether, but all the time you knew it could not be true, you believed in it because the writer made you believe it." She reads about two books a week, and only asks Miss _____ occasionally now because "she's got a pretty good idea herself what's in the library." She likes reading "for lots of reasons and nearly every book you read seems to give you a new one. Just to pass the time first and still is sometimes. But it widens your mind and makes you understand a lot more. I've got interested in a lot of new things this year. Anyway," she concluded, "it makes me blush to think a baby I was last year."

Barbara thinks she might like to be a teacher but "hasn't thought about it much yet." She plays hockey and tennis, likes swimming "very much," is a Girl Guide and likes painting. She paints pictures "for fun" and paints "the garage and things like that. You ought to help around the place a bit and it's better than washing up." She likes some television programs but never watches for long. "It's funny how I can sit still and read a book for hours, but I don't like sitting still by the TV for too long."

Comment:

It is impossible on the evidence available to look beyond the school and particularly the school librarian for what has made Barbara the good reader she certainly is. Barbara herself has no doubts about it! She is not from a "bookish" home, her interest in reading is comparatively recent and she was emphatic that it originated in the school library under the guidance of Miss _____. Miss _____ is in fact one of the few trained children's librarians in South

Australian schools, and both the quality of the books in the library and the quality of the reading done by the pupils are significantly higher than in most other schools. Barbara's attitude towards her parents seems one of cheerful affection but not much dependence. She impressed the interviewer in much the same way as she apparently impresses her teachers. She exudes physical health and enjoyment of life. She looks like a hockey player! She has a number of interests, works hard in school and successfully, though her I.Q. is not high. She spoke on all matters with engaging frankness. Barbara seems to feel that the good books she has read have done much for her development, and her unself-conscious remarks are often very revealing.

A "before-and-after" study of Barbara as a reader would have been illuminating. Finally, these two brief sketches:

Colleen reads books of excellent quality, has close familiarity with many good authors and titles and is motivated at all times by a strong sense of Christian duty and moral rectitude. She is the second of nine children. Her father is a radio technician who borrows books from the Public Library, while her mother, not surprisingly, has no time to read. There are a few shelves of books in the home, including school prizes. Colleen attends a convent school, finished 3rd out of 23 in a recent examination, and has an I.Q. of about 108. The Sister who teaches her thinks "reading is very good for you and helps you in general knowledge." There is a class library with "enjoyable books" and the teacher has mentioned some good authors. Colleen joined the Children's Library at a friend's suggestion three years ago and reads about 6 books a month during term, but twice as many during the holidays, though towards the end of the holidays she always studies "to get her brain in working order." She likes to read a mixture of history, poetry and fiction but dislikes "things too far-fetched." "My friends," she said disapprovingly, "are keener on comics and magazines. Though," she added: "I've not really time to have friends." In another context--"most of my time is spent in studying and helping Mum." However, reading is "interesting and enjoyable, it helps you in examinations and also takes your mind off things that aren't very nice." "I think I'd just be a drab sort of person if I didn't read books." "Other children say I think myself big because I use big

words, but reading helps with spelling and vocabulary and
is very good for English marks." Colleen plays basketball
at school, does no radio listening, has no television--"it
would interrupt work"--and goes once or twice a year to the
films. However, the family has a radiogram because "we
do enjoy good music." She is taking piano lessons.

The Sisters at the convent described Colleen as "a
quaint child in the pleasant sense of the word . . . a keen
student, ambitious but generous in helping less able students.
Colleen is a good girl, certain of it, secure in it and self-
righteous about it. Everything she does is intimately bound
up with moral purposes and her obedience to the will of
God. Books of good quality have become a part of her way
of life.

Paul is the only child of European migrant parents
who came to Australia about 10 years ago when Paul was
nearly four. His father, a lower grade white collar employee in Europe, is working as a laborer. The native
tongue is used at home, the only books are a few in that
language, and his parents read nothing but the newspaper.
When asked if they encouraged him to read, Paul replied
that "they're more keen on my studying."

He is in a middle stream at a large high school, was
placed 4th out of 41 at a recent examination and his I.Q.
was assessed at about 105. His teachers find him "an
excellent student in Science and Mathematics," think him
"very mature for his age" and that "his work indicates a
higher I.Q." Paul "likes school better than home," has
nothing to do with the school library and says the English
teacher does "absolutely nothing" to promote reading. His
own reading interests are largely in non-fiction, "to find
out things," and especially in books on radio, television and
solar energy. He owns a few books, among them Moby Dick,
War and Peace and Shakespeare's collected plays. He joined
the Children's Library about three years ago because he
was looking for a particular book and some boys told him
about the library. He used to borrow about once a fortnight
but has not been for a long time, firstly because he "has to
learn a lot" and secondly because he is reading War and
Peace. He is ambitious to go to the University and study
engineering.

He plays football and cricket, listens to the radio "a lot, especially Hit Parades and serials," but the family has no television because "school comes first." His parents listen to good music ("5AN and that stuff") but he likes "rock and roll."

The above sketch would, with variations in detail, fit other children of migrant families. The parents are projecting their ambitions and their hopes for upward mobility into their only son who will study hard, will try to get to the university and become a professional man. Paul is responding, he is an "excellent student," and his pursuit of knowledge permits relatively little other activity. It is significant that he seeks status even in "leisure" reading by concentrating on classics of famous name, though it is doubtful whether he can derive much pleasure or profit from doing so. (This peculiarity has been noted in the reading of other children from migrant families.) Yet inevitably Paul will grow away from his parents. They scarcely speak the same language already, and there are hints of the gap between generations. He seems to accept the absence of television but despises his parents' good music, and already he likes school better than home.

The foregoing portraits of individual children have been taken at random from a much larger number. They illustrate a few, but only a few, of the reasons why children read. These reasons may or may not be applicable to many of the children who use our libraries and there are certainly other reasons and combinations of reasons which have not emerged. I hope nobody will think that the studies quoted represent the last word on these boys and girls. I have collected some information about them and, on the basis of what is really very little evidence, have speculated about them. Some of the tentative conclusions I have drawn may turn out to be quite inaccurate.

Nevertheless, I hope that the studies may have some value in drawing attention to the vast differences among children who use our libraries. They might also be considered to support a case I have made elsewhere[2] --that librarianship is concerned with people as well as with books.

References

1. Discussion of the significance of this remark has been omitted here since it is featured in "The Role of Libraries in Education--Some Impediments and Potentialities," which is Paper XXXa in the published proceedings of the 1963 Hobart Conference.

2. For further argument, see Paper XXXa as above.

V: Ages Twelve to Nineteen

What Do They Read? An Inquiry
Into the Reading Habits of School Children Today

Part 1 by David Jesson-Dibley;
Part 2 by Robin Atthill;
Part 3 by Roland Earl

From English 13:55-8, Summer 1960. Reprinted by permission.

PART 1:

Though other activities and distractions may provide less time, these days, for reading at leisure, the facilities at a boarding-school are such as to make it inevitable for a boy to meet books and acquire some measure of habit in his reading. Here we have a School Library, libraries in each House, libraries in each classroom where form subjects are taught, and a useful supply of sets of books for classroom study. Moreover, television is a luxury of the holidays, and times for playing the radio and gramophone records are restricted.

Boarding-school life, however, provides less privacy and quiet for the boy who takes his reading seriously. Fortunately, most boys who want to read are like caterpillars: they can create their own "chrysalis of the mind," separating all thoughts from the bedlam background of ping-pong, radio, hobbies, and humanity.

To assist the writer of this contribution, a "snap survey" was made recently of boys' reading tastes in the school. Two questions were put to about 300 boys, representing every level of intelligence from the ages of twelve to nineteen:

    1. What books of any kind, apart from textbooks, have you read with pleasure during the last three months? Limit your answers to five.

2. What books have not given you pleasure, either because they proved to be too difficult, or trite, or they did not come up to expectation for some other reason? Limit your answer to two.

"Creating an impression" was discouraged by asking the boys to submit anonymous answers. Just under 2 percent were honest enough to admit that they had read less than three books. There was one "nil return."

Overwhelmingly--it seems, after examining the answers--the preference is for fiction, especially among the senior boys. Lower down the school what goes by the name of fiction is supplemented by travel books, war stories, animal stories, and "adventure." Detective stories are more popular among the under-fifteens, too. Writers who have the widest appeal would seem to be Dickens, John Wyndham, Nevil Shute, Hammond Innes, and Paul Gallico.

In the vanguard of "contemporary" reading in the sixteen-to-nineteen age-groups stand Huxley, Hemingway, Orwell, Waugh, Steinbeck--the latter much read but not all that greatly favored. Golding's Lord of the Flies and Salinger's The Catcher in the Rye are undoubtedly the "best-sellers," with Brave New World and 1984 still exciting curiosity. It seems that Penguins provide the chief source of reading in contemporary fiction for senior boys. Sir Charles Snow's The Masters and The New Men would not have swum into their ken had they not been recently republished in a paperback edition.

Novels that explore human relations do not appeal much, unless the principal characters are adolescent or younger. Lip-service is paid to E. M. Forster, to D. H. Lawrence and Graham Greene, though they have their supporters. A strong narrative line is preferred to analysis of thought and feeling; direct statement to the oblique. If asked what kind of novel I would hesitate to recommend to the average senior boy, I think I would reply: "Most of the novels of Jane Austen and Henry James, Conrad's Lord Jim, Forster's Howard's End, and Angus Wilson's Hemlock and After, not on any grounds of "unsuitability" other than those suggested.

Ages Twelve to Nineteen

Few classics are mentioned outside the sphere of fiction. But there, one may say, Dickens is "in"; the Brontës and George Eliot have also been read by older boys, though George Eliot is little favored. Hardy climbs up beside Dickens for fifteen- and sixteen-year-olds. In translation, the Russians are well represented by Tolstoy and Dostoevsky; <u>Dr. Zhivago</u> is much in evidence, too.

Plays, poetry, biography, social studies have been the exception rather than the rule. To most boys, I suspect, plays and poetry do not "count" as books.

The fantasies of T. H. White, J. R. R. Tolkien, and C. S. Lewis come further into the reckoning as one explores the middle and junior sections. The historical novel undoubtedly appeals there, especially if written by a modern writer, such as Alfred Duggan or D. K. Broster. They are found rubbing shoulders with Agatha Christie and Dennis Wheatley. War stories--H. M. S. <u>Ulysses</u>, <u>The One that Got Away</u>, and <u>Camp on Blood Island</u>--are relished. But furthest to the fore are such tried hands as C. S. Forester, Buchan, Conan Doyle, Jules Verne, and H. G. Wells, supported at lower levels by Henty and W. E. Johns. Rudyard Kipling is not mentioned; Charles Kingsley's <u>Westward Ho!</u> is out of favor; Scott, I believe, is "coming back."

The extent of a boy's reading, once he has acquired the habit, depends, I think, on two factors. An obvious one--often forgotten--is the <u>pace</u> at which he is able to read. The rapid reader is free to <u>read</u> widely and variously. The slow reader has to be "choosy." If he chooses poor stuff, more's the pity. And the other factor is the <u>will</u> to read. Shame on the fast reader who complains that <u>he</u> "can't find the time!" The best advice for the slow reader I believe to be this: "Take your time, regard it as precious, and don't be daunted by the length of a book, nor by the boasting of rapid readers. A good book is like a good meal--the longer you can savor it, the richer the experience."

<u>PART 2:</u>

The English Library at Downside is available to fourth- and fifth-form boys, and caters for their leisure reading: it consists of about 700 books, of which about one-third are nonfiction, and the rest are standard classics and modern popular fiction with a sprinkling of "juveniles." There are no separate House Libraries (except in the Junior House), but the main School Library contains a large fiction section as well as a full range of non-specialist books: these may be read in the Library, and reserved by fourth- and fifth-form boys, but not withdrawn.

I have analysed the borrowings from the English Library during the last two terms to discover what is being read by a cross-section of thirteen- and fourteen-year-old boys: only one-third of the fifth form, for instance, have borrowed books from this source. Of the last 500 borrowings, 75 have been nonfiction, ranging from Annapurna, The Bombard Story, and The Overloaded Ark to Undertones of War and The Reason Why. War books such as The White Rabbit, The Colditz Story, The Frogmen, Elephant Bill, The Jungle Is Neutral, and Cheshire V.C. are regularly borrowed.

Four authors easily lead the field in fiction: C. S. Forester 60, H. G. Wells 39, John Buchan 34, Conan Doyle 31 (with Sherlock Holmes and the historical romances in equal demand). This is a surprisingly conservative showing: except for Forester, it might be 1930, not 1960. Next in order come C. S. Lewis 20 (Out of the Silent Planet, Perelandra, That Hideous Strength), John Wyndham 19 (The Day of the Triffids, The Kraken Wakes), Nevil Shute 13 (four titles), Jane Austen and P. G. Wodehouse 12 each, Dumas 11, G. K. Chesterton 10 (mainly Father Brown), and Wilkie Collins 9. Jane Austen's clear lead among the classical novelists is surprising in view of the average age of the borrowers: of the other major novelists, Conrad's name appears 7 times, Hardy 6, Dickens 5, the Brontë sisters 4. No book by Scott or by George Eliot was borrowed in this period, though they have been occasionally read in other terms. Other occasional borrowings include Robbery under Arms, Lorna Doone, Captain Singleton, Moonfleet, Tom Brown's Schooldays, and Mr. Sponge's Sporting Tour.

Obviously, supply to some extent creates demand: if I bought more Shute, more Shute would be read; on the other hand, John Wyndham's total is achieved with two titles (I have hesitated to add The Midwich Cuckoos). I have been asked for War and Peace and (frequently) for 1984. I do not supply "whodunnits": these and other more or less lurid paperbacks appear to be in good supply in private hands, though unacceptable for silent reading periods or preps. ("Is Nevil Shute all right, sir?")

Again, to some extent, choice of reading is controlled by English masters: I myself issue an arbitrary "select list" of about a dozen titles to my forms each term, I insist on two of them being read, and follow this up with class-discussion or a short written commentary. The real controlling factor, however, is a sort of bush-telegraph of popular fashion and recommendation: this leads to unadventurous choice of books--hence the popularity of sequels (Buchan, Forester, C. S. Lewis), and of the well-tried favorites of yesteryear, though Hugo, Kipling, and Stevenson now find no readers, and even Frankenstein, Moby Dick, and The Old Man and the Sea ("the book of the film") have only been taken out once each in the past six months. Specific "juveniles" are scrupulously avoided; indeed the vagaries of taste are quite as perplexing as the variations of pace: one boy will read comfortably and intelligently two books a week, while his neighbor will reluctantly and unprofitably struggle through one a month. Nor are the best writers in a form necessarily the boys who read most.

What are they reading now? An impromptu reading poll taken in my fourth form (15 boys, average age 13.9, most of whom will probably eventually specialize in History or English) gave the following result: Great Expectations (four boys: a prompted response from last term's reading list?); David Copperfield as a Boy; A Tale of Two Cities; Dr. Jekyll and Mr. Hyde; War and Peace (my copy, and lost within a week); Pygmalion; Owd Bob; Elephant Bill; Lucien Fabre's Joan of Arc; An Escaper's Log (Grinnell and Milne); and An Old Captivity (Shute). After a month of term one boy had read nothing.

PART 3:

The discovery of bad spelling always makes headlines in the newspapers. Yet today, in an aural and pictorial age, far too many children only hear words. Outside school they would seldom see them. They pick up words by hearing them on the radio or television, rather than reading them in books. "I druw my weppen and fired," wrote a nineteen-year-old American airman asked to explain why he had illegally fired a pistol. The alarming thing was that the airman was a high-school graduate of above average intelligence.

Small wonder, then, that when I glance through a number of compositions written by a group of not so intelligent boys of ten I find St. Paul "pritching the gosbal" and "seeing a krat liet." I read "a cupl of days" and "he adventurly died." And someone, I find with interest, "rode a fune poime" as well as "an avnch book."

Hearing words, not seeing them: that is the problem. From home-time to bed-time stretch as many hours as a normal school day, and during that time how many children see the printed word? That is the problem of the primary school. "It is no use giving Auntie a book, she's already got one" is no joke with many of our children. In their homes there are few, if any, books; and seldom, if at all, does the family read. For many teachers it seems a losing battle.

Yet one of the greatest delights a child can have is the joy of reading. And it is one of the hardest jobs in the primary school to get the children to read a book at all. A boy who likes reading is no trouble. He will devour anything from The Swift to Gulliver's Travels, from the ubiquitous Enid Blyton to the expensive encyclopaedia, from the jampot label to Jennings at School.

For the boy who is not interested any distraction or diversion is an excuse to come out of his seat with "Please, sir, this is not a very interesting book. Can I change it?" Such children will do anything rather than read. They will do nothing rather than read.

Talking to them, when they are about nine or ten years old, one finds that they like to read adventure books, history books, and geography books. They like facts. They are not particularly interested in books about sport. They seldom look at a poetry book. And humor does not seem to interest them. But how to get them to read, that is the worry of the teacher in the primary school. Time and again at the bottom of school reports one reads: "Will not read."

Finding that even quite intelligent boys were slightly

Ages Twelve to Nineteen 245

horrified when I suggested that they should read (over two
nights) a book for homework, and that their parents thought
I was making an excessive demand, I decided to experiment
with the school tape-recorder. Getting some of the keen readers together, I gave them copies of "The Young Traveler"
series published by the Phoenix Press. Freshly requisi-
tioned, attractively presented, and with lively dust-covers,
these books were eagerly read, a brief review of their contents written, and "a spoken magazine" of book reviews
taped. With incidental music the magazine was fed through
the school loud-speaker system to the classrooms. "These
books are in the class library. Why not try them?"

  Reviews of other books came in thick and fast. Another "spoken magazine" was edited. A boy would describe
the book he had read. He would set the scene, tease the
listener, and in unison several voices would demand: "Did
Mowgli kill Shere Khan? Read Rudyard Kipling's Jungle
Book to find out."

  "Book reviews" caught on. It was surprising how
many boys found that they could read a book--and quite a
thick one--and write a brief account and opinion of it in a
night or two. The result is that, for some months now,
at least twenty boys in a school of 186 have read a book
a week at home.

  From "The Young Traveller" series we moved to
the Educational Supply Association's very fine "Information
Book" series of how things have developed, how things are
made, and how to explore churches or villages and towns.
From these, more factual books, we gradually slipped into
fiction. Christopher found The Overloaded Ark by Gerald
Durrell "a very interesting book, easy to read, worth reading, and I enjoyed it immensely." For David, Secret
Service by Norman Dale was "very exciting," and, if you
like mystery stories, Raymond is "sure you will like
Mystery at Witch End by Michael Saville."

  No Boats on Bannermere by Geoffrey Trease, The
Eagles Have Flown by Henry Treece, and books about secret
agents, thrilling exploits of modern adventure, and Wilkie
Collins's The Moonstone were soon being recommended as
"well worth reading." Not all criticism, however, was
favorable. Of Five Weeks in a Balloon Geoffrey wrote:
"This well-known books is very interesting, but I think the

events follow too quickly, because as soon as the interest is aroused by one escapade it is taken off to another." And writing of Stirring Deeds of the Twentieth Century by G. F. Lamb, Patrick remarked that "while this is not the best book I have read recently it was very good. . . . There is, however, one story which I do not think belongs in this book. It is called 'The First Atom Bomb' and tells of the horrible things it did. It should be in a book of disasters rather than a book of stirring deeds."

Incidentally I no longer leave the dust jackets on the books. I found one or two boys becoming just a little too good at reviewing. They were reading the "blurb"!

Deiches Studies of Pratt Library Examine Student Reading

Lowell A. Martin

From Maryland Libraries 29:9-11, Fall 1962. Reprinted by permission.

. . . Information about the reading of students was gathered in the three main settings in which they function as readers--as members of families, as students in school, and as library users. The family data comes from hour-long interviews in a sample of Baltimore-area homes, the interview usually with the mother of the family. Direct data about student use in the Pratt Library comes from question forms filled out by students entering Pratt Central and ten branches on four days scattered between the middle of November and the end of December, 1961.

Because the information obtained from students in school may well prove most helpful in understanding student library needs, this source will be described in just a little more detail. For the few highlights being reported here, we will treat only secondary students, both junior-high and senior-high. Questionnaires were filled out by a sample of 3,578 secondary students, in 111 classrooms in 23 schools. Both public and Catholic schools were included, in Baltimore City and Baltimore County, plus one school in Anne Arundel County. This is not the place to go into the question of whether the student responses were accurate and honest, except to point out that we had a cross check from information obtained in the homes and in the public library-- when students claimed they spend a certain amount of time reading, we could check this from the home interviews; when they claimed they visited the public library at certain intervals, we could check this by noting the frequency of actual public library visits.

Well, all this has led to boxes and boxes of punched cards. It will be some time before we digest all the statistics--and certainly I have no illusion that statistics alone are going to lead to full understanding and neat solutions to problems.

But let's just take the information we have on one simple, obvious starting question--just how much do high-school students read? Some critics say very little: librarians know that they are being swamped by students. What are the facts in the Baltimore area?

Note if you will that we start here with a rather obvious question. The answers at first may not seem very startling, but on analysis they lead to some rather significant implications.

Limitations of space permit consideration only of reading by the 75-80 percent of the high-school group who are engaged in academic, general and commercial curricula. The statistics below do not include the 20-25 percent in vocational and special programs, which usually call for less reading. Here, then, is part of the picture of the more-or-less typical teen-age reader in senior-high school:

>He devotes 15-16 hours per month to reading for homework outside the classroom.

>He reads almost six books (other than textbooks) in whole or in part each month for school work, two of which he gets in the school library and four in the public library (these six books are in addition to reference sources consulted briefly.)

>He spends 14-15 hours per month in libraries looking for materials, consulting references, reading books (part of the 15-16 hours of reading time mentioned above)--one-third of this time in his school library, two-thirds in the public library.

>In addition to the 15-16 hours of reading for school work, he spends 9-10 hours per month reading for personal interest or amusement.

>This 'free' reading time is devoted primarily to newspapers and magazines, although the

high-school student goes through 2-3 books of his own interest during a year (the books about equally distributed between material he finds at home, paperbacks he buys or borrows from friends, and books from the public library; the school library figured only rarely in this study as a source of free reading for students).

Taken individually, this is simply the outline of a young person devoting the major portion of his life to education and depending on reading as a major source for the purpose. And there is no point in being sentimental about the considerable amount of reading. Much of it is done under duress, to get good marks, to get the approval of parents and teachers, to get into college. Certainly the quality of free reading by students leaves much to be desired. But whatever their motives, substantial reading is being done by young people, at a strategic stage of their development, and for the worthy purpose of education.

In the coming school year there will be approximately 145,000 secondary students in the Baltimore area. From one-fifth to one-quarter turn to curricula where reading plays a lesser role, and 11 percent of those in the regular curricula somehow get along with very little reading outside the classroom. This leaves just over 100,000 "readers" among the junior and senior high-school students in the Baltimore area. From some source or sources they must get the staggering total of 5,000,000 books during the school year, and in some library or libraries they are spending a total of 11 to 12 million hours during the year! And during the next five years the number of secondary students may increase by as much as 50 percent.

I am sure such statistics raise for you, as they do for me, more questions than they answer. How in the world can we meet this demand? What part should properly be carried by the school library on the one hand and the public library on the other? Is it conceivably even more than a library job--should part of this vast student demand be met by non-library books, such as paperback books either provided or sold through the schools? And if we can meet this demand, what about the greater trend toward accelerated classes in some form (which the Deiches Studies show have a definite effect on library use), to say nothing of the growing number of college students living at home, and going full-time or part-time to local institutions with limited library facilities?

This is just the starting point in analyzing the question of student reading and library use. Here is the way the information to this point is put in a preliminary Deiches report:

> High-school students may well be the largest and most intensive group of purposeful book readers in our society. No one will understand the problem of library service for students until he grasps this fact. It is easy to play variations on the theme of 'Johnny can't read,' but if he can't he certainly spends an inordinate amount of time staring at printed pages.
>
> School officials and librarians (both school and public) have no alternative except to face the fact that it is going to take a lot of books, far more than has been recognized to the present time, to meet the reading needs of students--and more library hours and more librarians. Either that, or in good faith we should take steps to deter young people from reading. The so-called 'problem' of library service for students has its origin in nothing more subtle than the fact that there are many more students and they are doing much more reading.

Fortunately we have in the extensive data the answers to some of the questions that arise as we go into this problem. Not all the answers by any means, but enough to carry us forward. . .

A Study of Pupils' Interests: Grades 9, 10, 11, 12

Paul Witty

Reprinted from the October 1961 issue of Education. Copyright, 1961, by the Bobbs-Merrill Company, Inc.

Editor's Preface: This is part of a report based on a cooperative project carried on between Northwestern University and the Office of Education, U.S. Department of Health, Education and Welfare. Three hundred pupils at each grade level, nine through twelve, in schools in Evanston, Illinois, and in Gary, Indiana, were used in the study. Approximately equal numbers of boys and girls were included at each grade level. The questionnaires were administered during November and December 1958 and January 1959.

Reading

The pupils were asked to indicate how much time they spent in reading "outside school." Table 1 presents the averages for pupils in grades 9 through 12. It may be seen that the pupils spent on the average about one hour and one-third per day. The girls read more than the boys.

Table 1
Time Spent in Daily Reading Outside of School
(82% return)

Boys	Girls
	Grades 9 and 10
1.3 hours	1.4 hours
	Grades 11 and 12
1.3 hours	1.4 hours

Table 2
Percent of Pupils Who Have Library Cards
(96% return)

Boys	Per Cent	Girls	Per Cent
	Grades 9 and 10		
Yes	71.0	Yes	79.8
No	19.0	No	20.2
	Grades 11 and 12		
Yes	69.7	Yes	83.9
No	30.3	No	16.1

Table 3 shows the percentages of pupils who said that TV, radio, and movies had influenced their reading. The pupils reported that movies and television programs had influenced their reading of books to a greater extent than did radio. Movies ranked first and radio third in influence among these pupils. Some of the movies may have been seen on TV.

Table 3
Influence of TV, Radio, and Movies Upon Reading
(99% return)

Boys	Per Cent	Girls	Per Cent
	Grades 9 and 10		
TV		TV	
Yes	18.1	Yes	15.0
No	81.9	No	85.0
Radio		Radio	
Yes	1.5	Yes	2.1
No	98.5	No	97.9
Movies		Movies	
Yes	36.8	Yes	38.5
No	63.2	No	61.5
	Grades 11 and 12		
TV		TV	
Yes	15.1	Yes	16.7
No	84.9	No	83.3
Radio		Radio	
Yes	2.7	Yes	2.1
No	97.3	No	97.9
Movies		Movies	
Yes	45.8	Yes	63.4
No	54.2	No	36.6

Table 4 contains a list of the pupils' preferred types of reading. The girls gave fiction highest rank as the kind of reading they liked best. The boys' first choice was newspaper and magazine articles. Second choice for the girls at both levels was the reading of articles in newspapers and magazines. Fiction was the second choice of the boys. Relatively small percentages of the pupils reported a liking for poetry, plays, or essays. At both levels the girls expressed a greater liking for poetry or plays than did the boys.

Table 4
Kinds of Reading Liked
(98% return)

Boys	Per Cent	Girls	Per Cent
\multicolumn{4}{c}{Grades 9 and 10}			
Articles in newspapers and magazines	32.0	Fiction	30.4
Fiction	31.3	Articles in newspapers and magazines	26.0
Biography	22.4	Biography	17.9
Plays	5.7	Plays	13.3
Essays	5.4	Poetry	7.0
Poetry	3.2	Essays	5.4
\multicolumn{4}{c}{Grades 11 and 12}			
Articles in newspapers and magazines	30.9	Fiction	32.6
Fiction	30.7	Articles in newspapers and magazines	25.2
Biography	23.4	Biography	19.0
Essays	6.7	Plays	12.4
Plays	6.6	Poetry	6.2
Poetry	1.7	Essays	4.6

Sex differences were somewhat pronounced as shown in Table 5. Science fiction was among the preferences of the boys, but it did not appear among the girls' choices. Similarly, romance and career stories were chosen by the girls but not by the boys at these levels. The boys indicated a strong preference for adventure stories. Girls appeared somewhat more interested in humorous stories. In general, boys at all levels expressed a preference for stories involving action and adventure, while girls at all levels generally expressed a preference for romance, mystery, and humor.

Table 5
Kinds of Stories Liked
(95% return)

Boys	Per Cent	Girls	Per Cent
Grades 9 and 10			
Adventure	63.7	Romance	71.4
Mystery	55.4	Mystery	55.1
Science Fiction	44.9	Humor	49.3
Humor	39.3	Adventure	31.3
Westerns	19.1	Animal	10.9
Grades 11 and 12			
Adventure	67.3	Romance	64.6
Mystery	53.3	Humor	52.5
Humor	49.4	Mystery	47.1
Science Fiction	33.1	Adventure	41.7
Westerns	16.3	Career	22.9

The favorite titles of the boys in the ninth and tenth grades were The Yearling, Kon Tiki, and Around the World in 80 Days. The favorite titles of the girls in the ninth and tenth grades were Gone with the Wind, Little Women, Sue Barton, and Kon Tiki.

The favorite titles of boys in the eleventh and twelfth grades were Kon Tiki, Old Man and the Sea, Tale of Two Cities, Huckleberry Finn, Cry the Beloved Country, and 20,000 Leagues under the Sea. The favored title of the girls in the eleventh and twelfth grades was Gone with the Wind, with lesser interest in Tale of Two Cities and Jane Eyre. The boys' interests were broader than the girls'.

Table 6
Best Books Read

Boys	Per Cent	Girls	Per Cent
Grades 9 and 10			
The Yearling	3.8	Gone with the Wind	7.9
Kon Tiki	3.8	Little Women	5.6
Around the World in 80 Days	3.5	Sue Barton	5.0
		Kon Tiki	4.6
Tom Sawyer	2.9	Jane Eyre	3.6
Hardy Boys	2.9		
30 Seconds over Tokyo	2.4		
Robinson Crusoe	2.4		
Three Musketeers	2.4		

Table 6 (cont'd)

Boys	Per Cent	Girls	Per Cent
\multicolumn{4}{c}{Grades 11 and 12}			
Kon Tiki	5.2	Gone with the Wind	18.1
Old Man and the Sea	3.0	Tale of Two Cities	6.8
Tale of Two Cities	3.0	Jane Eyre	6.0
Huckleberry Finn	3.0	The Robe	4.4
Cry of the Beloved Country	3.0	Little Women	4.0
20,000 Leagues Under the Sea	3.0		
Gone with the Wind	2.6		
Tom Sawyer	2.6		
Mysterious Island	2.6		
The Yearling	2.6		

The boys and girls tended to select non-fiction books in similar categories although the rank order changed. Thus, the boys in grades 9 and 10 preferred in order books about famous people, travel, and space travel, while the girls favored famous people, careers, and people from other lands. Table 7 shows the favored nonfiction reading of both sexes.

Table 7
Books Other than Storybooks Liked
(91% return)

Boys	Per Cent	Girls	Per Cent
\multicolumn{4}{c}{Grades 9 and 10}			
Famous People	39.8	Famous People	53.5
Travels	24.6	Careers	37.1
Space Travel	21.4	People of Other Lands	35.6
Careers	17.3	Travels	24.3
People of Other Lands	14.2	Space Travel	6.0
\multicolumn{4}{c}{Grades 11 and 12}			
Famous People	47.0	Famous People	78.9
Space Travel	36.5	Careers	59.3
People of Other Lands	23.3	People of Other Lands	43.5
Careers	20.9	Travels	40.2
Travels	20.1	Space Travel	11.0

One of the major trends in the publishing of books has been the dissemination of paperback editions. The participants in this study were asked whether they read these editions. As shown in Table 8, these students frequently reported reading paperbacks.

Slightly more girls than boys said that they read paperback editions. However, the difference was small.

Table 8
Percent of Pupils Who Read Paperbacks
(92% return)

Grades 9 and 10	Boys	Girls	Grades 11 and 12	Boys	Girls
Yes	31.7	35.8	Yes	36.5	36.6
No	68.3	64.2	No	63.5	63.4

Table 9 gives the percentages of pupils who read series books. Table 10 gives the five best-liked series in the various grades. The Landmark series was the most widely read with Teen-Age Tales second.

Table 9
Pupils Who Read Series Books
(96.3% return)

Grades 9 and 10	Boys	Girls	Grades 11 and 12	Boys	Girls
Yes	45.8	47.8	Yes	37.2	30.0
No	54.2	52.2	No	62.8	70.0

Table 10
Series Books Read by Pupils

Grades 9 and 10	Boys	Girls	Grades 11 and 12	Boys	Girls
Landmark	63.4%	34.1%	Landmark	81.9%	37.5%
Teen-age Tales	19.0	28.3	Teen-Age Tales	5.3	--
Hardy Boys	5.2	--	First Books	2.1	--
Nancy Drew	--	12.3	Nancy Drew	--	20.8
			Cherry Ames	--	5.5

Ages Twelve to Nineteen

At all levels, the pupils consistently ranked the picture magazines Life and Look among their favorites. The Saturday Evening Post, news periodicals such as Time and Newsweek, and Seventeen also appeared frequently.

Table 11
Magazines Liked Best
(97% return)

Boys	Per Cent	Girls	Per Cent
Grades 9 and 10			
Life	44.4	Life	41.1
Saturday Evening Post	25.8	Seventeen	30.5
Look	21.9	Look	19.9
Time	12.2	Saturday Evening Post	19.9
		McCall's	9.9
		Ladies' Home Journal	9.6
		Reader's Digest	9.6
Grades 11 and 12			
Life	57.9	Life	53.1
Saturday Evening Post	31.3	Seventeen	46.0
Look	27.0	Saturday Evening Post	26.3
Time	19.7	Look	23.8
Sports Illustrated	15.0	Reader's Digest	14.6

The newspapers read regularly by these pupils consisted of the local morning or evening publications. The parts of the newspaper generally preferred by boys and girls were sports, comics, front page, and news.

Table 12 gives the favorite comic books of boys and girls in the two levels. Superman was clearly the favorite of the boys at both levels and Archie and Little Lulu were clearly the favorites of the girls at the lower level, and in reverse order were also the favorites at the higher level. The third favorite title of girls at both levels was Donald Duck, and the fourth favorite title was Superman. In general the boys tended to prefer thrillers such as Superman, whereas the girls tended to prefer humorous and romantic comics.

Table 12
Favorite Comic Books of Pupils
(90% return)

Boys	Per Cent	Girls	Per Cent
Grades 9 and 10			
Superman	23.6	Archie	19.1
Donald Duck	16.7	Little Lulu	16.9
Mad	12.8	Donald Duck	12.5
Batman	11.8	Superman	8.5
Bugs Bunny	8.8	Love Comics	8.5
		Katy Keene	7.7
Grades 11 and 12			
Superman	12.8	Little Lulu	16.5
Donald Duck	12.8	Archie	14.7
Bugs Bunny	7.0	Donald Duck	12.5
Mad	6.6	Superman	10.7
Batman	5.8	Bugs Bunny	8.5
Mickey Mouse	4.5		

Table 13 shows the favorite comic strips at the two levels. It may readily be observed that Dick Tracy was popular with both boys and girls at both levels. Nancy was popular with both boys and girls in the ninth and tenth grades, whereas Peanuts was popular with boys in the eleventh and twelfth grades. Both boys and girls liked Dennis the Menace. Here again, as in other categories, the girls manifested greater interest in romance than the boys.

Table 13
Favorite Comic Strips
(85% return)

Boys	Per Cent	Girls	Per Cent
Grades 9 and 10			
Dick Tracy	25.0	Dick Tracy	22.5
Nancy	14.7	Nancy	21.7
Steve Roper	13.4	Dondi	16.0
Dennis the Menace	12.3	Dennis the Menace	16.0
Peanuts	11.7	Long Sam	13.3
		Peanuts	13.3
		Brenda Starr	12.6

Table 13 (cont'd)

Boys	Per Cent	Girls	Per Cent
\multicolumn{4}{c}{Grades 11 and 12}
Dick Tracy	29.1	Dick Tracy	29.2
Peanuts	17.9	Peanuts	23.7
Nancy	17.1	Dennis the Menace	17.8
Dennis the Menace	14.5	Nancy	16.9
Steve Roper	14.1	Mary Worth	16.9
		Brenda Starr	16.4

"We Don't Even Call Those Books!"

Esther Millett

From Top of the News 20:45-7, October 1963. Reprinted by permission.

Recently, in a developmental reading class of ninth and tenth grade students, I asked the girls to name some of their favorite books. With scarcely a pause, the titles came tumbling over one another: The Good Earth, Jane Eyre, Hawaii, The Bridge at Andau, Wuthering Heights, Kontiki, The Jungle, The King Must Die, A Separate Peace, To Kill a Mockingbird, Travels With Charlie, To Catch an Angel. Since these students were slow readers--and some of them reluctant ones--I asked them if they were sure that they weren't trying to impress me. Didn't they secretly like some of the many teen-age novels published today? And almost in chorus came the answer, "Oh, Miss Millett, we don't even call those books!"

This experience was one of many that has convinced me over the years that we--librarians, teachers, parents-- are not offering enough challenging reading to the high school student of today. We are constantly being reminded of the gifted child and his ability to read and study in great depth and of the modern curriculum, with its increased demands, but we tend to forget that the average reader, and even the slow reader, also needs to be given books which appeal to the adult in him.

Even my thirteen-year-old neighbor surprised me this year. I have always given him books as gifts, and his thanks have often been lukewarm. So last Christmas I chose a different gift, and as I offered it said, "I know you don't like books much, Pobby, so here is something I hope you will like better." He replied, "Thanks, but I like to read now. I just finished The Townsman. Gee, it was great."

Ages Twelve to Nineteen

In my own library--serving grades nine to twelve--I have never stocked any but adult titles. Most of the girls read much voluntarily; in the words of one, "It is the fashion to read at Westover." All students are encouraged to buy as well as borrow books, and even with almost unlimited choice of books at their disposal, there are relatively few who own and enjoy made-to-order teen-age novels.

For years, when I showed some of our reading lists to other librarians, I was told that the students in my school were "special," that in public libraries and public schools one could not aim so high. As editor for a number of years of the Senior Booklist and the Junior Booklist of the Independent School Education Board (now called the National Association of Independent Schools), I was told that our lists were good but, of course, many of the books were too mature for the average high school reader. As a consultant for the Standard Catalog for High School Libraries, my plea that we include more adult books, and leave those labeled "14 to 18" or "14 and up" for the Children's Catalog, went unheeded. As I talked to many parents, they were concerned that their children were not ready for the mature reading I recommended.

We expect more and more responsibility from young people today, and I contend that we should expect more maturity in their reading tastes than heretofore. Perhaps they will not get as much meaning from a book as an adult, but who is to say what is the right age to read and enjoy War and Peace or Huckleberry Finn? The former is a great tale of adventure and a study in philosophy. The latter has been called both a children's book and one of the greatest of American novels. At different ages one finds different values in books. If a book is honest, is well written, is in good taste, is timely, it will appeal to a wide range, and that includes the teenager.

Not long ago I heard a college professor state that he was impatient with those who thought that some books should not be studied in high school, but should be saved for study in college. College courses, he said, can certainly deal with the same books in greater depth. If a book is a good one, if it can stand the test of time, it can be read again and again and new meaning found with each re-reading.

Happily, of late, I notice many signs that the high school reader is coming into his own, that he is at last being considered, not as being in a sort of no-man's-land between child and man, but as a person who is more adult than child. The Senior Booklist is now not one of few, but one of many, book lists for young people that aim high. Publishers send out more and more lists of "adult books for young people"; The New York Public Library's annual Books for the Teen-age has in each succeeding issue had a larger and larger percentage of adult books; The New York Herald Tribune Books has been printing excellent short reviews of adult books for young people under the heading "For Teenagers." Teachers and librarians in courses which I have taught in library schools have been more and more vocal in their requests for basic and current lists of adult books for high school libraries.

And finally, the H.W. Wilson Company's Standard Catalog for High School Libraries is embarking on a general upgrading of its selections. In the preface to the 1963 Supplement, the publishers state, "An increasing number of serious articles . . . have voiced concern that many high school library collections have failed to keep pace with the more advanced or upgraded curricula now in effect in high schools generally . . . It is hoped that a better balance will be found in the present Supplement as the result of this procedure, which will be continued in future Supplements."

I am glad to say that in checking the 1963 supplement against my own collection, I have found a much closer correlation than in the past. I am further assured, moreover, that this new policy will be incorporated in future editions of the basic catalog.

Such changes in approach to teen-age reading are encouraging. They are long overdue, and all of us in the book business must not only rejoice but continue as individuals to provide the best and the most challenging reading within our power for today's young people. High school students will continue to be bombarded with ideas from movies, television, radio. Increasing demands will continue to be made on students--and on libraries for them. Ideas from books have more permanence than all other media, for they are not flashed before us or heard only once but are in such a form that they may be referred to at will.

If the aim of education is to teach the student to think, then we must do all we can to provide young people

Ages Twelve to Nineteen

not with books that touch only the surface and have contrived situations, but with books that inspire them, excite them, give them lasting food for thought. Let us, as Lawrence Clark Powell says, "speak to the latent bookishness in young people . . . arouse and feed the bookish hunger which God mysteriously goes on putting into a number of human beings in each generation, year after year, from the time of the first clay tablet and papyrus roll to the day of doom."

Patterns of Young Adults' Reading

A meeting during an American Library Association convention; reported in Publishers' Weekly 190:29-32, August 8, 1966. Copyright 1966 by R. R. Bowker Company. Reprinted by permission.

Like virtually all of the meetings during the American Library Association's 85th annual convention, the one sponsored by the Young Adult Services Division and held at the New York Hilton on Thursday, July 14, was crowded. The main speaker was Dr. G. Robert Carlsen of the University of Iowa, Iowa City.

Dr. Carlsen analyzed the reading patterns, based on the content of a book, which he has found most prevalent among young adult or teen-age readers from early adolescence to age 20 or over. He drew, in part, on his own teaching experience at the University of Iowa, upon thousands of "reading autobiographies" from adults all over the world, and upon the response to questionnaires he submits frequently to young people in which he asks them what, if they could have a book written to order personally, they would like to find in it.

In early adolescence, from about ages 12 to 14, Dr. Carlsen said, almost inevitably the child finds that he likes a book of adventure in which an individual is cast adrift somewhere and makes his way back to security. He cited as an excellent example of this kind of fiction last year's typical Robinson Crusoe story, Pilot Down: Presumed Lost. Children of this age also like mystery stories, not the flamboyant James Bond type as yet and not murder mysteries, but the kind of stories that involve mistaken identity, a lost will or stolen papers. Too Many Sidneys, Dr. Carlsen said, was a particularly successful example of this type of fiction, including as well elements of slapstick comedy and a chase. Girls this age are intrigued by such mysterious atmospheric touches as old houses and dark corridors. Boys prefer their thrills in an exterior setting, perhaps on a mountain peak or in a desert.

What Young Adolescents Like to Read

    Thirdly, young adolescents, Dr. Carlsen said, still go for animal stories in a big way. Boys prefer primitive savage animals in their fiction. Girls like the kind of animal that is more dependent on humankind, horses or dogs. Girls of 12 to 14 love family stories. Boys hate them. The Village That Slept was especially popular with girls because of its introduction of elementary housekeeping. Girls rather than boys prefer books with a historical setting, "books about the olden times," that may be somewhat mystical and romantic. A Romeo and Juliet love story of prehistoric Denmark, The Far Away Lures, was very successful with girls. Both boys and girls at this age level are interested in tales of the supernatural. It is the best age at which to introduce them to Edgar Allan Poe. Dr. Carlsen mentioned Cape Cod Casket as a legitimate modern descendant of this kind of spookiness.

    Boys of 12 to 14 have a maximum interest in sports and nothing quite equals a John Tunis sports book in popularity. Girls enjoy stories of growing up around the world. Boys do so occasionally but generally require some other element of mystery or adventure in the plot first. Dr. Carlsen thought that a number of excellent foreign writers writing for young people in their own lands were now being translated very successfully for American teen-agers. He approved particularly of The Spinning Top of Naples. Broad slapstick humor is enjoyed by both boys and girls, books like The Pushcart War. This kind of thing is not easy to find, however, Dr. Carlsen said. At this age boys will usually discover science fiction. Some boys will be crazy about car stories such as the French The Nightmare Rally. Girls of 12 to 14 appreciate vocational stories, not because of the factual information included in them so much as because these tales almost always develop into glamorous success stories with strong human interest.

Reading Tastes in the 15-16 Age Group

    In middle adolescence, 15 to 16, Dr. Carlsen suggested that young people have five general areas of reading interest so far as plot is concerned. Girls begin to get interested in the true historical novel. Boys move over to accounts of actual real life adventure, stories of survival or exploration. Girls become passionately involved with the Gothic romances of such ladies as Mary Stewart and Victoria Holt. Boys admire stories of physical courage. They begin to take an interest in war stories that actually try to tell them something of what it feels like to be in battle under stress. Boys and girls become interested in stories of people like themselves, living lives not far different from their own. They prefer to have the hero or heroine a few years older than they themselves actually are, but the characters must have problems not too different from their own. The adult books they may begin to read at this age include The Catcher in the Rye, Anne Frank's Diary of a Young Girl, A Separate Peace or Look Homeward, Angel.

Pre-College and College Readers

In late adolescence, which Dr. Carlsen characterized as extending from age 17 or 18 to college or age 20 to even 22, preferences generally fall into four categories: 1) Books like Lord of the Flies in which readers can continue their search for personal values. 2) Stories dealing with deprived or persecuted people or social injustice. Highly successful books in this category for young adult reading have been Black Like Me, Seven Days in May, The Ambassador and The Ugly American. 3) Books that skirt the psychological fringes of the human soul, Kafka's Metamorphosis, Billy Budd or Crime and Punishment. 4) The surest point of interest for the late adolescent, however, is found in books that show others maturing into early adult life, books such as Of Human Bondage, Arrowsmith or Joy in the Morning.

Discovering the Unconscious Delight

In broader terms, Dr. Carlsen said, the adolescent reader is generally in the process of discovering the really unconscious delight that reading can offer him in terms of escape to a world of intensified action and emotion. He is often in search of a world that will assure him of his own importance and gratify his ego, a world in which the adolescent is idyllically free of adult supervision. ("Have you noticed," he asked, "how often the stories for teen-agers seem to be frequented by motherless kids?") Even in his

liking for animal stories the adolescent may be searching
for the noble, courageous beast who freely acknowledges
the superiority of a teen-ager over him. About 14 or 15
a youngster finds the book a safe way of seeking out some
of the answers to his own inner problems and fears. It
will not invade his privacy as a counselor would. Finally,
in late adolescence the reader begins to discover that literature has much to say about the basic dilemmas of mankind.
The aesthetic delight in perfection of form and literary technique comes late in the reading scale.

    Dr. Carlsen closed with a report on a reading study
made of juniors and seniors at the University of Iowa, all
especially selected students who were given absolute freedom to read what they wanted out of a list of nearly 2500
books. Of these students, 6% were still reading in the
adolescent category; 55% were reading popular adult books,
the sort of thing that appears on the best seller lists; 29%
were reading modern classics with some genuine literary
merit, books by Camus, Sartre, Hemingway, Kafka, McCullers, Steinbeck. Only 10% had yet gone on to the realm
of the great classics of all time.

"Duds and Dandies" in the YA Field

    Then the librarians met in groups to discuss informally, on the basis of their own experiences with young
adult readers, a list of "Duds and Dandies: Adult Books
that Did or Did Not Make It with Young Adults." The list
was prepared by the Publishers Relations Committee of
the Young Adult Services Division of the ALA, headed by
Julia G. Russell, Young Adult Services, Nassau Library
System, Hempstead, N.Y. The selection of "Duds and
Dandies" was based upon frank reports made by a group of
young adult services librarians especially polled for the
occasion, on the equally candid comments of the publishers
involved, and on a careful culling of various young adult
reading lists. It would be nice to report that after all this
there was unanimous agreement among the librarians present as to what really constitutes a dud or a dandy, but,
truth to tell, as one wandered from table to table at the
Hilton, it became quite apparent that many of the books
which were officially designated as "Duds" had been great
hits in certain libraries, while some of the "Dandies" were
being described in anything but flattering terms by other
librarians.

Lists Indicate Successes and Flops

Here, however, is the ALA Young Adult Services Division's own officially designated list of "Duds and Dandies." We might point out that the designation "dud," as used here, refers only to the book's apparent lack of success with young adult readers and in no way reflects on its reception by adults.

The list of "Successful Young Adult Titles from Adult Publishing 1960-65" as officially designated included: The American Way of Death by Jessica Mitford (Simon and Schuster, Fawcett); Black Like Me by John Howard Griffin (Houghton Mifflin, NAL); The Eighth Moon by Sansan (Harper & Row); Fail-Safe by Eugene Burdick (McGraw-Hill, Dell); The Hospital by Jan de Hartog (Atheneum); I, Keturah by Ruth Wolff (John Day); Life with Mother Superior by Jane Trahey (Farrar, Straus & Giroux); The Lightship by Siegfried Lens (Hill and Wang); Nigger by Dick Gregory (Dutton, Pocket Books); The Rebuilt Man by Fred Warshofsky (T. Y. Crowell); The Spy Who Came in From the Cold by John Le Carré (Coward-McCann, Dell); Travels with Charley by John Steinbeck (Viking, Bantam); Up the Down Staircase by Bel Kaufman (Prentice-Hall, Avon); Von Ryan's Express by David Westheimer (Doubleday, NAL); We Have Always Lived in the Castle by Shirley Jackson (Viking, Popular Library).

The official list of "Unsuccessful Young Adult Titles from Adult Publishing 1960-65" included: Dr. Ox's Experiment by Jules Verne (Macmillan); The Echoing Cliffs by Hjalmar Theson (McKay); Find the Boy by W. J. Canaway (Viking, Ballantine, as A Boy Ten Feet Tall); The Little Kingdom by Hughie Call (Houghton); Peter Freuchen's Adventures in the Arctic (Messner); Old Mali and the Boy by D. R. Sherman (Little, Brown); Raymond and Me That Summer by Dick Perry (Harcourt, Brace & World); The Serpent's Coil by Farley Mowat (Little, Brown, Ballantine); A Ship Called Hope by William B. Walsh (Dutton); Sword at Sunset by Rosemary Sutcliffe (Coward-McCann, Fawcett); To Catch an Angel by Robert Russell (Vanguard, Popular Library); A Very Small Remnant by Michael Straight (Knopf, Dell); When the Legends Had to Die by Hal Borland (Lippincott, Bantam).

Teen-Age Reading

From a National Library Week Conference; reported in Publishers' Weekly 176:12-5, November 30, 1959. Copyright 1959 by R. R. Bowker Company. Reprinted by permission.

What causes young people to give up book reading, either partially or completely, as they enter their teens?

Is this drop-off in reading as widespread as it is generally portrayed?

How can teen-agers be encouraged to continue reading and develop lifetime reading habits? . . .

The present teen-age generation is not dramatically different from previous teen-age generations. Perennially, teen-agers are viewed as "a problem"--in their reading habits no less than in other aspects of behavior. A number of factors work to discourage youngsters from continuing voluntary reading after they enter their teens. For the youth who never was a reader, these factors simply confirm him in the non-reading habit as he enters the teen years.

If books are not important to parents, they are not likely to achieve any importance for the teen-age youngster; reading will remain "a chore," school-imposed. In our high schools, the very way in which books are used often discourages teen-agers from undertaking any but "required" reading.

In our colleges, with their over-emphasis on courses-for-credit and their under-emphasis on courses-for-content, the prospects of a teen-ager becoming a confirmed reader are not much better. "Those iniquitous book reports!" said one conference participant. "Once the teen-ager has slaved through a dull book and ground out a report, he wants nothing more to do with reading."

The teen-ager's peer group appears to be a stronger inclucence on him than home or school, but this fact in itself offers little encouragement to those who would hope that more teen-agers will do more voluntary reading. Social life, athletics, family responsibilities and homework make compelling demands on the teen-ager's out-of-school hours. The free time he has left after these activities might be spent in voluntary reading, but the chances are not good.

Our culture does little to reinforce the appeal of book reading. The number of books read is unlikely to be an important status symbol in any given teen-age circle.

The teen-ager lives in a world he never made, true enough, but he appears to accept it on its own terms. If there is a significant difference between today's teen-ager and his counterpart of 30 years ago, it is in today's teen-ager's lack of intellectual curiosity. If he has any mental image of a library, it is an unfavorable one. More likely, he has no image of the library; he does not go there for answers to his intellectual questions because he never asks such questions. Grudgingly, he might admit that the library is O.K. for old ladies and "squares," but there's nothing in the library for him.

That is the generalized, stereotyped picture of the state of teen-age reading. How valid is it?

Reading can appeal to adolescents, if their curiosity can be engaged, as indulgence in fantasy or as a supplement to direct experience, or, more prosaically, as a source of information needed for scholastic or social advancement.

The major channels for appeal to teen-agers' curiosity are the mass media, particularly television and motion pictures. Current best sellers of the Campus Book Club include The Nun's Story, Green Mansions and Anne Frank's Diary of a Young Girl -- books which recently have been made into well-publicized motion pictures.

Nonfiction is becoming more popular with teen-agers than it once was--particularly books about science and space travel and "contemporized" biographies of historical figures. This trend is attributable in part to the increasing nonfiction content of television--the Walt Disney science programs, for example.

Polls About Teen-Age Tastes in Reading

Studies undertaken by the Boy Scouts and the Girl Scouts (covering nonmembers as well as members) found that 85% of the boys and 90% of the girls polled listed reading as a leisure time activity in which they engaged. In amount of time spent, reading ranked fifth among the girls, eighth among the boys. As a leisure time activity which they enjoyed, reading dropped off in this poll; 38% of the boys and 50-55% of the girls said that they enjoyed it.

A Purdue poll of teen-agers taken in February 1959 found that of those surveyed 8% read comics and cartoons, 54% read fiction and adventure stories, 11% read biographies and general nonfiction, 11% read science books, 3% read "classics" and 5% read religious books.

A survey of 10 high schools serving representative but widely differing socio-economic communities, found that 5% of the boys and 10% of the girls listed reading as their favorite pastime. Among various leisure time activities, reading ranked well behind watching television, participating in athletics, listening to records, pursuing hobbies and engaging in social activities.

From school to school, in this survey, the percentage of students who liked reading stayed relatively constant. From one socio-economic level to another, it was the quality of the reading that differed. (It should be noted that reading is not likely to show up strongly in a poll that asks teen-agers to list their favorite pastime. Among boys particularly, there may be strong reluctance to go on record as favoring an activity which is essentially non-social and could be criticized as "sissy." Because of this it may not be true, as is widely assumed, that girls read significantly more than boys. Rather, the boys feel ashamed to confess the amount of reading they actually do.)

The teen-agers who do go to libraries do so somewhat in violation of prevailing teen-age society mores. They come chiefly because of a subject that has caught their fancies, whether it be baseball or sports cars or rocket propulsion or World War II. "We start with their subject interests," one librarian at the conference said. "We worry about their potential subject interests later." "They need personalized reading guidance," said another librarian at the conference. "Book lists alone will not do the job."

Some adolescents are not readers and never will be readers. The job of National Library Week and other teen-age reading development programs is to reach the might-be teen-age reader and give him the push that will start him on the path of lifetime reading. The job is started when the teen-ager who comes to the library gains the confidence to stray beyond the subject area that brought him there in the first place.

Initially, the quality of reading is not important. "Poor" reading may have to precede "good" reading; any reading is better than none.

"Image" of the Library can be Recast

The image of the library can be recast for teen-agers in terms that are consistent with what a library actually is. The library is not--or it need not be--a gloomy place with "Quiet, Please" signs all over the walls. Within limits that can be made understandable to teen-agers, the library is a rather permissive place, allowing a large degree of freedom.

If there are social pressures that work to inhibit reading, there are others that can be employed to make reading an attractive and meaningful activitiy.

As the statistics presented at the conference indicated, reading may not be ideally popular among teen-agers; but it is not as unpopular as it is generally believed to be.

In attempting to make voluntary reading more widespread among adolescents, one great advantage is that teen-age society is a society, much more sharply defined than it was 30 years ago. Much is known about this society's habits and anxieties, and this information can be put to use in a campaign to build lifetime reading habits.

Encouraging the Development of Lifetime Reading Habits

The image of the teen-ager as a "rebel without a cause" has been overrated. Teen-agers basically are conformists. They want and need voices of authority. They are miserable unless they know their own limits, and they are willing to be told what those limits are. They look for guidance in the adult world, which they feel, often rightly, has let them down rather badly.

Teen-agers are not escapists. A pro-reading campaign addressed to them ought to include appeals to conformity as well as appeals to the "impulse life" embodied in reading. Teen-agers are concerned with the here-and-now. At most, the vision they project of themselves is one that extends only two or three years into the future.

In the field of music, teen-agers make the transition rather easily from rock-and-roll to ballads to jazz and classical music. Is there any form of literature which can perform a catalytic function similar to that performed by rock-and-roll? What is the significance of the fact that adolescents of all ages and socio-economic groups read Mad Comics, that zany, witty satire on adult life? Should more be written and published specifically for the teen-age group, to make the transition to mature, adult reading less difficult?

College Plans: A Motive for Teen Reading

Among the possible uses of anxiety available for a teen-age reading campaign, one of the most viable comes from the fact that an increasingly higher percentage of teen-agers plans to go to college. This increase in the percentage of hopeful college candidates, plus the "baby boom" of the 1940's, will make admission to college increasingly difficult in the 1960's. Stiffening their requirements, more colleges are going to put more emphasis on general reading in preparing their entrance examinations. This development should be publicized widely to teen-agers.

Parents should be reinforced in whatever desires they may have to stand up for their values in the face of prevailing community anti-intellectualism. If books and ideas are important for the parents, they can be made meaningful for their adolescent children. Does the youngster see his parents reading or do they do their reading only after the children have gone to bed? Does the family ever read aloud together? Does the house contain bookshelves for the children's own libraries?

Ultimately, if books are made available, and if book reading is made attractive, adolescents will develop lifetime reading habits. The Yale & Towne Manufacturing Company's experience with factory reading racks is a case in point (Publishers' Weekly, November 12, December 17, 1956). Racks of children's books were placed in the company's factories, and employees were invited to borrow the books, take them home, bring them back when they were finished with them. The turnover on the racks was terrific. Employees who might never go to a bookstore, who might avoid a public library because it made them feel "uncomfortable," queued up for books at the factory racks. Though they might not be book readers themselves, they considered it important that their children read.

Another case in point for book availability is the experience which several high schools and private preparatory schools have had with selling paperbacks in their libraries. In these schools, paperbacks were simply placed on shelves in the library, and students were invited to browse and, if they chose, to buy. In one school, this experiment was so successful that the librarian reportedly was slightly embarrassed at the amount of dollar turnover in the paperbacks-for-sale department.

A Role for National Library Week

In its first two years of existence, National Library Week has proved its ability to broadcast nationwide, through all media, the merits of books and reading. How can National Library Week's resources be applied specifically to the job of encouraging teen-agers to read? The conference came up with some interesting suggestions.

The teen-agers' image of the library must be recast, in terms consistent with what a library actually is. For example, there is a reason why libraries require a measure of silence, somewhere between absolute quiet and bedlam. This reason can be stated in terms acceptable to teen-agers.

The school library can be promoted as one of the freest places in the entire school. The school librarians' status should be reinforced, made more prestigious; more often than not, a school librarian is regarded by the school administration neither as a professional educator nor as a professional librarian. In national magazine and television National Library Week promotion, teen-age idols (entertainers, athletes, etc.) could promote a specific book as one that was meaningful to them and/or marked a turning point in their careers. If this were done with sincerity, without the taint of hokum, it could be an effective way of suggesting that teen-agers ought to read the book, too.

Through National Library Week, a pool of writers might be set up to supply teen-age publications with articles about books and book-related subjects.

In the adult book field, best seller lists exercise a subtle compulsion to buy the books which others are reading. In connection with National Library Week, libraries might compile lists of the books most borrowed by their teen-age constituents. The implication could be, "Many of your peers are reading these books. Maybe they contain something that you, too, would find interesting and valuable."

National Library Week Sunday could be promoted as Family Reading Sunday--with messages from pulpits and with local bookstores and libraries holding open house in the afternoon. ("Don't feel that you have to buy or borrow any of our books. Just come and see us, and see what we have here. You'll be welcome.")

Teen-agers themselves should be encouraged to participate in local National Library Week celebrations--as guides for school or public library tours, for instance, or as sales clerks at book fairs.

Without "knocking the product," magazine articles for teen-agers during National Library Week could point out that not all books are uniformly "great" and that indeed some of the "classics" that are required reading in schools are silly and dull. Such an approach would generate controversy and might make reading seem a bit less forbidding.

Debates and controversy about books--Dostoievsky vs. Tolstoi or pro-and-con arguments about a particular author's work--if effectively presented on TV or in the press or from the stage of the school auditorium, are more likely to capture the attention of teen-agers than reiterations of bland messages: "Reading is nice," "Reading is good for you."

      Teen-agers may resent being preached at. But they are ready to listen to sensible advice, sensibly presented.

"Teen" Reading Assessed in Scholastic's Survey

From Publishers' Weekly 175: 22-3, April 13, 1959. Copyright 1959 by R. R. Bowker Company. Reprinted by permission.

Two out of three teen-agers are "currently reading a book"--or so they say--according to a survey just completed by the Institute of Student Opinion, sponsored by Scholastic Magazines, Inc. Released for publication during National Library Week, the survey covered 10,149 young people in grades 7 through 12, in junior and senior high schools of all sizes and kinds. The poll was taken during February and March, 1959. The various answers were weighted and adjusted according to scientific polling principles. Says the Institute's report on its survey: "It was recognized at the outset that responses to questions about reading, book buying and book ownership would reflect some inflation. All possible steps were taken to minimize inflated answers."

Exaggerating or not, when the young people were asked, "Not counting school work, are you currently reading any book (not magazines or comics)?" 59.4% of the boys and 68.8% of the girls--or 64.3% in all--said "Yes." When they were asked if they had spent any time reading a book "yesterday," 41.7% of the boys and 49.6% of the girls-- 45.9% in all--said "Yes." Within this group 14.7% said they spent from 30 to 60 minutes reading a book; 11.3%, 15-29 minutes; 7.8%, 1-2 hours; 6.3%, under 15 minutes; 5.8%, 2 hours or more. Twice as many girls as boys (7.4% vs. 3.7%) claimed to spend 2 or more hours reading a book.

Asked where they got the last book they read, the teenagers mentioned primarily the school library (38.2%) or public library (23.9%); and 11.4% claimed to have bought it with their own money. In fact, 26.7% said they had bought a book or books for themselves during the 30 days preceding the poll. The breakdown here consisted of: 1 paperback, bought by 10% of the students; 2, by 8%; 3 or 4, by 5.2%;

5 or more, by 3.5%; 1 hard-cover book, bought by 10.6%; 2, by 4.3%; 3 or more, by 4.8%.

The young people also made some estimates about book ownership--other than schoolbooks and including both hardcover and paperbound books. In all, 92.4% of the teenagers owned some books, 38% owning 1-9 books, 28.4% owning 10-24 books, 15.8% owning 25-49 books and 10.2% owning 50 or more books. Also, 92.1% said their families owned books: 1-49 books in 54.1% of the families, 50-199 books in 27% of the families, and 200 or more in 11% of the families.

Book club membership of some sort was claimed by 13.4% of the teenagers questioned.

The questioners started off by asking about comic books, and found that 77.4% of the teenagers asserted they had not been reading any comic book "yesterday"; of the rest, half claimed to have spent under 15 minutes doing so. On the other hand, 67.1% said they had been reading in other magazines, and two-thirds of these said they had put in 15-29 minutes on that kind of reading. Some 78.1% read a newspaper "yesterday," almost half spending under 15 minutes and almost half, 15-29 minutes, on newspaper reading.

TV viewing was also covered in the survey. Some 21.1% of the youngsters said they did not "spend any time yesterday watching TV," but 24.8% confessed spending 2-4 hours in TV viewing; 18.8%, 1-2 hours; 14.1%, 30-60 minutes; 7.3%, under 30 minutes; 9.6%, 4-6 hours; and 4.3%, an appalling 6 hours or more. . . .

What Do They Really Want To Read?

Mary L. Smith and Isabel V. Eno

From the English Journal 50:343-5, May 1961. Reprinted with the permission of the National Council of Teachers of English, Mary L. Smith, and Isabel V. Eno.

"If you could have an author write a story-to-order for you, what would you have him put in it?" Five hundred and ten students in grades seven through twelve responded to this question. Thirteen types of stories were suggested by their responses, but so many students desired combinations that there was a total of 836 requests. (These multiple requests explain why percentage totals of students given below are above 100.)

In these schools English is a required course in all grades but the twelfth. Questionnaires were returned by the following numbers of students:

Junior High

Grade:	7	8	9	Total
Boys:	62	39	41	142
Girls:	70	43	47	160

Senior High

Grade:	10	11	12	Total
Boys:	51	20	21	92
Girls:	40	50	26	116

The per cent of students requesting a type of story revealed the following popularity ratings:

Junior High Boys:

Mystery	16%
Sports	15%
Science fiction	15%
Adventure	15%
Animal stories	13%
Sea stories	10%

Junior High Girls:

Romance	65%
Mystery	20%
Career	12%
Comedy	11%

Senior High Boys:

Adventure	46%
Mystery	25%
Sea stories	25%
Comedy	24%
Historical	23%
Science fiction	21%

Senior High Girls:

Romance	66%
Career	36%
Mystery	32%
Adventure	30%
Comedy	28%

(Smaller per cents of students selected other types of stories.)

Boys' favorites seemed to involve action, with this appeal reaching a climax in the tenth and eleventh grades. Sea stories maintained consistent interest for boys throughout junior and senior high school, but the appeal of simple sports stories and of animal stories declined. Biography was practically an added interest for senior high boys.

A persistent interest for girls was romance--very seldom requested by the boys. Mystery, comedy, and career stories allured girls of all grades. The interest in career stories seemed to reach a peak in tenth and eleventh grades. Sports, sea, animal, and western stories--so popular with the boys--were of negligible interest to the girls. The increasing appeal of adventure seemed to contrast with the declining interest in mystery as the girls grew older. High school girls showed added interests in novels with religious, historical, and biographical backgrounds.

What type of person would these students select for the leading character in their "made-to-order story"?

The boys showed a distinct preference for their own sex. Among the girls, those in tenth grade showed a similarly strong preference for a heroine. Twelfth grade girls, on the other hand, asked for more heroes than heroines; these requests may be partly due to their recognition of the need for two leading characters in a romance. Among the other girls, there were about twice as many requests for a heroine as for a hero. Does this preference for a leading character of his own sex enable a student to identify himself with successes and, perhaps, to solve present problems or to experiment with the future vicariously?

A protagonist between the ages of fifteen and nineteen had the best chance of popularity with the junior high students--37% of the choices. One between twenty and twenty-four was second in popularity--19% of requests. Twenty-seven percent of senior high students desired a leading character fifteen to nineteen years old; 23% asked for one twenty to twenty-four.

A student was the most popular leading character, preferred by 27% of junior high and 15% of senior high students. A secretary was second choice, requested by 6% of junior high and 8% of senior high students. 9% of senior high students asked that he be a service man. Although they engaged in a remarkable variety of activities, the heroes of 32% of the junior high and 30% of the senior high boys were men of action.

Junior high students described their heroes and heroines as attractive, kind and considerate, intelligent, physically strong, good natured with a sense of humor. Senior high students most frequently desired the leading character to be attractive, intelligent, physically strong, friendly, kind, and popular. (Characteristics have been listed in order of decreasing frequency of request.)

Except where the plot demanded another location, this hero or heroine lived in the United States, most frequently in a large city. Occasionally he travelled the Pacific Ocean, explored outer space, even ventured under the Polar ice cap in a submarine.

Except in the case of biographical, historical, and religious novels, there was an overwhelming desire for stories of the present or recent past.

Students revealed their individuality most clearly in outlining plots for the accommodating author. However, certain themes revealed themselves. The prevalence of the girls' interest in romance was emphasized by the number of problems involving boy-girl relationships. Junior high students' plots concerned getting the attention of "a certain boy," of overcoming parental objections to dating, of the complication of romance with popularity and school activities. They invariably had happy endings.

Senior high students devised romances of a more advanced stage which required the choice between "two men," between school and marriage, between marriage and a career. These "more mature" plots usually ended in marriage, but in several the girl did not "marry the first man"; in two, she did not marry at all. Three stories continued beyond the heroine's decision to show "what happened after." In eleventh grade, the girls revealed an awareness of the need for at least one character to make adjustments and moral decisions. Twelfth grade girls placed the characters of their romances in adult occupations. For example, one specified a lawyer and his client--"she's guilty, but he doesn't know it."

Younger boys outlined animal and sports stories. In the sports stories through the tenth grade, the problem was "winning against odds" or "overcoming a handicap."

Mystery plots for both boys and girls were the ordinary crime types involving murder, dope smuggling, robbery, etc. For girls, they were often combined with romance. Junior high boys occasionally demanded pirates. One girl specified that the chief character be a "baby-sitter." Mystery stories were to be solved successfully, sometimes by a surprise character such as "an old lady."

Younger boys more frequently outlined sea stories. War stories were increasingly numerous among the plots of the older boys. In these the eleventh and twelfth grade boys wanted a description of the effect of war upon the people as well as an account of the action. They showed a desire for development of the theme of "survival" and "self-sufficiency" in war stories and also in stories of exploration.

A more objective questionnaire would have been easier to tabulate and would have given more uniformity of results, but it also would have been less significant in revealing individual differences and range of choices.

Analyzing Reading Interests

Dean C. Andrew and Curtis Easley

From The Clearing House 33:496-501, April 1959. Copyright 1959 by Fairleigh Dickinson University. Reprinted by permission.

The Taylor School District of Arkansas is located in an area in which the International Paper Company owns and operates an industrial plant. In 1956, this company grew interested in helping the local schools improve their educational programs to the end that the schools might better meet the future needs of business and industry by producing better-prepared high-school graduates. . . .

It was decided that the purpose of the 1957-58 improvement program would be the initiation of an evaluation of the extent to which the school was satisfying the need of the youth of its school community to acquire a knowledge of the fundamentals of reading, language arts, social sciences, mathematics, and the natural sciences. . . .

The purpose of the study made by Committee I was to seek answers to the following questions: (1) What are the reading interests of the Taylor public school students? (2) What relationship exists between the cultural factors and the reading skills of these students?

To determine the reading interests of Taylor public school students, the committee (Mrs. Corrine Bryan (chairman), Mrs. Wayne Pickler, Mrs. Lucille Moore, Mrs. Virginia Wells, Mrs. J. V. Franklin, and Mr. Voyne Souter) prepared and administered to all students in grades 7 through 12 a reading-interest check list including books, magazines, and newspapers. Students indicated their first, second, and third choices. The lists were then scored to learn the number of students of the six classes preferring each of the three types of reading.

A second check list was used to determine the number of students in each grade preferring certain types of books. The list included books of autobiography, fiction, history, literature, science, vocational material, comics, and poetry. Students checked first, second, and third choices.

The students were next asked to list the magazines to which their families subscribed or which they bought regularly. They were then asked to submit their preferences for these magazines.

A fourth check list was used to learn the preferences in such newspaper materials as comics, editorials, front-page articles, local news, social news, sports, and advertising. Students indicated their first, second, and third choices.

Table I shows that the students find books and magazines much more interesting than newspapers. Books were checked as first choice by 273 students, magazines were checked as first choice by 276 students, while only 48 students checked newspapers as first choice. Books hold predominant interest for eighth- and ninth-grade students. The reverse is true for twelfth-grade students.

Table II shows a predominant interest in fiction, which was checked as most interesting by 318 students, with comics checked by 97 students, and history by 49 students. Of the four other categories, science was of the highest interest with 24 checks, vocational material next with 16, literature next with 8, while no students checked poetry as first choice. The data indicate that the reading interests tend to follow a developmental pattern, with autobiographies and comics holding greater interest for the younger students and interest in history and fiction increasing as students advance in age. Interest in comics tends to be high for students at all age levels.

Table III indicates that the interest of Taylor students in magazines tends to center around pictorial, sports, fiction, and human-interest magazines. Interest in these magazines appears to be fairly constant from grades 7 through 12, while interest in teen-age, radio, TV, and movie magazines, and in magazines of sensational content follows a developmental age pattern. Very little interest is manifested in

Table I

Reading Interests of Taylor Junior- and Senior-High-School Students in Books, Magazines, and Newspapers

Type of Reading Material	7th 1	7th 2	7th 3	8th 1	8th 2	8th 3	9th 1	9th 2	9th 3	10th 1	10th 2	10th 3	11th 1	11th 2	11th 3	12th 1	12th 2	12th 3
Books	43	28	28	54	25	20	67	4	28	40	28	36	44	20	36	25	39	35
Magazines	57	28	14	38	33	29	28	63	8	48	36	12	48	36	16	57	22	22
Newspapers		44	58	8	40	50	4	33	63	12	36	48	8	44	48	16	39	43

Table II
Types of Books Most Interesting to Taylor Students

Grade

Type of Book	7th 1	7th 2	7th 3	8th 1	8th 2	8th 3	9th 1	9th 2	9th 3	10th 1	10th 2	10th 3	11th 1	11th 2	11th 3	12th 1	12th 2	12th 3
Autobiography	28	18	11	4	33	8	28	16	25	4	24	32	8	20	16	4	39	30
Fiction	28	25	25	45	12	25	56	16	8	68	24		56	12	8	65	17	
History	8	11	14	12	12	20		20	20		16	20	20	20	12	9	9	22
Literature		7	7	4		12			16			20		12	8	4		4
Science	4	7	14	8	20	4	4	4			4	8	8	4	16			13
Vocational		11	11	12		4		4	12	4	4					4	4	13
Comic	32	21	18	12	20	16	8	40	16	24	24	16	4	28	32	17	26	13
Poetry						8								4		4	4	4

Table III

Types of Magazines Most Interesting to Taylor Students

Types of Magazines*	7th 1	7th 2	7th 3	8th 1	8th 2	8th 3	9th 1	9th 2	9th 3	10th 1	10th 2	10th 3	11th 1	11th 2	11th 3	12th 1	12th 2	12th 3
Chiefly Pictorial	8	9	6	13	11	6	4	7	1	7	9	5	2	4	10	5	8	7
Sports	6	3	2	3	3	6	6	6	6	6	2	3	5	9	4	2	4	2
Science	2	2	1		1		2		3	1	1	1		1	1	1	1	2
Teen-Age	7	6	3	3	2	3	1	3	1	4	5	1	3	2	2		1	
Radio, TV, movie		1	1				4	3	1			1	3	2		3	3	5
Fiction and human interest	8	1	6	4	7	6	5	1	8	1		1		2	1	6	2	3
Sensationalism			1	1					1	2	1	1	2	1	6	6	4	

* The magazines were grouped in certain classifications according to the predominant type of material they contained. The classification "Chiefly pictorial" includes such magazines as Look and Life; "Sports" includes such magazines as Field and Stream; "Science" includes such magazines as Popular Mechanics; "Teen age" includes such magazines as Seventeen and Boys' Life; "Radio, TV, and movie" includes such magazines as Radio and TV Mirror; "Fiction and human interest" includes such magazines as Saturday Evening Post and Reader's Digest; "Sensationalism" includes such magazines as True Confessions and Modern Romance.

Ages Twelve to Nineteen 289

Table IV
Types of Newspaper Materials Most Interesting to Taylor Students Grade

Section of Newspaper	7th 1	7th 2	7th 3	8th 1	8th 2	8th 3	9th 1	9th 2	9th 3	10th 1	10th 2	10th 3	11th 1	11th 2	11th 3	12th 1	12th 2	12th 3
Comics	78	21		50	28	8	67	25	4	80	12	4	44	24	12	52	22	17
Editorials			7	8		12			8		4	8	4		8		4	
Front Page	7	26	14	28	25	12	16	33	20	12	24	25	24	24	32	17	13	35
Local News	4		28	4	8	25		16	28	8	8	25		8	24	13	9	17
Society			14		4	12		4	12	20	20	4		12	8	9		
Sports	11	28	25	4	25	25	16	20	20	20	20	32	24	24	12	4	48	17
Advertisements		4	11	4	8	4			4	8	8	4		4		9		13

science magazines.

Table IV indicates that Taylor students' interests in the newspaper are limited primarily to the comics, the front page, and the sports section. While 371 students indicated comics as their first choice, 104 indicated the front page and 59 indicated the sports section as their first choice. Practically no interest is manifested in the editorials, society news, or advertisements. The data concerning interest in newspaper comics seem to corroborate the information relative to interest in comic books, but there seems to be no increasing interest in editorials or front-page materials as students advance in age.

To determine the relationship between certain cultural factors and the reading skills of Taylor students, the committee administered a standardized reading test and several questionnaires on various cultural factors. Through use of the scores on the reading test and the data compiled from the questionnaires involving cultural factors, the committee was able to draw certain conclusions about the relationship between reading skills and the cultural background of students.

Table V shows that the majority of the students scoring in the upper two quartiles on the reading test came from homes owned by their parents and that these homes were equipped with telephones and Deepfreezes. Table V shows that fewer students scoring in the two lower quartiles came from homes equipped with telephones, but the same relationship does not seem to hold in a comparison of reading test scores with Deep-freezes and home ownership. The data suggest that the relationship between cultural factors mentioned in Table V and reading achievement falls in the following rank order of importance: (1) telephones in home, (2) Deepfreezes in home, (3) home ownership.

Table VI shows that the number of people sleeping in the room with the student has little relationship to the student's reading achievement. The large majority of the students occupy bedrooms to themselves or with only one other person.

While an equal number of students scoring in the lower and higher quartiles have parents belonging to two

Ages Twelve to Nineteen

Table V
Telephones, Deepfreeze, and Home Ownership of Parents
and Reading Achievement of Students

Economic Factor

Reading Quartile	Telephone Yes	Telephone No	Deepfreeze Yes	Deepfreeze No	Home Ownership Yes	Home Ownership No
75-99	17	5	16	6	17	5
50-74	22	17	23	15	28	10
25-49	14	24	16	19	26	11
0-24	20	35	28	26	39	17

Table VI
Sleeping Conditions of the Students, Number of
Organizations to Which Parents of Students Belong,
and Reading Achievement of Students

Reading Quartile	Number of People Sleeping in Room With Student 0	1	2	3	4+	Number of Organizations to Which Parents Belong 0	1	2	3	4+
75-99	6	10	5	1	0	0	2	6	7	7
50-74	16	14	4	1	1	3	6	13	7	7
25-49	15	12	9	0	2	5	7	13	10	2
0-24	18	20	12	0	0	13	18	17	6	0

or more organizations, there are many more students scoring in the lower quartiles whose parents belong to only one or to no organization.

Table VII reflects a distinct relationship between the number of books in the home and the reading achievement of the students. Of the students scoring in the lower quartiles on the reading test, 42 had fewer than 25 books in the home, while only 19 students scoring in the upper quartiles had that few books in the home. Twenty-five students in the upper quartiles and 23 students in the lower quartiles had 50 or more books in the home. The data here, as in Tables V and VI, show that approximately 60 per cent of all the students involved in the investigation scored below average on the reading test.

The number of magazines regularly subscribed to appears to influence the students' reading achievement. Twenty-three students who scored in the upper quartiles had four or more magazines in the home, while only 15 students who scored in the lower quartiles had four or more magazines in the home. One rather startling discovery is that 58 students had only one or no magazines in the home (Table VIII).

Table VII
Number of Books in the Homes and Reading Achievement of the Students

Number of Books

Reading Quartile	0-9	10-24	25-49	50-74	100 or More
75-99	0	3	4	4	11
50-74	3	13	11	6	4
25-49	4	13	9	4	7
0-24	14	13	15	8	4

Ages Twelve to Nineteen

Table VIII
Number of Magazines in the Homes and Reading
Achievement of the Students

Number of Magazines

Reading Quartile	0-1	2-3	4-5	6-7	9 or More
75-99	4	6	6	4	2
50-74	10	16	11	0	0
25-49	12	20	6	0	0
0-24	32	13	8	1	0

Conclusions

The findings from the study suggest the following tentative conclusions:

1. While Taylor students' reading interests tend to follow a developmental pattern, the reading interests do not progress to the level normally expected of senior-high-school students.

2. The breadth of reading interest of Taylor students is somewhat limited regardless of whether they read books, magazines, or newspapers.

3. Taylor students do not tend to keep abreast of current events and developments. (Little reading interest is manifested in such materials as newspaper editorials, science magazines, and other materials that would tend to keep one up to date.)

4. This study verifies findings of other studies that there is a distinct relationship between certain cultural factors and reading achievement. The home environment appears to be a very significant factor in the cultural development and educational achievement of students.

5. The scores made by Taylor students on a standardized reading test reveal that the reading-achievement level of Taylor students is below the average.

Recommendations

The conclusions suggest the following recommendations:

1. An attempt should be made to improve the reading skills of Taylor students at all educational levels by improving the quality and increasing the breadth of their reading.

2. Considerable attention should be given to creating an interest or increasing the currently existing interest of students in such reading fields as current events, science, and literature. The use of current-event magazines, as well as special-interest clubs, book reports, term reports, and librarian visitations may facilitate the achievement of this goal.

3. A community program should be launched to acquaint parents with the value of an abundant supply of good reading material in the home. Such groups as the P.T.A., civic clubs, farm groups, and library personnel may be helpful in implementing a program for achieving this goal.

4. Emphasis should be placed on the reading interests and skills of Taylor students. Achievement of the school goal is possible only through continued evaluation and subsequent placement of students in appropriate reading groups.

A Study in Adolescent Reading

Joan W. Butler

From the Library Association Record 58:387-9, October 1956. Reprinted by permission.

As part of their studies on adolescent reading at two courses on library work with young people held at the Department of Librarianship, North Western Polytechnic, in 1954 and 1956, students were asked the discuss the books they themselves had read and enjoyed during their adolescence (roughly between the ages of 13 and 18). Every student in both courses contributed to the discussions which demonstrated, not surprisingly, that there is much common ground in adolescent reading, however different the home, school or geographical background. The accessibility of books and the approach to reading, however, did show some startling differences between the two groups.

The 26 students in the 1954 group covered a very wide age range and an equally wide range of experience and ability. There were three older and more mature students, one an American with much experience in work with young people, and two graduates, one from overseas and the other a teacher. The remaining students were drawn from all over the British Isles, including one from N. Ireland, and the majority were between the ages of 20 and 25. The 21 students this year included a Jordanian, three graduate librarians and one teacher; these students, too, were drawn from all parts of the country, Scotland and Wales being represented this year but not N. Ireland; again, the majority were between the ages of 20 and 25, although the age range of the whole group was less wide and students were much closer together in ability than the students at the earlier course. There was no one as mature and experienced as the older students of 1954, nor were there any as limited in their power of written expression as the younger students at that first course.

It must, of course, be realized that neither group of students could be regarded as having been in any way "typical" adolescents, if such there be. They were librarians, partly, at least, because they enjoyed reading, and though there was perhaps only one genuinely omnivorous reader in the two groups, they all read and enjoyed books and this fact alone rendered them unusual amongst their contemporaries according to their own evidence. Both groups included students who said they had done very little reading during their adolescence.

Books read by students in both groups included such titles as Three Men in a Boat, Daddy Long-Legs, Les Miserables, Tell England! and The Hill: authors mentioned included Doyle, Dumas, Buchan, A.E.W. Mason, L. M. Montgomery, Farnol, Wren, O. Douglas, Broster, Orczy and Arnold Bennett ("Five towns" series, but not Old Wives' Tale). Books by authors such as the Brontës, Jane Austen, Hardy and George Eliot, read for the English syllabus, were re-read and explored further for enjoyment by students in both groups. Thackeray, Scott and Dickens were read and enjoyed at home and school by many students in the first group, but the first author was not mentioned at all by the second group, Scott by only one Scottish student, and Dickens much less frequently than in the first group. Joan Grant and Elizabeth Goudge were mentioned by the second group, but not by the first, and one or two students in the second group said that they had read and enjoyed E. M. Forster, Graham Greene and Aldous Huxley, following the recommendation of these authors by teachers. One student in this group also mentioned disliking the works of Somerset Maugham during her adolescence and there appeared to be general agreement with this. Poetry, plays, ballet, travel, biography, and essays were mentioned by several students in both groups; politics, history and the lives of naturalists by the men in the two groups and women aviators, Octavia Hill, Scott and Antarctic explorers by the women. Books read in adolescence which were mentioned as vivid experiences were Room of One's Own in the first group, and Neville Cardus's Autobiography in the second. Books which had been read and re-read by students in the second group in their adolescence included Broster's Mr. Rowl, Hewlett's The Forest Lovers and Uttley's Traveller in Time; this question of the constant re-reading of a favourite book was not mentioned by the first group. Students in both groups read junior fiction as well as adult books throughout their adolescence. It will be seen that the reading of the two groups covered much the same ground; but their approach to books and their sources of supply showed some considerable differences.

Few students in the first group had made use of the public library until fairly late in adolescence, school libraries had not been extensive, but most of them had had books at home and the majority felt that their enjoyment of the older classics had arisen because of this early introduction to them. Only two of the second group mentioned books in the home as having any influence on their reading taste. The 1954 students were emphatic in their denial that other people's recommendations had influenced their reading to any great extent saying that if, following a recommendation, they read and enjoyed a specific title, they seldom attempted to obtain other books by the same author.

The 1956 students had had fewer books in the home, better school libraries and earlier access to public libraries, and almost without exception, they had relied for their reading on the recommendations of older brothers or sisters, teachers or contemporaries (at sixth form and university level only). Many students had been furnished with lists of "Required or recommended reading" at school and had read from these. Recommended authors, if enjoyed, had been conscientiously "read through." The only student who had not been provided with such a guide to reading, had few books at home and a poor school library, admitted to complete bewilderment when faced with a wide range of books at the public library after she left school. In this group, many students stated that they had read comparatively little during their adolescence because of the demands of their school work. One student, a graduate, stated definitely that she had not read for pleasure alone since the age of 13, as all her reading since then had been connected with the English syllabus for various examinations. The earlier group had not mentioned homework as a deterrent to reading but the later group had evidently found this burden heavy.

The 1954 students agreed that their reading taste had been conditioned by the books available. The range of these books had been, in most cases, limited, but within that range their explorations were unguided. The 1956 students had had access to an unlimited range of books but they accepted, and indeed sought, guidance in exploring that range. In any event, both groups of students had read much the same type of book.

It can be argued that the type of book which is provided for, recommended to, and read by, adolescents is perpetuated from generation to generation by these very recommendations. Nevertheless, it is an undoubted fact that books of this type--romantic, active, colourful, adventurous--are enjoyed by adolescent boys and girls from generation to generation. Their preference for books of this type was clearly demonstrated by the students in their remembered reaction against Maugham's urbane cynicism and realism, their tepid approval of such widely diverse writers as Huxley, Forster and Graham Greene, whose appeal had been intellectual only, contrasted with the warm emotional response, often of the same students, to the books re-read such as Mr. Rowl and The Forest Lovers.

In the light of the evidence about adolescent reading supplied by themselves, the 1956 students were asked to suggest what it was that young people sought in books during these years. They felt these requirements were: (a) a means of escape when unhappy; (b) excitement; (c) a hothouse and sentimentalized emotion; (d) picturesqueness; (e) genuine heroism; and (f) something to sharpen the mind.

Obviously, these findings have very little scientific or statistical basis: the discussions were open and informal; students may possibly have influenced one another, and the books discussed were read a decade or so ago. Nevertheless, I do feel that the students' own findings are basically true and are not confined to a small minority of highly literate young people.

Firstly, then, what significance has such an enquiry for us as librarians? Two main points seem to me to emerge. The 1954 enquiry provided evidence of the overwhelming importance of book selection for any limited range of books, since the reading tastes of these students had been conditioned entirely, for life in some cases, by the books made available to them. The 1956 enquiry, on the other hand, provides important evidence of the necessity of having in our schools and libraries an adequate number of adults, able and willing to provide some form of personal guidance to young people in their own book selection. Given the freedom of a large library, all, except those who have moved freely in the world of books from infancy, need some kind of help.

If we are to have specially selected collections of books for adolescents, then the librarians or teachers selecting those books must be imaginative enough not to deny young people the experience of reading books of the status of Room of One's Own or Neville Cardus's Autobiography. If we are to give our young people the freedom of the adult library, we must see to it that we have reader's advisers who have read widely enough and know young people well enough to be capable of the same feat of imaginative recommendation.

Finally, has this enquiry anything to offer to the wider world of "communications" outside the immediate purview of librarianship? I believe it has. If the truth of the students' findings about the reading needs of adolescence is admitted, it will be seen that points (a) to (d) deal with the markedly immature emotional needs of adolescence. Satisfaction for these is sought by the literate in books of the type discussed, by the illiterate or semi-literate referred to in such studies as Pearl Jephcott's Some Young People or Brian Reed's 80,000 Adolescents, in novelettes, cheap magazines, sensational newspapers and horror comics.

The moral and mental needs of adolescence are, I am persuaded, as valid for the less fortunate many as they are for the fortunate few. The emotions for the many are dulled, deadened or pole-axed by sensationalism and so there is rather less chance for them than there is for those from a richer cultural background to satisfy those needs. The generous desire to worship at the shrine of some worthy hero and the development of adult mental powers are as typical of youth and as widespread amongst all classes as are the romantic emotional urges so ruthlessly exploited by the commercial world, and these needs must be recognized and satisfied if we are to have a healthy adult population.

It is doubtful whether any of those agencies which tell the world of the world--film, television, radio, book, magazine, newspaper--provide enough tales of genuine heroism for hero-worshipping youth, not because there is a dearth of such everyday heroes, but because they are unsensational, do not advertise themselves and require rather more finding than the daring sunbather or the latest jewel-robbery. That young people correspond to tales of heroism is evidenced by the popularity of the Everest and Scott of the Antarctic films, the demand for books about Dr. Schweitzer following television programmes, the popularity of the Kon-tiki; these from all sections of the population. It should not be beyond the wit of writers, journalists, speakers and film directors to tell the tales of such modern heroes in those simple epic terms which will meet the emotional, moral and mental needs of youth and give to the many the enriching experience given to those two students for whom a new world opened when they read Virginia Woolf and Neville Cardus.

What Young People Want to Know About Themselves

Evelyn Millis Duvall

Summary of a talk given by Dr. Duvall at the "Youth Today" program sponsored by AYPL during the Miami Conference. From Top of the News 13:39, December 1956. Reprinted by permission.

> Today's young people ask many questions. Dr. Duvall collected twenty-five thousand of them as the basis for her books Facts of Life and Love for Teen-Agers and Family Living, a high-school text. Here briefly are the main areas of teen-age concern which she has described.

"How can you tell when you are really in love?" is a question that both boys and girls ask Dr. Duvall in ever-increasing numbers today. Now when so many young people are getting married right out of high school, and often while they are still in school, knowing when you are really and truly in love can be pretty important. The popular songs aren't much help. Yet, there is enough known about the differences between infatuation and the kind of love that lasts to give youth sound guidance.

Becoming a more attractive, likeable person is of course a major teen-age concern. The two questions which recurred most frequently in the Facts of Life and Love analysis were: "How do you get a date?" and "What do you do with a date when you get it?" There seems, too, to be more parental disapproval of dates and dating now than in the past two generations.

Sex, petting, courtship, marriage, and engagement are the five subjects which college freshmen find most difficult to discuss with their fathers and mothers. A nationwide study indicates that many can't discuss petting and sex at all with their parents, and more than half never talk over life's meaning and purpose with their parents. An even greater number never discuss sex education with them. Although the popular press is full of stories and references to sex, birth, babies, and bizarre pathological detail, simple, straightforward explanations of the facts of life are rarely available to youth in wholesome presentation. The librarian who honestly, wholesomely, and humbly attempts to help youth find answers to life's biggest questions finds parents, teachers, and communities grateful. Oncoming generations are helped to find the happiness that is possible for them, and to develop the strengths needed to take today's stresses and strains. These are the rewards that make up even for the books that aren't returned.

Some Results of a
Twelve-Year Study of Children's Reading Interests

George W. Norvell

From the English Journal 35:531-6, December 1946. Reprinted with the permission of the National Council of Teachers of English and George W. Norvell.

It is widely recognized that secondary-school children read below the standard justifiably to be expected for their ages and intelligence. Even more disconcerting, vast numbers of them fail to turn voluntarily to reading as a means of information and recreation. Faced squarely with the charge, we cannot deny that our schools in general and English teachers in particular have failed to attain a major objective of the nation's schools: to lead every normal child to a permanent reading habit based on a love of reading.

There is, I believe, a simple solution for the problem presented, simple but not easy: Make reading genuinely attractive to our students.

In the past, two mutually opposing principles have governed the assembling of classroom reading materials. In accord with the one, adults chose, from classic and contemporary literature, titles which they were convinced children should know. The resulting offerings, as English teachers know all too well, failed to satisfy pupils. Under the second plan of selection, which has had wide vogue, the supposed popularity with children of lightweight and ephemeral materials constituted the criterion. This time neither teachers nor pupils approved the results, for young people are seriously concerned with life's problems, their problems, and are not long content with the trivial.

A third plan is proposed. Discontinue reliance upon "expert" opinion, which has proved inadequate. For reading in common choose only selections known to be enjoyed by children through sufficient data coming directly from children. From the titles which children themselves endorse, exclude the trashy. To summarize: For reading in common choose only selections which stand where the lines of student and teacher approval converge.

In this discussion I wish to offer for consideration suggestions based on a twelve-year study of children's reading interests. I shall refrain from extensive detail respecting the statistical treatment given the collected data, first, because teachers are principally interested in practical applications rather than in statistical formulas and, second, because the study, fully documented, will be reported in book form, I hope, within the next year. A few of the basic facts seem in order, however.

More than 50,000 pupils and 625 teachers in all types of communities in New York State participated in the study. Tabulation of 1,590,000 reports on literary selections has been made according to the pupil's grade in school, sex, and level of intelligence.

In the belief that information is needed as to the level of interest that various literary materials have for children under actual classroom conditions, the procedure provided that pupils report on selections which had been read before the study was undertaken. To secure so far as possible uninhibited and honest responses from children, the following was included in the instructions:

> Announce to the pupils that we desire the frank opinion of each pupil without reference to what any other pupil thinks. This information will make it possible for recommended lists to be prepared which will contain reading materials genuinely interesting to the pupils who are to use them. <u>Be careful to impress upon pupils the importance of giving their own candid opinions. Also please see that pupils do not consult about their replies.</u>

The classroom blank provided columns that permitted the pupil by checking to indicate whether a listed selection was "very interesting," "fairly interesting," or "uninteresting."

The complete data, when published, will provide information concerning seventeen hundred literary selections commonly used for study in secondary schools and will suggest answers to such questions as these:

1. How important relatively, in influencing pupils' choices of reading materials are the following: age, sex, intelligence?

2. To what extent do various interest factors influence boys' and girls' choices?

3. Do boys enjoy poetry as much as girls?

4. How do the various literary types rank in children's interests?

Let us consider first the influence of increasing age or maturity on children's reading interests. Our data show clearly that much literary material being used in our schools is too mature, too subtle, too erudite to permit its enjoyment by the majority of secondary-school pupils. This error in the English field has been recognized for decades by certain leaders in the teaching profession. Unfortunately, reform has come slowly. Yet progress has been made. The data of the current study show that many selections still widely used should be abandoned and that others should be shifted to a more suitable grade level. For example, Shakespeare's As You Like It, perhaps the most widely used play in America's junior high schools, is so seriously disliked by boys as to make its general use indefensible. There are Shakespearean plays well liked by both boys and girls. Let us use them and use them at the right stage of the student's intellectual growth.

It appears advisable to discuss together, since they are closely related, (a) the differences in boys' and girls' choices of reading materials and (b) the factors affecting reading interests. Some factors of reading interest produce favorable reactions in both boys and girls; some produce favorable reactions in boys only; some produce favorable reactions in girls only; while some factors produce unfavorable reactions in both. Both sexes react favorably to adventure; humorous poems, stories, and essays (except where the humor is of the subtle type); poems and stories of patriotism; stories of mystery, of games, and of animals. Boys are more favorably inclined than are girls to strenuous adventure, including war, to stories of wild animals, to science, and to speeches. Girls react very favorably to romantic love, to sentiment in general, and to poems and stories of home and family life. Neither boys nor girls like subtle humor; descriptive prose and verse; letters; reflective, didactic, philosophical, or nature poems (though girls are more tolerant of them than boys). Of course, there are exceptions to these rules, but as general guides they can be very helpful.

Unquestionably, teachers who are genuinely concerned with leading children to a love of literature would not intentionally force upon them any large proportion of materials which are definitely disliked on the basis of a composite of boys' and girls' reactions. It might be argued that a few illustrative examples of disliked types should be offered to broaden children's acquaintance with literary forms and techniques. In any case, such materials should be restricted, I believe you will agree, to less than 10 percent of the total. Granting this, what must be our reaction to the actual teaching situation?

In common practice a high percentage of the titles provided for class study are in groupings definitely obnoxious to secondary-school students. By actual investigation and tabulation such materials constitute more than 50 percent of the titles commonly provided for study in the classroom. Is there not here a vital challenge to teachers and to the makers of courses of study in literature?

To the question, "Are there boys' books and girls' books?" the answer is clear. There are. The most powerful single influence in determining children's choices of reading materials in the high school is sex. During the primary- and elementary-school periods increasing maturity rivals sex as a determinant of what children choose to read. But even as low as the seventh grade children's reading tastes show a marked tendency to approximate the tastes of adults. This trend continues throughout the secondary-school period, so that by the time young people leave high school their reading preferences are substantially the ones they will follow through later life. By contrast, the potency of sex in governing reading interests reaches a high mark during the junior high school period and retains that power with little diminution to high-school graduation and beyond.

Almost invariably, discussions of reading interests deal with poetry. Is poetry disliked? Do girls like poetry better than boys? What types of poetry are satisfactory instructional material?

It will probably be no surprise to you that our study of several hundred poems shows that, in comparison with novels, short stories, biographies, and plays, poetry as a whole is not well liked. On the other hand, there are many individual poems that rank high. With many exceptions, we may generalize that narrative poems, patriotic poems, and poems of obvious humor are liked; poems of nature, sentiment, reflection, religion, philosophy, and didacticism rank low.

What accounts for this low estate of poetry among children? Is it primarily word choice, meter, rhyme, compression or other devices that distinguish poetry from prose? No doubt certain poetic usages, such as unusual word order and exotic or subtle vocabulary, occasionally interfere with pupils' understanding of a poem's meaning. Yet an examination of well-liked as well as disliked poems reveals, I believe, that, basically, not form but content is the touchstone of popularity. The vast majority of poems deal with themes and ideas which children would reject as decisively if offered to them in prose. Youth demands life in action; age is often content with sentiment in rose leaves, with mood, dreams, reflection, didacticism, and philosophy. Poems that present life dramatically or with humor rival in popularity with children prose selections that do the same. Examples: "Old Ironsides," by Holmes; "O Captain, My Captain," by Whitman; "The Messages," by Gibson; "It's a Queer Time," by Graves; "The Twins," by Leigh; and "The Highwayman," by Noyes.

As to poetry's standing with boys and with girls, the data speak decisively. Girls rate it markedly higher, in fact some eight percentage points higher, as Table I shows.

Of important practical significance is the question as to whether teaching materials in literature as now chosen are equally favored by boys and by girls. The data afforded by this study point unmistakably to the fact that they are not.

Table I

Literary Types in Order of Preference

Literary Type	No. of Selections	Per Cent Liking Boys	Per Cent Liking Girls	Per Cent Liking Average	Spread-Points	No. Better Liked by Boys	No. Better Liked by Girls	Per Cent Better Liked by Boys	Per Cent Better Liked by Girls
Novel	47	78.4	79.6	79.0	1.2	22	25	46.8	53.2
Play	62	71.3	77.2	74.3	5.9	13	49	21.0	79.0
Short Story	219	72.5	73.8	73.2	1.3	111	108	50.7	49.3
Biography	50	67.7	69.2	68.5	1.5	23	27	42.0	58.0
Essay	81	63.1	66.3	64.7	3.2	21	60	25.9	74.1
Poem	466	60.7	68.3	64.5	7.6	88	377*	18.9	81.1
Letter	12	60.6	64.9	62.8	4.3	2	10	16.7	83.3
Speech	13	63.9	59.7	61.8	4.2	11	2	84.6	15.4
Total	950	65.6	70.5	68.1	4.9	291	658	30.7	69.3

* One poem equally liked by boys and girls.

Ages Twelve to Nineteen

Two out of every three selections commonly used in the classroom are better liked by girls than by boys. This fact may well have much to do with the unfavorable attitude taken by many boys toward school in general and toward the English class in particular. Surely, in common fairness, this situation must be righted.

What is the relative standing in children's interest of the major literary types? A tentative answer is afforded by our data. The ranking for each type was found by averaging the scores for the various titles of that type; for example, the popularity of the novel as a type was found by averaging the interest scores for 47 novels. It seems reasonable to believe that 47 novels, 62 plays, and 81 essays provide a basis for assessing the relative popularity of these literary types. The numbers of letters and speeches are small, comparatively, and render conclusions as to these types less dependable than for the other six. The table shows the novel in top position, followed in rank-order by the play, the short story, biography, the essay, poetry, the letter, and, last, the speech.

The standings of the literary types with boys and with girls are given, in addition to the composite ratings. The data show that, judged by the literary materials commonly used in our schools, girls enjoy seven of the eight literary types better than do boys. The only type better liked by boys is the speech, though the spread between the rankings of boys and of girls is not great in the novel, the short story, and biography. Disregarding the groupings by type, we find that, of the 950 selections used in this part of the study, girls like 69.3 percent of them better than do boys.

It may be of interest to note the relative popularity rankings of a number of literary selections, extending from a high mark of 95 percent to a low of 36 percent. On this tabulation, the critical point dividing selections recommended for study in common from those to be reserved for individual reading is 70 percent. This point was decided upon tentatively when New York State's course of study in English was prepared. In actual practice it has not appeared too high. Obviously, the teacher using the study's findings can readily shift the standard, since the report will provide for each of the 1,700 selections interest scores for both boys and girls separately, in addition to a composite rating. May I add that, on the basis of the more extensive data now available, it seems that a standard even higher might well be practicable?

Chart I shows graphically the extreme spread of interest of the literary materials commonly assigned for class study in the junior-senior high school. This range from a high of 95 to a low of 36 is startling. And let us not complacently assume that the procedures of the classroom will suffice to supplant the boredom and even disgust produced by the majority of our offerings. Not even the skill of the superior teacher suffices for that miracle. The study indicates that educators sometimes act as though they were not dealing with human beings--with boys and girls--but with mythical, sexless robots whose tastes, inclinations, and interests can be assumed to be or must be made to be identical with those of the teacher. The budget of unattractive modern writings and generation-to-generation classics now constituting the major part of our reading program is kept going only by a rigorous, zealously pursued system of forcible feeding.

If all the superior literary materials were disliked and if only the trashy and ephemeral were enjoyed by children, the problem would be different. There is, however, an ample supply of literature approved by critics which is also approved by children. At the present time there are at least eight to ten thousand selections widely used for class study in the nation's secondary schools. No particular school or teacher can introduce the student to more than a fraction of that list during the six-year high-school period. Why not, then, winnow the titles which meet both standards for use in the classroom and relegate the selections that are popular only with a few to supplementary, individually chosen reading? Why should we insist on As You Like It or Shakespeare's sonnets when Macbeth, Hamlet, and other well-liked plays are available? Why Whitman's rejected "Song of Myself" when there is "O Captain! My Captain!"? Why "Comus" when there is Milton's "On His Blindness"; "The Bunker Hill Address" when there is "The Gettysburg Address"; The Rising of the Moon when we might choose Emperor Jones?

The question may be asked, "What are the implications of this study for classroom practice?" If the results of the current study are dependable (the data for judging

Ages Twelve to Nineteen

Chart I

Scale of Reading Interest- Junior and Senior High School

Per Cent

95 Tom Sawyer (Twain)
    Night of the Storm (Gale)
    Call of the Wild (London)
    "The Gettysburg Address" (Lincoln)
    Emperor Jones (O'Neill)
    "O Captain! My Captain!" (Whitman)
    "The Highwayman" (Noyes)
    Treasure Island (Stevenson)
    "The Barefoot Boy" (Whittier)
    "Mary White" (White)
    "Three Questions" (Tolstoy)
    "A Dissertation upon Roast Pig" (Lamb)
    Macbeth (Shakespeare)
    "The Man with the Hoe" (Markham)
    "On His Blindness" (Milton)

70 "Crossing the Bar" (Tennyson); "Birches" (Frost);
    "My Native Land" (Scott)

    "Passing of Arthur" (Tennyson)
    The Rise of Silas Lapham (Howells)
    "On Getting up on Cold Mornings" (Hunt)
    Julius Caesar (Shakespeare)
    The Sketch Book (Irving)
    The Rising of the Moon (Gregory)
    "Sounds" (Thoreau)
    "She Was a Phantom of Delight" (Wordsworth)
    "Sir Roger de Coverley at the Theatre" (Addison)
    As You Like It (Shakespeare)
    "Compensation" (Emerson)
    The Lady of the Lake (Scott)
    "Bunker Hill Address" (Webster)
    Sonnets (Shakespeare)
    "Comus" (Milton)
    "Old China" (Lamb)
    "Will o' the Mill" (Stevenson)
    Autocrat at the Breakfast Table (Holmes)
    "Rules for the Road" (Markham)
    "On Conciliation" (Burke)

Chart I (cont'd)

Per Cent

	Anglo-Saxon Chronicle
	"Song of Myself" (Whitman)
36	"The Land o' the Leal" (Nairne)

will be published), the following appear to be suggested:

1. That for assignment for study in common only selections be used that (a) meet the approval of both critics and teachers and (b) are genuinely enjoyed by children.

2. That, in addition to the study in common, there be much wide reading through which young people may enjoy the materials which appeal to them individually.

3. That teachers and course-of-study makers cease to choose classroom reading materials in accord with their own preferences and place the student first always.

4. That three-fourths of the selections in our current program be replaced with selections of equally high merit that children indorse.

5. That the new program give the boy, the forgotten boy, a break through the choice of selections which are as popular with him as they are with the girl.

6. That, to increase reading skill, promote the reading habit, and produce a generation of book-lovers, there is no other factor so powerful as interest.

What Does Johnny Read?

Lois B. Hall and William N. Rairigh

From Maryland Libraries 31:6-8, Fall 1964. Reprinted by permission.

Comic books, television and other forms of instant culture notwithstanding, evidence is mounting that not only can Johnny read, but what he chooses to read puts many adults to shame, both in depth and for catholicity.

A shred of evidence bearing out this fact was gleaned from an experiment conducted on the Eastern Shore. The Wye Institute, recently established to assist in the educational, economic and cultural development of the Eastern Shore, presented a collection of paper books to a ninth grade student in each of the Shore's 38 high schools. The 11 boys and 28 girls were nominated by their respective principals on the basis of their potential for future academic work and leadership in school and community activities.

The Book Awards were established experimentally to stimulate interest in reading of good books by young people, to recognize promising students and encourage them to deepen their education and broaden their intellectual interests, and to provide the student with the nucleus of a personal library. The Institute also hoped that the project would emphasize to young people, as well as school and public librarians, that a wealth of worthwhile reading--educational, informational and recreational--appealing to them is available in paper books at low cost.

To launch the Awards project the Institute convened a committee, comprised of three Eastern Shore school librarians and two public librarians with Sara Siebert, Coordinator of Work With Young Adults, Enoch Pratt Free Library, as chairman and Mae Graham, Supervisor, School and Children's Libraries, Maryland Division of Library Extension, as consultant. Other committee members, in addition to the authors, were Mrs. Elizabeth H. Baker, Talbot County Free Library; Mrs. Shirley McCloud, Kennard High School, Centreville; and Mrs. Rachel Weedman, Sudlersville High School. The committee compiled a classified list of 320 titles costing, except in a very few instances, less than one dollar. The only restriction placed on the student's choice of 40 titles was the requirement that he must select at least two from each of the ten categories.

Selections fell into the pattern as indicated in the table appearing on the following page.

Any effort to draw a conclusion regarding young adult reading patterns from such a small sampling would be preposterous; however there are some interesting facets when these results are compared with some other surveys.

A recent survey of 691 public, Catholic and private schools conducted throughout the country by Educational Testing Service shows that while students are being instructed in the "new math," and in laboratories may be performing experiments involving radio-active isotopes, they are still being assigned the classics in English classes; in fact, reading lists in the public schools surveyed reveal that the most universally assigned reading consists of Macbeth, which is on 90 percent of the lists, Julius Caesar 77, Silas Marner 76, Our Town 46, Great Expectations 39, Hamlet 33, Red Badge of Courage 33, Tale of Two Cities 33, and The Scarlet Letter 32.

Seventeen of the Eastern Shore students selected Shakespeare's Four Great Tragedies (Hamlet, Julius Caesar, Macbeth, Romeo and Juliet); 12 chose his Great Comedies (As You Like It, Midsummer's Night Dream, Tempest, Twelfth Night) and Hawthorne's Scarlet Letter; 10 picked Three Plays by Wilder (Our Town, Skin of Our Teeth, The Matchmaker); six wanted A Tale of Two Cities; and three The Red Badge of Courage. Other titles which were chosen by ten or more young adults from Categories II, IV and VI (Fiction) were Fifty Great Short Stories, Fifty Great Poets, Three Comedies of American Life (Life With Father, I Remember Mama, You Can't Take it With You), Tales and Poems of Poe. Gone With the Wind topped all of these three classes, while Lord of the Flies, Canterbury Tales, Pocket Book of Robert Frost's Poems, Inherit the Wind, and Mutiny on the Bounty only narrowly missed receiving "top ten" distinction. Only two titles were not selected by at least one: they are Bret Harte's Outcasts of Poker Flat and The Adventures of Huckleberry Finn (Tom Sawyer had only one friend).

Category		# Titles in Category	#Titles Chosen	Total# Books Chosen	Chosen by 10+
I.	Facts in Hand (Home Reference)	20	20	123	4
II.	Classics: Old and New	42	40	180	2
III.	Lively Arts (Art and Music)	33	19	93	1
VI.	Lively Beat (Poetry and Plays)	26	26	157	6
V.	Laughing Stock (Humor)	12	12	96	4
IV.	History: Fact	31	28	138	2
	Fiction	18	18	88	1
VII.	Inside USA	30	29	137	3
VIII.	International Scene	20	18	90	3
IX.	What is Important? (On Building a Philosophy of Life)	22	19	101	3
X.	Scientific Mind in Fact and Fiction	66	57	222	4
		320	286	1425	33

It appears that although the most popular choices of the classics on the Eastern Shore reflect classroom familiarity, such authors as Cather, Hemingway, Hudson, Orwell, Remarque, Hansbury, George Bernard Shaw, Costain, Fast, A. B. Guthrie, Renault, Richter and Robert L. Taylor elicited substantial followings.

Speaking of the pre-college reader, at a meeting during the St. Louis Conference of the American Library Association, Dr. G. Robert Carlsen reported on a series of polls he had conducted. He found that teen-agers are interested in books dealing with: the search for the meaning of life, the consequences of injustice in our world, the bizarre, the off-beat, the highly symbolic, and the story that moves adolescents toward adulthood. He further contended that their usual reading pattern progresses from teen-age novels, to popular novels, to writers with "messages," and finally to the classics; at this stage they read for content, not for technique and style.

Even on the limited basis of the books selected by these 38 ninth grade students, Dr. Carlsen's observations appear to have much validity. The group showed a strong interest in categories VII, VIII, and IX. The front runners in "Inside USA" were To Kill a Mockingbird, 14; Black Like Me, 12; The Ugly American, 11; with Up from Slavery and Making of the President, 1960 scoring near misses. Top honors in the "International Scene" went to Exodus, 14; I Am Fifteen and Don't Want to Die, and Inside Europe Today, both with 10; but Cry the Beloved Country and Rise and Fall of the Third Reich were close. President Kennedy's Profiles in Courage listed in Category IX was the selection of 16 of the students, followed by Diary of a Young Girl, 12; and The Night They Burned the Mountain, 10. Two novels, The Pearl and The Citadel, were runners-up.

"The Scientific Mind In Fact and Fiction" was the most popular class, with 222 volumes selected from the 66 available titles covering the scientific gamut. Top choices here were The Science Book of the Human Body, 14; A Dictionary of Science, 13; We Seven, 11; and The Sea Around Us, 10. Although the "Lively Arts" lacked the general popular appeal of other categories the most popular book of all the 320 comprising the list was one of its entries-- American Folk Tales and Songs by Richard Chase; it was the only title selected by a majority (20) of the Book Award recipients.

In presenting the Book Awards, Wye Institute hoped that the 38 students would share their libraries with their parents, neighbors, teachers and fellow students. It was not willing, however, for these personal collections to be the only source where these editions would be available. The Institute is now implementing the experimental Awards project by offering each county library and the two state colleges a collection comprised of each of the 320 titles.

Cynics may scoff that Johnny won't read what he has selected, but any school librarian or any public librarian serving a school clientele would bet even-money that Johnny will not only read these but anything else which will answer his "whys" about life and the world in which he lives.

Anybody Got a Good Book?

Thomas L. Kilpatrick

From Illinois Libraries 44:282-4, April 1962. Reprinted by permission.

With, "Hey, ain't cha got any good books in this library?" still echoing from the stacks, and my blood pressure a few points above normal as a result, I shall try, barring interruptions, to explain what a "good book" is to a high school student, and how we manage to meet the demand for reading material at Herrin Township High School.

Whether high school students read more or less now than students did ten, fifteen, or twenty years ago is hard to say. With television a commonplace fixture in every home, automobiles available to a majority of high school students simply for the asking, and the stepped-up pace at which most of us speed through life, one would be inclined to say that the reading activity would suffer at the hands of high school boys and girls. Most librarians will agree, after checking their circulation records, however, that this is a fallacy. Teen-agers are busier nowadays than ever before; yet they find time to read. This can be attributed, I believe, to three factors--the attractiveness of today's reading materials; the availability of books and periodicals made possible through school and public libraries, book stores, and newsstands; and the recent emphasis placed upon academic achievements in our schools.

It is the librarian's duty, then, to anticipate the reading interests of the teenager, to make books and periodicals available that are suited to both his reading and interest levels, and to guide the student in the selection of a good book when he wants to read.

The reading interests of boys and girls can generally be predicted by an experienced librarian. Although there are exceptions, girls generally ask for books with romantic themes. A freshman or sophomore girl may be well pleased with the writings of such ladies as Betty Cavanna, Anne Emery, Rosamond du Jardin, and Maureen Daly. As she matures, however, the girl should be encouraged to try books that offer a greater challenge to her mentality. Such books as the <u>Diary of Anne Frank,</u> <u>White Witch Doctor,</u> and <u>Song of Years</u> often serve as stepping stones to the more difficult <u>Jane Eyre,</u> <u>Scarlet Letter,</u> or <u>My Antonia.</u>

The reading interests of the high school boys are generally more varied than those of the high school girl; therefore, the boy's reading interests are more difficult to predict. While he may want a book about hot rods today, tomorrow he may request a good football story and next week a novel concerning the wonderful world of animals may be the only thing that will please his fancy. The librarian, of course, is expected to know what the boy wants, and must be able to produce it at a moment's notice when the boys asks that all important question, "Have you got any good books?" Just as the girl is encouraged to choose reading materials that will challenge her ability, so the boy should be guided gradually from the Walter Farley and Jackson Scholz books to literature that will stimulate his intellect. <u>A Bell for Adano,</u> <u>My Friend Flicka,</u> <u>Red Badge of Courage,</u> or <u>Kon-Tiki</u> often serve to lead the boy to greater achievements.

Most teenagers are aware of fashion and fad in current literature just as they are aware of the most recent clothing styles, the newest dance craze, and the top ten records on the hit parade. As each year sees hemlines making headlines, the twist replacing the stroll, and Elvis moving over to make room for Fabian, so it sees, also, a new book come into extreme demand, run its course, then fall by the wayside. Such was the fate of Pat Boone's <u>'Twixt Twelve and Twenty.</u> During the 1959-60 school year, Mr. Boone's literary accomplishments represented the ultimate in fashionable reading. Today, <u>'Twixt Twelve and Twenty</u> sits unnoticed on the library shelf next to <u>Between You, Me and the Gatepost,</u> a somewhat similar effort which never took hold or attracted the attention that its predecessor did. As interest in Pat Boone began to wane, a new novel came on the scene. <u>Exodus,</u> by Leon Uris, became, almost overnight, the book of the year to most teen-agers. Strangely enough, Exodus caused a revival of Uris' earlier novel, Battle Cry, which I read and praised during my high school days. Presently, the students seem to be in a period of transition. Most of them have read Exodus, seen the movie, and bought the Ferrante and Teicher recording of the theme music from the movie. Now they are ready for a new interest. What will it be? I will venture a prediction that Mila 18, Uris's most recent creation, and Franny and Zooey, by J. D. Salinger, will be next.

The established literature of previous years should not be overlooked in preference to fad reading, however. Perennial favorites such as 1984, Rebecca, Wuthering Heights, and Call of the Wild are as popular with teenagers today as when they were written. Margaret Mitchell's Gone With the Wind is by far the most outstanding example of a book which has maintained its popularity through the years. Although nearly twenty-five years old, Gone With the Wind still ranks first on the list for popular or leisure reading. When a questionnaire concerning reading interests was distributed to the students at Herrin Township High School last year, 173 of the 526 people who responded listed Gone With the Wind as the best book they had ever read. Les Misérables was second on the list, receiving nineteen votes, while Rebecca, Exodus, and Old Yeller followed, in that order.

Being able to supply these books as soon as they are requested has long been a problem confronting the high school librarian, who usually has to operate his library on a limited budget. This problem has been greatly alleviated at Herrin by the sale of paperback books in the library.

Paperbacks offer advantages to both the student and the high school librarian. They eliminate waiting for books that are in great demand; they never become overdue; they may be marked in, torn up, put away, or thrown away, as the reader wishes; they are easy to carry; and because of their reputation of a few years ago, there is a certain charm and daring in reading a paperback that cannot be achieved with a library book. Possibly because of their reputation, paperbacks in the library attract many teenagers who would never think of checking out a library book. What the boys and girls do not realize is that they are reading good literature and classics under the guise of the drugstore novel. The two major advantages for the librarian are that paperbacks ease the demand for popular reading from the library, and they contribute a small bit of revenue to the library which can be used to advantage either by the library or the library club.

The books that teenagers purchase from the paperback racks in the school library differ somewhat from what most people would expect them to buy. Strangely enough, the Webster's New World Dictionary has been the best seller for two years running. The Larousse French-English Dictionary also sells quite well, as does Hamilton's Mythology, Les Misérables, Green Mansions, and Exodus. Also popular, particularly with the boys, are such books as Street Rod, Battle Cry, I Was a Teen-Age Dwarf, and The Guns of Navarone.

Paperbacks seem to be the coming thing in the changing world of the high school library. And many librarians, recognizing the advantages of selling these books, are contacting their local newsstand supplier, or are taking advantage of the services offered by the Scholastic Publishing Company and others who have recognized the worth of paperbacks in the school.

We must remember that one of the major activities of our profession is the stimulation of reading. Whether he wants fiction or nonfiction, romance, western, hot rod, or any one of a thousand other types of reading material, when the teenager says, "Hey, ain't cha got any good books?", he expects and should receive a positive answer-- "Yes, just look around you. Come, I'll help you choose one."

Contemporary Literature Through
the Eyes of Upper-Grade Pupils [in Russia]

L. S. Aizerman

From Literatura V Shkole, 1964, No. 5; The Soviet Review 6:32-45, Spring 1965. Copyrighted by the International Arts and Sciences Press, Inc., White Plains, New York. Reprinted by permission.

We still do not know our pupil well, his interests and his tastes, the peculiarities of his perception of works of art, his attitude toward what is done in class. And without all this it is very difficult to teach literature and simultaneously to see to the upbringing of the pupils and their instruction.

> Study of the influence of the collective on the personality should be added to the investigations of other forms of social influences on the masses, such as, for example, the influence of belles-lettres, periodicals, movies, radio, television, and propaganda lectures. This has particularly great significance for pedagogy, for the work of rearing the rising generation. Not knowing exactly what radio programs the students listen to, what television programs please them, and how they perceive movies, it is difficult to mold esthetic tastes and a scientific world outlook, and to bring them up as collectivists. [1]

Compositions by Moscow students on the theme "Which of the Works of Contemporary Soviet or Foreign Literature I Like the Most and Why" provide interesting material for characterizing the literary sympathies of upper-grade pupils, their attitudes toward contemporary literature and their understanding of it.

Ages Twelve to Nineteen

This theme, among four others, was proposed in February 1964 by the Moscow Department of Public Education and the Moscow Advanced Teacher Training Institute as a city composition in the 9th to 11th grades. The compositions were written in all the districts of the city and in several schools of each district.

Written with the passionate directness peculiar to youth, these compositions also make it possible to judge the quality of the teaching of literature in the schools. Its task is to develop artistic taste, to teach the students to read literature, and to understand it fully. The extent to which the pupil studied and understood Gogol and Tolstoy can best be judged by how he perceives and evaluates the work of K. Simonov, A. Solzhenitsyn, K. Paustovskii, and D. Granin. Knowledge is tested in practice. And in our work, practice is independent reading.

At our disposal are 1,139 compositions on the theme "Which of the Works of Contemporary Soviet or Foreign Literature I Like the Most and Why." We shall try to be brief in our comments. Let the pupils speak more for themselves. And we shall not argue with them on each occasion: this must be done in class. Our main purpose here is to understand the pupils: what they like in literature and why.

Discovery of the World

What does the upper-grade pupil look for in a book? What does he expect from it? "I want to know life, people and myself"; this expresses concisely the thought of a great many of the authors of compositions. To see, unnoticed, to understand while still not being clear, to investigate one's surroundings and one's self--this is what the young reader wants; for him, a book is first of all an artistic investigation of reality.

> What do I seek in books, what interests
> me? Oh, many, many things. And,
> certainly, you can't enumerate them all.
> In the first place, of course, people. What
> are they like? How do they relate to each
> other, what do they think about, what do they
> live for? What are 'good' people and what
> 'bad'? Which should be taken as examples

and which not? And, in general: 'Just what is good and what is bad?' And again: Why are they so?[2]

Each literary work pursues two aims: first, to make the invisible visible, and, second, to make men think about these invisible or, often, simply unnoticed aspects of life.

That is why, when the upper-grade pupils give their reasons for naming a particular book as the work which they liked most of all, they write first of all about what they learned about life from having read it.

"I read many books about the war and saw many movies. But only after having read The Living and the Dead [Zhivye i mertvye] did I understand at what price victory was gained."

"To read the novel (the reference is to Silence [Tishina]) is an extraordinarily interesting experience. And not only because the subject and the fortunes of the heroes are interesting, but because the times themselves are interesting too; one wants to learn more about them, to understand them better."

"I could not conceive until then (until having read Salinger's novel Catcher in the Rye [Nad propast'iu vo rzhi] of a young American who could love Burns. I thought that they all loved baseball, that in the evenings they sat in bars and paid very little attention to the fact that poetry and young children exist in the world."

In a composition about Paustovskii, a pupil wrote emotionally and poetically about the significance of a book which reveals the world and teaches one not only to look, but also to see, not only to listen, but also to hear.

"A man lived in a great city. Each day he walked along the streets. The man hurried; he had no time to look around him. He, of course, knew that there were strange lands in the world and fantastic plants. But he was a serious man; he had no time to think about that. But then Paustovskii enters his life. He brings with him the white nights of Leningrad, the white and transparent woods of Scandinavia, the warm, caressing mists of the Baltic, the gaily colored days and the nights, black as soot, of Odessa, the quiet bashful nature of Meshcher. He brings people with him: fishermen and writers, meteorologists and pilots, sailors and artists, gardeners and actors, urchins and scholars--all such romantics as he himself. And the serious man can no longer go along the streets, hurrying and not looking about. He is infected by romanticism. He sees how deficient his life was, how much of beauty he cast out of his life; he cast out that without which in the end it is impossible to be happy. . . .

"It is a shame to admit, but previously I skipped over the descriptions of nature in books. But reading Paustovskii, you sense the salty smell of the sea, you hear how 'the first drops of rain beat upon the elastic leaves of the lilac,' you feel the piercing Northern wind. Perhaps this sounds too gradiloquent, but, on my word of honor, my heart stops beating at such words as these: 'All the beauty in the world I would give away for the willow bush, wet from the rain, on the sandy bank of the Oka.' I have never been on the Oka, but this willow bush, this sandy bank, I see as clearly as if I had passed my whole life on this bank . . . . My life can be divided into two parts: the period up to the time I read Paustovskii, and my life after."

To see the world in all its complex diversity, to understand people, to introspect--this is not only a natural desire of youth to understand their environment. To see the world in order to make it better; to understand people in order truly to be friends with them and passionately to struggle with them; to look into one's self in order to develop oneself--this is what the students write about in their compositions, which distinguishes the citizen's personal involvement, the citizen's enthusiasm for personal participation and personal responsibility. In this respect, the compositions on the narrative by A. Solzhenitsyn, One Day in the Life of Ivan Denisovich [Odin den' Ivana Denisovicha], are characteristic.

"In order to truly understand what a terrible thing it is when people begin to create gods and what a tragedy this can become for the nation, the youth need such books as One Day in the Life of Ivan Denisovich. They evoke many arguments, thoughts and conclusions, and the main one is: 'This must not happen again!'"

"I will say honestly that for me this narrative was not only a revelation, but, to a certain degree, a blow. Perhaps I am not right, but it seems to me that this narrative, One Day in the Life of Ivan Denisovich, is an appeal directly to us, to the youth. We must not allow this a second time; we are obligated to know where this can lead."

To understand in order to construct life better; to know in order to be able to organize it wisely and humanely:

"In a year and a half we tenth-graders will finish school, our childhood will end, the time will pass when adults decided all matters, big and small, for us. We will enter into an independent life. It is said that a life to live is not a field to cross over. But, surely, even a field can be crossed in different ways: it is possible to walk along the edges of pits and hummocks, or one can go straight across. And so with life: one wants to set a direct course, so that the conscience may never be tormented that somewhere the soul was twisted.

"A great many works are devoted to the young generation. We will learn from them; they will help us in the future not to make mistakes and to go along the right path, to find our 'place in life.' For this, I like the writers who tell of boys and girls who are entering or have already entered into life"; thus begins a composition on the story by V. Aksenov, Colleagues [Kollegi]. This approach to literature determines the attitude not only toward books which deal with yesterday's students entering into the larger world. Here are some interesting reflections from a composition on K. Simonov's novel The Living and the Dead.

"Before this, I had read a great deal about the war, but I imagined it to be completely different...Simonov's book changed my attitude in many ways toward that terrible grief through which the whole nation, the whole land, lived while repelling the barbaric attack of the fascists....I have often heard it said by people of the generation that lived through the revolution and then through the war, that modern youth does not value and cannot evaluate the great feat which our fathers performed. In my opinion, this is not true. It is simply a prejudice. I do not doubt that we, too, are capable of such feats....Among us there are petty bourgeois, scoundrels and Philistines, but, indeed, when didn't they exist? And how would it be if all books brought as much to us as the books by Simonov!"

The author of this composition did not express his thought with sufficient clarity. But this thought is comprehensible: it is not true that the Philistines, the petty bourgeois, and the scoundrels define the character of our generation; it is not true that we cannot evaluate our fathers' feat; but we would value it all the more if it were always recounted to us as truthfully and convincingly as Simonov did.

The students' aspirations and ideals also characterize their attitude toward the heroes to whom they have given their sympathies in the books they have read. Our upper-grade pupils are attracted to strong, honest, manly, noble heroes. Serpilin, Bakhirev, Krylov, Sasha Zelenin, Andrei Sokolov, Sergei Vokhminstev, Naval Captain Buinovskii--these are the ones they named when writing about heroes close to their hearts. This list, of course, could easily be expanded. The principle upon which the favorite hero is selected is important.

And here is something interesting. Even when the students write about people very far from us in many ways, they speak first of all of the genuinely human things that are close to them, the youthful readers of the Soviet Union. In this respect, the compositions on the novels of E. M. Remarque are characteristic. "Oh, Remarque," I have heard a number of times, "why do they even publish him! Constant carousals. All the time bars, wine, women. This arouses an unhealthy interest in him." I read everything that was written by the students about Remarque: the interest in the writer is healthy and the understanding is correct.

"The friendship of the three comrades arouses admiration. True friendship, without superfluous words, without loud protestations! A friend is having a hard time of it. And they help, they help, whatever it may cost them. Pat has to be taken to the doctor, and Kester does the impossible, but he carries out his mission. Pat is doing poorly, and Robbie should be with her, but for this money is necessary. The friends sell 'Karla,' their own creation and, perhaps, the only thing remaining to them. Really, is this not healthy? Indeed, let us look at many things in different ways; let us live in different worlds. This does not prevent us from valuing genuine people in whatever country they live and regardless of what language they speak. We can love, we can be friends, we can stand up for ourselves and for our friends; therefore, the heroes of this work are close to us."

No, it is not calvados and not bars that attract our children to Remarque; they seek in a book first of all positive spiritual values. Here is yet another characteristic meditation. This is about Hemingway's The Old Man and the Sea [Starik i more].

"An old emaciated man, weak and alone; it seems that he needs nothing from life, and life nothing from him. Everything has been experienced, everything has been tried, in everything there is a bitter aftertaste. But this old man, it turns out, puts up a real struggle with what he understands as his place and role in life. He is old and weak, and he envies the power and dexterity of a fish he has caught, but he firmly believes that in the end he will triumph because he is a man. Don't you experience a true feeling of pride in this understanding of the power of man? And in the words of the old man that it is possible to kill a man, but impossible to conquer and to subjugate him? Is this not a principle of life? Can't this be the program of every real man?"

And, here, in another's experience, the youthful reader seeks his own; in remote experience he finds what is close to him. This personal identification with the heroes is characteristic of many of the compositions. It is not surprising that many compositions on the works which the students liked most became not only analyses of these works, but also meditations on the times and on the students themselves. Even if these reflections are often debatable, even if the comparison of the book with their own lives is not always justified, still it is a natural desire to think of oneself when reading.

Here is a composition on Salinger's novel Catcher in the Rye.

"I feel very sorry for Holden, because he is essentially a very good person. Behind his outward display of carelessness and undue familiarity, one senses an unusually fine and tender soul, a purity of thought. It enrages him

Ages Twelve to Nineteen

that a scoundrel corrupts the pure souls of children and disturbs their peace. He erases some obscene words written on a wall, but they appear again elsewhere. He wants to rub them off but he is unable to do so. He is indignant because he doesn't want little ones to be touched by this depravity. But this, most likely, will lead to nothing. For Holden is alone and there are hundreds of scoundrels. Looking at his conduct, it is difficult to imagine that he can change anything. He should find effective methods of struggle. But, perhaps, he will not find this path and will go downhill and become a habitué of some bar or other and, there, will cry about the vices of society... To be truthful, I do not think he will become a scoundrel, but, as he himself says, he is a coward, and this trait could lead him to baseness. Besides that, his complete skepticism has a rather unpleasant effect. I cannot say about myself that I am distinguished by a kind of special esteem or respect for my elders, or that I am possessed by a sacred trembling when I see historical relics. But such a scornful attitude, in my opinion, is also intolerable. Most likely, this scornfullness is basically a pretense, but, nevertheless, a person should have something which he is unable, which he does not have the right, to respond to casually."

Here is a composition on the novel Goodbye, Boys [Do svidan'ia, mal'chiki] by B. Balter.

"Involuntarily, you compare yourself with those boys and girls, and, it seems, our generation matured earlier, perhaps because we saw and heard more. We know more about life than Balter's hero, and our complex understanding of life does not boil down to simple concepts of good and evil, it does not fit into a ready-made scheme--'our generation has grown up.'"

Here is a composition on Aksenov's novel Colleagues.

"When you read about them, you think: "But we are their contemporaries, we are younger than they by some five or six years, and we are just like them, you know. But why are we so bored? We are not dawdlers; we are interested in many things; we burst into performances of plays, even without tickets; we are carried away by literature, English, technology; we run to the exhibitions and the creative evening get-togethers; we read newspapers and... we are bored. We are bothered by our studies and by idleness;

we want to live with a KPD [efficiency coefficient] of 100 percent. We want to do something, to do something useful for our Motherland, for people. You know, we, 'the light-headed' youth, love people. . . ."

One can disagree with what is written in these and many other papers, and, possibly, sometimes one should take issue with them. But one thing is beyond question: it is important to know not only what our student reads (this, by the way, is the easiest of all to learn), but also how he reads, how he relates to what he has read, what he ponders over, and what thoughts the book arouses in him.

"In educating the youth, it is necessary to know with what they live, with what thoughts, and what attracts them and what repels them"--this I read in one of the compositions. What is said is provocative and controversial, but essentially correct.

Reading these compositions, you understand especially well why a study of classical literature does not always satisfy our pupils. It sometimes happens that for the students, classical works represent only knowledge of the past, and that during their study in school, there is no spiritual contact between the writer and his modern readers. But without this there is no genuine contact with art.

Only the Truth

One concept is encountered more often than any other in the compositions in which the boys and girls ponder over the merits of a literary work. This concept is truth. But what does truth mean to the young reader? What connotations does this concept have for him? To write truthfully, as he sees it, means not to embroider upon life.

"When you are only seventeen, you are just entering life, you still judge everything in your own way.... And, for all that, you seek answers to many questions; you seek a man no less fine than the heroes of past years, but alive and contemporary. You always expect a great deal from books. Each person has his own needs, but all expect honesty from a writer. He should just not embroider on life."

"The novel The Living and the Dead attracted me because, in it, a difficult period for the Soviet people is described directly and honestly, without any embellishment."

The upper-grade pupils believe that to write the truth means not to describe life in a facile way. This is what particularly attracted them in D. Granin's novel I Go into the Storm [Idu na grozu].

"It pleased me that the author did not go overboard when he wrote about Agatov. It seemed that at any minute the crime would be discovered, good would triumph, the guilty would be punished, and the whole effect of the work would be ruined. But here is the end, and Agatov remains with a stain on his conscience and, perhaps, no one will learn what he did."

"Having read the novel, many will most likely be astonished. What is this? Agatov at liberty and still going strong? But this is what I liked most of all in Granin's novel. We are all accustomed to the fact that, at the end of a book, good triumphs and evil is punished. This is not so in the novel I Go into the Storm. The writer as much as warns us: 'Be on guard, such Agatovs still walk among us, ready to make their way under communism, without difficulty, at someone else's expense!'"

To write the truth, in the opinion of the girls and boys, means to speak honestly and directly about the most bitter and difficult aspects of life.

"This book (One Day in the Life of Ivan Denisovich) is difficult and terrifying to read; you do not want to believe that these things ever happened. You don't want to. But all the strength of this book lies in the fact that you believe everything in it, right up to the end--from the first to the last line."

"Steinbeck (in the novel The Winter of Our Discontent [Zima trevogi nashei] shows the destructive, poisonous influence of capitalist morality. It penetrates everywhere, spreads throughout the whole country, and gets into the narrowest and most remote crannies. I liked his candor in portraying his native land and the bitter truth about it. Indeed, a man must have fortitude to write in such a way about his native land."

To write the truth means to give a full-bodied, three-dimensional portrayal of life in all its variety and contradictions. It is precisely this which attracts the youth to the works of Sholokhov:

"With Sholokhov everything is natural, like life itself." This is, for them, the merit of Granin's I Go into the Storm. In connection with this, it is interesting to note how the present-day student relates to the portrayal of Germans in the war. He wants to learn how the German became a fascist, why he came to wage war against us, whose son he is and whose father. That is why many of them write on The Adventures of Werner Holt [Prikliucheniiakh Vernera Khol'ta], the novel The Bridge [Most], the narrative The Passenger [Passazhirka], and the poem "The Court of Memory" [Sud pamiati].

The students strive for a many-sided cognition of the world in all its complexity and contradictions. And from us, their literature teachers, the students also expect a many-faceted investigation into life and its reflection in art (both the art of the past and of the present). Therefore, they are not satisfied by a schematic and simplified presentation of literature, in which the good and evil of the world are fitted neatly and thoughtlessly into standard pigeonholes.

One's Point of View

"There are a great many problems about which one can think and argue and this is one of the merits of Granin's novel I Go into the Storm."

"Many parts of the book are very debatable, and this is also to the author's credit. I have had occasion to argue with many persons who have read this book, and I am glad that it provoked arguments and disagreements. This means that it is real, this means that it is powerful." This is about the novel Death Calls on Engel'khen [Smert' zovetsia Engel'khen].

These statements are symptomatic. The authors of the compositions like literature which compels them to think and to debate. For them, good books are not ones that leave their spirits calm, that do not disturb their intellects

Ages Twelve to Nineteen 333

or incite interesting debates and discussions.

And this is not accidental. Youth, which Pushkin so aptly named "restless," is the time for assertion of the personality, the years when, as never before or after, it is desired to unravel all the contradictions in the world, to find the exits of the labyrinths of life.

But there is more to this than just age. In the compositions, "the era and contemporary man are reflected." The aspiration for independence, the defense of one's position, and disputes with what is read and heard--all these things are a reflection, in the school compositions, of a time of good changes in our life, of its renewal and purification.

There are constant references in the compositions to newspaper and journal reviews and to opinions heard in debates and discussions. The children pay careful attention to what is said or written about books which have interested them. They listen, but they by no means always heed what they hear. When I read the compositions, I constantly felt the passion of the arguments and discussions. The compositions defended, the compositions attacked, the compositions upheld.

"Balter, in my opinion, writes so warmly and purely about the love of Inka and Volodia. But many, on the other hand, find this thing immoral and think that it 'will corrupt our Soviet youth.' In my opinion, this is absolute nonsense. Only people with dirty minds can see anything bad in this book."

"Let us remember his touching love for Tina Karamysh. Some will object: 'Really, what love can there be between a married man and a married woman?' But G. Nikolaeva depicted this love as so touching, so pure and bright, that even the most violent opponents of this love should, in my opinion, show some feeling of sympathy for these good people."

Especially heated arguments were provoked by Solzhenitsyn's One Day in the Life of Ivan Denisovich. (But let us not forget that no matter what point of view is expressed by the students writing about Solzhenitsyn, they all named the narrative as their favorite work. We should also remember that the compositions were written at the beginning of February, when many of the things that are now said about One Day in the Life of Ivan Denisovich had not yet been printed.)

"Shukhov is a most commonplace person," we read in one of the compositions. "His range of interests is very narrow. Only one thought occupies Ivan Denisovich: to survive, no matter what happens. Life outside the camp seems to him strange and incomprehensible. Shukhov doesn't even think about why he is serving a term. This is an ordinary punitive camp. And such a man became the main hero of the tale. I can't completely understand this.... Nor is Shukhov's spiritual world rich. And here is how that day ended. What gladdened Ivan Denisovich so? He received two servings of watery soup, bought some tobacco, was not caught with a hacksaw at the gate search. These are all the cares of the main hero."

And the author of the composition contrasts Ivan Denisovich to Naval Captain Buinovskii.

"In the camp, where the wardens mock a man's will, Buinovskii found the strength in himself to defy Lieutenant Volkovoi. In this hero, Solzhenitsyn depicted a real Communist, a real fighter."

We encounter similar contrasts in other compositions, but not all share such a conception of Ivan Denisovich:

"Ivan Denisovich is not a fighter; he does not come forth with disclosures and protests. He simply remains a man. But under camp conditions this was not simply a great deal, this was everything."

And in another composition:

"I saw the people imprisoned in the camp on the most absurd, unsubstantiated charges. Some of them became despondent, lost their dignity, their human appearance, became 'bootlickers'; others mastered themselves and remained people. Shukhov is an example of such a man. He remained the same as he was before imprisonment in the camp. His sense of personal worth did not fail him. He did not start begging cigarette butts as did Fetiukov, who was the director of some enterprise. I especially like the episode of the work of the 'Zeks' during the construction of the thermal electric power station. Shukhov and the other bricklayers no longer felt the frost and the wind rushing over their heads. Ivan Denisovich worked profitably, smoothly, surmising in advance where the most mortar should be put and how to place the bricks sideways. Now everyone had only one concern--to bring in the mortar and bricks in time, so that the bricklaying would not be brought to a standstill...."

The students <u>think</u>, the students <u>argue</u>, the students talk about <u>their</u> opinion, <u>their</u> attitudes toward what they have read, and <u>their</u> understanding of it. Behind all this stand good changes in the teaching of literature.

That is why it is impossible to agree with those articles in which it is asserted that teaching literature in school kills independence and thinking and condemns thoughts and words to standardization.

There are hundreds of compositions. One cannot agree with the evaluations of many of them; you can dispute the teachers' reviews. But surely this is a fact: in no case has the evaluation of a composition been lowered because the student expressed his thoughts in a nonstandard way, wrote provocatively and combatively, or defended positions which the teacher does not share.

Here are 9th-graders defending modern literature, contrasting it to the classics: "These books, which had a revolutionary trend in their time, are read now only for an understanding of the past or because they have become part of the school work. And it seems to me that I would not have lost anything if I had not read <u>Woe from Wit</u> [Gore ot uma]."

"At the beginning of the composition," writes a teacher in a review, "very strange views were expressed on classical literature which could serve as a basis for argument." The evaluation was not lowered.

This from two more reviews: "Interesting, although one would like to argue with you." "I do not share your tastes. The narrative...does not seem to me to deserve such a high evaluation. But you wrote well, frankly, and simply."

Of course, the students' independent thinking is not always and everywhere treated both with exactingness and respect. However, there are more and more thinking teachers who are educating thinking students.

A considerate and respected attitude toward the student's own opinion not only does not exclude but often presupposes the necessity of arguing with the student in a rational and convincing way; for the upper-grade pupils have not always examined the complex phenomena of life and their (also far from always profound and faithful) representation in art.

In this connection, the compositions devoted to V. Aksenov's Star Ticket [Zvezdnyi bilet] went into more detailed discussion. For our critics and, in truth, for the author himself, Star Ticket is already past. In any case, in filming the novel, the author shifted many accents. But the book lives, it is read, and is debated. And so for us, the teachers, it is not past, but present.

What in Star Ticket attracted those students who selected it as their favorite work? First of all, there was the fact that the author described characters whom the students had had occasion to meet more often in life than in art.

"A great deal has been said about the narrative Star Ticket by V. Aksenov. The thirty-year-old critics wrote about it in the same way as the forty-year-olds. They wrote with bitterness: 'The book does not reflect reality;' 'the hero of the book is not a hero of our times!' And what do the seventeen-year-olds think? Did they like it? I will say directly: 'Yes--I did.' The reason is that Dimka, Galka, Iura and Alik live next door to us, they study in our school. The author showed the life of some Moscow kids who are about seventeen with startling exactness."

But it is not only, and not so much, a question of whom the author described as of how he described his heroes. Strictly speaking, we have met them before, most often in the newspapers; teddy boys [stiliagi], scum, riff-raff. No, said Aksenov in his novel, this is not all (and in many respects he is correct in this). Often all this is only external, superficial; look deeper--these are good kids. It is this rehabilitation, I would say more--this idealization--of the character which attracted part of the students. There is enthusiasm in their compositions in defense of the heroes of the narrative:

"Aksenov very correctly understood our youth. He knows that we love the sun and music, that we want to work, that we have the strength to do a great deal. To those who say that the youth of the sixties are not able to do anything, I would like to ask a question: 'Do you know anything about us, about the youth?'

"They go along the right path in life, they make mistakes, but by their actions, their views on life, it is clear that from them come real Soviet people."

"Victor was killed, but in parting he left Dimka his punched ticket. I think that whatever road in life Dimka chose, the star ticket left him by his brother would permit him to go along it with honor, and he was worthy of this gift because, despite his boyishness, he took from his brother all his best traits."

As regards the external appearance, the language, conduct and manners to be adhered to, the students' opinions differ. Some students consider that in this there is much that is superficial, temporary, on the surface:

"Here is the environment of the heroes, the inhabitants of 'Barcelona': the troublemaker Aunt El'va, the speculator Tima, the perpetually drunk yardkeeper, and the other Philistines. Such an environment gives rise to a completely legitimate protest: 'You do not recognize modern dances? Then we will dance to spite you! You object to narrow pants? Then we will wear only narrow ones,' and so forth. A primitive protest, the antithesis, gives rise to that appearance which is 'alien to us' and to an imaginary spiritual emptiness."

Other students see in everything the signs of the times, the traits of the generation:

"The awareness that it is not for nothing that they eat their bread fills their souls with pride. The fact that they, having received a secondary education, work with simple stevedores does not antagonize them. For them the consciousness of their own independence, of their own strength, is important. They are proud of their tired hands. And the fact that they look like 'fops' as usual, go to cafes in the evening and drink wine there does not lower the significance of labor in their lives. This, in my opinion, is a distinctive trait of our generation: the youth do not want to renounce pleasures, good, stylish clothes, and at the same time they do not avoid work, but, on the contrary, they seek it. It is always pleasant to realize that you are of use to people and do not live in the world for nothing."

However, even those who think that the skeptical attitude toward adults and the nihilistic perception of established traditions and views are all only temporary and superficial (and this is exactly what is shown by the hero of the novel) arrive at peculiar conclusions:

"In our house there lives a fellow. Formerly, he was the terror of the whole house. He was just like the hero of Star Ticket; once he fell in with a gang of 'fartsovshchiks.' He discussed everything with such cynicism that it was disgusting to listen to. Everyone said that this was an 'arrant type.' But, look, he finished school. He became tempered in the virgin lands. And, arriving in Moscow, he entered the Bauman Institute. I am sure that exactly the same fate awaits the hero of this tale."

Thus, there is no need to be disturbed. Foppishness, cynicism, a nihilistic attitude toward suffering humanity, a caddish impertinence--there is nothing terrible in this; it is a childhood disease and will pass.

And there is more. Authors of the compositions affirm that the "star boys" represent not only a portrayal of certain characters who actually exist, which is, of course, a correct description, but also a portrait of the better part of our youth (can it be shown that this is not so?), more than that--a picture of the life of all young people:

"The author revealed to us the real side of the life of the youth. He revealed their thoughts, aspirations, and desires. Aksenov showed the youth as they really are; nothing is omitted, nothing is concealed."

As far as criticism of the novel is concerned, it did not convince the authors of these compositions. Here is a characteristic statement:

"It happened that when I was in the library this year, I came across an article, more correctly, a review of the novel in which it was criticized in every possible way. Since I was of a completely contrary opinion, I decided to read everything that other critics had written about it. I read four or five articles; in all of them the novel is abused. These articles even outraged me a little. I reread the novel. I went more deeply into the events occurring in it, and, nevertheless, I held to my own opinion.... Judging by the articles, one might think that the critics do not know life, that they were never young or that they now have no young acquaintances, and that they do not go out on the street, and never look about them."

We are speaking now about the students' perception of the novel and not about the novel itself. Of course, a one-sided and often incorrect understanding comes, in large part, from the book itself. But now it is important for us to emphasize the other aspect: <u>the independent judgment of the students is not always a true judgment.</u> And in order to instill genuine independence, it is not enough to teach the students to say what they think, to "have their own opinions." N. D. Moldavskaia wrote well about this:

> The students' independence of judgment and appraisal of artistic works can be formed only on the basis of literary development, the development of figurative thinking, powers of observation, imagination, and a feeling for poetic language, on a firm foundation of historical and historical-literary knowledge and concepts, on the basis of a serious orientation in the already existing points of view that have been shaped in science (at the present level of its development) and in the collective experience of Soviet readers.[3]

<u>What Is Most Popular</u>

"Which of the Works of Contemporary Soviet or Foreign Literature I Like the Most and Why." This was how the theme suggested to the upper-grade pupils was formulated. Hitherto we have talked about how they answered the second part of the question--the why. Now that we have become clear about the criteria from which the students proceeded in naming the works which they liked most, we should speak about the books that they have named. Let us begin with the poetry.

Comparatively few wrote about poems. Of the 1,139 compositions, only 110 were devoted to poets. But two factors must be taken into consideration here. It is very difficult to write about a poet, without having his poetry at hand. And, secondly, it is more difficult to discuss poetry in a composition than prose.

About whom were the compositions written? Sixteen poets were named. There were 3 compositions on A. Voznesenskii, 3 on E. Yevtushenko, 8 on E. Mezhelaitisa, 15 on A. Tvardovskii, 17 on R. Rozhdestvenskii, 22 on the poem by E. Isaev, "The Court of Memory" [Sud pamiati], and 32 on the poetry of E. Asadov. Let us see how the upper-grade pupils substantiated their choices.

Students were attracted to Rozhdestvenskii's poetry because it expresses "an ardent civic concern in feelings and thoughts, an aggressive romanticism." "They have in them something of Mayakovsky. But this is not the main thing. The main thing is the very great and unaffected feeling of the poet, who unites in himself both feelings of love for our motherland, and for our Revolution, and a tremendous sense of responsibility to our contemporaries, in particular, to contemporaries of our own age....I cannot say exactly what pleases me in Rozhdestvenskii's poetry. Most of all, perhaps, I like the crystal honesty and lofty civil courage in the poet's verses."

The girls wrote about the verses of Eduard Asadov, and they wrote rapturously:

"Softly the pages rustle. Around me the words ring, fate takes its course, and feelings are expressed in song. I discover a new world, the soul of man, I am lost in reverie. Softly the pages rustle... "In the Name of a Great Love" [Vo imia bol'shoi liubvi]. Eduard Asadov."

What is attractive in the poetry of E. Asadov was described best of all by a boy--the only one among the writers on this poet:

"Why do the majority of the people, in conjunction with the word love, use the words morals, ethics? What is this? If we begin to speak about love, then, in my opinion, it is worth talking about morals too, as one newspaper did. It seems to me that morals, in the sense in which this word is now used, is a congealed and atavistic conception. Morals--most often this word can be heard from the petty bourgeois. He was born, grew up, loved, married, had children, the children grew up--this is how this citizen pictures to himself real love. This, of course, is all good, even very good, when everything turns out this way, but surely it is not always so simple. So why is it considered immoral to be divorced and moral to live with a man whom you do not love? This, perhaps, is everything and nothing, but the whole trouble is that often scoundrels and vulgar, petty people take refuge in these words. And they will say all these words with such ardor that you can't distinguish them from real men. And it is here that the concept of morals is lost. It seems to me that for morals there should be substituted sincerity. In our society, moving towards communism, sincerity is needed in everything, and first of all in love, in the relation of one person to another.

"Sincerity in everything: in poetry, in thoughts, in feelings, in actions--this is the main theme of Asadov's poetry. In his poetry, Asadov carries on an open conversation with the reader. He does not flatter, he does not embellish, he does not idealize love. But, despite this, his poetry breathes with spring and life and optimism."

It does not have to be proven that the author of this composition was taking a stand not against morals, but against the morals of the bigoted, the morals of the Philistines, the petty bourgeois representation of respectability. He is for purity and sincerity in human relations. And this sincerity is what he values in Asadov's poetry. Others also write about the same thing. That is why the students forgive the poet (or, perhaps, simply do not see?) for the artistic shortcomings of his poetry.

Now let us turn to prose. Here are the Soviet writers about whom more than ten students wrote:

M. Sholokhov--58 (of which, 34--Virgin Soil Upturned [Podniataia tselina], 20--Fate of a Man [Sud'ba cheloveka], 4--Silent Don [Tikhii Don]).

D. Granin, I Go into the Storm--53.

Iu. Bondarev, Silence [Tishina]--49.

V. Aksenov--47 (of which, 28--Colleagues, 18--Star Ticket, 1--Oranges from Morocco [Apel'siny iz Marokko]).

K. Simonov, The Living and the Dead--36.

A. Solzhenitsyn, One Day in the Life of Ivan Denisovich--34.

B. Balter, Goodbye, Boys--29.

Chingiz Aitmatov, Tales [Povesti]--27.

A. Fadeev, Young Guard [Molodaia gvardiia]--23.

N. Ostrovskii, How the Steel Was Tempered [Kak zakalialas' stal']--22.

G. Medynskii, Honor [Chest']--18.

K. Paustovskii--18.

G. Nikolaeva, Battle on the Way [Bitva v puti]--18.

A. Andreev, Judge Us, People [Rassudite nas, liudi]--18.

Iu. German, My Good Man [Dorogoi moi chelovek]--15.

A. Chakovskii, Light of a Distant Star [Svet dalekoi zvezdy]--14.

I. Efremov--13 (Nebula of Andromeda)]Tumannost' Andromedy]--11, Razor Blade [Lezvie britvy]--2).

A. Kuznetsov, Continuation of a Legend [Prodolzhenie legendy]--12.

B. Polevoi, On the Wild Shore [Na dikom brege]--11.

As regards compositions on foreign literature (203 in all), most of them were written on the following authors:

E. M. Remarque--30 (wrote about Remarque "generally," but in the first place named Three Comrades [Tri tovarishcha] and All Quiet on the Western Front [Na zapadnom fronte bez peremen]).

Dieter Noll, The Adventures of Werner Holt [Prikliucheniia Vernera Khol'ta]--30.

D. Kiusak, Hot Summer in Berlin [Zharkoe leto v Berline]--26.

John Steinbeck--15 (of which, The Winter of Our Discontent [Zima trevogi nashei]--13, Of Mice and Men [O myshakh i liudiakh]--2).

Harper Lee, To Kill a Mockingbird [Ubit' peresmeshnika]--12.

J. D. Salinger, Catcher in the Rye [Nad propast'iu vo rzhi]--10.

As is evident from the data given, the majority of the books named by the upper-grade pupils are really good, high-quality books (this is also true of those works which are not mentioned here). In any case, the compositions completely refuted the opinion that contemporary upper-grade students prefer The Copper Button [Mednaia pugovitsa] and not The Copper Horseman [Mednyi vsadnik]. Only three compositions were devoted to Sergeant of the Militia [Serzhant militsii], and three to the novel And One in the Field Is a Warrior [I odin v pole voin]. Not more than ten votes were given to all the books of this type. And the very choice of the book says a great deal about the taste of the writers.

Especially pleasing were those compositions in which an endeavor was made to speak about the artistic originality of the work, about the peculiarities of the author's creative style. Here a girl writes about the novel Catcher in the Rye:

The book is written in a very original and interesting manner. The story is told in the first person, and all the people and the events are interpreted through the eyes of Holden.... Not once in the whole narrative does the author attempt to evaluate Holden. He simply portrays some mad days in his life, filled with petty, seemingly disconnected events. But from these events and from fragmentary memories, Holden rises before us as a man. The language of the novel is rather coarse. It shocks respectable readers who are sure that their children do not speak and think like that. But, along with this, the book is unusually poetic, and the whole book somehow warms one inside. There are no landscapes, no vast descriptions of the city at night, no tearful scenes by the fireside. But the poetry of the novel is concentrated in Holden's soul, a pure, sensitive and easily wounded soul, which he hides behind an affected coarseness and cynicism. At first, when you are just beginning to read, the brokenness of the thoughts and details, to whose description whole pages are devoted, is somewhat startling. But then you understand: so it is in life, exactly so. The teacher talks with Holden about life, and Holden thinks about ducks on a lake and about how repugnant it is to see the white legs of an old man. Real detail, and in such quantity in the novel, and the character of Holden becomes ever more clear...."

Here is a composition on V. Tendriakov's Short Circuit:

"Tendriakov's method of portraying events and heroes is interesting. I would like to make a small digression in order to compare various literary methods. Take Sholokhov, for example. He lives alongside his heroes. We get to know them through their deeds, through their interactions. The characterization of the hero is shaped by the hero himself. The author does not impose anything on us. Fadeev has another method. Fadeev himself judges his heroes, gives them the author's characterization, and then, as if for confirmation of their thoughts, adds their actions and interrelations. Tendriakov proceeds in quite a different way. He characterizes his heroes at the beginning with a few strokes. It is as if he himself does not know what will happen later. The characters of the heroes are completed for him by the events, in which the complete essence of the people is manifested. And only in the end do we hear the

voice of the author, who judges his heroes as if passing
sentence on them. All their subsequent life is absolutely
clear for him and for us. I like this method very much.
He compels the reader to participate actively in events."

And here is something interesting. Sometimes the
student says nothing about the peculiarities of the author's
style, about the peculiarities of his poetics, but by the way
in which the student himself writes, by the style of his composition, you see that he really sensed the creative style of
the artist to whom his composition is devoted.

"Reading these books, you become aware of the scent
of fresh breezes, the riotous display of blooming lilacs, the
somber beauty of the cliffs of Kara-Dag, the dazzling snow
of Scandinavia, the rusty ancient earth of the Crimea, the
eternal roar of the sea"--this is from a composition on
Paustovskii.

"And Holden's life is not at all sweet! It seems his
parents are well-off and they love their son, but there is
no pleasure in life. Why is this? Even Holden cannot
answer this question. He's simply very sad and depressed.
He has not yet entered the mendacious and hypocritical
world of adults, but he is standing on the 'precipice,' one
step more and--the fall...

"Everyone who surrounds Holden, even the children,
is infected with either skepticism or cold calculation. Take
Sally, for example. She seems to be a gay, joyous girl,
but actually she is a calculating, fully adult and prudent
person. When Holden proposes that they marry and go far
away to live somewhere by the side of a stream, she answers very judiciously that they will have time to marry
when Holden has finished the university, and that they will
go on a honeymoon somewhere more pleasant than living
'somewhere by the side of a stream.' But, please, do not
think that Holden is in love with Sally!"--this is from a
composition on the novel Catcher in the Rye.

However, there are comparatively few compositions
in which an understanding of the artistic peculiarities of
the work is expressed in some form. Perhaps this is not
so strange in the present case: the theme of the composition was not announced ahead of time, and the majority of

the writers did not have at hand the books which they analyzed. It is very difficult to write about the poetics of a novel without having the novel itself.

Reading the compositions, you see how much we still have to do. And together with this there is a great deal which is heartening.

The civic maturity of many of the students' papers, the good taste, the free and unfettered quality of the exposition, the honesty of thought, the picturesqueness of language--all these things give one pleasure.

A young Philadelphia teacher, David Mallory, decided to find out how the personality of a student in a contemporary American school is formed, and what influence the school has on his life and the form of his thinking. He talked with the students in a relaxed setting and, on the basis of his investigations, he wrote a book.

While talking about teaching literature and independent reading, Mallory observed "how assiduously the students discriminated between reading for school and reading for themselves." When the talk got around to what the students read for themselves, "sometimes, with an apologetic smile, someone would introduce (in a list of books which were not read for school--L.A.) such books as A Farewell to Arms [Proshchai, oruzhie] by Hemingway or Catcher in the Rye by Salinger. I asked the question: 'Why do you name these books in such a way as if to ask forgiveness?' Some answered: 'In them, things are written about which have no place in school'; others: 'These are contemporary books; I mean to say, they are written in our times. These books are not for the ages'; still others: 'The teacher does not suggest such books.'"[4]

Mallory was acquainted with teachers who paid a great deal of attention to out-of-class reading. But, in his words, "more often...the students maintained that school was not the place for conversations about personal interests."

The article from which I took these statements is entitled "High School Students Speak" [Govoriat ucheniki srednikh shkol]. If you like, our account of the compositions of Soviet students might have been called the same thing. And it is pleasing that our school has become a place for conversations about personal interests, and that a teacher suggests for reading and talks those books that are close to the student and excite him.

I am glad that the study of classical literature has improved in the school. Classical? But all the compositions are about contemporary literature. Yes, but here is what the students themselves say about this:

"The main thing is that the study of literature in the school helps us to understand not only the works in the curriculum, but also all the books which we read. You are reading something quite unrelated to school work and suddenly you begin to think: 'What is unconvincing in this, why did he act in that way? How can she do this? You think about the milieu in which the heroes live, about their interrelations, and about what kind of a man the author was and what his views were on various things."

"Would I have understood all of The Living and the Dead if at the literature lessons we had not studied Tolstoy's novel War and Peace?"

"The truly excellent works of Pushkin, Lermontov and Tolstoy enabled me to examine contemporary literature and poetry." And this is actually so.

More than a thousand compositions were written. There is a great deal in them that does not satisfy, that disturbs and saddens one.

But it is impossible not to see the main thing: they reflect good changes in the teaching of literature in the school.

Notes

1) L. F. Il'ichev, "Metodologicheskie problemy estestvoznaniia i obshchestvennykh nauk," in Metodologicheskie problemy nauki, "Nauka" Publishing House, Moscow, 1964, p. 175.

2) All the compositions are quoted without stylistic corrections.
3) N. D. Moldavskaia, "Znaniia, opyt kollektiva i sobstvennoe mnenie," in Literatura v shkole, 1964, No. 2, p. 30.
4) David Mallory, "Govoriat ucheniki srednikh shkol," in Amerika, 1964, No. 92, p. 50.

Tell It As It Is

Nat Hentoff

From the New York Times Book Review, p. 3+, May 7, 1967. Copyright 1967 by the New York Times Company. Reprinted by permission.

When Ursula Nordstrom of Harper & Row suggested a few years ago that I consider writing a novel for teenagers, I had grave doubts. After all, by the time a reader is 12 or 13--and certainly by the time he is 15 or 16-- he is reading adult fiction. It seemed like a factitious journey into imagination, but since I was assured there would be no limitations as to subject matter or style, I went ahead and wrote Jazz Country.

Since the book was published, I've talked to some of the young people who read it. At schools, at libraries, and through correspondence. I've also looked at a variety of other fiction directed at readers 12 and over. I'm still not entirely sure of the need--the organic need--for fiction specifically aimed at this age group, but I am beginning to think there may be.

It is true that McLuhan notwithstanding, there are many teen-agers who get great pleasure--atavistic kicks, he might say--from reading. And a sizable number of them do move naturally into adult fiction. But there are others who seldom read--either because their schools have effectively made reading synonymous with forced labor, or because few books they have seen sufficiently speak to their basic concerns to warrant their taking time away from listening to the Lovin' Spoonful, the Mamas and the Papas, Bob Dylan or the Beatles. The latter minnesingers do speak directly to the young, and one of the more literary of the folk rockers now predicts that the song may be the new form of the novel to come. (A development apparently unsuspected by Robbe-Grillet.)

Yet I don't believe that printed fiction is an entirely anachronistic medium for those of the young who, so far, have not felt drawn to it. There are questions and ambivalences endemic to adolescence that songs and even films have not begun to explore in ways that are compellingly meaningful to the young. Perhaps fiction still can.

Jazz Country, for instance, focused on the discovery by a white middle-class teen-ager that he needed credentials he had never thought about to be accepted on probation in the black world of jazz. Some young black readers of the book found it surprising that jazz could be considered of such value. The music and the subculture behind it had been ignored in their schools; and from watching television, they also knew it was ignored or dismissed as merely "entertainment" by the white-run outside world. By contrast, young white readers in all-white schools were surprised at the possibility that there were Negroes who wouldn't accept them, that there were Negroes whom whites had to prove themselves to.

But in other respects, Jazz Country failed, as have most books directed at teen-agers. "How come," one young reader asked me, "no one in Jazz Country ever felt hung up or got kicks from sex?" "And why," said another, "was there nothing about marijuana or any kind of drug in the book?" "I just don't believe," a third pointed out accusatorily, "that the white boy in your book had parents who didn't bug him. Not only about hanging out with black people, but about everything."

My point is that the reality of being young--the tensions, the sensual yearnings and sometime satisfactions, the resentment against the educational lock step that makes children fit the schools, the confusing recognition of their parents' hypocrisies and failures--all this is absent from most books for young readers.

Oh, yes, these days a girl does occasionally get pregnant in such a book--or, rather, a friend of the protagonist does. Or a boy slips into what the therapists call antisocial behavior. But the point of view of the author, even when intended as that of the beleaguered youngster, is closer to Rose Franzblau or some other Dr. Pangloss than it is to the complicated sense of being young in America that adolescents feel.

Where is the book that copes with the change in
sexual values--if not yet sexual behavior on a large scale--
among adolescents? Where is the book that even mentions
an erection? And what of marijuana and LSD and banana-
highs? What is there about society that is leading more
and more of the young to drop out of it, if only momentarily
and experimentally? And some do take the whole trip.
What is life like among the Diggers in San Francisco? What
are the losses as well as the releases in being "free" in
that way?

There are others of the young, some of them as
young as 12 and 13, who are wondering what alternatives
there are to tuning in and dropping out. They go on peace
marches; they picket; the boys among them worry about the
draft. Not only about being killed but about killing. Where
is the novel that copes with a teen-ager's revulsion to this
particular war in Vietnam and with his exceedingly difficult
array of choices when the time comes? What is involved
in being a conscientious objector, inside one's self as well
as outside? Will Canada be an answer? Or maybe jail?
Do adults have the right to make you kill? And if not, how
do you assert your right to live and let others live?

There are so many parts of the lives of the American young that are alien to books for them, and to many
books of adult fiction for those who do read adult fiction.
There are many black youngsters experiencing a rush of
black consciousness through the example of a Stokely Car-
michael, or the legend of Malcolm X, or the sounds and
fury of neighborhood black nationalists. But what happens
then to such a youngster--in his relations with his parents,
in his school, when he's through with school?

And what of the many white, middle-class youngsters
who have not yet been processed into the McNamaras and
Humphreys and Goldbergs and Dirksens of the future? They
know what they don't want to be--like their parents, for one
thing--but they are far from certain they will find other
ways of making it which don't require the suppression of
spontaneity, sensuality, honesty. Where are the books
about them?

As a result of Jazz Country, I've talked to youngsters from many different neighborhoods and backgrounds, and the questions and issues they raise are precisely those which are either ignored or evaded in books for young readers. Should marijuana be legalized? If not, why not, when all of you smoke cancer, lift yourself through a day on pills and get to sleep with other pills or with liquor? Why should I have to marry a girl to sleep with her, if we both want to sleep with each other? How did you let this country get to be in such a state that Lyndon Johnson could be elected President? (That question comes from the full spectrum of political belief and lack of political belief.)

This is an unprecedented time in which to be young in America. On the one hand, there is--not in all but among many adolescents--a healthy, witty skepticism about the conventional wisdom of adults. Along with it exists a free-flowing reaching out to experience, to the textures of being, that is vividly evident in the dress, the speech, the music, the very gait of the young. I mean not only many of those now 16 and 17, but, even more so, those starting their teens. For all their sometimes exasperating defiance and prickly confusions, they are beautiful in their possibilities.

On the other hand, there is the society waiting for them as they leave their teens. A society which may lead some of them to murder or be murdered, or is otherwise efficiently equipped to kill their spirit. How will they be able to keep their possibilities alive and maybe--a very remote perhaps--really change that society? Where is the book concerned with that?

To read most of what is written for young readers is to enter a world that has hardly anything to do with what the young talk about, dream about, worry about, feel pain about. It is indeed a factitious world, and that kind of writing for teen-agers is not worth doing, because it is not worth their reading. But there may be a place in writing for the young for those authors of whatever age who have not forgotten the exultancy and the fear that are intertwined in possibility, who are neither didactic ("I was young once myself") or lost in the illusion that they can be young again. Who, in sum, are still struggling themselves with the question of what life is--and who feel there are things they can still learn along with the young.

It is a challenge few adults can begin to fulfill, but it is not impossible. As I said, in many respects Jazz Country failed. But parts of it did bring me into a dialogue with some of the young, and that experience has been among my most satisfying and instructive as a writer.

And so, I expect, I'm going to try again. Not writing at them, but about them and about myself, about possibility, about the good, kind, decent grown-ups who once were young and now allow napalm to fall on children. About what one person, one naked human being, can do to stay as whole as he can in a time of the banality of evil.

But if I preach, I fail. However, if I can find in fiction the truth that only fiction can tell, I may be able to continue that dialogue. Even--to be utopian--with one or two of my own children.

"Well, What Did You Think Of It?"

Bruce C. Appleby and John W. Conner

From the English Journal 54:606-12, October 1965. Reprinted with the permission of the National Council of Teachers of English, Bruce C. Appleby, and John W. Conner.

Yesterday, Dave walked into our English office, pushed aside a pile of books and papers, sat down and remarked, "Well, I finished reading the book. What did you think of it?" The lavender dust jacket of a current novel by a local writer's workshop instructor came into focus, and we began to trade impressions of the book, exchanging critical assumptions, finally trading titles of books we have enjoyed which our conversation about this book brought to our minds. Fifteen minutes later, Dave stood up, smiled wistfully, and said, "I wish I were taking 'Individualized Reading,' again this semester. I've only read about five books so far this semester and last semester, by this time, I had read over thirty." Next week, or the week after next, Dave will be back to exchange impressions about a book or books we have suggested, and to ask us what we thought of a book he had suggested to us. Dave has the individualized reading bug. He has been bitten, infected, and constantly reinfects himself by his informal visits with us. We hope he never recovers from his current illness!

Dave is a product of a one-semester course in individualized reading which is offered on an elective basis to junior and senior students at University High School. Dave's wistful wish to re-enroll in "Individualized Reading" is typical of a growing number of our students who are so pleased with their progress that they automatically re-enroll for a second semester. It is gratifying to report that, although four semesters of English are required for all junior and senior students at University High School, five and even six semesters are becoming the average. And "Individualized Reading" is a prime reason for this growth in student interest.

How do you teach individualized reading? Jeannette Veatch (Individualizing Your Reading Program, New York: G. P. Putman's, 1959) and Dwight L. Burton (Literature Study in the High School, New York: Holt, Rinehart and Winston, 1964) provide excellent sources for tailoring a variety of programs. Our own program is based upon the ideas in such sources as these and the planning of the English department head at University High School, G. Robert Carlsen.

Our students are introduced to individualized reading through a curricular strand of units which begin in Grade 7 and extend through Grade 10. With this background of specific individualized reading experiences, they are ready at the eleventh and twelfth grades for the fuller experience of an entire semester devoted to personal reading development.

Practice and Procedure

On the first day of class, we explain to the students that the nature of the course is found in its title, "Individualized Reading." Each student starts a reading profile sheet by answering two questions: "Where have you been in your reading?" (What titles have you read for enjoyment the last few years? What type of book do you enjoy reading?) and "Where are you going in your reading?" (Do you have a particular plan in mind? Are there authors or themes you are interested in or curious about?) Students are told to sign for individual conferences on the schedule sheet, where they indicate their names and the titles and authors of books. During a classroom period, the students sit and read. If a student finishes what he is reading during the period, we give him a library pass so he may find another book. Conferences are held in the back of the room or in the hall, in order that nothing interferes with the students' reading. Allowing approximately ten minutes per conference, we find we can talk to four students each day. If two students have read the same book, conferences are arranged for both at one time.

The first task for the teacher is to develop a list of suggested titles for each student by perusing his reading profile sheet, determining his areas of interest and the type of book he is curious about. This list can be developed from many sources, the most important being the teacher's personal reading background. Of the many good reading lists and sources available, we have found the following most helpful: Books for You (NCTE, 1964), Patterns in Reading (Jean Carolyn Roos, ALA, 1961), Good Reading, (The Committee on College Reading, New American Library, Mentor, 1964), and Reading Ladders for Human Relations (American Council on Education, 1963). By guiding the student throughout the semester, we encourage him to deepen, then widen his reading interest, noting the direction and growth of his reading maturity.

Patterns of Reading

We have noticed that there are group and individual patterns of reading which develop within any given class. The group pattern occurs when one student tells another who tells another about a book which he has discovered. For example, Joyce started reading Green Mansions. Within a week and a half, seven students who sat around Joyce were reading and had signed up for conferences on Green Mansions.

Local showing of a movie based on a novel, such as Golding's Lord of the Flies, will prompt several students to read it. Scripts of new plays will arouse interest. For example, the February 1, 1964, Saturday Evening Post's publication of Arthur Miller's controversial play, After the Fall. Titles suggested by the teacher to an individual will pass around the class with astounding rapidity, as has been observed with Daphne du Maurier's Rebecca, Heller's Catch-22, Steinbeck's The Winter of Our Discontent, or Carson McCullers' The Heart Is a Lonely Hunter.

The individual patterns which develop fall into three categories, according to the student's ability.

Students above average start out reading popular adult novels about which they have heard, but have not had the time to read. They then tend to read more esoteric books, often by controversial writers. An outgrowth of this phase is to read as much as possible of what has been written by one author; the student is trying to form a personal critical opinion of that author even though he may not like all of that author's writings. Rather than interest in a particular author, sometimes the student will turn to a

Ages Twelve to Nineteen

theme, such as social criticism in the 1930's or the Negro in contemporary American fiction. Often, the above-average student will become more definitely part of the group pattern after this point. He will notice what others in the class are reading and become curious as to why.

Typical of the above-average student's reading pattern, Al started by reading Fail-Safe (Burdick and Lederer), Seven Days in May (Knebel and Bailey), The American Way of Death (Mitford), Franny and Zooey (Salinger), and Clock Without Hands (McCullers). The Plague (Camus), Les Jeus Sont Fait (Sartre) which he was also reading for third year French, The Doctor in Spite of Himself (Moliére), After the Fall (Miller), and An American Tragedy (Dreiser) were next. Curiosity led Al to Faulkner, who fascinated and aggravated him. The Sound and the Fury; Sartoris; The Hamlet; As I Lay Dying; Light in August; The Unvanquished; Absalom, Absalom; Go Down, Moses; A Fable; and some short story collections seemed to satisfy Al's curiosity. Several books by Carson McCullers, some more Salinger, and Shadow on the Rock, Song of the Lark, Lost Lady, and O Pioneers by Willa Cather rounded out the semester. Al is obviously not an average student, having read a total of 35 books. The pattern of his reading, however, is typical of the academically able in a course of this nature.

Students of average ability often start out reading popular adult novels which are currently being widely discussed. Generally, the average student will then fall into a pattern of reading based on his favorite type of book, such as war stories, historical romance, or adventure stories. Here, the teacher has an excellent opportunity to help the student develop this interest and to lead him gently to new areas and ideas within it. Often the average student indiscriminately samples books following his investigation into a favorite type. Generally, we encourage this in order to help him widen his reading interests and knowledge.

Typical of the average student's reading pattern, Ben started by reading West Side Story (Shulman), On the Beach (Shute), and Black Like Me (Griffin). Catcher in the Rye (Salinger) followed, as Ben wanted to know why it was so popular. PT-109 (Donovan), Kon Tiki (Heyerdahl), Mutiny on the Bounty (Nordhoff and Hall), and Call of the Wild (London) were next read, as Ben investigated his "favorite" of war and adventure stories. A few more of these were followed by A Connecticut Yankee in King Arthur's Court (Mark Twain). Ben enjoyed this novel as a good adventure story, but was also able to see some of its satirical implications. Depending on the student's ambition and personal motivation, the number of books read during the course of the semester by the average student will vary from around eight to 16.

Below-average students offer what is perhaps the greatest challenge and the greatest reward. Generally, the pattern of the below average student centers around his particular preference in reading to the exclusion of other types of books, i.e., war stories, romance, true adventure, hot-rodding, or mysteries. The teacher can do a great deal with and for this student by suggesting a variety of titles within his interest and by helping him to see the wealth of materials available. In working with the below-average student, even in the upper grades, a knowledge of literature for the adolescent can prove most valuable.

Typical of the below-average student, Bob indicated on his reading profile sheet that he liked "war stories. Nothing else--war stories." A preliminary conference revealed "I've read all the war stories that have been written." Bob was asked if he had read The Strong Men (Brick). Since he hadn't, Bob started with it. Rifles for Watie (Keith), April Morning (Fast) and Behind Enemy Lines (Sanderson) followed. As a tangent to his interest, Bob struggled through One Day in the Life of Ivan Denisovitch (Solzhenitsyn). Bob tackled Battle Cry (Uris) next. The length of the novel and the number of characters proved difficult for Bob, but he did enjoy the book. At the teacher's suggestion, Bob read All Quiet on the Western Front (Remarque). A new world of literature was opened to Bob, based on his interest, yet completely different from the type of story he had previously read.

Another and even more dramatic example of what this approach to literature can accomplish is seen in the case of Barb, a junior with an I.Q. of 89. On her reading profile sheet, Barb indicated she liked romances, yet insisted, despite other suggestions made by the teacher, on reading To Kill a Mockingbird (Lee). Barb's reading was not controlled by her interests, but by what her peers were reading. Observe a student like Barb trying to read something beyond her ability, struggling to complete two pages a class period, and you will see how we reacted. Finding a book for this high interest-low ability student proved a problem. Many excellent adolescent novels were rejected, because they didn't seem right for Barb's ability or personality. Finally, Vivian Breck's excellent novel Maggie was suggested to Barb, with the idea that the teacher was curious to have Barb's opinion. The day Barb finished this book, she sat in class and cried. Why? She understood it. She enjoyed it. The book was able to meet and combine her interest, ability, and rate of reading and yet hold her curiosity. Most importantly, "It's the first book I ever finished all on my own."

Conferences

For the teacher, the most heartening aspect of this entire program is found in the conferences. To be able to sit and talk with our students about what they are reading, and what they are getting out of the books they have chosen is stimulating, delightful, and enlightening. Student-teacher rapport runs very high and, because the teacher is reading what the students are reading, the students feel and know the teacher is genuinely interested in their reading and their progress. When we began this course, we feared that discipline might be a problem, particularly with those students we considered bad risks. Because of the rapport, there has been no problem.

During the conference, the student and teacher discuss the book on a number of levels. We try to ascertain how much the student has enjoyed the book by asking questions which will reveal such things as: (1) How many different levels of meaning has he employed in approaching the book? (2) How does he associate the book with his previous reading? (3) What relations to his experiences were implied in the book? (4) How has he progressed in his reading as a result of having read this particular book? (5) How does this book fit into his general reading program and plan?

Each conference results in a student's answering a question about or indicating an opinion of a particular aspect of the book on a 4 x 6" card. These cards are not book reports; instead the student discusses a particular aspect of the book such as characterization, handling of theme, fidelity, comparison to a similar book. etc.

Since the student will have finished a book before the conference, we often end it with a question on what he is now reading and what he plans to read next. Here the teacher can guide the student into a wider and deeper approach to reading based on his interests and abilities.

Reading Project

The reading project is an outgrowth of the students' interests and patterns in that each one chooses an author, theme, or genre in which he is particularly interested. He reads a minimum of four books which center in his chosen topic. The project then consists of the student's writing an analysis of his chosen topic. We want students to make up their own minds about the material read, not to parrot the opinion of others, so usually we limit the students to the books they have read. We do sometimes encourage the better students to use outside references. (An alternative we offer the students on the reading project is to do an oral report, although relatively few students choose this option.)

Approximately three weeks before the end of the semester, our students are to have finished their reading projects. They are told about the project at the beginning of the semester, but are not encouraged to begin active work until the beginning of the second quarter.

A widely divergent and rather amazing range of topics results from the reading project. In one semester, a far above average senior did his reading project on "An Interpretive Study of Twentieth Century Man as Seen in the Plays of Arthur Miller"; an average student investigated "Realistic Language in Four War Novels"; a below-average student was concerned with the fidelity of "Hot Rod Terms in H.G. Felsen's Novels."

Grading

An inevitable question is "How do you grade students?" We have found that the best answer is to let the students decide how they will be graded. Five years ago, when our present English curriculum was initiated, the students enrolled in Individualized Reading decided there should be three criteria for grading: (1) number of books read, (2) quality of conferences and cards, and (3) the level of each book. Each class has been offered an opportunity to modify the grading system. Our present system, which follows, reflects these modifications.

1. Number of books read. This measure alone is unreliable in that books vary so greatly in length and difficulty. Nevertheless, the students have always felt that quantity of reading is important.

2. Number of books is multiplied by an estimate of the student's perceptiveness into what he has read. The student is graded on the conference and card on a cumulative 1 to 4 scale; 1-no understanding beyond plot; 2-some application to his own life; 3-some implications for larger human ideas; 4-understanding of levels of meaning, esthetic values, and relationships with other reading.

3. The product of criteria one and two is multiplied by an estimate of the level of the book. Each book is given a numerical rating on the following scale:

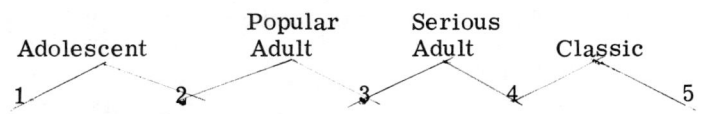

	Popular	Serious	
Adolescent	Adult	Adult	Classic
1	2	3	4 5

By multiplication of the three factors, a student reading adolescent materials which he understands completely may achieve as high a grade as one who reads serious adult materials which he does not completely understand. To be sure, the grading is based on subjective evaluations by the teacher, but it does standardize procedures and provides a quantitative score.

It is very important, in using this grading system, to modify it to the grade level and ability of each group. The scale must be applied in a sense of being completely movable. What would be judged and placed on the serious adult level in seventh grade might be placed on the popular adult level for eleventh grade. For example, Hawaii (Michener) is serious adult level reading to the seventh grader, but popular adult to the eleventh grader. Making the scale movable allows for differences in reading ability in any particular grade.

Teacher Preparation

What special preparation does an individualized reading program require of the teacher? Essentially, this program requires (1) a knowledge of the developmental tasks of adolescents (see Robert J. Havighurst, Human Development and Education, New York: McKay, 1953), (2) a knowledge of the reading interests of young people (see Geneva Hanna and Mariana McAllister, Books, Young People, and Reading Guidance, New York: Harper, 1960, or George W. Norvell, The Reading Interests of Young People, Boston: D.C. Heath, 1950, and What Boys and Girls Like to Read, Morristown, N.J.: Silver Burdett, 1958), and (3) a wide acquaintance with good books. A good book is here defined as any book which is right for one of your students at this time in his life. Generally, the right book for most seventh through tenth graders will be found in that large body of literature labeled literature for the adolescent, and the right book for a tenth through twelfth grader is more likely to be found in adult literature. We have suggested some sources for learning about good books. However, there is no substitute for personal reading and evaluation. A file including book cards for each book you have read is an invaluable aid in assisting students with further reading suggestions.

Code of Procedures

We believe that the success of our program is directly related to the following code of procedures:

1. The teacher has read or skimmed most of the books that the students read.

2. The teacher must resist the temptation to recommend a "better quality" book than the one the student has just finished reading simply for the sake of "quality." The next book read must be read because it is of interest to the student, not because it is of interest to the teacher.

3. The teacher must resist the temptation to present any planned classroom activity which prevents individual reading and book conferences.

4. There is no specific level where reading must begin. The individual reading level is dictated by one's

interest and ability.

  5. The basis for a book conference can be a difference of opinion between the student and teacher and may end with unresolved differences.

  6. A summary of the book's plot (oral or written) is probably a waste of time for all but the slowest of students.

  7. The teacher must be supportive in the conference and avoid making derogatory evaluations of books which have meant much to the student.

  8. The teacher must leave each conference feeling the student has gained a clearer understanding of the book and his program.

Conclusion

  Although many teachers and administrators agree with an individualized reading program in essence, they are reluctant to start the program on a complete semester basis because of administrative problems or simply through fear of being unable to cope with the awesome task of reading all the books adolescent readers might consume during a semester period. Aware of this, we recommend starting with two-week to four-week units of individualized reading within the regular English curriculum. The total number of books to be read by the teacher will be less oppressive and when the success of the short unit has been evaluated, another unit or units can be scheduled.

  A related feature of this program concerns the use of the school library. We have found it valuable to ask each student to keep a list of the books he would like to have checked out of the school library if he could have found them there. We turn these lists over to our librarian to use as one basis for buying new books or for stocking additional copies of existing titles for the school library. This practice builds better student relations with the school library as well as provides us with the books students really want to read.

  It would be unwise to conclude without asking: Is individualized reading a valuable way for students to become acquainted with literature? Perhaps one way to answer this question is to recall the top forty books which NCTE Achievement Award winners for 1960, 1961, and 1962 believed most significant for them. Heading the list is Salinger's The Catcher in the Rye. We don't believe that this book was introduced as common reading in many English classes. Irwin Edman (Saturday Review, November 4, 1950) writes of the joys of unrequired reading for students and adults: when the pleasure of reading includes the pleasuure of knowledge and thought. James R. Squire (The Responses of Adolescents While Reading Four Short Stories, NCTE Research Report No. 2, 1964) believes that teachers need to develop better techniques for assessing the quality of an individual's responses to literature (italics ours). Individualized reading has provided the students at University High School with the opportunity to discover the pleasure of learning through reading they enjoy. They have shown their enthusiasm through such heavy enrollment that the course must be offered every semester rather than alternate semesters as originally planned. Even then, it is impossible to include all students who would like to take this course. Individualized reading has become an important way of reading at University High!

VI: Ages Fifteen to Nineteen

What High School Students Say About Good Books

Nick Aaron Ford

From the English Journal 50:539-40+, November 1961. Reprinted with the permission of the National Council of Teachers of English and Nick Aaron Ford.

Today many serious thinkers fear that the best elements of American culture are deteriorating. They are appalled by the charges that juvenile delinquency is increasing at a frightening pace, that American education is turning soft, that the daily literary diet of our teenagers is the comic book and the Western, and that the will to attend to matters that require intellectual concentration or mental discipline is fast declining. And, what is worse, they profess to see no signs on the horizon to contradict these omens of approaching doom or to give the faintest hope that salvation is still possible.

A booklet prepared for seven thousand delegates to the White House Conference on Children and Youth, March 27 to April 2, 1960, by thirty-four departments and agencies of the Federal Government, asserts that the child today has very little independence, and he is seldom alone. Most of his time is regulated by adults, and most of it is spent with other children. His parents' concern is almost wholly for his physical welfare and comfort, with no attention to the cultivation of inner resources of character. "Does a regime such as this," the editors ask, "teach children that to be born, to reproduce, and to die, is the whole duty of man?"

With such pessimism expressed in many different ways, it is only natural for thoughtful citizens to begin to wonder if there is another side of this picture which offers some ground for hope. Is there any considerable segment of our present school population which exhibits disesteem of what is cheap and trashy and impermanent? In short, is there any hope that a reasonable number of teenagers now in training has high standards of what is excellent and durable and a strong desire to maintain such standards?

In this article I propose to make a limited examination of "the other side." Since attitudes toward books are usually regarded as a test of the taste and cultural values of an age, I shall be concerned with such attitudes as manifested by a representative number of the most articulate students in American high schools, students who in all probability will be the artistic, scientific, educational, political, and moral leaders of tomorrow. I shall base my conclusions on the comments and opinions of more than two hundred senior high school students, representing one hundred and fifty-four schools in forty-nine states. These young scholars, almost equally divided as to sex, range in age from sixteen to eighteen years. Each is represented by an impromptu essay on "What Is a Good Book?" selected at random from more than five hundred compositions submitted in competition for the 1959 NCTE Achievement Awards in English, sponsored by the National Council of Teachers of English.

What is a good book? What are its most satisfying qualities? Who are the writers that can best touch a responsive chord in the youthful reader? What specific books deserve immortality? These are some of the questions that this discussion shall attempt to answer.

Qualities of Content

Of all the satisfying qualities of a good book, the teenagers represented in this survey give the highest place to intellectual stimulation. From a small town in Georgia one girl writes, "A book is good to me when it touches off new questions in my mind, when it makes me stop, and wonder, and seek an answer. It deepens my awareness of my own ignorance, my own narrowness; yet it does not discourage me, but encourages me to grow, to wake up. It is like a mental ice-cold shower." A boy in Alaska declares, "There are times when one prefers to relax physically but keep his mind sparkling. On such occasions there is no more satisfying diversion than an essay on some aspect of life." Approximately two-thirds of the youthful scholars listed intellectual stimulation as one of the chief requirements of a good book.

Moral and social insight ranks second in the hierarchy of satisfying values that a good book can offer. "If one is able to believe in a reality different from his native one," writes a student from Kansas City, "to see truth from a new vantage point, to be a person other than himself when he reads, the book is good, because it makes the reader realize more fully the possibilities of his humanity." A girl in a Minnesota town confides, "I very seldom get angry with anyone. How does it feel to be angry, or to lose a lover? And what are the consequences of such experiences? I prefer to learn these things from a book-- from an author who knows--rather than from real life. I want to learn how to live, how to grow up." From Seattle comes a confirmation of this philosophy with an added suggestion: "Nearly all books are, in a sense, good books, because they present varied experiences which expand awareness of both the ugly and the beautiful." As an illustration of the significance of a writer's ability to reveal new insights, a boy from Illinois suggests, "Because they were intent upon explaining human nature, Dostoevsky and Hawthorne were able to create characters of greater depth than any characters ever created merely as spokesmen for plots."

The third quality of a good book is its emotional satisfaction. A student from Kentucky insists, "Real literature is spiritual, an outcry of one spirit to another." A girl in Maine says, "A good book is deep and powerful. It causes furrows to appear on otherwise placid brows. It causes tears to fall on serene cheeks, and it brings a smile to calm lips." A small-town boy in the state of Washington believes, "No matter what the subject, all readers will say that a good book gives them the thrill of an experience they have never had before." A Missouri girl is sure that "through good books one can become educated emotionally."

A fourth satisfying quality of a good book is the opportunity it offers for escape from overbearing tensions. A Chicago girl thinks, "Many people seek refuge from this world of tension and turmoil by indulging in alcohol or drugs. However, men and women such as Shakespeare, Austen, Burns, and Bronte have supplied far superior means of escape from life's perplexities. Unlike some other methods, books do not cheapen and weaken men's minds and souls, but rather they build, strengthen, and enrich. Soon the path of escape supplies courage and wisdom to face adversities."

A fifth satisfying quality of a good book is its embodiment of beauty, sensual and spiritual. From New York, Wisconsin, Arkansas, California, Iowa, and South Carolina come almost identical suggestions that "a good book should glow with the inspiration of beauty." A boy in Massachusetts adds, "A good book should display beauty for its own sake."

Qualities of Form

But intellectual stimulation, insight, emotional depth, opportunity for escape, and a sense of beauty are not enough to completely satisfy these teenagers' requirements if these qualities are to be found in content only. They demand a fitting style commensurate with a satisfying content. A New Mexico boy says, "I consider the author's style one of the factors that make a book good or bad. A clear, concise presentation makes reading a pleasure." From a town in Oregon a girl explains: "Usually a good book has a mixture of moods. Seldom is an interesting book so shallow that there is a laugh on every page. On the other hand, a light moment of humor or entertaining romance can break the monotonous heaviness of a tragedy." A girl in Phoenix, Arizona, maintains, "The writer's use of language is an important part of every good book. The writer must know how to paint word pictures so vividly that we feel we are actual participants in the incidents of the plot." Of a good novel an Iowa boy demands "a plot wide enough to include several ideas, and characters with depth that reach down, pull out, and reveal every elusive human trait, quality, and emotion of the persons they represent." A fitting summary of the importance of style is well stated in the comment of a Philadelphia student: "It is the author's privilege to put into words what the reader has always known but been unable to say. A good book is one which expresses these dumb feelings at the crucial moment when the less gifted reader can think of no way to bring them forth."

Specific Titles

One hundred and two different titles, ranging from the works of Aeschylus written nearly twenty-five centuries ago to the latest best-seller, were listed as qualifying for the appellation of "good book." Typical reactions to specific choices attest to the values these articulate teenagers possess. A girl in Westport, Connecticut, says of War and Peace, "It exemplifies the 'great' book. Tolstoy has created a magnificent panorama of history, wherein life is discussed as a myriad of details and also as a flowing universal river." From Jacksonville, Florida, a boy writes concerning You Can't Go Home Again, "I luxuriated in Wolfe's gorgeous style, the flow and rhythm of his language." A student from Greenwich, Connecticut, calls James Joyce's Finnegan's Wake "a remarkable account of a man's dream." An Arizona girl declares, "A classic like Of Human Bondage or The Brothers Karamazov could not have been written by a small mind; the ideas in these books are too profound." From an Illinois town a boy asserts, "My reading in Bertrand Russell, Einstein, and Huxley on the nature of science interested me in the philosophic importance of science and the scientific method."

A fitting summary of this entire discussion might well be the thoughtful conclusions of a student in Libby, Montana: "One of the most important things that a good book accomplishes is the arousing of its reader to an awareness or appreciation of life itself. . . . A good book must arouse in its reader the desire to develop all his abilities, to fulfill completely his potentialities, to accomplish every deed worthy of him and attain every good within his power, and to live to the fullest extent his life as long or as short as it may be."

Private Reading in the Fifth

W. Stephen Jones

From the Times Educational Supplement 2626:506, September 17, 1965. Copyright 1965 by Times Newspapers Limited. Reprinted by permission. The author wishes readers to note that the school referred to in this article is not the school at which he presently teaches.

After the O level examinations this year, I asked my form to compile a list of the novels that they had read during the year; I asked them to include all the novels that they had read, however trivial and non-literary they might think that I would consider them to be. I also asked them to say, if they wished, why they had read the books, what they thought about them and if they could discover any significant pattern in their reading.

Above all, I stressed how necessary it was that their answers were honest, that they did not include books because they felt that they ought to have read certain novels, or exclude books which they thought might reflect badly upon themselves. I am fairly confident that their answers were honest; they understood why honesty was necessary and I believe that the relationship that they and I had established during at least two years' work, and in many cases a longer period of previous teaching, enabled them to answer honestly.

The form was an A-stream form in a two-stream independent school; although everyone in it should have passed his O-level language paper (they do not take the literature paper) I would hesitate to describe them as an academic form. The form's average age was 16.5; they form a relatively homogeneous group, the oldest boy being 17.1 and the youngest 15.10. There are 19 boys in the form, but one was missing at the time when this was done.

They had read 248 books during the year; the most prolific reader had read 28 books, and one boy who is able at English had read only one, saying:

> The type of literature that I am most interested in is reference books; e.g., electronic catalogues, radio and car magazines, etc. This is why I want to do economics, not English, in the sixth form.

The average number was 13-14 books each. The most popular author--need one say it?--Ian Fleming--33 books. He was followed by Hammond Innes (16), Golding (12), Hemingway (11), Orwell (10), and Shute (9). If one classifies the books by titles, instead of authors, there is an interesting difference, with Fleming less influential, in general, and largely confined to two boys, both of whom said: "I wanted to read all Fleming's books." One of them then added: "All his stories are the same and I have difficulty in remembering which story had which title." His most popular book was On Her Majesty's Secret Service (5), presumably because it first appeared in a paperback version during 1964, for I think that even the most ardent Fleming fan would not regard it as his best book, and Dr. No., which, of course, has been filmed.

The most widely-read novel was Lord of the Flies (10)--that is to say, by more than half the form--followed by For Whom the Bell Tolls (5), 1984 (5), The Lonely Skier (5), On Her Majesty's Secret Service (5), Fanny Hill (4), Brave New World (4), The Perfumed Garden (4), The Doomed Oasis (4), Dr. No (4), The Moon and Sixpence (4), A Farewell to Arms (3), The Ginger Man (3), The Go-Between (3) and three more Fleming novels (3).

Most of their reading was of books that one might describe as modern. Outside the twentieth century, Fanny Hill was the most popular, but not for literary or historical reasons. Dickens occurred only twice: A Tale of Two Cities and, by another boy: "I felt very sincere and so tried to read a novel by Dickens, Dombey and Son. I read the first two hundred pages: my will had given in by then." (All had, however, read Great Expectations during the year.) Two boys had read Plato's Republic; incidentally, one of them is intending to read English in the sixth form, the other biology, physics and chemistry. One boy had started, but given up The Mayor of Casterbridge.

Perhaps the most surprising choice of all the books mentioned was from outside the twentieth century: Malory's Morte d'Arthur.

> I enjoyed this book, but it had to be read carefully as the English was in the style of the old translation of the Bible. I read it because I saw it in the house library, and as the title was in French I decided to see if I could translate any, and found that the book was in English. As I enjoyed it, I read the second book in the series.

But otherwise their reading was almost exclusively of modern novels. This is explained, partly, by my policy. I recommend books to them during the year and particularly at the beginning of the Christmas and Easter holidays; most of the books that I recommend are twentieth-century novels because I believe that they will enjoy these books more than earlier novels, from which I think they will derive more benefit when they are older. Consequently I concentrate on Hemingway (although one parent wrote this year to say that he was writing to the headmaster to complain strongly that his son was reading "pornography by a man called Hemingway; my son tells me that you have told him to read this stuff"), Orwell, Huxley, Golding, Cary, Maugham, Hartley, Conrad and Greene; this, of course, is only a selection of authors, but reflects the popularity of choice among the year's pupils.

Of those who said why they chose certain novels, it is perhaps not surprising that the most common reason was "by recommendation". In 34 cases, the recommendations were by me, in 20 cases by their friends, and in nine cases by their parents; the parental recommendations may seem very small, but all the boys were boarders and so such recommendations were restricted to the holidays. It is interesting that the second influence in choosing a book was "because I enjoyed another book by the same author"; this was so in 42 cases. Naturally, Fleming occurred occasionally here, but less often than one might have expected, for most boys did not give any reason for going from one Fleming novel to another.

After reading Lord of the Flies, one boy read Free

Ages Fifteen to Nineteen

Fall and Pincher Martin. One boy had enjoyed an extract, in form, from Homage to Catalonia; this led to his buying and reading it, and also buying and reading Down and Out in Paris and London and Keep the Aspidistra Flying. After we had read The Diamond as Big as the Ritz in form, another boy read The Great Gatsby ("I have now re-read it three times") and This Side of Paradise. For Whom the Bell Tolls frequently led to A Farewell to Arms (although one boy described For Whom the Bell Tolls as "the best novel I've read this year" but was not prompted to read any more of Hemingway's works) and 1984 often led to Brave New World and frequently provoked the request: "Are there any more novels like these?"

Twenty-two novels were chosen specifically because they were thought to be "sexy"; I will return to these later. Nine were read because they were lying about, often on the floor. There are seldom books of any sort lying around in this school, and I constantly wonder why schools are so parsimonious in the provision of books, when they spend large sums on laboratory equipment; furthermore books are often too carefully guarded. I like my books to be clean; but I would prefer them to be dirty and read, than neatly displayed on the shelves with the pages uncut. Books are "the precious life-blood of a master spirit"; but need they be embalmed in a guarded, and sometimes even locked, library? Accessibility to books is essential if reading is to be encouraged and to occupy its rightful place in the curriculum; and both the initial expenditure and the depreciation should be greater than they often are.

Four books were read after a boy had seen the film made from the book: Dr. No, The Lord of the Flies, The Cruel Sea, and Lord Jim. A Portrait of the Artist as a Young Man was read by a boy, who had seen the television programme about Joyce, when he found the book lying on my table; this was the only example of television influencing directly anyone's reading. Three books were read because of their covers; this figure was surprisingly low, and included The Card, whose cover was modern but not in any way lurid. Finally, on three occasions boys started to read a book in a bookshop, were interested by it, and bought it. These reasons for reading books are not complete, for in many cases, the boys did not state their reasons, but they are probably representative.

The reactions of the boys to books which they read because the boys thought the books would be sexy are interesting and support the view that such books are not, in themselves, likely to corrupt or deprave boys; it does seem, from this group of boys, that boys take from the books only what they bring to them in the first place. Three boys read The Ginger Man, and all did so because they had heard that it was sexy; although one said "It was stolen before I could finish it," which sounds regretful, the other two said: "I gave it up as it was far too vulgar; sex was just carried to an extremity," and "It was despicably boring and unpleasant to read."

Of Lady Chatterley's Lover it was said: "I was curious about the contents, but found it very boring." Perhaps, when he reads it for more mature reasons, he will not be bored. Similarly, The Perfumed Garden was dismissed as "a disgusting book, crude, &c.," and "I did not finish it; it was too full of sex which was very boring." Fanny Hill was regarded as "Repetitive and boring" and, by another boy: "I read it to see what it was like as my brother bought it in Germany; I found it very boring and did not complete it." All these remarks were written by different boys. It is, I think, a cynical rather than a sexy book that is harmful.

It was encouraging to find how often a book which the boys had started to read only because they felt "I must read this as it was recommended by 'Sir'" became the book which they had most enjoyed reading this year: "I found For Whom the Bell Tolls was much better than I expected, and I think that it's the best book I've read this year"; of the same book, "Very much better than I had expected; it was thoroughly interesting." A Farewell to Arms: "One of the best books I have ever read." The Old Man and the Sea: "Very good, but too short." Dr. Zhivago: "A very moving book which was interesting and contained a good story, although it had too many complicated Russian names for my liking." The Great Gatsby, as I mentioned earlier, was re-read three times. Two of the three boys who read The Go-Between found it "hard going for some time, but it became very interesting and exciting towards the end."

Not all, of course, found the recommended books re-

Ages Fifteen to Nineteen

warding: "The characters in Father and Son were too Puritan and there was no excitement in the book at all." Only one out of 10, however, did not enjoy Lord of the Flies; the other nine all approved of it, largely because, as one boy put it:

> This book was very good because when you ask someone what he would do if wrecked on an island, he would say that he would build houses, cultivate the land, and become another R. Crusoe. But this book gives a true idea of what it would be like, as the children eventually become wild, idol-worshiping savages.

This does not purport to be an authoritative survey. It is merely the result of a period or two spent discussing the reading of one O level form of 18 boys who, heaven knows, were under a great deal of pressure from many of their masters to "do some hard work this year", and who found little enough time left to read in their leisure hours. But they did read some books, and enjoyed most of them; if they did nothing else, between them they bought at least 63 books this year.

Table I

The most popular authors

Fleming	33
Innes	16
Golding	12
Hemingway	11
Orwell	10
Shute	9

Table II

Reasons for reading books

Recommended		63
(by me:	34	
friends:	20	
parents:	9)	

Table II (cont'd)

Reasons for reading books

- Enjoyed another book by the same author — 42
- Because it was thought to be a sexy book — 22
- It was lying around — 9
- After seeing the film — 4
- Because of the cover — 3
- Started to read it in a book-shop — 3

Why Do They "Hate" the Classics?

Lewis S. Gannett

From Child Study 34:16-7, Spring 1957. Copyright 1957 by the Child Study Association of America. Reprinted by permission.

"I hate books," a Williams College graduate began the literary autobiography which I had asked the students in a graduate school of journalism class to write. As he remembered it, he had enjoyed reading as a child, but the home-reading assignments imposed upon him in high school had soured him on literature for life.

It was a Harvard graduate who told me that he had disliked reading from kindergarten all the way into his postgraduate years in the Army. There he fell sick. In the Army hospital there was nothing to do but read. Books were abundant, and nothing was prescribed. He said he discovered, for the first time in his life, that reading could be fun.

Another presumably bright young man (students at the Columbia school are picked from a long list of applicants) explained: "My real awakening to books came about 14 when I began to notice the half-naked women on the covers of the 25-cent paper-back books." He confessed later that he had at first been disappointed at the failure of the texts of these books to live up to the lurid promise of their jackets, but had soon found that, regardless of their sex content, many books which he had heard described as classics were surprisingly interesting.

A few students wrote evocative pictures of family readings aloud at home, of sympathetic small town librarians, or of inspired high school instructors who aroused the imagination of a whole class and set them all to acting Shakespeare. But far more declared that they had hated Shakespeare and all other classics in schools.

A surprising number reported on the usefulness of "Classics Comics". With their aid, they tell me, it is possible to pass high school tests in required reading without going through the drudgery of reading the books. A few insisted, however, that the "Classics Comics" stimulated them to look at the originals, and they had been delighted to discover that classics were not always as sappy as both their teachers and the "Classics Comics" had indicated. (The only student in this year's class who had not at one time or another read comic books was a girl who had grown up in Ireland.)

These students, I believe, have been honest with me, and I suspect that what they remember of their own experiences with books is significant. Not one has ever thought to complain of the techniques by which they had been taught to read. Most of them seem to have learned to read avidly, especially if they had an older brother or sister who achieved the magic of deciphering print ahead of them. Not one admits that his early experiences with comics hurt him. Most remember their first children's books with pleasure. An impressive proportion, however, recall that they virtually stopped reading, or at least enjoying reading, in high school, and not all of them have even yet recovered from that trauma. Most have a vague feeling that they have somehow missed out on something worthwhile, and hope some day to "find time to catch up."

One of the games I have played with these classes is to take a census of their reading. They all have read something of Hemingway, Faulkner, Steinbeck and Sinclair Lewis. About half have read a bit of Dreiser, Sherwood Anderson and Dos Passos. When I ask how many have read any George Eliot, every hand in the class goes up. How many have ever read a book by George Eliot which was not prescribed for them in school? Hardly a hand shows!

What does it all mean? Casual contacts with a limited group of more or less picked graduate students in journalism are scant basis for generalizations. But they at least suggest that there may be serious errors in the curricula of high school courses in English. The students are forced to read, and are puzzled and dismayed by, Shakespeare and Milton before they are ready for them.

Ages Fifteen to Nineteen

(I think the same may be true of Moby Dick, which has crept into the curricula since my day.) They are still asked to read Silas Marner, Ivanhoe and Evangeline; and they find them dull and pallid fare. Most of them emerge from the discipline with little gain in knowledge, but an impressive distrust of anything called a classic, and, all too often, with an actual dislike of books--any kind of books.

I have never met in a classroom the type of youthful cynic who spills over so many pages of recent fiction. These students are healthily suspicious of authority, but they are not instinctive amoralists, as the novels would have us believe. They may have read less, but in other ways they are more adult than my own remote pre-war generation. They are far more familiar with the "facts of life" than we were, though we knew more than our parents and teachers dreamed. Indeed, I suspect that they go through in grade school the types of adolescent courtship I first observed in high school, and many of them marry before they leave college.

Explain it as you like: television, movies, world wars, atom bombs, sunspots, what you will. We used to be told that our grandparents had matured younger than we, and that boys and girls ripened faster in the tropics than in these temperate climes. Maybe that is no longer true. At any rate, I tend to believe that the selected reading lists of today--whether selected by parents, librarians, teachers or school boards--and even the well-intended "Classics Comics"--are based on an out-of-date picture of the childishness of young minds. Give the kids stronger fare than bowdlerized Shakespeare, immaculate Milton and womanless Melville, and they may respond by more, and more eager, reading.

The capacity of the young mind to survive and even profit by tough experience in and out of books can hardly be exaggerated. I am still haunted by the remark of an able and positive girl barely graduated from a New York City college who told how her father had tried to limit her reading to the Bible, and how, still in her teens, she had discovered and read by herself, and had been excited by, Hemingway's The Sun Also Rises. It was, she said, the greatest experience of her life; obviously she felt it had been the beginning of a new world for her. "I don't know if I have ever felt quite the utter uselessness and aimlessness of life," she wrote, "that I did then."

At first it seemed a frightening remark. But as the girl talked on it seemed rather that she had discovered at 13 what some people discover only at 30, and too late. She had already recovered from the experience. She was triumphantly on her way. She had picked the forbidden fruit, read the forbidden books, made adolescent discoveries on her own, and moved into an adult world. So few of us ever do!

Free Reading and Book Reports--
An Informal Survey of Grade Eleven

Donald R. Gallo

From the Journal of Reading 11:532-8, April 1968. Reprinted with permission of Donald R. Gallo and the International Reading Association.

When three eleventh grade students out of 142 of average ability select Goldfinger as the best book they have ever read, when one boy selects The Carpetbaggers and another Fanny Hill as the best books they have ever read, when 16 percent of the students in two different schools select The Scarlet Letter as the worst book they have ever read either for school or outside of school, when 17 percent of the students in another school select The Scarlet Letter as the best book they read in English class this year, and when twice as many students in one school are influenced by movies as by teachers in their choice of books...we need to reevaluate the impact of teaching on our students' reading.

An informal survey--by questionnaire--was recently conducted in the entire eleventh grade at two different central New York State schools, involving a total of 262 students-- 128 boys and 134 girls--In English classes taught by six different teachers. Included were: one honors group in each school, one basic (slow) group in each school, and nine "average" groups (five in one school and four in the other). Admittedly, this informal survey was of limited scope--only one grade and two schools; but probably the students involved represent a cross-section of American youth. Both schools are central schools; that is, each is the main school for a district that includes more than one town. The students come from varying backgrounds. The fathers of some students are farmers; some are employed in the small businesses and services of the towns; and, because both schools are within easy commuting distance of an industrial city, many fathers are engaged in big businesses and professions or employed as blue-collar workers in the city. There are neither very rich nor very poor.

The questions were divided into a number of broad areas: (1) numbers, kinds, and titles of books read; (2) reasons for reading; (3) books and movies; (4) attitudes and procedures involved with book reports; and (5) influences on reading choices and attitudes. Some of the findings are corroborated by previous research; some are not. Nevertheless, many of the replies provoke vital questions and urge broader research into reading habits.

Books Read

Always of interest are the current reading choices of students--the amount and kinds of reading. In the ten-months period preceding the questionnaire, students reported that they had read for their own private reading (not for school work) an average of 13 books each. The basic groups averaged 11 books each, while the top groups averaged better than 20 books each. Fewer than 8 percent of the students had not read a book on their own. The range within each class was tremendous: in most classes some students said they had not read a book while others reported fifty or more. In all groups, girls read more than boys, a finding corroborated by all previous research.

The most important finding regarding amount of reading is that on the day of the survey 47 percent of the students were reading a book on their own volition. In one school 37 percent of the basic class, 38 percent of the average classes and 67 percent of the honors class were reading at the time. But almost the opposite was true in the other school: 81 percent of the basic class, 47 percent of the average classes and 40 percent of the honors class were reading. Although girls usually read more than boys, more boys than girls were in the process of reading a book at the time of the survey. But the questionnaire did not request the kind of information that would suggest reasons for this. What is startling is the amount of reading being done, especially in the light of the heavy assigned reading schedules these students had, plus the threat of the New York State Regents Examinations which were about a month away.

Few students were reading the same titles, but of

Ages Fifteen to Nineteen

those mentioned by more than one student, the following appeared: Lord of the Flies, 1984, The Pearl, Harrison High, The Agony and the Ecstasy, and The Green Berets. Other titles ranged from Atlas Shrugged to Street Rod to Up the Down Staircase to Fanny Hill. Other popular titles were Catcher in the Rye, Black Like Me, Gone with the Wind, The Diary of Anne Frank, Goldfinger, To Kill a Mockingbird, Thunderball, A Tree Grows in Brooklyn, Animal Farm, and Death Be Not Proud. Obviously, the titles do not fall into any single category.

Preferences, especially among teen-agers, change rapidly. Among these books noted by students, only two-- To Kill a Mockingbird and Gone with the Wind--were chief among the books enjoyed most by students surveyed by Fulton in 1964.[2] Among recent best sellers, Up the Down Staircase and The Green Berets appealed most to the eleventh graders. But spy thrillers dominated their readings. Goldfinger and Thunderball led the list, but many other James Bond books were mentioned.

Although many of the titles mentioned most frequently are serious fiction, the majority of all titles mentioned are light fiction. The students indicated this also on a checklist of preferences. Serious fiction and true stories follow, except in one honors class where serious fiction was preferred over all other kinds. Then follow short stories, humorous essays, and science fiction.

Gone with the Wind led the list of the best books ever read; it was noted best by 22 students, 17 of them girls. Next in frequency of mention was Catcher in the Rye, 1984, and To Kill a Mockingbird. There was little further agreement as to best titles. Among those listed as "best ever" were Exodus, Another Country, Up the Down Staircase, Huckleberry Finn, The Longest Day, Kon-Tiki, Lassie Come Home, A Thousand Days, Hawaii, The Diary of Anne Frank, Harrison High, Animal Farm, Peyton Place, and The Scarlet Letter. Tastes ran from very serious, adult, "significant" novels to simple, very youthful adventure stories.

The implications of these titles are many and varied. But the dominating one is that many English teachers would shudder to hear some of those titles mentioned as the best book a student has ever read. (Conversely, many students shudder at the thought that Great Expectations, The Scarlet Letter, Julius Caesar, and The Mayor of Casterbridge are great books.) More than 16 percent of the students noted The Scarlet Letter as the worst book they had ever read. Perhaps if more students had been forced to read it, and were thus in a position to pass judgment on it, the percentages might have been even greater. Other titles rated "worst" by many students are The Red Badge of Courage, The Mayor of Casterbridge (44 percent of one class!), Great Expectations, and Lord of the Flies (disliked by mostly girls). Not so understandable is that four boys disliked The Yearling most, one boy hated Treasure Island, one Huckleberry Finn, and another noted The Bible as the worst book he had ever read.

What is very confusing is that three of the four "least liked" books appear as three of the four most liked books in this survey, with The Scarlet Letter at the top of the list! Obviously, "What is food to one man may be fierce poison to others." But what is not obvious to many teachers and administrators is the futility of submitting all students to the same bill of fare all the time. The need for flexibility in required and suggested reading is certainly indicated here.

Reasons for Reading

In answer to the simple question "Do you like to read?" a majority of both boys and girls, though more girls than boys, said Yes; a few said it depended on the material; and slightly more than 20 percent of the students said No. In the honors classes, 100 percent of the girls and 94 percent of the boys liked to read. In the basic groups, 56 percent of the girls said they did not like to read, while only half as many boys said they did not like to read. So, while in the top and average classes more girls than boys liked to read, the reverse was true in the bottom groups.

Young people--all of us for that matter--have many reasons for reading. Chief among them is enjoyment. Exactly what enjoyment means is another matter, beyond the scope of this investigation. But, without a doubt, most students read primarily for enjoyment, and a book ceases to be worth reading as soon as it ceases to be enjoyable. In these two schools, 62 percent of the students read primarily for enjoyment. Another 19 percent read because "books tell you a lot about life." Two girls said they read primarily to get into college; and three boys and one girl read to satisfy their parents.

Books and Movies

Movies, contrary to many beliefs, have a positive effect on reading. More than 62 percent of the students had read a book after seeing the movie version. In one school there was little difference among groups, while in the other school 81 percent of the honors group and only 53 percent of the basic group had read a book after seeing the movie version.

Television has its place here, too, since many of the movies were seen there rather than in a movie theater. Among the chief titles seen on television and then read were The Diary of Anne Frank, The Manchurian Candidate, Wuthering Heights, 1984, The Grapes of Wrath, Green Mansions, For Whom the Bell Tolls, On the Beach, Jane Eyre, and Inherit the Wind. Slightly more girls than boys read books after seeing the movie version, but girls read slightly more than boys anyway.

It might be an interesting idea for a school to provide free movies each weekend and then to have the paperback book versions available for sale in the school store. Perhaps influential teachers can persuade their local educational television station to run a series of films selected jointly by students and teachers. If the films do not lead to more reading, they should be enjoyable in themselves and might, with the proper follow-up, lead students to better understanding and appreciation of films. After all, many students prefer movies to books anyway; in fact, about 44 percent of the eleventh graders stated a preference for movies over novels.

Book Reports

There is very little debate among students when it comes to deciding whether or not they like book reports. They do not. As a matter of fact, in these two schools 79 percent said no. A few sometimes did and sometimes didn't, depending on the material read, and 17 percent liked to give book reports. If the teacher's goal in assigning outside reading is to broaden every student's background and to strengthen his reading abilities, then a completely individualized reading program, with the teacher encouraging students to read diversified materials that he might enjoy, rather than assigning specified titles that everyone must read, is a much more sensible way of attaining that goal.

Students were also asked to state their preference for one of a pair of possible assignments for book reports. When given a choice between an oral report and writing a short review on a 5 x 8 card, 84 percent chose the latter; in three classes, the girls were 100 percent for the short review. The most popular choice (when paired with oral reports) was discussing the book in small groups of students who had all read the same book or a book by the same author. Given the choice of small group discussions or talking about their book privately with the teacher, 74 percent favored the small groups.

Influences on Reading

What students have to say to each other about the books they read has far more influence on future reading than any other person or any other device. This was demonstrated both in Smith's[5] study of grades 10 through 14 and in this survey of grade 11. For suggestions of good books to read, a majority of the eleventh graders go most often to friends. In classes where students have book lists of good books (good from their point of view), they go to the lists. If good lists are not available, students go to members of their class and to book displays.

The influence of the English teachers in these two schools is very interesting--perhaps even disturbing. In one school the teachers were at the bottom of the list of sources; no boys and only 3 percent of the girls there go most often to teachers for suggestions of good books to read. By contrast, in the other school, the third largest percentage of students listed teachers first, with the boys noting them second after friends.

Smith noted other motivating factors; they are, in order: "parents, librarians, book displays, book clubs, relatives, knowledge of the authors, the scoutmaster, hobbies, and advertisements."[5] In this survey, book displays were more important than parents; relatives and hobbies didn't count; and advertisements were far down the list.

Farthest down the list in both schools was the influence of the librarian. Fewer than 5 percent of the students go most often to the librarian for suggestions of good books to read!

Students most often discuss their reading with friends. Almost 55 percent of the students go most often to friends and classmates. Next come parents, then brothers and sisters. Teachers rank sixth on the list, chosen first by only 3 percent of the students in one school and by 4 percent of the girls and 16 percent of the boys in the other school.

When asked about the book they were presently reading or had read most recently, "What prompted you to read it?", the largest percentage (21 percent) was the suggestion of friends. Although this is a very small percentage, the influence of friends dominates here. Next in frequency is that the student "just picked it up" either at the library or at home. The recommendation of an English teacher was far from significant in general, although, in one school, 14 percent of the boys were reading a book recommended by an English teacher. A few students were reading a book after having seen the movie or after having read another book by the same author. A few were reading something recommended by other teachers--all were history teachers. Only one boy was reading a book that had been suggested by a librarian.

But when it comes to a problem that arises in reading, most students no longer go first and most often to a friend. Parents take the lead here even though they have very little influence in other areas of reading. More girls than boys go most often to parents. Boys go most often to resource books. Teachers rank second, followed by friends.

Conclusion

The tremendous influence of friends on reading and discussing books is something that a wise teacher takes advantage of through classrom discussions with small groups. Eliminating the threat of grading, minimizing the amount of required writing, and encouraging free discussions about books ought to produce more enthusiasm for reading. But a word of caution is necessary. Previous investigations[1, 3] have shown that completely free reading, although it increases the amount of reading, does not necessarily lead to improvement of taste or appreciation. Reading must be guided; students must be taught how to read better. But first they must be encouraged to read, and that is often the most difficult part. They need a start. Norvell[4] advocated letting students read what they want to read, except the "morally objectionable," to get them started and to keep them reading.

Spiegler[6] supplies an enthusiastic comment that fittingly summarizes the direction teachers should take:

> Give Johnny a title, a book jacket, a theme that rings true. Talk to him colorfully about the world of books. Don't limit him to the confines of prescribed book lists and prescribed formulas for making book reports. Let the world and its infinite wonders be the subjects he may choose from. Let him read what he likes, appeal to his interests-- and Johnny reads (p. 183)

If the students at the two schools in this survey could have reacted to that statement, they probably would have said "AMEN!"

References

1. Bruning, Herbert I. "A Study of the Readability, Interest, and Usefulness of Selected Materials for Retarded Readers in Grades Seven to Twelve," unpublished doctoral dissertation, University of Kansas, 1954.

2. Fulton, Jennie E. "An Annotated Bibliography for Giftted Senior High School Students," unpublished master's thesis, University of Kansas, 1964.

3. Handling, Bertha. "The Fallacy of Free Reading as an Approach to Appreciation," English Journal, 35 (4), 182-188.

4. Norvell, George W. "Developing Reading Interests and

Attitudes Among Adolescents," Conference on Reading, University of Pittsburgh Report, 1959, 125-147.

5. Smith, Helen K. "A Survey of Current Reading Interests--In Grades Ten Through Fourteen," in Helen M. Robinson (Ed.), Developing Permanent Interest in Reading, Supplementary Educational Monographs, No. 84. Chicago: University of Chicago Press, 1956, 65-68.

6. Spiegler, Charles G. "Johnny Will Read What He Likes to Read," in Helen M. Robinson (Ed.), Developing Permanent Interest in Reading, Supplementary Educational Monographs, No. 84. Chicago: University of Chicago Press, 1956, 182-186.

What Does Research Reveal
About Reading and the High School Student?

John J. DeBoer

From the English Journal 47:271-81, May 1958. Reprinted with the permission of the National Council of Teachers of English and John J. DeBoer.

We know today that reading is not an isolated skill, but a complex ability that is closely interrelated with the general personal development of the individual. Physical well-being, emotion, thought, mood, experience, rate of general maturation, and similar factors are all involved in reading growth. For this reason, no study of the reading process is complete without a close look at the characteristics and needs of the learner himself.

Winnowing from the now vast professional literature about the adolescent and his reading those generalizations which have general acceptance is no easy task. Much of the research is inconclusive; some of it is contradictory. This article undertakes to report a number of facts and interpretations about young people which may throw some light on the difficult task of helping them to read better.

The Concerns of High School Youth

There have been numerous listings of needs, characteristics, "developmental tasks," and concerns of adolescents. Among those commonly described are the following:

Physical Development

The chief task of the adolescent, of course, is to grow into adulthood. Part of this task is performed with the benevolent cooperation of nature itself. The boy or girl who enters into the period of puberty and sexual maturity has little to do with the changes that occur in his or her muscular, skeletal, glandular, and physiological makeup. But the individual's attitude toward these changes may make a great deal of difference in his social behavior and general outlook. Especially adolescent boys are much concerned about being "normal" in physical dexterity. For example:

"Among adults it is often difficult to realize what it means to an adolescent when through illness, late development, or other factors, he is unable to play a usual part in the physical activities of his fellows. Such a boy may turn his interest to other goals. It is a critical question whether, in so doing, he will lose contact with his classmates, or, on the other hand, will find a socially adequate use of such favorable traits as he may possess. When it becomes feasible for the teacher to provide guidance in such situations, the adolescent appraisal of physical prowess need not be accepted as an inevitably sound scheme of values."(24)

Personal Appearance

Many youth of high school age have anxiety about their physical appearance. Poor complexion worries many adolescents, both boys and girls. Being "unattractive," too fat, too thin, too tall, or short worried seventeen percent of respondents in one study (8). In another study (11) the responding male youth expressed concern about complexion, lack of beard or heavy beard, scars, irregular teeth, protruding or receding chin, large or protruding ears, and even freckles! Female respondents named similar sources of anxiety, although none seem to have been disturbed by the beard problem.

Being Accepted and Loved by Parents and Peers

Tryon puts it this way: "The peer group, whether it is a neighborhood play group, a social clique, or a delinquent gang, offers the child or adolescent greater continuity in terms of time, and more understanding than he finds in adult-directed groups... Next to the family in childhood, and probably equally with the family during adolescence, the peer group provides satisfactions to the basic urges for security in the warmth of friendship and the sense of adequacy that come from belonging..."[1] Thus also the security of the home and the love and guidance of parents remain important, even while the youth strives to gain emotional independence from his parents.

Having Confidence in Himself and His Own Abilities

Many factors operate to promote feelings of insecurity among young people. The imminence of military service, conflicts between cultural standards of the older and younger generation, conflicts between ethnic and racial groups, fear of not being accepted by the peer group, anxiety about vocation, and the contradictions in social examples and ideals make many an adolescent wonder whether he can measure up to the expectations of those to whom he looks for approval.

Assuming an Acceptable Sex Role

Since adolescence marks the beginning of strong sex interests, it is a period of stress and often of perplexity because of the young person's normal sex desires and the restrictions placed upon him by the moral standards of the adult society. The new problem calls for a kind of intelligence, judgment, and quality of character never before required in the child's experience. Moreover, he is called upon to enter into socially approved roles for boys and girls which, whether justified or not, are essential to happy accommodation to our culture (17).

Developing an Acceptable Set of Values, a Faith for Living

Young people are concerned, not only about how they will make a living, but also how they will make a life. Underneath the surface frivolity of adolescent youth, there is usually a strong desire to come to terms with the realities of life and to find a path to direct their ways. They want to know what things are of most worth, what their feelings about human beings should be, what constitutes real success, and how they can best bend their efforts toward the achievement of their cherished goals.

In this connection it is interesting to note the revival of an old-fashioned idea that has been given scientific respectability in an important new volume by Daniel Prescott

(25). This student of child development rehabilitates a word long shunned by psychologists--the word "love." With his permission we quote a part of his discussion of love in the development of children and youth:

"Some seven years ago I was quite bothered by the fact that the term "love" occurred so infrequently in psychological writings dealing with human motivation. Scientists seemed to have a deep distrust of the term. This led me to read extensively in psychiatric literature in the attempt to discover whether love is a genuine human reality or only a romantic construct within our culture, for cultures do exist in which love is not practiced. My search was very rewarding and led not only to the conclusion that love is a genuine human reality but also to the conviction that it plays a most important role in human development. Very cogent affirmations of the nature of human love appear in the writings of Harry Stack Sullivan and Erich Fromm.

Perhaps it will be worth the space here to include a brief summary of my conclusions regarding the nature of love so that teachers may know what to look for in relationships between parents and children. Valid love seems to include the following components:

    1. Love involves more or less empathy with the loved one. A person who loves actually enters into the feelings of and shares intimately the experiences of the loved one and the effects of these experiences upon the loved one.

    2. One who loves is deeply concerned for the welfare, happiness, and development of the beloved. This concern is so deep as to become one of the major organizing values in the personality of self-structure of the loving person. Harry Stack Sullivan wrote, 'When the satisfaction or the security of another person becomes as significant to one as is one's own security, then the state of love exists.'

    3. One who loves finds pleasure in making his resources available to the loved one, to

be used by the other to enhance his welfare, happiness, and development. Strength, time, money, thought, indeed all resources are proffered happily to the loved one for his use. A loving person is not merely concerned about the beloved's welfare and development, he does something about it.

4. Of course the loving person seeks a maximum of participation in the activities that contribute to the welfare, happiness, and development of the beloved. But he also accepts fully the uniqueness and individuality of the beloved and, to the degree implied by the beloved's maturity level, accords to the latter full freedom to experience, to act, and to become what he desires to become. A loving person has a nonpossessive respect for the selfhood of the loved one.

By permission from D. A. Prescott, <u>The Child in the Educative Process</u> (New York: McGraw-Hill), pp. 357-358.

Individual Differences

The foregoing discussion undertook to describe some of the common concerns of high school youth. But the differences among the youth are perhaps as important as the characteristics which are common among them. The young people differ widely in their height, weight, color of hair and eyes, temperament, background of experience, intelligence, socio-economic status, and in every other identifiable characteristic. They differ especially in their reading interests and abilities.

Differences in Reading Ability.

All teachers are aware that their pupils differ widely in reading ability, but few are familiar with the astonishing range of the differences. Most pupils in American high schools are grouped roughly according to chronological age. In the typical eighth grade English class, therefore, we are likely to find a range of eight or more grades in reading ability. Thus in one study (21) it was reported that among more than 50,000 eighth grade pupils only fourteen percent had eighth grade reading ability. Eight percent had less than fifth grade reading ability, and almost seven percent had twelfth grade reading ability. The rest were distributed between these two extremes. The sample is so large that it is reasonable to assume that these differences are typical of high school students generally.

Other studies yield similar results. In a St. Louis study only slightly more than fourteen percent scored at the eighth grade level, while thirty-seven percent scored above, and forty-eight percent scored below the eighth grade level. Of 4,236 eighth grade graduates, eighty-six scored below the fourth grade level, and ninety-nine scored at the thirteenth grade level or above. Just about as many of these students scored at the ninth grade level as the eighth, and far more of them scored at the seventh grade level than at the eighth (20). Apparently, knowing that a pupil is in the eighth grade, or a graduate of the eighth grade gives no clue to his reading ability.

Ernest Horn reports an extensive study of the reading comprehension of 6,000 sixth, seventh, and eighth grade children in a variety of school systems.[2] He found that the lowest score in grade eight was as low as any in grade six. The range of ability in grade seven was eleven times the difference between the medians of grades six and seven. The difference between the best and poorest pupil in the middle half of grade seven is nearly three times as great as the difference between the medians of grades six and seven.

That the range of abilities is equally wide in various sections of the country is illustrated in another study.[3] Simpson compared the spread of reading ability among 565 tenth graders in a large midwestern city and of 380 tenth graders in a Southeastern city. The grade distributions for both groups resembled those in the other investigations.

The range of differences in reading ability represents only one aspect of the problem. Students who score at the same grade level vary widely in the nature of their difficulties and needs (23).

The existence of such a wide range of reading ability

is not to be deplored. Even many experienced teachers often feel that the wide differences are unusual, and try very hard to bring the very retarded pupils "up to the norm" or to the appropriate grade level. Obviously if they succeeded in this endeavor the class average itself would rise, and the range of the class would be greater than ever. The purpose should not be to bring the most retarded "up to the norm," but to help every child to read up to his full capacity. Individual differences are increased, not diminished, by good teaching.

There is no way of escaping the fact of individual differences in our classes (and, consequently, the need of adapting instruction to individual differences). We can keep the element of chronological age constant. Many people think that children learn best in association with their age mates. But if we do, the spread of reading ability will be very great. We can keep the "reading age" constant. But if we do, the range of chronological age, social maturity, and special abilities will be very great. In any case, it will be necessary to deal with individuals. At the same time, however, we must be concerned about the social experiences of the children. The conclusions are inescapable: (1) our groups must be socially compatible, and they must be reasonably homogeneous in physical maturity and general development; and (2) we must provide for individual instruction, permitting each child to master the needed skills at his own rate.

Sex Differences

Girls are generally superior to boys in reading ability, especially at the elementary school level. While boys tend to excel in such subjects as science, arithmetic, and history, girls are more proficient in all kinds of verbalistic activity. Apparently these differences are not attributable to any differences in the intelligence of boys and girls, but (1) to the slower maturation of the boys, and (2) to the cultural influences which assign diverse roles to boys and girls. Certainly the number of boys in remedial reading groups and clinics far exceeds that of girls, often by a ratio of ten to one. Moreover, larger numbers of boys than girls of the same chronological age appear to be unready for beginning instruction in reading.

Socio-economic and Cultural Differences

How well the child succeeds in reading depends in large measure on what he brings to the printed page. His attitudes toward people, books, and school itself; his stock of meaningful impressions; his knowledge of language; his vocational aspirations and prospects--these and many other factors will determine the degree of his success in reading. All of these are profoundly affected by his social, economic, and cultural background.

For example, the part of town in which a child lives will affect his standing in the community, the way in which others think of him, and the way he thinks of himself. If he comes from the district on the "other side of the tracks," he will not only lack many of the images and concepts he encounters in his reading, but he may lack also the self-confidence and the motivation which are needed for successful reading and which the child from the "Gold Coast" is more likely to possess. The child of first or second generation immigrants, often the butt of cruel nicknames, may feel inferior academically to his age mates of native stock. Especially if he comes from a bilingual home, he is likely to be at a disadvantage, since the average performance of bilingual children is lower than that of monolingual children. (Please note the word average, since also in this respect children differ widely.)

Family income, too, plays a large part in the child's attitudes toward his peers, not only as a result of the amount of money he has to spend, but also as a result of the social standing of his parents. In a typical school the differences in family income are very great. For example, in Illinois, according to the 1950 census, the median family income was $3,267, with nineteen percent of the families earning less than $2,000 per year, and 28.1 percent of the families earning $5,000 or more per year. The fact that even in a fairly homogeneous wealthy community the children of the business executives sit side by side with the children of the family servants is a tribute to the democratizing influence of the public school; but it also presents an instructional problem of the first magnitude.

Low social, economic, and cultural status interferes with all school learning, but especially with learning to read. Unfavorable conditions at home have been shown to be a major factor in many cases of reading retardation (27). It is of the utmost importance, therefore, that the school attempt to supply the favorable conditions of which children are deprived at home. These conditions include an abundance of good, attractive books, suitable physical surroundings, time and encouragement to read, and an atmosphere of acceptance, security, and affection.

That the school can succeed in overcoming the effects of unfavorable social, economic, and cultural conditions in the teaching of teading has been repeatedly demonstrated. However, superior educational statesmanship, imagination, adequate facilities, and skilful teaching are required to cope with the reading problems of children who live under these conditions.

Reading Interests[4]

The interests of young people are as varied as the young people themselves. They are the product of many interrelated factors--intelligence, general maturity, home background, geographical location, past experiences, cultural opportunities. These interests vary in kind, diversity, and intensity. Happily, they can be kindled, sustained, enriched, redirected, and heightened through skilful guidance.

The interests of young people are characterized by change as well as range. They change from one generation to the next, and of course they constantly change within individuals. Not only increasing maturity and experience, but external events and social change affect profoundly the interests of youth. Who knows what combination of factors caused the progression from the Charleston to bebop and rock 'n' roll? The causes may lie deep in the fears and uncertainties of our time.

Obviously the subject matter that engages the interest of young people will reflect the changing aspects of the passing scene. Aviation and space travel may have their basic appeal in youth's immemorial love for adventure, but the specific forms of these interests are derived from inventions of the last half-century. If girls are turning today to stories of careers for women and read less about domestic scenes, it is because women have entered into industry, business, and the professions on a scale not known before in Western

culture. If junior high school girls wear lipstick earlier
than ever before, it may be because they sit up late enough
to ponder the Revlon commercials. Surely the interests of
youth are in large part learned interests.

Each generation, each great social change, finds its
reflection in literature, including the literature for children.
The greatest of the literature survives the generations and
the social changes, but the more ephemeral books serve
important purposes. New issues arise and old ones die.
The old titles are forgotten and new ones take their place.
Thus Charters found very few titles that continued at the
head of the list of best-liked books for boys over a period
of thirty years. Only three survived throughout the period--
Tom Sawyer, Huckleberry Finn, and Treasure Island. More,
of course, have survived as favorites with many children
and youth. Robinson Crusoe, Little Women, The Five Little
Peppers, Alice in Wonderland, Heidi, Hans Brinker, Uncle
Tom's Cabin, and The Call of the Wild are examples. But
just as it is right for our impressions of reality to keep
fading as new ones constantly make their impact upon us, so
the books, the chief conveyors of these impressions, are
properly and promptly replaced and forgotten. Only those
with universal themes that transcend specific events or periods survive.

In all this diversity we do, however, find traces of
unity. Despite the wide range of individual interests and
the changes that occur outside and inside the reader, certain
general statements can be made safely. A great body of research on children's interests has been accumulating over
the years. While some of the findings are inconclusive or
contradictory, certain major conclusions may be drawn from
the numerous studies. Thus at the junior high school level
the themes of adventure and humor command well-nigh universal appeal, while the theme of romantic love, particularly
as found in adult fiction, is making a strong beginning in
the affections of the young. From these studies, as well as
from informal observations, we know, too, that there are
sharp differences between the interests of boys and girls.
Boys like vigorous action--exploration, pursuit, conflict,
triumph, surprise. They like the David-and-Goliath type of
story, the real life or fictional hero in either the Edison or
Daniel Boone category. Often they enjoy stories of sports
and science. Many come to love Stevenson, Dickens, Dumas,

Mark Twain. Girls, on the other hand, read stories of home and school life, romantic love, careers for women, mystery stories, and sentimental fiction. Girls are more likely to read boys' books than boys are to read girls' books.

Curiously, the factors of intelligence and socio-economic status do not markedly affect young people's interests. Bright and slow-learning pupils tend to like the same kinds of books, movies, and radio and television programs. Of course, the age at which they acquire the various interests will vary, and the quantity of reading is greater in the case of the brighter pupil. The reading of comic strips and comic books is very much the same among pupils of varying levels of intelligence. Moreover, the choices of adolescents among the various media are similar in the various socio-economic classes. Many investigators comment upon the poor quality of the selections made by many youths. Fiction predominates over non-fiction in the voluntary reading of junior high school students. And, contrary to common opinion, the amount of voluntary reading is approximately as great among boys as among girls. The interest patterns of young people in reading are strictly individual, the product of hereditary, maturational and environmental factors, all interrelated and interactive.

Perhaps the most significant of the findings relating to young people's interests is the fact that voluntary reading reaches its peak at about age 12 and tends to decline during the senior high school years. It is comforting to know that with this decline appears also a sharp lessening of interest in the so-called comic books.

It should be noted also that the particular medium of communication does not essentially affect the nature of young people's interests. The appeal of the content, rather than the specific medium of communication, is the determining factor in young people's interests.

Nevertheless, we cannot overlook the revolutionary effect of television upon the lives of children and youth. Paul Witty's annual surveys of the TV viewing habits of the young are startling and fraught with significance for the teacher. If it was thought in earlier years that TV viewing would decline after the novelty had worn off, we now know that this has not been the case. For example, in 1950 Witty found that children devoted twenty-one hours per week to television viewing. In 1956 it was still twenty-one hours.

Fortunately TV viewing falls off during the high school years, and we may reasonably assume that the decline begins in the junior high school.

Much discussion has centered about the question of the effect of television on the reading habits of young people. The reports have been contradictory. Some librarians think there has been a decline in the amount of young people's reading. Others report that reading among children and youth has reached record heights. Here again we must deal with the fact of individual differences. Certainly some boys and girls are reading less because of the hypnotic charms of the TV screen. Others, however, have been introduced to new worlds of knowledge and imagination, and are now reading more. Witty's latest study suggests that nearly half of the children read more than before the era of TV. Soon a comparison will not be possible because TV will have been an accepted part of children's lives since their earliest memories. It is hard to know whether one should pity or envy them.

A good general characterization of young people's interests in reading has been given by Berry: "In this adolescent period, reading interests are broad. Students are beginning to wonder what it feels like to give one's life to religion, to be poverty-stricken, to be corrupt in politics, to die, to give birth, and to fight lions in Africa" (4).

Interrelationships Between Reading and Other Factors

Reading and Intelligence

As most teachers know, there is a high correlation between reading ability and intelligence as measured by existing tests. While it is true that many students of average and above-average intelligence do not read well, and many more fail to read up to their capacities, in general the brighter students are the better readers (Traxler, p. 65). The correlations range between .40 and .60. Since most intelligence tests involve reading tasks or at least linguistic ability, such high correlations are to be expected. Some evidence suggests that the correlation between intelligence and reading rate is low (3).

Reading and Emotions

A close relationship exists between reading and personality problems (42). It is not clear whether personality problems cause reading difficulties or whether the reverse is true. Some investigators stress the crucial role of personality and emotion in reading retardation. Certainly it is true that family relationships play a major part in many cases of reading difficulty (Robinson). It is probable that there is frequently an interactive relation between the two factors (42).

Other factors such as physical development, diseases, sensory acuity, socio-economic status, bilingualism, and experience background have been studied in relation to the reading problem. A summary of the research on all of these would carry us beyond the purpose and scope of this publication. It has been our purpose merely to describe some of the major findings of research workers relative to the characteristics of the student in reading in the secondary school.

References

1. Caroline M. Tryon, "The Adolescent Peer Culture," Adolescence. 43rd Yearbook of the National Society for the Study of Education (Chicago: The University of Chicago Press, 1944), p. 236.

2. "Current Issues Relating to Reading in Various Curriculum Fields," Recent Trends in Reading. Supplementary Educational Monograph, No. 49 (Chicago: The University of Chicago Press, 1939).

3. Ray H. Simpson, Improving Teaching-Hiring Processes (New York: Longmans, Green and Company, 1953), p. 289.

4. The section on Reading Interests is quoted in part from the author's article in Reading in Action (Nancy Larrick, Editor.) Conference Proceedings of the International Reading Association, 1957.

Bibliography

1. Armstrong, Chloe, "Reading Tastes of Waterloo Seniors," Applying Linguistics. 2nd Yearbook of the Iowa Council of Teachers of English (Champaign, Illinois: National Council of Teachers of English, 1957).

2. Association for Supervision and Curriculum Development, Growing Up in An Anxious Age (Washington, D. C.: National Education Association, 1952).

3. Barbe, Walter, and Werner Grilk, "Correlations Between Reading Factors and IQ," School and Society, 75 (March 1, 1952), pp. 134-135.

4. Berry, Elizabeth, Guiding Students in the English Class (New York: Appleton-Century-Crofts, 1957), p. 305.

5. Burton, Dwight L., "The Relationship of Literary Appreciation to Certain Measurable Factors," Journal of Educational Psychology, 43 (November 1952), pp. 436-439.

6. Buswell, Guy T., "The Relationship between Rate of Thinking and Rate of Reading," School Review, 59 (September 1951), pp. 339-346.

7. Clark, Willis W., "Evaluating School Achievement Ability," Journal of Educational Research, 46 (November 1952), pp. 179-191.

8. Elias, L. J., High School Youth Look at Their Problems (Pullman, Washington: The State College of Washington, 1949). The tabulated results of a statewide survey of the opinions of 5,500 high school youths concerning their schools, their families, their friends, and their futures.

9. Ephron, Beulah Kauter, Emotional Difficulties in Reading (New York: The Julian Press, 1953).

10. Frank, Lawrence, and Mary H. Frank, Your Adolescent at Home and in School (New York: Viking Press, 1956).

11. Frazier, Alexander, and Lorenzo K. Lisonbee, "Adolescent Concerns with Physique," The School Review, 58 (October 1950), pp. 397-405.

12. French, Will (ed.) and Associates, Behavioral Goals of General Education in High School (New York: Russell Sage Foundation, 1957).

13. Gann, Edith, Reading Difficulty and Personality Organization (New York: King's Crown Press, 1945).

14. Gesell, Arnold, Frances L. Ilg, and Louise B. Ames, Youth, The Years from 10 to 16 (New York: Harper and Brothers, 1956).

15. Gray, William S., "Reading-II. Physiology and Psychology of Reading," Encyclopedia of Educational Research, Walter S. Moore, Editor. Revised edition (New York: The Macmillan Co., 1950).

16. Gray, William S. (ed.), Reading in Relation to Experience and Language. Supplementary Educational Monographs, No. 58 (Chicago: The University of Chicago Press, 1944).

17. Havighurst, Robert J., Human Development and Education (New York: Longmans' Green and Co., 1953).

18. Havighurst, Robert J., Eugene Strivers, and Robert DeHaan, A Survey of the Education of Gifted Children (Chicago: The University of Chicago Press, 1955).

19. Jones, Harold E., "The Development of Physical Abilities," Adolescence. Forty-Third Yearbook, Part I, of the National Society for the Study of Education (Chicago: The University of Chicago Press, 1944).

20. Kottmeyer, William, "Improving Reading Instruction in the St. Louis Schools," Elementary School Journal, 45 (September 1944), p. 341.

21. Lazar, May (ed.), The Retarded Reader in the Junior High School (New York: Board of Education, City of New York, Bureau of Educational Research, 1952).

22. Lennon, Roger T., "The Relationship between Intelligence and Achievement Test Results for a Group of Communities," Journal of Educational Psychology, 41 (May 1950), pp. 301-308.

23. McCullough, Constance, "What's Behind the Reading Score?" Elementary English, 30 (January 1953), pp. 1-7.

24. National Council of Teachers of English, Commission on the English Curriculum, The English Language Arts in the Secondary School (New York: Appleton-Century-Crofts, 1956), pp. 16-20.
25. Prescott, Daniel A., The Child in the Educative Process (New York: McGraw-Hill Book Co., 1957).
26. Robinson, Helen M., "Some Poor Readers Have Emotional Problems," Reading Teacher, 6 (May 1953), pp. 25-33.
27. Robinson, Helen M., Why Pupils Fail in Reading (Chicago: The University of Chicago Press, 1946).
28. Russell, David H., "Reading Disabilities and Mental Health: A Review of Research," Understanding the Child, 16 (January 1947), pp. 24-32.
29. Sheldon, William D., and Lawrence Carrillo, "Relation of Parents, Home, and Certain Developmental Characteristics to Children's Reading Ability," Elementary School Journal, 52 (January 1952), pp. 262-270.
30. Townsend, Agatha, "Interrelationships between Reading and Other Language Arts Areas," Elementary English, 31 (February 1954), pp. 99-109.
31. Traxler, A. E., and Agatha Townsend, Another Five Years of Research in Reading: Summary and Bibliography (New York: Educational Records Bureau, 1946).
32. Traxler, Arthur E., and Agatha Townsend, Eight More Years of Research in Reading (New York: Educational Records Bureau, 1955.) (Covers period from 1945-1953).
33. Traxler, A. E., and Others, Ten Years of Research in Reading: Summary and Bibliography (New York: Educational Records Bureau, 1941).
34. Tryon, Caroline M., "Evaluation of Adolescent Personality by Adolescents," Monographs of the Society for Research in Child Development, Volume 4, No. 4 (Washington, D. C.: National Research Council, 1939).
35. U.S. Department of Health, Education, and Welfare, Improving Reading in the Junior High School (Washington, D. C.: U. S. Government Printing Cffice, 1957).

36. Warner, W. L., American Life (Chicago: University of Chicago Press, 1953).
37. Wattenberg, William W., The Adolescent Years (New York: Harcourt, Brace and Co., 1955).
38. Wheeler, Lester R., "The Relation of Reading to Intelligence," School and Society, 70 (October 8, 1949), pp. 225-227.
39. Witmer, H., and R. Kotinsky, Personality in the Making (New York: Harper, 1952).
40. Witty, Paul (ed.), Mental Health in the Classroom, 13th Yearbook of the Department of Supervisors and Directors of Instruction of the National Education Association (Washington, D. C.: National Education Association).
41. Witty, Paul A., (ed.), Mental Health in Modern Education. 54th Yearbook of the National Society for the Study of Education, Part II (Chicago: The University of Chicago Press, 1955).
42. Witty, Paul, "Reading Success and Emotional Adjustment," Elementary English, 27 (May 1950), pp. 281-296.
43. Zolkos, Helene H., "What Research Says about Emotional Factors in Retardation in Reading," Elementary School Journal, 51 (May 1951), pp. 512-518.

Reading Interests and
Informational Needs of High School Students

J. Harlan Shores

From The Reading Teacher 17:536-44, April 1964. Reprinted with permission of J. Harlan Shores and the International Reading Association.

The primary purpose of this study was to find out what high school students are looking up in books, what they want to read about, and what they want to find out about. A secondary purpose was to find whether the teachers of these youth have a realistic picture of their reading interests and informational needs. A third purpose was to look for trends in the relative strength of reading interests and informational needs by comparing the results of this study with studies conducted in a similar manner at earlier grade levels.

The Population

The schools providing subjects for this nationwide sample were distributed in fairly equal proportion in each of the nine census areas of the United States. Approximately equal representation was taken from rural, urban, and metropolitan communities. About one-third of the student population was in each of the tenth, eleventh, and twelfth grades. Actual selection of schools within these categories was done with a table of random numbers.

In comparison to most nationwide sampling by mail, the percentage and distribution of responses were quite gratifying. A total of 74 percent of the packets of student inventories was completed and returned, and the distribution of the returns closely approximated the original sampling plan. The population included 6,614 students from grades ten, eleven, and twelve in 240 English, science, and social science classes in 240 schools. The distribution of 235 teachers was: 112 English teachers, 67 social science teachers, and

56 science teachers. Each of these teachers taught one class of the student population. Five teachers did not return usable inventories.

The Method

The inventory questions were in open-ended form to discourage stereotyped and forced responses in terms of a rigid classification. They were as follows:

Reading interests. If someone were to give you a book (not a dictionary or encyclopedia), what would you like it to be about?

Ask-about interests. If you had a very good friend who could answer any question you asked, what would you ask about?

Reference behavior. (1) Every student must from time to time look up information needed for use in school. What did you look up recently (not in a dictionary), in connection with your school work? Tell exactly what you wanted to find out. (2) Most people sometime or other need information for their own use and not in connection with school work. What did you look up recently (not in a dictionary) that was not needed for school work? Tell exactly what you wanted to find out. (3) I'm sure you can remember trying to look up something recently (not in a dictionary) and not finding what you wanted. Tell exactly what you were looking for and couldn't find. (4) If you had a good encyclopedia by your side and were told to look up anything that you wanted to find out about, just for your own use, what topic would you look up?

On the basis of the returns a three-place classification scheme was devised. Fourteen major categories were selected to contain the responses and thus are only generally suggestive of the data classified within each. The major categories were: Literature, Social Sciences, Science, Personal and Social Adjustment, Recreation and Hobbies, Vocations, the Arts, Religion, Psychology, Mathematics, Philosophy, Language Arts, Money Economics and Banking, and Schools. The minor categories and the minor subcategories under each major heading are more closely descriptive of student behavior, interests, and needs. For example, Social Science minor categories included Social Problems, War and

Peace, Government and Ideals, Future of the World, Cultures, History, Famous People, Geography, and Current Events. Within such a minor category as Social Problems were such subcategories as the International Situation, Space Race, Education, Prejudice, Crime and Prisons, Conservation, and Employment.

Five persons analyzed and classified all the data. Following a two-week training period, during which the five-man team analyzed approximately five hundred returns, classification rules were developed and the classification scheme was revised to better represent the data. The five hundred inventories used for refining the scheme were analyzed again according to the rules and the revised plan.

The questions asked the teachers were patterned closely after those asked the high school students. The teachers, however, were giving their judgments of what students would read about, ask about, or look up.

Data were summarized in terms of the percentage of total response to each question. Categories receiving less than one-third of 1 percent were not reported.

The findings of this study are summarized according to the type of response sampled, i.e., reading interests, ask-about interests, and reference behavior.

Reading Interests

Most high school students want to read literature (57 percent) and especially fiction (49 percent). However, considerable reading interest was apparent in the major areas of social science (14 percent), science (13 percent), and recreation and hobbies (6 percent). There was only a scattering of interest in reading about vocations, the arts, personal and social adjustment, religion, psychology and philosophy.

Within the field of literature the strongest interest was in mystery stories, followed by adventure, novels not specified as to type, and stories about young people. There was also considerable interest in biography, historical fiction, fiction not specified as to type, romance, science fiction and sports fiction. There was less interest in humor, war stories, classics, stories of the outdoors, westerns, sea stories, short stories without mention of type, poetry, travel, and drama.

History, especially United States history, ancient history, and European (mostly English) history, was the strongest of the social science reading interests. However, there was also considerable interest in stories about the Civil War and World War II. Interest in reading about cultures was scattered, with the strongest interest in foreign cultures. There was some interest in reading about famous people and about government and political ideals, especially communism. The international situation was the strongest interest in the area of social problems.

More high school students wanted to read about biological and applied science than about physical science. Animals, especially horses, dogs, and wild animals, dominated the biological science reading interests. Most of the applied science interest was in automobiles, aircraft, space travel, and medicine and drugs. In the physical sciences students wanted to read about electricity and electronics, chemistry, and space exploration.

Reading interest in recreation and hobbies tended to fall in the areas of camping, hunting, and fishing. There was also considerable interest in the sports of football, basketball, baseball, and auto racing. Cars accounted for most of the hobby interest.

Sex differences. These differences in reading interests were more pronounced than those found in a similar study at the elementary school level.[3] In grades 10, 11, and 12 girls more than boys wanted to read literature (especially mystery, novels, stories about young people, romance and biography), about foreign cultures, vocations, personal and social adjustment, and religion. Boys more than girls wanted adventure, science fiction, sports, and war stories from the literature category. The interest of boys was several times greater than that of girls in each science category, and boys were also much more interested in mathematics and in sports and hobbies.

Comparison with other studies. Comparison of the present study with three studies employing a similar classification scheme and almost identical methodology indicates a remarkable degree of consistency of reading interests through the grades from 4 to 12. However, it is important to note in this regard that the elementary school data combines grades 4 through 8 [2,3,4] and the present study combines data for grades 10 through 12. In each of these studies mystery was followed by adventure as the most prominent literature reading interest. Also, reading interests were remarkably constant throughout these grades in biography, social science, applied science, physical science, recreation and hobbies, personal problems, and the arts.

Except for the expected shift away from cowboys and westerns and fairy tales and mythology in the junior and senior high school, the only really noteworthy shift in reading interests through the grades was in stories about animals. The elementary school studies indicated nearly three times as much interest as did the junior high school study, and the junior high school interest was more than twice that shown at the senior high school level. Reading interest in biological science other than animals was weak but remained fairly constant through the grades.

Teacher Reports. High school teachers' reports of the reading interests of their students differ more from the students' own reports of their reading interests than is the case in the elementary school studies mentioned above. Following the same trend, neither do junior high school teachers[1] report reading interests as closely to the students' own choices as do elementary school teachers. High school teachers see choices in literature much as the students report, except that teachers underestimate the strong interest in mystery stories. Secondary teachers seriously underestimate reading interest in the social studies. The tendency of high school teachers to see students' interests in terms of their own field of specialization undoubtedly accounts for some of the discrepancy between their reports of student interests and the reports of the students themselves.

Ask-about Interests

When the area of personal and social adjustment is interpreted broadly to include concern about vocational choice, further education, the more personal aspects of religion, and the part of philosophy concerned with goals in life and morals and ethics, in addition to the more obvious concerns of personal and social adjustment, this area looms as the largest one to ask about. However, the categorization scheme used in this study gives separate consideration to many of these concerns, which results in the appearance of the social sciences as the largest major area about which youth would ask.

The major areas of social science (28 percent), personal and social adjustment (20 percent), and vocations (9 percent) hold nearly three-fourths of the topics youth would like to ask about. When religion, recreation and hobbies, schools, and philosophy are added, the total runs to 90 percent. The remaining 10 percent is accounted for in psychology, the arts, mathematics, money, economics and banking, literature, and the language arts.

Many of the questions of high school students in the social studies area are related to the cold war and to the likelihood of actual war. There is interest in the international situation (usually U.S. and U.S.S.R. relations), the space race, keeping the peace, atomic war and survival, communism, Russian government and Russian culture, the future of the world, and current events. As a group these probably indicate real concern for troubles centering in United States-Russian affairs.

Some attention was directed to the social problems of education and prejudice. There were also questions about the United States government, politics, United States subcultures (states and regions), and cultures of foreign countries. Although history was not a large area of ask-about concern, it is interesting to note that there were a few more questions about the prehistoric era than about United States history. There were also questions about famous people and about geography.

Youth have many questions about personal and social adjustment--questions about one's own personal future, the opposite sex, teen-age problems, questions requiring a personal evaluation and those dealing with study habits and getting along with people. Lesser but still important attention was given to home problems and to personal appearance.

What youth say they would ask about in science gives

almost equal attention to the physical and applied sciences and somewhat less attention to biological sciences. In the physical sciences, space exploration and astronomy are the strongest areas, but some questions were directed toward chemistry, physics, geology and physical geography, and electricity and electronics. Questions about nuclear energy are conspicuously absent. Applied science questions were mainly about automobiles, space travel, and disease, health and hygiene. There was less interest in engines (probably related to the automobile category) and in radio and TV. Questions in the biological sciences were largely concerned with life in space and the human body.

High school youth of both sexes are seriously concerned about vocational choice: 1035 questions comprising 8.6 percent of the total response were concerned with vocations. Most of the questions were simply concerned with vocational information. Among the specific vocations frequently mentioned were the armed forces, nursing, medicine, and teaching.

About 5 percent of what youth would ask about was concerned with recreation and hobbies. The sports most frequently mentioned were football, and camping, hunting and fishing. The only hobby interest drawing much attention was cars.

It is interesting to note that as many questions were directed toward religion as were given to sports and hobbies. These youth wanted to ask about God, creation, the different faiths, the Bible, and eternity. Their questions in the realm of philosophy were concerned with goals in life, morals and ethics, and death.

The questions high school students have about schools are largely in anticipation of college. One percent, however, concerned high schools.

Sex differences. While there were differences between the sexes concerning the questions they would ask, boys and girls evinced about the same interest in the various social studies categories, vocations, and schools. Girls directed more attention than boys to questions about personal and social adjustment, religion, and disease, health and hygiene. Boys were more interested than girls in all other aspects of science and in recreation and hobbies.

<u>Grade differences.</u> Differences in interests by grade level are much more apparent in the questions children and youth would ask than they are in reading interests. Comparison with the earlier Rudman and Shores reports and Johnson and Shores reports indicates a steady decrease in questions about both biological and physical sciences through the grades from 4 to 12. There is a corresponding steady increase in concern with the social sciences and a shift from questions about cultures in the elementary grades to concern with national and international problems in the junior and senior high school. Junior high school youth are much more concerned with personal and social adjustment than are elementary school children, but the senior high students had even more questions in this area than did the junior high students. There is a slight increase in interest in recreation and hobbies and applied science in the junior high school over the elementary school, but this interest levels off at or slightly below the elementary level in the senior high school. There would appear to be slightly more interest in religion and ethics and values among elementary and senior high school students than among junior high students.

Most of the drop in questions about biological science through the grades is accounted for by the marked decrease in interest in animals, especially horses and dogs. In fact, interest about biological science other than that classified as "animal" interest probably increases slightly in the junior high school and then drops back to the elementary level in the senior high school.

<u>Teacher reports.</u> In general, the high school teachers saw their students' ask-about concerns realistically. However, the teachers did tend to overestimate questions about personal and social adjustment, especially referring to the opposite sex, and to underestimate questions in social science.

<u>Reference Behavior</u>

In connection with school work, high school students report doing more than twice as much reference work in social science (46 percent) as in science (21 percent) or literature (17 percent).

Social science topics most frequently assigned as reference tasks are, in order: famous people, history, government and ideals, war and peace (especially the Civil War), cultures, social problems, and geography.

High school students report nearly twice as much reference work in biological science as in physical or applied science. Reference work in science is largely in connection with study of the human body, disease, health and hygiene, and chemistry.

There is a tendency for reference assignments in the social sciences and literature to increase through the grades from elementary to senior high school, while the opposite trend is apparent in science and in connection with recreation and hobbies. Reference work in connection with animals decreases markedly through the grades. Junior high school students do more reference work in the physical and applied sciences than do elementary or senior high school students.

Reference assignments reported by high school teachers substantiate those reported by the students. It is interesting to note, however, that teachers of English make nearly one-fourth of their reference assignments in the social studies area--most frequently in the area of history and especially English history. Social science and science teachers infrequently assigned reference work beyond their own discipline.

Reference work not in connection with school assignments fall mainly in the science (30 percent) and social science (27 percent) categories. About half as much attention is given to recreation and hobbies (13 percent), and considerably less falls in the categories of literature, vocations, the arts, religion, personal and social adjustments, and schools.

Out-of-school reference work in science is devoted much more to applied science (14 percent) and biological science (10 percent) than to physical science (5 percent). Within the applied sciences students are seeking information about disease, health and hygiene, and automobiles. There is also considerable interest in radio, TV, and engines. The biological science concerns are scattered. Chemistry drew largest attention in the physical sciences.

In marked contrast to school oriented reference work the most frequent out-of-school reference area in the social sciences was geography, and especially map work connected with distances and place locations. Famous people, cultures, and history were also frequent out-of-school reference concerns. Students also wanted to look up information about governments and political ideals, war and peace, and social problems.

Out-of-school reference in sports emphasized basketball, baseball, and football, but there was also interest in camping, hunting and fishing, and in swimming and diving. The hobbies looked up most frequently were sewing and cooking, cars, guns, and card games.

What students would like to look up in "a good encyclopedia" follows closely what they are looking up in connection with out-of-school concerns. However, they would apparently like to do more reference work than they are now doing with respect to foreign cultures, communism, Russian culture and government, and history, especially ancient and prehistoric periods.

The unsuccessful reference attempts of high school students tend to fall in the same areas, and with approximately the same percentages, as those in which they are doing the most reference work. The minor exceptions to this generality are in mathematics, novels and biography, fields in which little reference work is done but where youth seem to be unusually unsuccessful in finding that for which they are looking.

Summary and Conclusions

An adequate description of the interests of youth requires a multidimensional model. The few dimensions investigated in this study indicate that youth are not necessarily interested in asking about the same things that they want to read about. Their reference behavior is different from both of these, and their reference desires differ in some respects from their reference behavior. Thus reading interests are not identical with informational needs as youth see each of these.

Each dimension of interest tends to highlight only a

part of the total configuration. For example, problems of personal and social adjustment are not predominant in either the reading interests or reference behavior of youth, but these concerns show up prominently in what they would ask about. However, it is interesting to note that while these stronger areas of interest are not prominent in certain dimensions of interest measurement, they do not disappear. It would seem that if an interest is strong enough it will show some response even in unlikely circumstances.

The picture of mid-twentieth century youth, brief and incomplete as it is shown in these data, is an altogether encouraging one. It is unlikely that the generations of their fathers and grandfathers indicated as much maturity of interests, especially in national and international problems. It has been several decades since the interests of children and youth have been advocated as a primary criterion for the selection of curriculum content, and it is not so advocated here, but it is altogether likely that the social science content of the secondary school could be considerably improved by giving more attention to some of the topics with which high school youth have strong concerns.

Taken as a whole, social science interests are at least as strong and are perhaps a bit stronger among high school students than are science interests. Only in out-of-school reference work did science show stronger than social science, and this difference was only three percentage points. In the dimension of ask-about concerns, the social sciences led by ten percentage points. High school students also have more than twice as many reference assignments in social science as in science.

The apparent general decrease in interest in science through the grades as something to read about, ask about, or do reference work about deserves closer attention. In the biological sciences most of this drop is accounted for by the marked decrease in concern with animals, and it may be a classification error to include interests in horses and dogs as science interests. Studies by interview would clarify the nature of these interests. Reading interests in the physical and applied sciences are not strong at any grade level and are fairly constant through the grades. The physical sciences as something to ask about do show a steady decline through the grades, and yet there was more interest in asking about than reading about or doing reference work with respect to the physical sciences.

As the grade level increases, youth direct a larger percentage of their questions to the social sciences. From elementary to senior high school the nature of social science interests shifts from cultures to concerns with United States-Russian relations and ways to "keep the peace" or maintain the cold war status quo.

Elementary school teachers apparently predict both the reading choices and questions of their students much more accurately than do junior or senior high school teachers. The junior high teachers are slightly less accurate in these predictions than are senior high teachers. A better understanding of students is an advantage long claimed by the self-contained classroom of the elementary school. Assuming other pertinent factors equal, the results of this study would support this claim.

Junior and senior high school teachers consistently underestimated the interests of youth in the social sciences and overestimated their concern with personal and social problems, especially those related to the opposite sex. It may be that some students were reluctant to indicate questions about the opposite sex. However, many of those indicating such questions were frank and explicit in the information desired. Teachers of both children and youth underestimated the strong reading interest in mystery stories.

References

1. Johnson, Charles E., and Shores, J. Harlan. "Reading and Reference Interests of Junior-High Students," Illinois Education, 51 (May 1963), 297-303.

2. Rudman, Herbert C. "Interrelationships Among Various Aspects of Children's Interests and Informational Needs and Expectations of Teachers, Parents and Librarians." Unpublished doctoral dissertation, University of Illinois, 1954.

3. Rudman, Herbert C. "Informational Needs and Reading Interests of Children in Grades IV Through VIII," Elementary School Journal, 55 (May 1955), 502-12.

4. Shores, J. Harlan. "Reading Interests and Informational Needs of Children in Grades Four to Eight," *Elementary English*, 31 (Dec. 1954), 493-500.

VII: Exceptional Children

The Library Looks at the Gifted

Howard W. Winger

From Illinois Libraries 42:287-96, May 1960. Originally a talk given at ILA Conference, Chicago, November 19, 1959. Reprinted by permission.

"The library looks at the gifted" is a topic evoked by the current public concern with the education of gifted children. This present general interest dates from October, 1957, when Soviet scientists rocketed the first artificial earth satellite into orbit. The American people were impressed and dismayed by that achievement. The dramatic step toward the conquest of space and the demonstration of scientific mastery and technological skill were impressive. The feeling that a hostile power had gained a sinister weapon and that American science and technology had been left far behind was a cause for dismay. The uneasiness, reinforced by well-publicized rocket attempts and failures in the following months, aroused a real public concern for the development and utilization of the best American talent.

How to develop American talent became a national issue. Popular magazines and newspapers contrasted our public school system with that of Russia as one clue to the Soviet success. The reports emphasized the Russian procedures for fostering the growth of scientific talent. In the Soviet program budding scientists enjoy the benefits of hard courses in science, mathematics, and languages that would jar loose the back teeth of some of our teachers--not to speak of students who have not been required to run on all cylinders. Although educators have for forty years been concerned with the problems of developing the most talented American school children, the recent public concern has given their ideas new force. More special classes that group children according to ability--called "track systems"-- were introduced. New courses in algebra and foreign languages entered the elementary school curriculum. A report

420

was issued on the American high school. These are signs of changed emphasis.

An altered educational emphasis directly affects school and college libraries because they are dependent on the school and college programs. It also quickly affects public libraries as educational institutions. When George Ticknor, at the beginning of our public library history, urged the city fathers of Boston to establish a library that would be "the crowning glory of our system of City Schools . . . opening to all the means of self culture through books,"[1] he was thinking of citizens continuing their education in libraries after completing school. As things have worked out, the connection of the schools with public libraries is closer than he anticipated, because so much of public library use is related to school tasks. School children are heavy users of public libraries, and they use the public libraries to complete school assignments.

The Issue for Libraries

The emphasis on the education of gifted children raises the old issue of special services to a small group as opposed to widespread services to the general public. If librarians recognize the special needs of a group selected according to talent, they may have to alter the emphasis of library work or add some new services. The idea of putting libraries to the service of genius is an attractive one. No doubt every librarian has dreamed of contributing to great intellectual achievements by just such practice. The thought of helping a brilliant few develop important ideas brings a relief we often seek from the pressure of statistics and mass circulation. Edwin Wolf, librarian of the Library Company of Philadelphia, said he would "rather have had one Thomas Jefferson pore over books on politics and government in the room of the Library Company on the second floor of Carpenters' Hall in the spring of 1776, getting ideas for a certain Declaration of Independence. . ." than serve hordes of less serious users.[2] So might we all! But the distinction lies not so much in Jefferson's genius as in his seriousness of purpose. Thousands of people, with less genius than Jefferson, somewhere acquired the ideas he put in the Declaration and by their dedication and sacrifices made those ideas effective. The librarian has an obligation to minister to their intellectual needs, too.

The peculiar educational virtue of a library is that it is geared to the individual who wants to forge ahead by his own efforts. As Justin Winsor wrote over eighty years ago, "It appeals to and nurtures every idiosyncrasy. Like the soil, it imparts this quality to that grain, and others to the different fruits."[3] If they have initiative to match their talent, the gifted should be best able to exploit the self-held feature of libraries. Our problem is to learn their characteristics of talent and the special library needs they have. It does not necessarily follow that we have lesser obligations to the common user who comes with similar seriousness of purpose.

Characteristics of the Gifted

Gifted people are a small minority of the population who stand well above their fellows in some kind of talent. Scholars have used different measures and devices to identify the group. Lewis Terman, who directed the genetic studies of genius, selected the one school child in a thousand with an intelligence quotient above 132.[4] In his report on the American high school, James Bryant Conant dipped below the genius level to concentrate on the 20 per cent of high school students who make the highest grades.[5] Robert Havighurst and his colleagues included high general intelligence, special ability in useful subject areas, and talent in the creative arts to distinguish the gifted child.[6] Interest focuses on the school child and most definitions are based on intelligence tests, school grades, and school counselors' reports.

In trying to serve the gifted, the librarian is faced with a problem in identifying them. The qualities which place a child in the class are often hidden from himself, from the public, and from the librarian. Identification often rests on refined testing techniques and on sophisticated counseling, and public behavior such as unrestricted rummaging in a public library is not a sure sign. Identification based on the raw observation of such public behavior runs counter to two confusing types of people mentioned in an ancient proverb. One is he who knows and knows not he knows. Another is he who knows not and knows not he knows not.

Ordinarily the librarian has to depend on his observation of library use to identify a gifted child. School librarians in good systems may have access to pertinent school records, but most other librarians do not. In addition to the conundrum of latent abilities, dependence on observation of library use presents another problem, because only a minority of the potential users of any library make free use of it.

Insofar as library users are concerned, however, some signs are indicative of talent. The ten-year-old boy who is always edging into the adult collection for his books probably has an intellectual maturity in advance of his years. That is the meaning of the high intelligence quotient. If we are interested in the gifted child, we will react to this imp with sympathy, rather than with exasperation at his disturbance to the order of things that be. Because he is young and because talent develops unevenly, he will also want his full share of juvenile books. And he should have them. Library users who have a consuming, persistent, and masterful interest in a particular subject field are also recognizable. Beyond such simple observations, we would need access to pertinent personal records in order to plan a complete program to specially serve the gifted child. We would also need time to make use of such records and adequate resources to put a program into effect.

Correlation of Talent with Library Use

Like gifted people, library users are also a minority. Less than a tenth of the adults and not quite a third of the school children use the public library as often as once a month.[7] College students have to go to the college library to read for their assignments, but a recent study of a college library showed that half the students accounted for 90 per cent of such course-related use.[8] The same study revealed that less than a third of the students used the college library for reading not related to their courses. Similar conclusions can be drawn about high school libraries. Students go to the library to complete course assignments, but they are likely to remain away in large numbers without such specific incitement.[9] It is to be expected that college and school libraries provide materials for course assignments and reserve lists and for whatever enrichment objectives are inherent in the curriculum. Although the librarian undoubtedly has to exert ingenuity in acquiring materials to meet such specific needs, the impetus for such acquisition is from outside the library and fairly specific. We are more concerned here with the free or individually motivated use of the library, and in every case the free users are a minority.

Since both are minorities of varying sizes, it is a good question to ask whether library users and gifted people are not consequently identical with each other. Little evidence has been uncovered to answer this question. Although studies of public library use show that the heavy users are better educated than average, they do not show, for example, that they were in the top 20 percent of their classes. The most pertinent studies have been made of college library users. Such studies yield a positive correlation between the measurements of high grades and high intelligence scores and use of the library, but the correlation is a slim one.[10] We have to conclude that a "C" student with average intelligence is almost as likely to prove a heavy library user as an "A" student with high intelligence. Library users as a group and gifted people as a group are not at all identical.

Other evidence shows that the conscientious plugger makes heavier use of the library than people who are merely bright. G. Donald Smith demonstrated that with what he called a "relative achievement" scale. Relative achievement is a measure of effort and motivation as well as performance. By comparing grades with intelligence scores, Smith made a rating which placed a "B" student with average intelligence, for example, higher than a "B" student with high intelligence. When he compared relative achievement with the use of the library for materials related to courses, he found that every student in the top group used nearly all the titles assigned or suggested, while there was a wide variation of use among the students in the bottom group.[11] This supports a theory that a library is the most useful educational instrument for the well-motivated student, even though his intelligence be average. Any proposal to develop library services for genius which would neglect normal services for the consistent pluggers is open to question. To refer again to the example of Jefferson's genius, the somewhat duller men who made Jefferson's ideas effective have intellectual needs, too.

Library Needs of the Gifted

A library supplies the user with two basic services. First, it offers him a wider range of books and other materials than he has at his personal disposal. That is the function of the library collection. Second, it can provide him with a guide and advice for the efficient use of the collection. That is the function of the library staff. To illustrate the meaning of these basic services to gifted users, I would like to recall two of my experiences in the circulation department at the University of Illinois Library.

One experience involved a high school student who had acquired a permit to use books in the university library. I first remember his coming to ask for Gardiner's Egyptian Grammar. After spending many pleasant Friday afternoons with it, he went on to books about other obscure languages. He illustrates the need for a far ranging collection. Although the Egyptian Grammar may be a standard reference book in a university library, it is not commonly found in private homes or in small public and high school libraries. Nor could he have been satisfied with that book alone, because when he went on to study other languages he used books that were much more uncommon than Gardiner's.

Another case illustrates the need for personal guidance to the user. The student actor who was going to play the leading role in King Lear asked me for a book that would help him get the feel of the way the play had been acted. Because my desk in the stacks was near the Shakespeare books, which I liked to scan, the young actor's request went to my head. I happily carried volume after volume out of the stacks for him to enjoy. Somewhat unhappily he rejected them all as fast as I carried them out. He left me to go to the reference room where a kind and wise librarian directed him to an encyclopedia. Apparently it had just the article for him, judging from the subsequent fine performance he gave of the role. He demonstrated the need for a librarian who is sensitive to the learner's thought processes and who suggests appropriate books. Many of the most brilliant students are answered in the World Almanac, a reference source so good and so cheap that most libraries could afford to have several copies to circulate. The trick lies in knowing when to use such sources and when to select more uncommon references.

Library Collections for the Gifted

Library collections with range and significance are essential for good service to the gifted. Although it is an imperfect measure, the most readily available standard of range and significance is the size of collections. The public library standards are based on library systems serving populations of 100,000 as the smallest fully effective units. The standards call for library collections of 100,000 currently useful volumes as a minimum. They also call for the yearly acquisition of 4,000 to 5,000 new titles with enough duplicate copies to make 20,000 new books for the minimum collections.

The book collections of most Illinois public libraries do not begin to approach the standard. Of 480 public libraries reporting in 1958-1959, only 10 had collections as big as 100,000 volumes and only 13 more had collections exceeding 50,000 volumes. There were 66 libraries with collections under 5,000. As for new acquisitions, only 22 libraries had book budgets exceeding $10,000.00. You could hardly buy 4,000 significant new titles, not to speak of extra copies, for less than that. Many reporting libraries spent less than $100.00 for books. With such weak collections and such low rates of acquisition we cannot furnish an adequate range of reading matter.

The handicap of weak library collections for a serious user can be shown from a specific case. A person enrolled in an adult education course with a specific list of readings to follow fits the definition of a serious user. Last summer the University of Wisconsin offered a course in liberal education for adults for which the registrants met on the campus. Books for the extensive reading lists were in the Memorial Library of the University. However, a person without access to a large book collection would have had a hard time getting access to the rather widely known books listed. From one list of 51 titles, 23 were in print in paperback books. The University Co-op Bookstore, a fine store with extraordinarily comprehensive offerings of paperback books, had 13 of the 23 in stock. The Union Bus Depot, with 139 paperback titles on display, had none. The public library in a town of 12,000 had 8 of the books. [12]

We cannot generalize that the serious library user would have to go to a scholarly collection to get even half the titles on every worthwhile reading list, but the books in question were not unusual for the purpose. They included such titles as: Randall, The Making of the Modern Mind; Brinton, Ideas and Men; Taylor, The Medieval Mind; Haskins, The Rise of the Universities; Winship, Gutenberg to Plantin:

a History of Printing; Willey, The Seventeenth Century Background; Gamow, The Birth and Death of the Sun; and Whitehead, Science and the Modern World. Although any collection of 5,000 volumes is almost sure to have some important books I have not read, I question whether such a collection would have the eight well-known books listed above.

Public Library Collections
The Key to Variety

In most communities where public libraries exist the public library collection is the largest in the community, and it is the key to the range and variety of books and other library materials available to the citizens. Academic centers like Madison, Urbana, and Chicago are the exception. School libraries, where they exist, have collections that are focused on a specific function. Their users are the wide range of school children, and they cannot predominate in adult books which are required by gifted minds, both young and old. Many school librarians are also forced to keep well in mind the parent who is likely to regard even Pearl Buck's The Good Earth as too spicy for high school students to read. Consequently, in a standard list of books recommended for purchase by a school library, we find Mackinlay Kantor represented by The Voice of Bugle Ann, but not by Andersonville. The "Notable Books" selected each year by the Notable Books Council of the Adult Services Division of ALA provide a measure of the difference between public library book selection and school library book selection. In the four-year period from 1954 through 1957, the Standard Catalog for High School Libraries recommended only a third of the "Notable Books."[13]

I am not prepared to say that the selection of books for school libraries is wrong, nor am I ignorant of the fact that alert and well-supported school librarians go beyond and in advance of standard minimum lists in buying books. My point is rather that the basis of selecting books for school libraries differs from that for public libraries. The two kinds of collections ought to complement each other to provide the most complete community resources possible. Cooperative planning might result, for example, in one of the libraries taking the responsibility for preserving back files of periodicals. As things work out now, there are many communities where no back files of periodicals exist.[14]

There is hardly anything harder to obtain from private resources than a six-year-old magazine.

Librarians to Serve the Gifted

A good librarian can improve the use of the best library collection and take fuller advantage of one which is not so strong. The inquiring beginner needs help to find his way into a field. The avid researcher requires bibliographical assistance to reach the printed sources of knowledge. Both need very badly the catalogs and indexes which are prepared and selected in the back room of the library and which are interpreted every day on the public floor. The librarian's task involves an understanding of the procedures and directions of inquiry in a large variety of subjects, a mastery of bibliography, and insight into the motivations of the learner. The nature of the task fully justifies professional education, but the library schools have not been able to supply librarians for all the libraries. A glance at public library statistics will hint at some of the reasons for this. Figures already cited indicate that many positions do not warrant the full application of professional skills. Other figures show that salaries are frequently too low to justify the expense of professional education. Of the 480 Illinois public libraries reporting in 1958-1959, nearly half, 222, had total salary budgets below $3,000.00!

Questions of professional preparation aside, many libraries do not have enough workers of any qualification to permit time for personal assistance to readers. It takes time to find out, when a student asks for a book about King Lear, that what he really needs is an encyclopedia article. It takes time to show him how to find books about Shakespeare in the catalog. It takes time to lead him to the indexes. And while you are helping him with that, another equally gifted student has finished studying the Egyptian grammar and wants your time to help in finding a book on the Gaelic language.

It is time well spent, but time you do not have if you are submerged in charging and discharging books and performing the vital mechanical routines necessary to keep the library open for business. The librarian who handles a 300,000 annual circulation has a big supervisory job. The selection and purchase of 5,000 to 6,000 new books a year is also time consuming. If he is shaking down a new building, that is another drain on his time. The task calls for at least seven professional assistants. If he has four full-time clerks, two part-time clerks, a half-time cataloger, and some pages, and if he is skilled at training clerks, talented at inspiring his staff with loyalty, alert to short cuts in routine, and filled with devotion above and beyond the call of duty, he can conduct a valuable community service. He will not, however, have much time left for aid to readers, and neither will any of his staff. This is a problem in a public library.[15]

School libraries are sadly understaffed when compared with the new school library standards. The new standards call for one librarian and one library clerk for every 300 students or major fraction thereof up to 1,000 students. There should be one librarian for every 400 students above 1,000. As I interpret these standards, a high school with 2,900 students should have eight librarians. According to figures compiled by Sara Innis Fenwick, a Chicago suburban high school with 2,900 students enrolled has only two librarians. Another with 2,500 students has only one. Such understaffing is consistent in the suburban area. In some places it has turned the librarian's job into a disciplinary nightmare, marked with fruitless struggles to keep irresponsible students from stealing 600 or 700 books each year. Adequate staffs might permit the librarians to concentrate on their true role of acquiring appropriate library collections and directing students in the use of them. Adequate book collections with an appropriate range and multiple copies would relieve the pressure on both books and librarian.

Summary and Conclusions

At this point it may appear that I have presented the gifted looking with a jaundiced eye at the library, instead of the library looking at the gifted. However, as a person engaged in the study of libraries I have tried to compare the apparent needs of gifted users with the resources we have at hand to satisfy them. In doing this, I have assumed that good library service to the gifted is based on the essentials of all library service--good library collections and expert librarians. From that point of view, the following observations seem in order:

1. Gifted children have an intellectual maturity beyond their years; therefore, they need to be admitted to collections of adult books.

2. However, abilities among gifted children are not evenly spread. They may be more highly developed in some areas than others. Therefore, gifted children will continue to need the full complement of juvenile books.

3. Gifted children like other users need guidance in the use of materials and, depending on their stage of thought, the most common sources may often best satisfy their needs.

4. To supply gifted children with the full range of materials they require, we need to make co-operative use of all library resources in the community. Librarians in every type of library need to familiarize themselves with all the library resources of the community--by study, visits, and contacts with other librarians.

5. Although library co-operation is vital, the distinctions between different kinds of library service are also important. The public library cannot be a good public library if it also has to be a school library. The scholarly library cannot appropriately serve crowds of high school students writing themes. By the same standard, school libraries cannot perform the functions of public and research libraries. That is to say, co-operation makes more effective use of different kinds of services, but it does not eliminate the need for any one of them.

6. Weak public libraries should take advantage of the Illinois state law permitting them to consolidate in larger units of service. Tax bases are too narrow to support 480 good public library systems in Illinois. At the same time, Illinois public libraries should seek the maximum tax rates allowed by Illinois law. Although the maximum rates, set in a bygone day, are too low for the support of adequate library service in most communities, few public libraries in Illinois even receive the low maximum.

Many special aspects of serving the gifted merit further study and discussion. For one thing, we need to study ways of convincing people that they need good book collections and good libraries. Public understanding of the need is not now adequate. For example, James Bryant Conant in his recommendations for improving the American high school failed to mention the school library or librarians. Such lapses are all the more discouraging in the face of rising taxes and mounting tax resistance. Even the small increases in financial support required to bring our public library tax rates to the legal maximum meet with opposition.

A second avenue of inquiry is concerned with the effect of librarians' attitudes and school and library policy on the free use of libraries. Although the proportion of students who use the library freely is regrettably small, it may not be students' impercipience or laziness which is responsible. Some librarians have been reported to discourage students from coming to the library for pleasurable exploration. Others have barred students with textbooks from the door, although some assignments logically require the use of textbooks in conjunction with library materials. Often, too, the most gifted students have the least chance to use the library. They take extra courses requiring extra class attendance and have no period left in the school day to visit the library. At the same time, early closing hours for the school buildings and the lack of enough library staff to cover a longer schedule prevent the offering of school library service in the evening. Presumably the public library is expected to fill the gap. However, to use the public library as a school library is to lay on it a responsibility for which it is neither best fitted nor legally obligated.

Finally, we might study the programs begun by some librarians especially for gifted students. Some of these programs are in the best traditions of librarianship. All of them, however, depend on good book collections administered by persons of competence, intelligence, and imagination.

References

1. Report of the Trustees of the Boston Public Library, 1852, p. 21.
2. "Libraries and Librarians: an Address," Drexel Library School Series, No. 2 (Philadelphia: Drexel Institute of

Technology, 1959), p. [10].
3. Justin Winsor, "Free Libraries and Readers," Library Journal, I (1876), p. 66.
4. Lewis Terman (ed.), Genetic Studies of Genius: Vol. I, Mental and Physical Traits of A Thousand Gifted Children (2n ed:, Stanford University Press, 1926).
5. James Bryant Conant, The American High School Today: A First Report to Interested Citizens (New York: McGraw-Hill Co., Inc., 1959).
6. Robert J. Havighurst, Eugene Stivers, and Robert F. DeHaan, "A Survey of the Education of Gifted Children," Supplementary Educational Monographs, No. 83 (University of Chicago Press, 1955), p. 3.
7. Bernard Berelson, The Library's Public: A Report of the Public Library Inquiry (New York: Columbia University Press, 1949), p. 21.
8. Patricia Knapp, The Role of the Library in a Given College (University of Chicago: Unpublished Ph.D. Dissertation, August, 1957), pp. 34-40.
9. E. Moore, An Analysis of the Uses Made of a Public Library by High-School Students (University of Chicago, Unpublished Master's Dissertation, June, 1959), p. 37.
10. Knapp, op. cit., pp. 98-99.
11. G. Donald Smith, The Nature of Student Reading (University of Chicago: Unpublished Ph.D. dissertation, December, 1946), p. 58.
12. Nelson F. Harding, Unpublished term paper, Library School of the University of Wisconsin, Summer, 1959.
13. Vera Cerny, Unpublished term paper, Library School of the University of Wisconsin, Summer, 1959.
14. Sara Fenwick, "School and Public Library Relationships," Library Quarterly, January, 1960, pp. 63-74.
15. Park Forest, Illinois.

Reading Interests of Retarded,
Reluctant, and Disturbed Readers

Louise Moses

From the Claremont Reading Conference--26th Yearbook, 1962, pp. 74-84. Copyright by Claremont University College. Reprinted by permission.

The development of an adequate correctional educational program for the socially maladjusted and the emotionally disturbed children is one of the most pressing problems facing civic minded persons and educators today. [4] An intensified search for causes and for better means of prevention and treatment is continuously being made. The greatest advance in the development of a program to help the mentally ill and disturbed children has been accorded to institutions and facilities offering residential treatment. More than 100,000 emotionally disturbed children are receiving care in some kind of residential facility in the United States. [1] The National Probation and Parole Association has devoted many years to the improvement of detention services for juvenile delinquents. Standards and Guides for the Detention of Children and Youth were established in 1958. Along with medical services, guidance, school, religious, and recreational programs, and library services are also recommended. [13]

The Juvenile Hall Branch Library of the Institutions Region of the Los Angeles County Public Library was established over twenty years ago. In 1954, Juvenile Hall enlarged its facilities and for the first time employed a County librarian full time.

The library maintains separate library reading rooms for boys and girls. The book collection for both groups exceeds 3,000 volumes; a small professional book collection for the Juvenile Hall staff is housed in one of the reading rooms. The librarian coordinates her program around the school, but also offers recreational reading for other juveniles who visit the library. The collections include easy books and juvenile books as well as literature for young adults and adults. Books and magazines are selected on the basis of the reading interests and needs of the Juvenile Hall population. In 1960, the average daily population was 651.[14] More than 14,000 books were circulated between December, 1960, and December, 1961.

Profile of a Juvenile Delinquent

It is very difficult to define juvenile delinquency. The term has many connotations. It usually refers to a specific legal status, meaning an offense committed by a juvenile in violation of a law. Some statutes are vague and do not clearly distinguish between juveniles who are delinquent, and those who are disturbed, dependent, and neglected.[11] Although there are many types of juvenile delinquents, many of them fall in the category of the socially maladjusted and the emotionally disturbed.

More than 1,200 juveniles are admitted to the Los Angeles County Juvenile Hall each year. The ages of the children usually range between ten and eighteen. Most of the children are teenagers, although there are a few cases of children under ten. Most of the children have committed serious delinquency offenses. Many of the behavior problems stem from poor home conditions of a socio-economic nature, such as neglectful and inattentive parents, and unsatisfactory home atmospheres. Juveniles create many of the problems themselves through association with gangs and through the development of wrong, or false ideas.[2]

Like the many faces of Eve, the profile of the juvenile delinquent may be wide and varied. Boys are usually institutionalized because they have committed crimes injurious to property or people, or have stolen. Girls differ in that they are usually incorrigible, runaways, or have committed anti-social sex offenses. Although most juvenile delinquents tested by psychologists are found to be normal in intelligence,[3] many can be classified as emotionally disturbed. A few suffer from retardation, school failings, personality deviation, physical handicaps or disabilities, physical, psychological, and neurological disorders.

The juvenile delinquent personality possesses no traits

which may not also be found to characterize non-delinquents, except that he has presumably been adjudged a violator of the law. They are not all alike in any respect, except that they are children and youth with problems.[12] It has been thought that mentally retarded children are predisposed to delinquent and criminal behavior. Research evidence by Levy has not confirmed this belief.[8] The emotionally disturbed child is one who cannot meet his own needs in environmental situations in which he finds himself without problems.

The reading interests of the children and young adults at Juvenile Hall are largely the same as non-juvenile offenders, since most juvenile delinquents transfer reading interests from their home community life. Some nonreaders have developed reading habits because of the isolation and confinement.

The Reading Interests of the Retarded

The reading interests of the retarded child usually are reflected in his readiness to read books centered around himself and his experiences. The books selected for the retarded should be chosen to suit the child's levels of interests and comprehension. If the reading age of a child is below the chronological age, it is retardation. Since reading capacity is a function of the intellectual level of the child, all mentally retarded children are retarded in reading.[9] Patrick J. Groff recommends the individualized method in which the child gains the satisfaction of being able to choose which books he wants to read, and of reading them at a pace comfortable for him.[6]

The retarded reader usually has a short retention span and usually has to be motivated by some type of stimuli. Griff L. Jones, in "An Experiment in Library Instruction for the Retarded," suggests the use of audio-visual aids.[10] This may be movies, bulletin board displays, or any other aids. The librarian or teacher may also tell stories or read poetry.

The retarded reader may range from a reading level of preschool age to any level below his chronological age. Most retarded readers prefer picture books or beautifully illustrated books with clear, large print. Picture books should be true to life in color and form, with few printed words which explain each picture. A juvenile retarded boy of ten to twelve years of age is interested in such subjects as animals, sports, drawing, lettering, magic, adventure, fables and folklore, Bible stories, jokes, and automobiles. If the subject matter of an easy book represents his interest level, he will not be embarrassed to read an easy book on the pre-school or early elementary level. Easy books about Indians, cowboys, dogs, snakes, trains, aeroplanes, and cars fascinate him. Suggested books for this type of retarded reader are the See About Books; First Books; Golden Books; Real Books; Nan Hurley's Dan Frontier with the Indians; Edna Chandler's Cow Boy Sam and the Aeroplane, or The Buffalo Boy, are popular with him. Books designed for adult schools may also be used with the shy and serious retardee. Boys in this retarded group will take Boys' Life Magazine and Hot Rod and will reproduce pictures from them.

A retarded girl whose chronological age ranges between twelve and fourteen, will read fairy tales, dog and horse stories, humorous books like the Madeline and Eloise series, Dr. Seuss, easy juvenile books on manners, people, travel, and romance.

Both boys and girls who read on the Easy Book level liked J. I. Ayer, Donald Duck and His Friends, T. S. Geesel, The 500 Hats of Bartholomew Cubbins, Mother Goose, The Tall Book of Mother Goose, and H. A. Rey's Curious George books.

The Reluctant Reader

Like the retarded child, the reluctant reader has to be stimulated or motivated into reading. Books arranged by subject interests may stimulate him, or the librarian may guide him along by pointing out to library groups new and attractive books on various subjects, or by giving book talks. Terman points out that most intense reading occurs at twelve or thirteen, and that interest falls off at fifteen; likes and dislikes are set at fifteen. Early adolescent girls prefer fiction and boys like non-fiction. Dislikes are set about sixteen.[15] Many reluctant readers have reading difficulties, have feelings of insecurity, or personality disturbances. Through puberty, boys are interested in travel, adventure, and technical books. Girls are interested in romances, mysteries, and problems of social relationships.

The Disturbed Reader

The therapeutic effect of reading has received much attention in the last few years. It has been used by librarians in connection with doctors and psychiatrists in mental hospitals, in penal institutions, schools, and guidance centers. Richard L. Darling writes that bibliotherapy, as used with children and adults, gives therapeutic effects for the reader in terms of identification, catharsis, and insight.[5] Disturbed readers, many times, are interested in finding solutions to life problems, information explaining human behavior, and an opportunity to get away from life's stresses. Margaret C. Hannigan, in an experiment with "six furious children" at the National Institute of Health Clinical Center, discovered that disturbed children experienced security and gratification by reading books in the Institute's library.[7]

Reading needs and interests change as children grow. The books in which small children who are emotionally distressed show an interest are Mother Goose rhymes, fairy tales, and humorous picture books with brief stories. In the intermediate years, children become interested in stories about girls and boys, heroes, folk tales, horse and dog stories.

Pre-adolescent and adolescent boys and girls who are disturbed show more interest in social problems such as sex, family stories and etiquette books. Boys particularly like westerns, mysteries, weight lifting, adventure, lives of famous athletes, explorers, aviation, hobbies, and hot rods. Girls like vocational books, books on romance, child care, physical exercises, personality development, biography, and poetry.

Names of books which illustrate the basic interests of disturbed teenagers and adolescents are:

Alcott, Louisa, Little Women.

Boyston, S., Sue Barton series.

Cooke, David, Bomber Planes That Made History.

Daly, Maureen, Seventeenth Summer.

Dickens, Charles, A Tale of Two Cities.

Doyle, A. Conan, Sherlock Holmes.

Emery, Ann, Popular Crowd.

Frank, Anne, Diary of a Young Girl.

Gottlieb, Bernhardt Stanley, What a Boy Should Know About Sex.

Gottlieb, Bernhardt Stanley, What a Girl Should Know About Sex.

Haislet, E., Boxing.

Humpries, R., Poems Collected and New.

Keller, Helen, The Story of My Life.

Landis, P. M., Your Dating Days.

O'Dell, Scott, Island of the Blue Dolphin.

Paine, Albert, Joan of Arc.

Reynolds, E., Custer's Last Stand.

Stolberg, D., First Book of Chess.

I should like to read letters, written at various times by boys and girls with whom I have worked in the library at Juvenile Hall, as evidence of the therapeutic effect of books on these young readers--disturbed, delinquent, or retarded.

> When a person is lonesome or by themself, a book can keep them company. Some books tell what other people's lives are like. My vocabulary is getting a little better since I have been reading.

I lose my troubles in the books I get out
of the library.

You can learn about authors and the way
they think about people and things, like
some authors write about love. And some
authors write books in anger to hurt people
or because they have been hurt. I learn
things when I read. Well, that's what the
library means to me.

At the library we have a chance to choose
our books which seems very interesting to
me. Some of the sections I like to choose
from are fiction, mystery and romance.
When we check out books it gives us a sense
of responsibility because we have to return
them on a certain date and we are held responsible. I enjoy reading and since I am not
on the outside I think the Juvenile Hall library
is a great privilege to me.

It helps a lot to read stories and get your mind
off your own problems.

I think the library is helpful to girls who are
sad and homesick. When one's mind is occupied one forgets sad and unhappy things.

The library helps me when I need to find something out and understand the meaning of it. I
like to read in my spare time. It keeps me
from arguing with someone.

The library is a good thing. It is interesting
to find out what's in books. It helps to understand life more easily and it helps girls to
understand why they shouldn't be here. Girls
find out the hard way. But it is good for
girls to have a library to take their minds off
other things.

The library means a lot to me because if there
were no books to read then people would be
less educated, less happy, and would not have

the power of speech or the peace of mind that books can give. With books I can read and imagine myself to be anywhere in the world, in the Tropics, in Oz, in the sunny land of Hawaii or in the mountains skiiing down the slopes. The land of books is a world of wonder and song and happiness.

* * * * *

Books, truest and most silent companions, how can we thank you for your ever-present readiness, for this eternally uplifting, infinitely elevating influence of your presence! What have you not been in the darkest days of the soul's solitude! In military hospitals and army camps, in prisons and on beds of pain, in all place, you, the eternally wakeful, have given men dreams and a hand's breadth of tranquility amidst unrest and torment.[16]

References

1. Alt, Hershel, Residential Treatment for the Disturbed Child, (New York, Internation Universities Press, Inc., 1960). P. IX.
2. Bogen, David, Statement in personal interview, Jan., 1962.
3. ----------- Statement in personal interview, Jan., 1962.
4. Cruikshank, William M. and G. Orville Johnson, Education of Exceptional Children and Youth (New York: Prentice-Hall, 1958), p. 557.
5. Darling, Richard L. "Mental Hygiene and Books," Wilson Library Bulletin, XXII (Dec., 1957), p. 293.
6. Groff, Patrick J., "The Librarian and Individualized Reading," Wilson Library Bulletin, XXIV (Jan., 1961), p. 3.
7. Hannigan, Margaret C., "Furious Children," Top of the News, XVI (March, 1960), pp. 13-15.

8. Hutt, Max L. and Robert Gwyn Gibby, The Mentally Retarded Child, (Boston: Allyn and Bacon, Inc., 1961), p. 184.

9. The Mentally Retarded Child, (Boston: Allyn and Bacon, Inc., 1961), p. 73.

10. Jones, Griff L., "An Experiment in Library Instruction for the Retarded, Wilson Library Bulletin, XXXI (Jan., 1961), p. 3.

11. Miller, Haskell M., Understanding and Preventing Juvenile Delinquency, (New York: Abingdon Press, 1958), pp. 15-17.

12. --------------- Understanding and Preventing Juvenile Delinquency, (New York: Abingdon Press, 1958).

13. Norman, Sherwood, Detention Practice; Significant Developments in the Detention of Children and Youth (New York: National Probation and Parole Association, 1960), pp. 101-102.

14. Ibid. p. 106.

15. Timm, Charlotte, "Reading Guidance in Adjustment," Wilson Library Bulletin, XXIV (Oct., 1959), p. 148.

16. Zweig, Stefan, "Thanks to Books," Wilson Library Bulletin, XXXII (March, 1958), pp. 477-78.

Author Index

John W. Adams, 209-16
L. S. Aizerman, 322-48
Dean C. Andrew, 284-94
Bruce C. Appleby, 354-64
Robin Atthill, 241-3
Robin B. Bateman, 82-9
Joan W. Butler, 295-300
R. S. Buzzing, 90-5
Helen S. Canfield, 116-8
John H. Coleman, 174-91
John W. Conner, 354-64
Richard Crosscup, 132-41
John J. DeBoer, 390-406
Evelyn Millis Duvall, 301-2
Roland Earl, 243-6
Curtis Easley, 284-94
Nancy Elsmo, 164-6
Isabel V. Eno, 279-83
Nick Aaron Ford, 365-9
Donald R. Gallo, 381-9
Lewis S. Gannett, 377-80
Roma Gans, 122-5
Patrick J. Groff, 108-15
Lois B. Hall, 313-7
Nat Hentoff, 349-53
Patricia Hill, 68-74
Richard J. Hurley, 96-7
David Jesson-Dibley, 239-41
Charles E. Johnson, 157-63
Lois V. Johnson, 98-107
W. Stephen Jones, 370-6
Ann Jungeblut, 174-91
Thomas L. Kilpatrick, 318-21
Ethel M. King, 143-56
Lowell A. Martin, 247-50
Sister Mary Consuelo, O.S.U., 65-7

Mrs. Robert Mead, 19-26
Esther Millett, 260-3
Louise Moses, 433-41
George W. Norvell, 303-12
Bette J. Peltola, 44-54
Bernard Poll, 119-21
William N. Rairigh, 313-7
H. Alan Robinson, 55-64
Ernest Roe, 217-38
Helen E. Rogers, 55-64
Monroe Rowland, 68-74
J. Harlan Shores, 157-63, 407-19
Sylva Simsova, 15-8, 27-32
Mary L. Smith, 279-83
Ruth C. Smith, 33-43
Anthony T. Soares, 169-73
Jo M. Stanchfield, 200-8
Beryl I. Vaughan, 192-9
Iris Vinton, 126-31
Elizabeth N. Wade, 75-8
Howard W. Winger, 420-32
Paul Witty, 251-9

Subject Index

age and reading interests. See age breakdown in Table of Contents
animal books, 128-30
ask-about interests, 411-8

Baker, Emily L., 144
bibliotherapy, 437
biographical selections--preferences, 177-8
book club membership, 278
book discussions, 164-6
book fads, 319-20
book lists, 262, 356
book ownership, 278, 292
book reviews by children, 79-81, 126-31, 245-6
  by young adults, 323-47, 370-6
books used in discussion groups, 165-6
Boys' Clubs of America, 126-31
Brueckner, Leo J., 152
Butler, James C., 75-8

Cappa, Dan, 145, 149
Carlsen, Dr. G. Robert, 264-7, 315-6, 355
Children's Book Council, 167-8
children's laughter and literature, 82-9
city boys' reading, 126-31
classics and reading interests, 377-80
classroom book collections, 94
Coast, Alice B., 149
comic books, 257-8, 278
comic pictorial image and laughter, 85-6
comic strips, 258-9
concerns of young adults, 301-2, 349-53, 390-4, 411-4
conferences with students, 359-60
Cutright, Prudence, 152

Deiches Studies, 247-50
dictionaries for preschool children, 27-32
discussions of books, 164-6
disliked books, 130, 268, 378-9, 384

445

disliked selections, 311-2
disturbed readers, 437-8
Dunn, Fannie W., 150

economic status and reading interests, 290
emotionally disturbed readers, 437-8
emotions and reading difficulties, 402
encouraging reading, 272-6, 312
encyclopedias and reference work, 161-2
English courses, 303-12, 354-64
escapism, 91
external influences on reading, 92-5

factory reading racks, 274
favorite books, 19-26, 79-81, 117, 122-5, 133, 167-8, 240-3, 245, 254-6, 260, 264-8, 296, 311, 320, 323-47, 368-9, 375, 383, 436-8
funny incidents and laughter, 83-5

general interests and reading interests, 144-5
geniuses, library service to, 420-32
gifted children as readers, 420-32
Great Books discussions, 164-6
Gunderson, Agnes G., 145

horse stories, 119-21
Howes, Virgil E., 145
humorous literature and children, 82-9
Humphreys, Phila, 149

identification with heroes, 90-1
illustrations and racial bias, 68-74
imagery and reading, 135-6
individual differences, 217-37, 394-8
individualized reading program, 354-64
influences on reading, 90-5, 297, 375-6, 386-7
informational needs. See: reference interests and needs.
Institute of Student Opinion, 277-8
intelligence and reading ability, 401
intelligence and reading interests, 147-8, 171, 194-7, 214-5, 356-9, 420-32

Jordan, Arthur M., 150
Junior Book Awards, 126-31
Junior Great Books discussions, 164-6
juvenile delinquents' reading interests, 434-5

Larrick, Nancy, 145
Lazar, May, 147
Lehman, Harvey C., 152
leisure pursuits and reading, 92
libraries and gifted children, 420-32
library use, 197-8, 252, 297-8, 423-4
library visits, 95
library's image, 272
Lima, Margaret, 146, 152
literary form and preferences, 150
literary types and reading interests, 308-10
ludicrous nonsense and laughter, 87-8

Mackintosh, Helen K., 150
magazine subscriptions and reading achievement, 293
magazines, 197, 209-16, 257, 278, 284-8
mass media and reading, 92, 252, 270, 278, 385, 400-1
Mauch, Inez L., 145
McAulay, J. D., 146
McCracken, Ruth U., 152
McKenzie, Edwin, 147, 152
movies and reading. See: mass media and reading.

National Library Week, 274-6
Negro children and reading, 68-74
"neutral" reading, 134
newspapers, 98-107, 197, 257, 278, 284-6, 289-90
Norvell, George W., 146, 147, 150

paperbacks, 256
  sold in school libraries, 274, 320-1
picture dictionaries, 27-32
poetry, 307
poor readers. See: retarded readers.
preprimers, content of, 33-43
preschool dictionaries, 27-32
primers, content of, 33-43
print, type of, and preferences, 150
psychological factors and reading, 119-21
  case studies, 220-37
public library collections, 426-8
publicity, 275-6

qualities of books. See: values of reading.

racial bias and reading materials, 68-74.
radio and reading. See: mass media and reading.

Rankin, Marie, 152
reader guidance to the gifted, 425
readers as individuals--case studies, 220-37
reading ability, 394-8
  and intelligence, 401
  and reading interests, 62, 214-5
reading aloud, 19-26, 93
reading as an outlet, 90-1
reading atmosphere, 94
reading improvement classes, 208
reading lists, 262, 356
reading patterns, 96-7, 151-3, 248-50, 251-9, 271, 277-8, 356-9, 370-6, 377-80, 382-3
reasons for reading, 90-5, 116-7, 384-5, 438-40
  case studies, 217-37
  See also: values of reading.
reference interests and needs, 160-2, 407-19
reluctant readers, 436-7
research studies on reading interests, 142-56
retarded readers, 207, 435-6
Russian students' attitudes toward reading, 322-48
Rudman, Herbert C., 146

Scholastic Magazines, Inc., 277-8
school library, 94-5, 318, 363, 373
science books, 126-8
sense of superiority and laughter, 86-7
series books, 256
sex and reading interests, 60-1, 77-8, 96-7, 146-7, 171, 193-7, 214-5, 253-9, 280-3, 305-9, 319, 410
sex education, 301-2
sexy books, 374
Shores, J. Harlan, 144-5
short story preferences, 170-2
Sizemore, Robert A., 149
Smith, Dora V., 153
social environment and reading interests, 77-8, 121
  case studies, 220-37
Standard Catalog for High School Libraries, 262
Stone, C. R., 148
subject interests and preferences, 33-43, 55-63, 75-8, 126-31, 159-60, 181-90, 193-7, 202-7, 253-4, 280-3, 287, 315-6, 409-18
subjectivity and reading, 134-5
subtlety and laughter, 88-9
Swenson, Esther J., 145

teaching literature, 303-12, 354-64
television and reading. See: mass media and reading.
Terman, Lewis M., 146, 152
textbooks versus trade books, 108-15
Thorndike, Robert L., 146, 147
trade books versus textbooks, 108-15
typical teenage reader, 248-9

values of reading, 132-41, 323-47, 366-9
  See also: reasons for reading.

Whipple, Gertrude, 151
Wightman, H. J., 149
Witty, Paul A., 149, 150, 152
writing style and preferences, 150
Wye Institute, 313-7

Yale & Towne Manufacturing Company, 274
Young, Doris, 144